W9-AAV-822

ORM

Kitchen Collectibles

Kitchen Collectibles

The Essential Buyer's Guide

Diane Williamson Stoneback

WALLACE-HOMESTEAD BOOK COMPANY   Radnor, Pennsylvania

Designed by Adrianne Onderdonk Dudden
Manufactured in the United States of America

Library of Congress Cataloging In Publication Data

Stoneback, Diane Williamson.
    Kitchen collectibles: the essential buyer's guide / Diane Williamson Stoneback.
        p.   cm.
    Includes index.
    ISBN 0-87069-668-8
    1. Kitchen utensils—United States—History.   2. Kitchen utensils—
United States—Collectors and collecting.   I. Title.
TX656.S76   1994
683'.82—dc20   94-13885
                                                                          CIP

1 2 3 4 5 6 7 8 9 0   3 2 1 0 9 8 7 6 5 4

To Margaret Cline Horn, who kept the past alive.

To my parents, Frances and Richard Williamson, who schooled me in the ways of the past so that I could live it for a few weeks each year.

To my husband, Bruce Stoneback, and children, Margaret and Ian, who endured patiently while this book was "in the oven."

Contents

Acknowledgments   x

Introduction ⤜ 1
Farmhouse Memories   1
About this Book   9

PART ONE
A RECIPE FOR SUCCESSFUL COLLECTING

1 A History of American Kitchens ⤜ 13
The Center of Home Life   15
The Colonial Era   17
The Victorian Era   19
Early Modern Times, 1900–World War II   23
Postwar to the 21st Century   33

2 Collecting Considerations ⤜ 40
The Collector's Kitchen of the 1990s   40
  THE EVOLUTION OF THE COUNTRY STYLE   41
What to Save from the 1990s   44
  THE THIRTY YEAR RULE   44
  DEVELOPING A SAVINGS PLAN   46

State of the Market   49
CURRENT TRENDS   50
TODAY'S COLLECTOR   53
THE INTERNATIONAL MARKET   54

3 Resources for Collectors ❧ 57
Museums and Archives   58
Price Guides, Reference Books, Collector's Clubs and Newsletters   62
SPECIALIZED SUBJECT REFERENCES   63
OTHER BOOKS YOU'LL ENJOY   77
REPRINTS AND FACSIMILES OF EARLY COOKBOOKS   78
COLLECTOR'S CLUBS AND NEWSLETTERS   78

4 Factors Influencing Price ❧ 85
Affordability of the Category   86
Collecting Crazes   87
Condition   87
Scarcity   89
Completeness   90
Repairs and Restoration   90
Geographic Location   91
Cross-market Appeal   93
Using Price Guides   93

5 Tips on Buying and Selling ❧ 95
Building a Supply Network   96
Hitting the Road   97
FLEA MARKETS, GARAGE SALES AND SECOND-HAND SHOPS   97
AUCTIONS   99
Focusing in on Your Treasure   105
DEALER CONTACTS   105
EFFECTIVE BUYING   106

6 Using Your Kitchen Collectibles ❧ 109
Inspiration from the Past   109
IDEAS FROM OLD COOKBOOKS AND MAGAZINES   112
Considerations for Use   116
KNOW THE ITEM'S VALUE   116
SAFETY FIRST   117

7 Decorating with Kitchen Collectibles ❧ 126
Country Decor   127
Creating a Personal Statement   130

8 Cookbooks, Culinary Ephemera and Advertising ➥ 133

Cookbooks   *133*
   A GLIMPSE OF HISTORY   134
   REPRINTS AND FACSIMILES   136
   ETHNIC, REGIONAL, COMMUNITY AND CHARITY BOOKS   137
   COOKBOOKS MAKE GOOD READING   138
   WHO COLLECTS COOKBOOKS?   139
   SPECIALTY COLLECTIONS   141
   TIPS FOR COLLECTORS   143
Culinary Ephemera   *146*
Advertising   *147*

9 Electrical Appliances ➥ 150

Starting Your Collection   *152*
Factors Influencing Value   *156*
Buying Tips   *157*
The New "Classics"   *159*

10 Modern Reproductions ➥ 161

Some Basic Definitions   *162*
Reproduction Market   *164*
Avoiding Pitfalls   *165*

PART TWO
KITCHEN COLLECTIBLES PRICE GUIDE

Alphabetic Listings   *168*
Index   *233*

Acknowledgments

You've heard the saying that too many cooks spoil the broth. I have never believed it. And that is why I interviewed dozens of wonderful people who gave freely of their time and knowledge. My heartfelt thanks go out to:

Julia Child, Cambridge, Mass.

William Woys Weaver, Devon, Pa.-based, nationally known culinary historian whose books stir history, recipes and photographs of culinary antiques into a feast for the mind.

Jane and Michael Stern, Connecticut-based authors who have chronicled the food culture of America in numerous books.

Chef Louis Szathmary and Barbara Kuck of the Culinary Archives and Museum of Johnson and Wales University, Providence, R.I.

Karen Hess, culinary historian, New York, N.Y.

Jean LemMon, editor-in-chief of *Better Homes and Gardens* and former editor-in-chief of *Country Home*.

Raymond Waites, pioneer of the American Country movement and co-founder of GEAR, Inc.

Betty Groff, author of numerous cookbooks that are flavored with Pennsylvania Dutch culinary history.

Chuck Williams, founder of Williams-Sonoma.

Jan Longone, antiquarian bookseller and cookbook expert, Wine and Food Library, Ann Arbor, Mich.

Nahum Waxman, bookseller and cookbook expert, Kitchen Arts & Letters, New York, N.Y.

Mary Barile, cookbook expert, Arkville, N.Y.

Dana and Darlene DeMore, publishers, *Kitchen Antiques & Collectibles News,* Harrisburg, Pa.

Carol Bohn, a founder of KOOKS (Kollectors of Old Kitchen Stuff), kitchen collector and dealer, Mifflinburg, Pa.

Phyllis and Jim Moffet, kitchen collectors and founding members of KOOKS, Modesto, Ill.

Don Thornton, eggbeater expert and founding member of KOOKS, Sunnyvale, Ca.

Chuck and Bonnie Badger, kitchen collectors and founding members of KOOKS, Lakeview Terrace, Ca.

Brian Howard, a Carlisle, Pa.-based museum conservator.

Caroline Sloat, director of publications at Old Sturbridge Village, Mass.

The staff of the Landis Valley Museum of Early Pennsylvania German Life, Lancaster, Pa.

Carolyn Travers, director of research, Plimoth Plantation, Mass.

Mary Thompson, curatorial registrar for Mount Vernon.

The Stowe-Day Foundation, Hartford, Conn.

Christopher Bensch, curator of furnishings, Strong Museum, Rochester, N.Y.

Eugene Kosche, curator of history, Bennington Museum, Bennington, Vermont.

Dick Roller, author of *The Standard Fruit Jar Reference* and *The Fruit Jar Newsletter,* Paris, Ill.

Tony Curtis, publisher of Britain's *Lyle Official Antiques Reviews,* Galashiels, Scotland.

Mike and Tessia McCurdy, Cooks Books, Rottingdean, Sussex, England.

Wendy Johnston, cookie jar collector, Brooklyn, N.Y.

Philip D. Kennedy, Hoosier cabinet expert, Indianapolis, Ind.

Steve Stephens, cast-iron expert, San Anselmo, Ca.

Sue Erwin, publisher of *The Cookbook Collectors Exchange,* San Jose, Ca.

Judith Snyder, director, Victoria Society of America, Philadelphia, Pa.

Kitchenware dealers and collectors including Bob Cahn, The Primitive Man, Carmel, N.Y.; Bob and Kaaren Grossman of B&K Kitchen Primitives and Collectibles; Joan and Warner Johnson of Kitchen Cupboard Antiques, Randolph, N.J.; Kathy Schneider, Pearl Washington's Cookware, Whitman, Mass.; Dale Schmidt, Salem, Or.; and Lyle Krug, Cedar Rapids, Iowa.

Cookbook dealers Phyllis King of MCL Associates, McLean, Va and Marian L. Gore, San Gabriel, Ca.

Corporate representatives of Armstrong Industries; American Harvest; Waring; Hamilton Beach, Inc.; Farberware; National Presto Industries, Inc.; KitchenAid and Oster who searched their archives for material and information.

There's much research to be done and examples to be found in the production of a book like this one. Support team members included: Frances Williamson, Quakertown, Pa.; Angus and Donna Sturrock, Poole, England;

Elizabeth Strunk, Perkasie, Pa.; Betty Heinbach, Pine Grove, Pa.; Denise Reaman, Whitehall, Pa.; Matthew Brown, Allentown, Pa.; Susanne Kessler, Easton, Pa.; and Georgianna Anderson, St. Michaels, Md.

Special thanks to Harry Rinker and Ellen Tischbein Schroy of Rinker Enterprises, Inc., Vera Cruz, Pa., for their invaluable guidance, advice, encouragement and resources; and to Harry Rinker, Jr., who provided much of the photography used in this book.

✈ Kitchen Collectibles

Sketch showing front view of the Williamson farm, constructed in 1840, near Salladasburg, Pa.

Introduction

Farmhouse Memories

A dime-store skeleton key, rather than a car's ignition key or a 21st birthday party, signaled my passage to adulthood. Given to me by an elderly cousin, its value far exceeded its price.

The key opened the kitchen door of a north central Pennsylvania farmhouse that remained in my family for 151 years. Built by my great-great-grandfather in 1840 and last occupied, year-round, by my great-grandmother in 1923, the old white clapboard structure became a vacation home for any family member who wanted to get away from it all, including indoor plumbing and electricity.

The hollow thuds of our footsteps crossing the raised wooden back porch and the metallic clicking of the long and slender key in the primitive brass lock of the kitchen door still echo in my mind. As the old plank door swung open, it welcomed us to the past. I didn't have to imagine how my great-grandmother lived. I could live it. Because her estate went unsettled for 68 years following her death, the rambling five-bedroom house remained much the way she had left it. Still furnished. Still full of memories, stacked as high as the family photographs in the parlor.

The only running water came from a rickety pipe and faucet on the back porch—an arrangement so fragile that we were afraid to turn the water off. As evening sunsets faded, kerosene lamps and candles gave the rooms a pleasing glow that matched the sepia tones of old photographs. A schoolhouse clock rhythmically marked the passing of time for there were no radio or television announcers to do so. Reading material was as diverse as the 1911 Sears Roebuck catalog, tattered *Saturday Evening Posts,* primers, readers and almanacs, along with stacks of old letters. The parlor still contained the Eastlake rockers, chairs and a settee that, according to family legend, my great-grandmother had hated from the day my great-grandfather surprised her with them. Her grand piano, stacked high with sheet music and song books, hadn't been tuned since the 1940's. Subjected to the cruel abuse of winter's cold when no one was there to feed the wood fires, it still helped warm every occasion—whether a family birthday party, a summer sing-along or a winter caroling session. Upstairs, bedrooms contained the standard washstands, dressers and rope beds softened with feather ticks or straw mattresses, which rustled loudly with every turn and gave meaning to the phrase "hitting the hay."

But the farm's pantry and kitchen remain at the heart of my memories. The two rooms were filled with the furnishings and equipment needed to feed a family of 10, plus assorted farmhands during the harvest season. The pantry really was the equipment room. In its dish cupboard were enough assorted patterns to make up a china sampler. Each succeeding generation also had added enough pots, pans, roasters, pie and cake pans and mixing bowls to make the search for a particular pan much like an archaeological dig through layers of time. Suspended simply from nails and old iron hooks were assorted slaw cutters, tin graters, cast-iron frying pans and griddles, dish pans and cake turners, as well as strainers and eggbeaters. A weathered, gray dry

Herrick Dry Air system Refrigerator featured in a June–July 1918 advertisement was apparently a joy to own because its manufacturers had designed it to be the answer to every householder's wishes.

Interior photograph of a portion of the farm kitchen, showing the dough box and the cherry dropleaf table as well as the "modern" Kalamazoo cooking range.

sink concealed stoneware and assorted fruit jars. Its top, no longer in daily use, contained a collection of coffee pots that easily documented nearly a century of man's search for the ultimate cup of java. In the kitchen, a massive corner cupboard displayed what remained of great-grandmother's collection of fancy dishes, including ironstone platters, tureens and bowls. Although many of the pieces were cracked, chipped or crazed, they looked good from a distance and were even more pleasing to the eye when they were heaped with foods and traveling from hand to hand around the table.

A freestanding, four-legged dough tray contained assorted rolling pins, pastry cutters, crimpers and powdery flour dust that hinted at the hearty loaves of bread and rolls started in its depths and kneaded and shaped on its plank top. Next to the dough tray stood a cherry dropleaf table that had the family's culinary history etched in its surface. There were cuts from paring knives, semicircular burns from hot pots, grooves and scratches where cherry pitters and food grinders had been attached and dents and cracks that may have come from wielding wooden beetles to tenderize meats.

The gaping old leviathan of an icebox devoured ice blocks faster than we could find them in a day when most people simply wanted a few cubes to chill their drinks. It also imparted an aroma of musty dampness to all the foods it stored. Great-grandmother's black cooking range emitted curls of smoke from cracks and holes. When the family grew tired of worrying about possible asphyxiation (and of smelling like smoked slabs of country bacon), her original stove was replaced by a "modern" beige and green Kalamazoo range, as well as a temperamental kerosene stove.

The kitchen table stretched from one end of the room to the other, and still had enough additional leaves to have gone well beyond the doors.

A photograph of the Williamson farm, near Salladasburg, Pa., during the harvest season of 1898. The author's great-grandfather is atop the hay wagon and her grandfather is the boy seated on the ground. To the rear of the picture, left to right, are the barn, wagon shed, summer kitchen, main house, woodshed, smokehouse and garden.

Covered with bright red oilcloth it was the main worktable, whether it was time to peel potatoes, shell lima beans or cut corn from the cob. But the table looked its best when every chair was filled. During summer gatherings, our family's oral history was passed from generation to generation, right along with the cake and coffee.

The same cousin who gave me the key to the kitchen door was the last family member to know and remember my great-grandfather. As a girl, she had enjoyed many a summer on the farm with her grandparents. She described Sunday afternoons spent making ice cream on the back porch. The sessions always began with great-grandfather sending two sons to fetch ice

Ice-cream freezers, like this triple-motion one from White Mountain, provided many an afternoon's or evening's entertainment as everyone took turns at the crank and anticipated the treat that would emerge.

The English-style coffee mill was always handy and ready for duty when mounted on the wall. It was an alternative to the square, boxlike, French-style mills that sat on cupboard or pantry shelves until needed.

from between layers of sawdust in the icehouse. They rinsed the sawdust away and then broke the ice into small chunks for the freezer. Everyone took turns cranking. Grandchildren hovered less than a spoon's length from nearby bowls. Great-grandfather was equally enthusiastic about the ice cream, except that he sprinkled his dish with a coating of black pepper so thick that it resembled cinders on snow. As he ate spoonful after spoonful (not because he liked it but for the shocking effect it had), grandchildren watched in wide-eyed disbelief. In summer, food was cooked in the summer kitchen. Just before it was carried to the farmhouse kitchen, the women formed a line and marched from one end of the kitchen to the other while waving their full-length aprons to shoo black flies out of the room. Thank goodness for today's window screens!

Great-grandfather believed meat platters should not be passed. He ceremoniously carved the meats and doled out generous portions, one by one. But woe to the grandchild who glanced away from his full plate after falling for great-grandfather's favorite trick of mentioning he heard an approaching wagon on the narrow dirt road that snaked past the front of the house. He'd snatch the meat from the child's plate and return it only after he'd extracted the appropriate number of yowls. (I won't discuss how his curious sense of humor was passed along to succeeding generations.)

I also learned the mysteries of the bent kitchen forks and the pigs that never gained weight, no matter how much they were fed. Both were tales from my father's youth when he and his family summered on the farm. My grandmother became an amateur sleuth when she noticed that the fork tines were pointing in as many directions as a crossroads signboard. She finally grilled my father and his brother, and they confessed that they had been fastening forks to long sticks and using them for fish spears in a nearby creek. They also were the culprits in the case of the skinny pigs. Seems dad and his brother would wait in ambush on top of the low pigsty. When a pig came out the door, the young "cowboys" from the city jumped onto the pigs' backs and rode until they were bucked off, rodeo style.

Dad took us to summer at the farm, too, and that's when I first learned that the kitchen's rusticity made cooking both novel and challenging. The rewards, however, were mouth-watering. I've never eaten better than I did on those summer days of my childhood. Although it wasn't a working farm by the time we vacationed there, we suffered no shortage of food. What we didn't have or couldn't buy was provided by friends at the neighboring farm.

I scoured the orchard of gnarled trees for buckets of golf-ball-sized apples. To avoid disappointing me, my mother turned those apples into sauce enriched with sugar, vanilla and a few tablespoons of butter. Still warm from the stove, the applesauce was heavenly. Encouraged, I headed back to the orchard. When I returned with another bucketful, mom got out great-grandmother's rolling pins and we produced fresh pie crusts to encase them.

On another visit to the farm, we discovered several bushes of wild plums like those used to produce Cape Cod's beach plum jelly. A few hours later, our plums produced a shimmering jelly that matched the shade of dark garnets. We sealed the jelly jars with melted paraffin. (Although this method

German-made pie crimper with wooden handle and slender brass blade "prettied up" pies by giving their top crusts nicely finished edges.

Square cast-iron frying pan served a multitude of purposes, from the frying of country bacon to the browning of crisp potato slices.

of preserving jams and jellies is no longer recommended nor considered safe, it didn't kill us at the time).

Cucumbers from the neighboring farm family's garden became bread-and-butter pickles; string beans were packed with vinegar and dill; fresh tomatoes became sauce that slow-cooked on the range. Whole heads of cabbage were streamed and the leaves were filled with ground beef and rice for baking in tomato sauce. Home-cured country ham, so salty that just one serving was enough to nearly pickle a person, was wonderful with pan gravy and fresh biscuits. Bacon crisped beautifully on the griddle. Hash brown potatoes in the cast-iron frying pan became so crusty they could barely be cut with a fork. Sun-warmed blueberries, fresh huckleberries and black raspberries were floated in a thick layer of fresh cream. No wonder our appetites reached Paul Bunyan proportions during those days.

Our kitchen experiments even inspired my father to tackle a few of his own. He stalked the farm's flower beds and harvested a bucketful of tiger lily buds. As he sauteed and served them, he informed us that Euell Gibbons had described them as a natural delicacy. I wish Euell had been there to eat my share. Dad, who included wilderness outfitters' catalogs in his evening reading material, ordered wild rice pancake mix for one of our farmhouse breakfasts. The box said it made six pancakes so dad mixed it all. After all, there were four in our family. He ladled more and more batter onto the griddle, but the level of batter in the bowl seemed never to drop. By the time he finally tired of this culinary experiment, each of us faced a lumberjack-sized portion of pancakes, and the family basset hound looked more mournful than usual as she faced her second stack with a decided lack of enthusiasm. Apparently, the pancake mix was really designed to make six griddle-sized pancakes.

Once I married, my husband, too, was charmed by the farm. Summer or winter weekends and vacation days were spent there. Despite all my mother's culinary schooling, I quickly found out that I hadn't learned everything about cooking in the old combination wood/coal range. My two-tone turkey—raw on one side and overdone on the other—was evidence that it should have been rotated so both sides spent time close to the stove's fire box. Baked beans, so thoroughly baked that they had to be chiseled from the casserole for the next two days, taught me that regulating the old range's oven temperature

This small, blue-banded pitcher once was in a set of three. But stoneware, because it was utilitarian, was hard-used and often suffered cracks, chips and larger catastrophes.

The term "window box" didn't always mean a planter that was attached to a house's outdoor windowsill for growing flowers. Instead, it was a city dweller's answer to winter food storage because the box (of wood or galvanized iron) was built to fit a kitchen or pantry window and was secured to the building by brackets. Its door opened into the room so that the contents of the box were accessible when the window was raised.

was something of a necessary art. The yeast dough that overproofed and oozed from the range's warming oven offered a lesson on why quick-rise yeast really wasn't necessary in those days.

Eventually, my husband and I became confident enough about our country kitchen skills to host our entire family at an annual early Christmas. During the first week or two of December, we'd invite a houseful of adults and children for the weekend, ask still more relatives from a nearby town to come for the festive dinner and deck the old house with fresh greens, candles and a Christmas tree. It was a time to add leaves to the table and lines to our generation's family history. I imagined our early celebration of Christmas was a scene my great-grandparents would have enjoyed. One year, in particular, I was sure of it: a localized snow storm blanketed the farm with a fresh layer of snow. A mile away, the ground was bare.

Cooking in the farm kitchen gave me a feeling of my roots. I expected to share those happy feelings with my children. But it wasn't to be. At long last, word came that the estate had to be settled. As I waited for word of the impending auction, I consoled myself with thoughts of the utensils and furniture I would buy from the kitchen. Because notice of the auction was printed in a newspaper 150 miles from my home, and because no relatives thought to notify us, the furnishings were sold without my being able to buy so much as a rolling pin. The news was devastating. I blame the suddenness of it all and missing out on buying something of my family's culinary history for my current obsession with collecting.

There aren't many days when I walk into my own kitchen and eye the collectibles I've accumulated without thinking of great-grandmother's kitchen. In a minute, I'd drive the 150 miles to once again taste a hearty stew slow-cooked on top of the range; to knead some bread on her dough tray, bake some fresh cinnamon sticky buns for a breakfast treat or pass another platter of salty country ham around the table. It's a feeling so strong that I'll probably spend the rest of my life and thousands of dollars collecting utensils and furnishings to recreate some of those memories.

My excuse for wanting kitchen collectibles is the blending of my culinary memories with preserving a link with my mother, grandmothers and great-grandmothers. But there are many other reasons for people to be in the market for kitchen collectibles. Some collect kitchenware simply because it is something to collect and there are many tools, utensils and furnishings that remain affordable, if not downright inexpensive. Some don't even have to be purchased because the makings of many a collection still can be found in the

Animal-shaped cookie cutters with sharp edges and easy-to-use handles were particularly popular with Pennsylvania Dutch housewives. Of course, the finished cookies were a hit with the children who devoured them, too.

White-painted sifter with red apple decals made a utilitarian item more appealing to look at and to use.

Hand-carved wooden butter molds were used by cooks who not only put plenty of effort into making the butter but also wanted to make it look attractive when it was placed on their tables at mealtime.

attics, basements and cluttered kitchen drawers of family homes. Sadly, some people acquire kitchen collectibles simply because they're part of a decorating strategy, a fast ticket to the country look without any personal meaning. Others may have an interest in a specific food, such as ice cream or chocolate, and the desire to collect everything associated with it. It's a hobby that can be just as habit-forming as the foods.

Practical collectors go after older kitchen utensils, equipment and furniture for their looks, craftsmanship and quality. Many intend to use them and will stop at nothing to have the best tools for their culinary tasks. Good cooks covet tools of the past in the same way a violinist would covet a Stradivarius. A person who makes paper-thin Christmas roll-out cookies will seek clean-cutting cookie cutters with charming designs, as well as good rolling pins, to make the job less tedious. A pastry chef might search for the prettiest madeleine molds or the most ornate pie crimpers—items he or she can display as well as use. Social historians are gathering the tools and books about kitchen practice because they recognize them as important clues in the study of women's roles in society. Finally, when a turn-of-a-century is imminent, authors have documented people's tendency to rediscover earlier centuries as they search for "the good old days." In the late 1800's, for example, there was a revival of interest in the 1700's. And now, as the 20th century comes to an end, the times make recalling the early 1900's, as well as the 1800's, very appealing. Call it comfort food for the mind.

There are many ways to start accumulating kitchen collectibles. All it takes is one butter mold, or even an old fruit jar, to catch the imagination. The bleached lines of hand-carved butter molds tell the story of a cook who cared enough to go a step beyond simply churning butter and make it edible art. In less time than it takes to spread a pat of soft butter on bread, this example of folk art will stimulate an urge to acquire more. The mind flies. Soon, butter churns, stoneware butter firkins and butter paddles will become part of the quest. Before long, all kinds of dairy collectibles will be added to the collection and a vast category like ice cream will begin to look as appealing as a double-scoop of butter pecan. You see what happens, of course. Collecting kitchen equipment becomes a lifetime pursuit.

About This Book

In writing this book, I have made the assumption that many of the people who are interested in kitchen collectibles are good cooks, too. They'll take on collecting equipment with the same fervor they've used to gather recipes they'd like to try. That's why the first half of this book reads a little like a cookbook: Read it closely and follow it through. The basic ingredients and directions for becoming a collector are there. Assembling a basic library on kitchen collectibles, developing an understanding of pricing and today's markets, as well as buying, selling and trading, will get you started. After you have tasted success, you will develop the confidence to improvise, just as seasoned cooks do with recipes all the time. Page through the book's second half and you'll find that using the alphabetically organized Price Guide is as easy as checking a cookbook's index for a favorite recipe. The Price Guide will appeal to many tastes. Bakers, happiest when the flour is flying and bowls are full of batter, can check the categories from cookie cutters, dough boxes and dough scrapers to eggbeaters, flour sifters and rolling pins. Readers who are interested in beginning a cookbook collection will find prices for big books, little books, special books and booklets. And those who like nothing better than waking up to hot waffles and fresh coffee will find selected prices for waffle irons, coffee makers and all kinds of other electrical kitchen appliances, which were once designed to make life easier and are now destined to make life more interesting for collectors.

Naturally, the dimensions of a person's kitchen and home will limit the number of cabinets, cupboards and tables that can be acquired. But there always will be room for a few more little cookie cutters, pie crimpers or ice-cream scoops. Kitchen collectors who are worth their salt always are able to find another shelf, a little more wall or ceiling space or some room in a cabinet for cookbooks, canisters, baskets, fruit jars, reamers, seeders and parers.

Although many authors of books on kitchen collectibles include equipment from the kitchen's darker side as wash-day headquarters, other than a few notations within the Price Guide, I have focused on happier times and tasks. Thoughts of cinnamon buns, fresh bread, warm blueberry cobbler or even a new batch of strawberry jelly, after all, will stir far more pleasant memories for most of us than boiling the wash, starching the shirts or wielding the iron.

Even if you've never cooked more than a frozen dinner in a microwave oven, consider using your new collection and the old cookbooks that will inevitably find their way onto your shelves. Feeding your memories will never taste any better.

PART ONE

A Recipe for Successful Collecting

1

A History of American Kitchens

Average cooks may have a hard time picturing the kitchens of earlier times. But there are many ways to get a taste of life in 17th, 18th, 19th or even early 20th-century kitchens. You can do your own research by studying appraised household inventories of old estates, scanning old cookbooks and books on household management, examining catalogs and newspaper advertisements for kitchen goods and paging through old magazines for articles and advertisements about cookery and the kitchen. You can also visit historic sites such as Plimoth Plantation, Colonial Williamsburg, Mount Vernon and Old Sturbridge Village where staff members are conducting ongoing research into kitchens, their contents and their inhabitants. No matter which way you choose to study, you'll surely come away with an appreciation for your modern gadget-and-convenience-filled kitchen that enables you to prepare a meal and clean up the remains in a matter of minutes.

But much more awaits those who are willing to give kitchens of the past more than a passing glance.

Caroline Sloat, director of publications at Old Sturbridge Village and the editor of *Old Sturbridge Village Cookbook* (Globe Pequot Press, 1984, 254 pp.) jokes, "Anyone who spends a day cooking on the open hearth won't have to worry about attending exercise classes." Dawn Fetter, in charge of the hearth cookery program at Landis Valley Museum of Early Pennsylvania German Life (near Lancaster, Pa.), said, "Your arm, back and leg muscles ache from bending over the hearth, from tending the fire and lifting the heavy cast iron pots full of water or food." On an even less glamorous note, she describes the

Colonial cooks needed plenty of muscle to move iron kettles in and out of the fireplace because such cookware was heavy even before food or water went into it.

Wood was a readily available raw material for early settlers, who carved it into many utilitarian household items like this bowl for kitchen use.

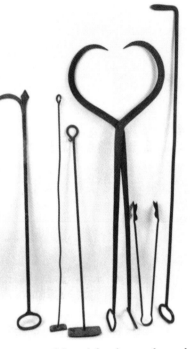

Assortment of forged fireplace tools needed by early cooks who mastered embers and flames to produce meals for their families.

difficulty of getting soot out from under fingernails and the risk that the fire in the hearth will singe anything from a hand to an apron. Spinning an oven dial or punching a few numbers on the microwave's control panel is a much simpler, but a much less romantic, way of accomplishing similar tasks. But the romance is apparently as enticing as the aroma of wood smoke on a brisk autumn afternoon. Hearth cookery programs, while they may not be totally accurate in every way, have never been more popular. Whether a person merely observes a working kitchen in an historic site or spends a day working with the staff to cook a meal over glowing embers and a crackling fire, such events do provide a small taste of the challenges early cooks faced.

Staff members at historic sites report visitors are asking greater numbers of more detailed questions, either because they're fascinated with the country's rich culinary history and the roles women played in it, are serious about mastering hearth cookery or simply want to give their families a taste of an old-fashioned stew that simmers slowly in a timeworn cast-iron dutch oven (even if it has to be heated on an electric stove). As one hearth cookery instructor said, "It's as if people are determined to compensate for the shortcomings of this hurried and convenience-filled world [and] they're looking for texture to enrich their lives."

The Center of Home Life

From the earliest days of this country's history, there can be little doubt about the kitchen's importance in life. Usually, it was the only room, or one of two rooms in the house. Simple New England dwellings were divided into two rooms by a very large central chimney. The "hall," or keeping room, was the kitchen, dining room and living room while the other room was the master bedroom but also served as a daytime parlor, or sitting room, when guests stopped by. Kitchens often were built onto the back of the house when settlers began to prosper and could afford larger dwellings. Often, the kitchen

Large, hardwood cookie/cake board had the design of a woman carved in one side and an image of a man cut into the other.

Wooden mortar and pestle were an early cook's way of grinding and mashing spices and other ingredients for the recipes to be made.

addition continued the steep slope of the roof and gave rise to the now-famous saltbox design for homes.

In early southern homes, kitchens were either in the basement or in a completely separate building, reducing the risk of fire in the main house and keeping the heat out of the house during the oppressive summer months. (Judith Snyder, director of the Philadelphia-based Victorian Society in America, said the custom of putting a kitchen in the basement—particularly for use during the summer months—was sometimes practiced north of the Mason-Dixon line, too. Several old Philadelphia mansions were built this way).

William Woys Weaver, probably the nation's foremost culinary historian and author of several fascinating books on the kitchen equipment and recipes that make up America's culinary history (*America Eats,* Harper & Row, 1989, 198 pp.; *Sauerkraut Yankees,* 1983; and *The Christmas Cook: Three Centuries of American Yuletide Sweets,* Harper Perennial, 1990, 268 pp.), provided an overview of basic kitchen equipment through the centuries:

> Most people in the 17th century were poor, with only the barest of hearth cooking essentials. But by the 18th century, average households owned a boiler, a four- or five-gallon, three-legged stew pot with a bail handle, as well as an even larger pot for laundry and a smaller one (a quart or two) for light cooking. They probably had a frying pan or skillet, if not both.
>
> Pennsylvania farmers, who were pretty well equipped, had a gridiron and a baking surface as simple as a large flat stone that could be heated in the hearth or a hanging griddle or bakestone (a piece of soapstone with metal around it). They also would have had a skimmer, a ladle, a flesh fork, some knives and some pottery like earthenware pie plates.

The "modern" ranges used by women at the turn of the century were far from automatic. Operating them correctly required skill and presented some challenges to coax the best foods from their stovetops and ovens.

Large breadboard shows a telltale sign that it endured some abuse—a hot pot that burned its outline into it.

By the end of the 18th century, most farmers had one of two kinds of bake ovens because these were status symbols. The English-style ovens were built out from the back of the hearth. The Pennsylvania Germans built their bake ovens outside the house, in separate structures, as they'd been required to do by fire regulations back in Germany. Then, if the bake oven split apart, at least the house didn't burn down.

Bake ovens, of course, required special equipment too, from peels to move breads and pies in and out of the oven to wooden rakes to clear the ashes.

By the end of the 19th century, people were better off. They had more money and the cook stove had been introduced. But changing from hearth cookery to the cook stove was a little like skiing. A cook suddenly had to buy all kinds of new equipment to go with the stove, including a boiler, stew pot, dripping/roasting pans, bread pans, frying pans and some kind of large iron, copper or brass tea kettle for boiling water.

Actually, the cook stoves, rather than making life easier, made slaves of Victorian women. Once a woman was lucky enough to have one, she felt she had to do all kinds of creative things with it.

The Colonial Era

Carolyn Travers, director of research for Plimoth Plantation, which depicts life in 1627, said, "Earliest cottages consisted of one room with a loft above it. This kitchen, called the 'hall' measured about 20 by 20 feet or more. It was the center of family life. Meals were prepared, cooked and eaten in the hall. But it was also the place for everything from giving birth to the children to making a new handle for a plow. The kitchen had a packed dirt and clay floor that was covered with rushes. There were some candles, some oil lamps and some rush lights. It was equipped with iron or brass cooking pots, pans and trivets brought from England, along with knives, cleavers, spoons and ladles. Some homes may have had andirons and spits for roasting meats. Most heavy-duty baking was done outdoors in clay 'beehive' ovens."

Not every kitchen contained a table. According to Travers, "Sometimes families simply put boards over the top of barrels at mealtime and then took it all apart when they had finished eating. And, just because a household had a dining table didn't mean there were enough chairs for everyone. Often, family members sat on chests, benches or stools gathered around the table. Children often stood when they ate, so they could serve their parents." (Tell that to today's teenagers!)

It comes as a shock to many people to learn that one-third of the Mayflower's families had a servant or servants. Travers said, "These servants often were other people's older children, apprenticed for training in running a household. A 16-year-old girl could really be a help to a woman who had several children under the age of six. And she'd also take direction from someone else more happily than instruction from her own mother." (Times haven't changed all that much!)

Much of a woman's day was spent on food, according to Travers who explained, "In springtime, there was gardening and field planting to be done.

There were animals to be milked and butter and cheese to be made. In summer and fall, there was harvesting and preserving to be done, if a family were to have enough food to make it through the winter. Pork was smoked or pickled. Fruits and vegetables were dried." She added, "Foodways were critical and entailed far more than cooking. It was the whole process from obtaining the food stuffs to preserving or cooking them. It was more than simply passing on recipes for bread, duck or beef stew. A woman had to know how much dried fish she'd need for an entire year and how to preserve it, as well as how to cook it."

Colonial Williamsburg staff members have examined the 18th century, and particularly the third quarter's kitchens, in great detail. Jane Carson's book, *Colonial Virginia Cookery,* offers a detailed view of Virginia kitchens including their furnishings (everything from pewter and crockery to the big brick fireplaces and built-in brick ovens) and sketches and descriptions of hearth cooking equipment. Early chapters provide more information about tin dutch ovens, clockjacks, griddles and wafer and waffle irons.

A look at the kitchen section of the *Inventory of the Contents of Mount Vernon,* conducted in 1800, provides another look at the well-equipped kitchen of the late 1700's. Mary Thompson, curatorial registrar for Mount Vernon, said, "Martha Washington's grandson claimed she made daily trips to the kitchen [a separate, two-story building at the end of a covered walkway] to supervise the cook. She may have been discussing the foods she and George wanted for their meals. She also may have been issuing supplies since things tended to be locked." The brick-floored building, about 20 by 40 feet, consisted of three areas: the kitchen and open hearth where the actual cooking was done, the larder (slightly below ground to keep foods in storage somewhat cool) and the scullery where dishes were washed. The second floor was divided into a storage area and living quarters for the cook or house-keeper.

A sampling of the utensils and dishes listed on the inventory of the building included china pickle plates, china custard cups, cups and saucers, a teapot, china mugs, soup dishes, tart molds, iron stew pan, Naples biscuit pans, copper egg boiler, three dutch ovens, cake pans, tin kettle, sugar cake pans, clay milk pans, waffle irons, pewter plates, copper saucepans, spits, fish kettle, grid iron, frying pans, a marble mortar as well as a slab, skillets, iron stew pans, two colanders, a griddle, pot hooks, trivets, supports for the spit, coffee roasters, kitchen boiler, pewter ice-cream pots, scallop cups, coffee-pots, knives and forks, skimmer, three ladles, two cleavers, four tubs, five buckets, iron spoons and skewers. And that wasn't all, by any means. Washington's estate, on a hillside overlooking the Potomac River, also included a separate smokehouse and an ice house, among other outbuildings.

The cooks in villages, such as the one Old Sturbridge Village depicts, worked with many similar hearth tools in their kitchens during the 1830s. Sloat said, "Kitchens were good-sized rooms because laundry and ironing also were carried on in the room. When natural light faded, the hearth provided most of the light in the room. Our ancestors were used to living with less light. It was one of the reasons why they did the bulk of their cooking in the morning for the noon meal, which was the biggest of the day."

Here is the chopper that cuts coarse, medium, fine or pulverized ~

The daintiest of dishes, with that added touch that makes one hostess more favored than another, can be prepared with this new chopper. Simply set the lever for the size cut you desire. There are no wing nuts to take off or cutters to change.

The Dandy can be taken apart and cleaned with a turn of the wrist, and the new, sloping clamp permits attaching to a narrow ledge table.

If your dealer does not carry the Dandy, it will be mailed anywhere post paid for $2.25 (large size) or $2 (smaller size).

NEW STANDARD CORP.   MT. JOY, PA.

Manufacturers of the
NEW STANDARD TRIPLE-WHIP FREEZERS

A stickler for efficiency and saving steps in the kitchen, Catherine Beecher also designed a sink and cooking area that put much of what a cook needed very close at hand. Courtesy of the Stowe-Day Foundation, 77 Forest St., Hartford, Conn.

This chopper was a "Dandy" in name and intended to be "dandy" for the housewife because it cut ingredients into coarse, medium, or fine shreds—or even pulverized them. According to the manufacturer, any of this could be accomplished by making a simple lever adjustment. It was manufactured by the New Standard Corp. of Mt. Joy, Pa.

The Victorian Era

As Weaver so aptly explained, the cook stove's introduction in the 19th century led to all kinds of innovations as more modern kitchens began to evolve.

In her book, *The American Woman's Home* (reprinted by the Stowe-Day Foundation, 1991, 500 pp.), Catherine Beecher, with her famous sister Harriet Beecher Stowe, enumerated the proper layout, equipment and labor-saving devices for efficiency in the up-to-date kitchen of 1869. Here is her description of the kitchen and stove rooms:

> Between the two rooms glazed sliding-doors, passing each other, serve to shut out heat and smells from the kitchen. The sides of the stove room must be lined with shelves. Boxes with lids, to receive stove utensils, must be placed near the stove.
>
> On these shelves, and in the closet and boxes, can be placed every material used for cooking, all the table and cooking utensils, and all the articles used in housework, and yet much spare room will be left. The cook's galley in a steamship has every article and utensil used in cooking for two

hundred persons in a space not larger than this stove room, and so arranged that with one or two steps the cook can reach all he uses.

In contrast to this, in most large houses, the table furniture, the cooking materials and utensils, the sink and the eating room are at such distances apart, that half the time and strength is employed in walking back and forth to collect and return the articles used.

Reproduced in many books and articles is Beecher's design for the area of the kitchen around the sink. She explains:

This is an enlarged plan of the sink and cooking form. Two windows make a better circulation of air in warm weather, by having one open at top and the other at the bottom, while the light is better adjusted for working, in case of weak eyes.

The flour-barrel just fills the closet, which has a door for admission, and a lid to raise when used. Beside it, is the form for cooking, with a molding-board laid on it; one side used for preparing vegetables and meat, and the other for molding bread. The sink has two pumps, for well and for rain-water—one having a forcing power to throw water into the reservoir in the garret, which supplies the water-closet and bathroom. On the other side of the sink is the dish-drainer, with a ledge on the edge next to the sink, to hold the dishes, and grooves cut to let the water drain into the sink. It has hinges, so that it can either rest on the cookform or be turned over and cover the sink. Under the sink are shelf-boxes placed on two shelves run into grooves, with other grooves about and below, so that one may move the shelves and increase or diminish the spaces between. The shelf-boxes can be used for scouring materials, dish-towels and dish-cloths; also to hold bowls for bits of butter, fats, etc. Under these two shelves is room for two pails, and a jar for soap-grease.

Under the cook-form are shelves and shelf boxes for unbolted wheat, corn-meal, rye, etc. Beneath these, for white and brown sugar, are wooden can-pails, which are the best articles in which to keep these constant necessities. Beside them is the tin molasses-can with a tight, movable cover, and a cork in the spout. This is much better than a jug for molasses, and also for vinegar and oil, being easier to clean and to handle. Other articles and implements for cooking can be arranged on or under the shelves at the side and front. A small cooking-tray, holding pepper, salt, dredging-box, knife and spoon, should stand close at hand by the stove.

The articles used for setting tables are to be placed on the shelves at the front and side of the sink. Two tumbler-trays, made of pasteboard, covered with varnished fancy paper and divided by wires save many steps in setting and clearing table. Similar trays for knives and forks and spoons, serve the same purpose.

The sink should be three feet long and three inches deep, its width matching the cook-form.

Obviously, Catherine Beecher had some very definite ideas about how the efficient kitchen should look. She also had strong ideas about the equipment it should contain. Here's what she had to say about kitchen furniture and equipment ratings:

When restoration of the Harriet Beecher Stowe house was underway, there were no records of the layout of the actual kitchen. It was decided to organize the kitchen along the lines advised by Stowe and her sister Catherine E. Beecher in *The American Woman's Home*. After all, Stowe's kitchen could very well have been a testing ground for some of their recommendations. Courtesy of the Stowe-Day Foundation, 77 Forest St., Hartford, Conn.

Crockery—Brown earthen pans are said to be best for milk and for cooking. The pans are lighter, and more convenient, but are too cold for many purposes. Tall earthen jars, with covers, are good to hold butter, salt, lard, etc. Acids should never be put into the red earthen ware, as there is a poisonous ingredient in the glazing which the acid takes off. Stone ware is better and stronger, and safer every way than any other kind.

Iron Ware—Many kitchens are very imperfectly supplied with the requisite conveniences for cooking. When a person has sufficient means, the following articles are all desirable: A nest of iron pots, of different sizes (they should be slowly heated when new), a long iron fork, to take out articles from boiling water; an iron hook, with a handle to lift pots from the crane; a large and small gridiron, with grooved bars, and a trench to catch the grease; a Dutch oven, called also a bake-pan; two skillets of different sizes; a skimmer; iron skewers; a toasting iron; two tea kettles, one small and one large one; two brass kettles, of different sizes, for soap boiling, etc. Iron kettles lined with porcelain, are better for preserves. The German are the best. Too hot a fire will crack them, but with care in this respect, they will last for many years.

A box and mill, for spice, pepper and coffee, are needful to those who use these articles. Strong knives and forks, a sharp carving-knife, an iron cleaver and board, a fine saw, steelyards, chopping tray and knife, an apple parer, steel for sharpening knives, sugar-nippers, a dozen iron spoons, also a large one with a long handle.

Tin-Ware—Bread pans; large and small patty-pans; cakepans, with a center tube to insure their baking well; pie-dishes (of block-tin); a covered

Wooden beetles came in many shapes and sizes, perhaps to suit the hands and strength of various cooks who wielded them to tenderize meat, work the dough for beaten biscuits or mash or pound potatoes.

butter-kettle; covered kettles to hold berries; two sauce-pans; a large oil-can (with a cork); a lampfiller; a lantern; broad-bottomed candlesticks for the kitchen; a candle-box; a funnel, a reflector for baking warm cakes; an oven or tin-kitchen; an apple corer; an apple-roaster; an egg-boiler; two sugar scoops, and flour and meal scoop; a set of mugs; three dippers; a pint, quart, and gallon measure; a set of scales and weights; three or four pails, painted on the outside; a slop-bucket with a tight cover, painted on the outside; a milk-strainer; a gravy strainer; a colander; a dredging box; a pepperbox; a large and small grater; a cheese-box; also a large box for cake; and a still larger one for bread, with tight covers. Bread, cake, and cheese, shut up in this way, will not grow dry as in the open air.

Wooden Ware—A nest of tubs; a set of pails and bowls; a large and small sieve; a beetle for mashing potatoes; a spade or stick for stirring butter and sugar; a bread-board, for molding bread and making pie-crust; a coffee-stick; a clothes-stick; a mush-stick; a meat-beetle to pound tough meat; an egg-beater; a ladle for working butter; a bread-trough, (for a large family); flour-buckets, with lids, to hold sifted flour and Indian meal; salt-boxes.

Basket Ware—Baskets of all sizes, for eggs, fruit, marketing, clothes, etc.; also chip-baskets.

Clearly, equipping a kitchen according to Beecher's directions could keep a collector going for a lifetime!

In 1881, another household adviser enumerated her ideas about a kitchen's location in a model home. Lydia McNair Wright, in her book *The Complete Home*, said, "Be sure and do not put the kitchen in the basement or cellar; this makes too many steps for the housewife; too much heavy carrying for the maids; the fumes of the cooking rise through the house and are driven back toward the furnace-cellar, and rise also with the heat. If the kitchen is beside the dining-room, do not have a door opening between them, but through a lobby; if dining-room and kitchen communicate, the dining-room is apt to be filled with steam, smoke or flies, as the door is constantly opened, and the people at the table get a view of the kitchen whenever a waiter passes between the two."

Although much attention was devoted to the proper equipment needed to cook and the right location for the kitchen, very little was said about decor. Most sources note that Victorian kitchens, particularly those in upper-class and upper middle class homes, were rather bleak. Servants worked in these rooms, and the family rarely ventured "below-stairs." (Those who watched the popular Masterpiece Theater series "Upstairs, Downstairs" will recall that Mrs. Bridges and Ruby rarely were visited by Mrs. Bellamy or the other women in the family).

Kitchens often were painted in dark colors such as green or gray to conceal the accumulation of dirt that included soot from the household cook stove as well as from the polluted outside air. Farmhouse kitchens, however, were brighter and more pleasant than those in the more well-to-do homes because family members ate their meals in the room.

After reading about these depressing kitchens, it's not hard to understand why Victorians get the credit for taking dining out of the kitchen. The Victorian Society's Snyder said, "In Victorian times, not many people ate in the kitchen. People had to be in a pretty low station of life to eat there. Dining rooms were for dining. Victorians made a great spectacle of taking their meals in these separate rooms, perhaps because theirs was the first generation of luxury homes in which a dining room could be separate from the kitchen. Before those times, the kitchen was the place where people gathered."

The women no longer had to toil in the fields or make the cloth for the family's clothes. Instead, they were responsible for directing the family's morals and religion and ensuring domestic bliss. Cookbooks of the times were dedicated to helping women make their men happy and healthy. The Victorian woman who had a cook was still responsible for reviewing menus, overseeing the food budget and making sure the cook prepared the latest recipes for molded foods and frozen desserts when guests were expected.

Victorians' new-found knowledge of microbes, bacteria and disease gave them a fascination for cleanliness, too. Although the kitchens weren't pretty, they were designed to undergo regular scrubbings.

Early Modern Times, 1900–World War II

The utilitarian Victorian kitchens carried over into the earliest years of the 20th century. Jane Celehar wrote in her book, *Kitchens and Gadgets 1920–1950* (Wallace-Homestead, 1982, 144 pp.), "The old-fashioned kitchen was dominated by the range. Unless gas was available, cooking would have been done on a cast-iron, iron-wood combination or coal range; all were inconvenient and inefficient. Flat irons were heated on the stove, toast was made on the open fire or in the oven. All beating was done by hand. The kitchen lacked adequate storage and often had no provision for keeping fresh food

BOLO

B I G   OVEN - LITTLE   OVEN

Bakes perfectly
In half the time—with half the fuel

Use it on top of your range, oil stove or gas plate—
Saves its cost in one season—Bakes bread, beans,
pies and roasts over the same fire at the same time.

The Adjustable Circulating Air Chamber
found only in the BOLO enables you to do this—no
other oven has this wonderful feature. *Say BOLO
to your dealer—if he's a good one he has it, or he will get
it for you.*

There is only one BOLO

IF YOUR DEALER CANNOT FURNISH WRITE FOR BOOKLET

The Griswold Manufacturing Company
Erie, Penna.

Although most people know about the
Griswold Manufacturing Company's fine
cast-iron cookware, they might not know that
Griswold also manufactured a stove-top
oven.

unless there was an icebox or 'cooler' (a passage in the wall fitted with strong wire shelves). Almost everything was stored in a pantry, requiring a lot of trips and endless miles of walking. It took a great deal of walking, stooping and bending to prepare a family meal in the large, old-fashioned kitchen."

Gustav Stickley, influential in the Arts and Crafts Movement, had different ideas about the kitchen, which he expressed in his writings in the early 1900's. He didn't like the idea that the kitchen had become the "dump heap of the whole household, a place in which to do what cooking and dish washing must be done and get out of as soon as possible." He advocated combining the kitchen, dining room and pantry in smaller homes, to make a single, large room that would be attractive, very clean and full of "homely cheer."

Gas ranges, with their ready and steady supply of fuel, liberated women without servants from such tasks as carrying wood or coal and feeding the stove, as well as trying to regulate oven temperatures. They simplified cooking and enabled these women to get out of the kitchen once in a while.

With the start of World War I, most household servants took jobs in factories to help with the war efforts. And some women, who had never done more than visit the kitchen long enough to make sure the cook was doing her job, suddenly found themselves thrust onto the culinary frontline. They were in unfamiliar, rugged territory, with totally new responsibilities: There was much to be learned and much to be changed, now that "milady" was suddenly cook and scullery maid. As one might expect, these women suddenly became concerned with eliminating some of the drudgery and making the kitchen attractive.

Beautifying the kitchen and making it more efficient was the subject of several articles in *American Cookery* (formerly the *Boston Cooking School*

Magazine) in 1916 and 1917. The author of "The Up-To-Date-Kitchen," in a 1916 issue, said that the kitchen should be a clean, well-ventilated place where food could be cooked in a sanitary manner and with the smallest amount of labor and warned, "It is negligence of these facts that makes it hard for the house mother."

Other essentials were porcelain or enamel sinks (the "most sanitary ones"), a wall table ("a kitchen table that lets down like a drop leaf and can be raised when needed for work"), a table, a chair, a long-legged stool and the new kind of kitchen cabinet ("that few modern housekeepers are able to resist because they're movable, are not as high as built in closets, are lined with tin and utilize every bit of space for storage of things like flour, bread, cake and everything that the mice might get at"). In addition, the coming of electric irons, toasters and other conveniences apparently made it "quite plausible to install two lights, one socket to furnish the light and the other to attach the plugs to."

Cooking utensils could be aluminum, nickel, porcelain, agate and enamel. The article noted, "They come in artistic shades and a wide variety of shapes, allowing the housekeeper ample choice. The first cost of these new wares may seem prohibitive, but there is no economy in purchasing utensils made of cheap material. . . . The newer wares vary in price—the most expensive being aluminum, while the cheapest is nickel. . . . Cost depends upon the grade. Enamel comes next to aluminum in price, followed by porcelain, blue agate and gray, all of which are advisable for use. A kettle of aluminum costs $3. . . . A very attractive ware is enamel. Its pure white finish gives it a clean look. It has practically superseded the old crock jar and the advantage over it is undeniable."

Other handy items were a two-and-a-half-foot long shelf for the holding of spices ("Today we can purchase porcelain jars with names lettered in gilt, that will hold just this kind of groceries") and a circular-shaped kitchen reminder with pointers and dials, which do away with pencil and paper ("All a housewife has to do is turn the hand to the articles needed, and make out her list at her leisure") and a chest of drawers for kitchen linens and aprons.

The following year, Jane Vos wrote "Kitchens Real and Make Believe," and described what women longed for in a 1917 kitchen: "A real white-tiled wall-and-floor one, with an automatic electric range and fireless, in fact, full electric equipment including the wired cooking table with all the small utensils; a rapid electric dishwasher; refrigeration without ice; innumerable cupboards of the drop-leaf type; marble-topped tables, and above all, plenty of windows with air, light and sunshine."

Although she acknowledged that few women would be lucky enough to achieve this ideal, there were things every woman could do to make her kitchen more convenient and attractive. The first step, she preached, was sacrificing a bit: "Pass the silk hosiery and lace counters with your eyes closed for the rest of the summer so that in the end you can afford aluminum pots and pans and glazed earthenware, especially if you do your own housework. Even if you have a maid, you will be more apt to keep her, if you make her domain convenient."

Vos claimed "the well-equipped, up-to-date kitchen comes nearer to solving the difficult servant problem than any other factor, for the efficient housewife knows the maid should not be expected to take charge of a kitchen in which the equipment is out of repair or hopelessly deficient."

It also had to be clean. "Nowadays, we, at least, insist on having our kitchens light, the woodwork painted white, if possible, to make our food laboratory or workshop, sanitary and wholesome. We furthermore insist that every part of the room must be washable, that the colors must, at least, be light if not white, with no effort to conceal dirt; that surfaces must be smooth without cracks or crevices, and that there must be no dark corners or closets." (Obviously, Vos would not approve of my kitchen where closets hide almost everything I haven't had a chance to finish and dark corners mercifully conceal the rest.)

The first principle of an ideal kitchen in 1917, according to Vos, was compactness—the maximum of utility in the minimum of space. She advised keeping stove, sink and worktable as close together as possible. Stove utensils were to be suspended on hooks over the range. Flour and sugar and spices were to be near the worktable. She also claimed exposed shelves are always better than closed ones in dark closets, and besides, she added, "they may be decorative, if their contents are arranged with an eye to color." (This lady, no doubt, was delighted by the addition of kitchen color in everything from the walls to the smallest of utensils, midway through the 1920's.)

Vos was ahead of her time in other ways, too. She talked of making sure that the kitchen also contained a much-needed "rest corner" for either housewife or maid, where a moment may be snatched for reading, perhaps, "while waiting for the teakettle to boil or the potatoes to cook." Here was the forerunner of today's modern kitchen "planning centers."

She wrote of "kitchens of the buffet or kitchenette type becoming more numerous and popular in the new apartment houses and studio buildings" but mentioned that not everyone was fortunate to have one. Despite fire laws that prohibited the making of even so much as a cup of tea or coffee in anything but a bona fide kitchen, she described daringly how a closet could be turned into a kitchenette. She asked: "Who says we can't have kitchens adapted to our needs? No one, we unfeignedly surmise, but the pudgy fire commissioners."

During the 1920s, authors continued to emphasize cleanliness and compactness. Ruth Peck MacLeod declared in her article in *American Cookery* called "Furnishings for the Kitchen," "The beauty of the kitchen lies in the cleanliness of it. The more white surfaces you have to reflect the light, the more pronounced the effect will be. The luxury of a spotless kitchen is well worth striving for. The charm of a domestic science laboratory or hospital depends on the whiteness and sanitary appearance of the whole." (One wonders what MacLeod would think of the modern country kitchens, if she found charm in such sanitary appearances.)

Although she acknowledged that some kitchens could be as large as an entire apartment, she added that all cooks had such similar needs as built-in storage cupboards, the sink and a working surface. She wrote, "The small

The up-to-date 1918 kitchen was the workshop of the house and needed to be clean and attractive. It was laboratory-like in appearance and design, with uncluttered surfaces that could be sanitized easily. Courtesy of the makers of Armstrong Floors.

kitchen in the modern apartment or average bungalow depends upon the use of cupboards to supplant the old-time roomy pantries, where one had to run for every spoon or utensil that was needed in getting a meal." "Some theorists," MacLeod added, "talk of a kitchen where one may sit on a stool and reach stove, cupboards, tables, etc., in preparing a meal without taking a single step."

Here's a sampling of her suggestions for kitchen furnishings:

Tables—A shelf, on a hinge, which may be converted into a table when needed is very convenient, especially where space is at a premium. A table of some kind is needed in the kitchen, unless one relies entirely upon a wide shelf. A tile-topped table, really enameled finish over metal, is what I recommend. Hot dishes do not effect it. Nothing could be more sanitary, nor more economical.

Chairs, stools etc.—Every kitchen should have a working stool, of the proper height, for washing dishes at the sink or working at the table. Kitchen chairs should be a part of the furnishings. They should be enameled to harmonize with the woodwork.

Sinks—The white porcelain sink, with porcelain drain board, is indispensable in the kitchen. It should be much higher than the average sink so that the housewife can wash dishes without having to bend over at her task.

Refrigerator—The refrigerator may, of necessity, be placed in the kitchen, although it is better if it can be situated in a built-in cabinet, pantry, or closet, where it may be filled from the outside, and where the heat of the room will not help hasten the melting of the ice. . . . The refrigerating box should never be placed on a back porch, unless it has some protection from the weather, as the dampness, frost, heat of sun, etc. will soon cause the box to warp and swell, so that it will waste ice rather than keep it. The tiled or

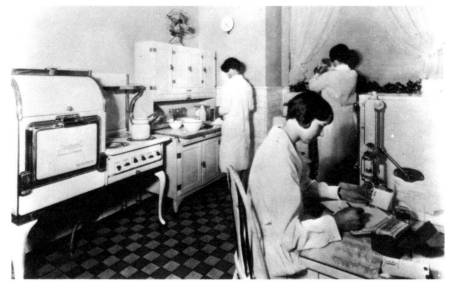

Home economists working in the Betty Crocker Kitchens in the 1920s were using a Hotpoint Electric Range, side by side with a Hoosier-style kitchen cabinet, as they created recipes for home cooks that showed off the baking qualities of Gold Medal Flour.

enameled ice box, outside and in, is the best type, as it is more porous and is easily cleaned, therefore, sanitary. The next choice is the one with white enamel inside only. This prevents absorption of odors by box. . . . The box with the ice compartment opening at the top keeps the food colder than that with side-door ice chamber."

(In her crusade for sanitation, MacLeod recommended painting an oak refrigerator with white enamel. She may be the one to blame if you have ever had to strip an old icebox.)

MacLeod liked aluminum ware for cooking utensils because it was "sanitary, easily cleaned and practically indestructible" but she also liked glass utensils because she could see how food was cooking on the bottom as well as the top. Also included in her suggestions for kitchen equipment were an iron skillet, deep-fat frying pan and enamelware for food storage.

However, she had strong reservations about using graniteware for cooking: "It is being used less and less. The fact that its composition consists of layers of a glass-like material over iron reminds us that a chip off the lining would be equivalent to a piece of glass. Because of its construction, granite ware, when heated, frequently breaks or swells to form a blister because of the uneven expansion of the glass and the iron. A blow to graniteware will often shatter it. Enamel pans are useless (or should be considered so) after the enamel has begun to chip off. On the other hand, enamelware bowls are excellent for the storage of foods and are used in preference to aluminum when acid foods (such as salads) are to stand for some time."

As the decade evolved, cooks were giving more thought to color and efficiency, according to Marion Brownfield. In "Kitchen Considerations," another article in *American Cookery,* she wrote: "As the kitchen has two

"Professor Goodfood"

A most important member of the faculty is Professor Goodfood! Growing girls at college get more out of his courses than they do out of Greek, geometry, and golf. Professor Goodfood's laboratory is aluminum-equipped.

Smith, Sweet Briar, and many other noted women's colleges cook in aluminum utensils. They use aluminum, some of them exclusively, because it does such good cooking and — thanks to its imperviousness to food acids — such healthful cooking, too.

The home kitchen needs these good gifts of aluminum. And the durability and economy of aluminum, and the ease with which it may be kept silvery bright, are added virtues which the thrifty housewife will consider in selecting the utensil equipment of her kitchen. . . . . The best cooks use aluminum.

MAIL COUPON FOR BOOKLET
ALUMINUM WARES ASSOCIATION
Publicity Division, 844 Rush St., Chicago
Please send booklet, "The Precious Metal of the Kitchen," to the address written below.

Aluminum manufacturers even used the names of Smith and Sweet Briar, noted women's colleges, to sell housewives on the durability, economy and wisdom of buying such cookware. After all, "The best cooks use aluminum."

functions in the home—the workshop and the temporary sitting room—for the average homemaker without help, it should be attractive as well as convenient." Good spirits, according to this article, "depend so much on cheerful surroundings that the housekeeper in a dark kitchen will be astonished at the unaccountable buoyancy she will feel, if the kitchen be repainted in a fresh, light enamel."

She also wrote of the considerable debate occurring at the time about the size of a convenient kitchen. Many people, she said, maintained that the shortest distance from the range to the sink and cupboards simplified work. She warned that a kitchen large enough to permit the introduction of numerous pieces of equipment, such as cabinet, refrigerator, table and so forth, is likewise apt to be a stumbling place that makes for extra steps at cleaning times. She concluded, "The ideal amount of floor space, probably, is just enough to walk, without interference, to all the necessary daily equipment, as stove, sink and cupboard, and enough extra space for a comfortable chair, while cooking food must be watched. The built-in breakfast nook, according to the author, was a naturally cozy corner.

Earl Lifshe, in *The Housewares Story, A History of the American Housewares Industry* (National Housewares Manufacturers Association, 1973, 380 pp.) talks about the other significant trend of the 1920s—the addition of color to kitchen utensils and appliances. Electric refrigerators could be handpainted by aspiring home artists, but if no one in the family was so inclined, one could even buy a refrigerator already decorated in vermilion, with parrots perched on green branches.

Although the scrubbed white, laboratory look for kitchens was being replaced with lots of color, the 1930s was a time for a sharp, scientific focus on efficient kitchen design. In 1935, an *American Cookery* magazine article

The kitchen of 1928 looked much less like a laboratory. It had become a cozier place for the home cook who had room to move and work, and also a cheerful corner in which to sit, relax, and study cookbooks for new ideas. *Courtesy of the makers of Armstrong Flooring.*

suggested the ultimate in convenience for the homemaker—the made-to-measure kitchen. According to the author of "A New Deal for the Home-maker," one of the most important factors to be considered in avoiding unnecessary fatigue was the height of the work surfaces. The article discussed in detail the 1929 findings of Dr. Lillian M. Gilbreth, an internationally famous industrial engineer, who believed that motion and fatigue studies were as necessary in the home as in industry because "the homemaker's time and energy are as valuable to her and her family as those of the industrial worker are to his employer and himself." Dr. Gilbreth defined two kinds of fatigue. The first was unavoidable fatigue that resulted from using up the normal energy spent on work that must be done. The second was avoidable fatigue resulting from work that didn't have to be done.

The kitchen Dr. Gilbreth analyzed measured 9 by 12 feet, had two doors, two windows and had everything arranged incorrectly from a motion-study viewpoint. Using a yardstick, T-square, compass, templates and process charts, she plotted the number of steps, motions and operations a home-maker performed just to make a cake. The total effort required to bake the cake included making 50 motions and walking 143 feet. (Desserts wouldn't have been included on my menus!)

She developed a plan using circular workplaces, or workstations, where all the important working equipment was to be kept in predetermined positions so that it was within easy reach of the homemaker. The circular workplace was placed in one corner of the room with the refrigerator beside one wall, the planning desk in the corner, the kitchen cabinet next to the other wall and the oven part of the range beside the cabinet. The top-stove circular workplace, consisting of the top-stove, drain board and sink, was

In the early 1930s, some cooks turned to the White Cross electric range, which was compact and quickly cooked, fried, baked and broiled foods for the affordable price of $44.

Labor-saving features were the focus of the Glenwood gas ranges like this one advertised in 1932. It turned the gas on and off by itself, so that a meal could be cooking while the lady of the house went out to play bridge all afternoon.

arranged along the side wall. Then, she used her tape-measure and yardstick to measure the homemaker for height, reach from fingertip to fingertip, space needed to move about freely at each workplace, hip measure, height to highest shelf the homemaker could reach, height of most comfortable horizontal plane for working surface, distance from elbow to floor when standing, length of forearm and distance from elbow to floor when sitting in an ordinary kitchen chair.

After everything was rearranged according to convenience and efficiency for the homemaker, Dr. Gilbreth again charted the effort necessary to bake a cake. This time, motions were reduced from 50 to 24 and the distance walked went from 143 to 24 feet—a saving of 119 feet of fatigue. She declared, "Think of the leisure time you could have every day if you saved 83 percent of your walking distance on every operation you performed! With a kitchen made to your own measurements, who of you wouldn't enjoy spending a part of each day working there? With unnecessary fatigue eliminated, equipment efficiently arranged, wouldn't a kitchen so planned be an inspiration for your creative work?"

Although it sounds heavenly, it's easy to understand why standardization came about: A kitchen made-to-measure for someone who's five feet tall could not be easily used by a six-footer.

In *American Cookery*, a 1938 house-tour article, "A House in Step With The Times," made particular comment on a breakfast nook and kitchen design. "What a breakfast nook. I'd risk serving friend husband burnt cereal

Worlds apart is the only way to describe the kitchens of the 1920s and 1930s, when scientists and efficiency experts turned their attention to saving steps and convenience for home cooks. This compact kitchen, a trend-setter in 1934, featured built-in cabinets, work area and stove all within easy reach of the cook. It also had a cozy breakfast nook for two that could be expanded to four, by using a larger table. Courtesy of the makers of Armstrong Flooring.

and cold coffee in a nook like this. Sunshine everywhere . . . and bright yellow paint. But this nook has more than synthetic sunshine to put friend husband in a good humor. There's a telephone at his elbow, a cabinet for his magazines, a special outlet for his reading lamp. But this breakfast nook is simply a 'teaser' for the kitchen of which it is really a part. A streamlined kitchen. A scientifically planned kitchen. I had the same sensation in this kitchen that I had in the kitchen of the streamliner City of Denver."

The room that drew such breathless praise was long and narrow with built-in cupboards running the full length, on both sides. Electric equipment was arranged according to the latest scientific ideas. "There was no retracing of steps. No walking two and a half miles in preparing the day's meals. And far from being a white enameled laboratory, this room had the cheeriness of a grandmother's kitchen. The walls were covered with gay canary linoleum, in happy contrast to the royal blue linoleum on floors and cupboard counters. The cupboards were of natural birch with pulls of black enameled wood."

In the 1930s, the Victorian "essential," the dining room, was shrinking or being eliminated from house plans because kitchens were becoming more colorful and pleasant. Electric and gas stoves were much nicer to have around and a good deal cleaner than earlier wood and coal ranges, inviting the family to linger well beyond simple meal hours.

Kitchens during the World War II years changed little from those of the 1930s because most factories had been converted to wartime production, sacrifice and frugality were the hallmark of the early 1940s. By the war's end, however, a culinary revolution began in America.

Jane and Michael Stern, authors of *American Gourmet, Classic Recipes, Deluxe Delights, Flamboyant Favorites and Swank 'Company Food' from the '50s and '60s*, (Harper Collins, 1991, 286 pp.) explained the impact of World War

II on American cuisine. "The war helped create the technology for current frozen and convenience foods. It also de-provincialized this country's palate. When the GIs were sent overseas, they tasted a range of foods that was new to them and when they came home, they wanted more. They helped get us out of the chicken croquette and cream gravy, pre-Eisenhower era of boring foods. In the 1920s, 1930s and early 1940s, a person who was considered well-bred and refined ate very bland foods. Only uncouth immigrants used garlic or anchovies or ate highly spiced foods. God forbid that anyone might burp!"

Postwar to the 21st Century

In the 1950s, the family was getting re-established and the baby boom was in full swing. Mom was in the kitchen, like Harriet Nelson and Donna Reed, cooking all kinds of homey dishes for family and friends. She didn't seem rushed and even had time to get together with neighbors for midmorning conversation and coffee.

She was happier, too, perhaps, because kitchen designers of the 1950s no longer kept her isolated. Although no one was directly underfoot, the family was within easy view, thanks to an open concept in design. Architects and homeowners discovered that an open arrangement of the dining room, living room and kitchen made all three rooms look larger. Some kitchens included a special play area for the children, well away from the hissing pressure cooker, the hot oven and the whistling tea kettle. There was a design that even included plans for a model railroad platform that dropped down over the top of the washer and dryer when not in use.

New homes with formal dining rooms still had "cozy kitchen eatspots" because homemakers had decided eating in the kitchen was more convenient than carrying food all the way to the dining room. (What would the Victorians have thought!) The kitchen designs could be anything from a restaurant-style booth or banquette to a combination table/island jutting into a section of the kitchen. Either arrangement, with family members sitting

After World War II ended, companies could again turn their attention to producing equipment and appliances for domestic use. This bright kitchen from 1947, was brimming with the latest electrical appliances, including a roaster, blender, toaster, coffeemaker and mixer. Courtesy of the makers of Armstrong Flooring.

across from one another or in a semicircular pattern, was more sociable than some one-sided breakfast bars of the 1950s that seated the family in a row, all facing a kitchen wall.

Conversation may not have been necessary because kitchen designers often placed the increasingly popular television sets within easy view of tables. Televisions were also to play a major role in changing Americans' tastes. Stern said, "Television probably was the best culinary machine of the day because it brought cooking shows into the home."

Color choices, rather than decor, made the rooms bright and cozy. Kitchens were done in shades of sunny yellow, coral and orange, along with pink and raspberry. Large appliances added to the rainbow of splashy colors because they could be delivered in white, turquoise, yellow, pink, blue or brown.

Other than canister sets, spice racks, a bowl of fruit and a few potted plants, kitchens had a clean, uncluttered and homey look that was a far cry from the country style of the late 1970s and the 1980s.

Steel, rather than warm wood, was featured in many advertisements for kitchen counters and cabinets. One 1955 advertisement from United States Steel read:

Show any girl, from 18 to 80, a modern, custom-designed all-steel kitchen . . . the kitchen that's a Wife-Saver . . . and watch what happens:

The all-steel kitchen brightens her eyes . . . because it's beautiful.

It lightens her heart . . . because it lightens her housework.

And it tickles her sense of thrift . . . because it's the most kitchen for the money there is.

A steel kitchen, remember. It has to be a steel kitchen. Because, in the kitchen, as elsewhere, only steel can do so many jobs so well.

Steel gives you those smooth, easy-to-clean kitchen cabinets that open and shut so quietly, that adjust so readily to your storage needs, that can't possibly crack or come apart.

Steel gives you those strong, durable built-in conveniences: broom closet, mixer compartment, cutlery drawer, flour bin. And those smart, long-lasting accessories: breakfast bar, corner cabinet, kitchen desk. And that stainless counter edging that never needs polishing, never wears off.

And most important of all, steel gives you a colorful custom-made kitchen at ready-made cost.

So make your kitchen a Wife-Saver . . . for beauty, for duty.

Whether or not she had a steel kitchen, the 1950s housewife surely was trying all kinds of new gadgets that were becoming available, from electric griddles to portable oven rotiseries. Tabletop appliances were popular, too, perhaps because the homemaker could cook and serve from her seat at the table, rather than carrying it from stove to table, or, worse yet, from stove to dining-room table. (Clearly, America was still a few decades away from the exercise craze and its emphasis on walking.)

Designer kitchens of the 1950s also featured such amenities as a rolling work counter/family fun bar; prefabricated fireplaces; a built-in barbecue

In the 1950s, kitchens got much of their character from the use of bright colors on walls, floors and basic furnishings, rather than from a large assortment of decorations. Electrical appliances were out of sight. Ovens were built in. A breadboard and a cheery window view (somewhat obscured by the mandatory spice rack and a few ornamental containers) were focal points in this kitchen of 1957. Courtesy of the makers of Armstrong Flooring.

corner; cabinet storage for sewing, toys and games; laundry centers incorporating washer and dryer into the overall kitchen design; as well as infrared bulbs (usually used by restaurants to keep food hot until it could be carried to the table). By the mid-1950s, consumers could buy such large appliances as built-in wall ovens with French doors; a stacking refrigerator and freezer that could also be placed side-by-side or across the room from each other (modular refrigeration units are expected to emerge again in the 1990s); a gas range with a fifth burner; foldaway electric cooking units that were recessed into a backwall panel to free up counter space when they weren't in use (so much for the newness of today's so-called appliance garages); a hinged stovetop for easy cleaning; a massive side-by-side refrigerator-freezer; and kitchen centers that grouped major electric appliances (oven and range, dishwasher, sink and garbage disposal and washer and dryer) all in a row.

In the 1960s, as families moved to the suburbs and into the middle class, airfares became affordable. Not ones to miss opportunities, Americans packed their bags and knives, forks and spoons so they could learn more about their world. According to the Sterns, The New York World's Fair of 1964 was even more of an impetus when it came to inspiring Americans to try foods they'd never tasted before:

The 1960s found women cooking happily in their L-shaped, U-shaped or corridor-plan kitchens creating a world of new recipes. When they ran out of recipes collected while on summer vacations, they tuned into the television. As the Sterns recount: "James Beard started it with his appearances in 1946 on the Borden Company variety show, "Elsie Presents." And when Julia Child went on the air in the 1960's with her show called "The French Chef," the gourmet era was on its way."

The Sterns also credit "Galloping Gourmet" Graham Kerr with making a contribution to the era. "He was sexy—not overly sensuous, but playful enough to making cooking seem like a swinging activity." A number of lesser known, but well-watched personalities such as the Philadelphia Electric Company's Florence Hanford, also took to the airwaves to supply recipes. Home cooks watched the television demonstrations and cooked the foods they'd learned to make. Cookbooks they owned weren't so-called coffeetable cookbooks, existing only to be scanned and admired. They were used, splattered with food and full of turned-down corners indicating favorite recipes.

Home cooks began to consider themselves gourmets and joined gourmet clubs. Ironically, these same gourmet cooks who prepared beef Wellington and lobster Thermidor on weekends were content to combine ingredients from boxes, cans and bags to create weeknight dinners. Kitchens designed for these gourmet cooks opened onto larger family rooms, separated only by a chest-high serving bar, for example. Spices and frequently used foods were out in the open, on open shelves. A cook's pot and pan collection no longer had to be hidden behind closed doors, either. Favorites were suspended above the stove on a restaurant-style rack. A center for mixing and baking (women were still cooking from scratch, as well as taking a few shortcuts) included a wood counter for chopping, mixing, rolling or kneading dough, while the upper cabinet contained staples, canned goods and mixes.

Corning introduced platinum-edged Centura, "the first ceramic without worry of breakage" that could go into the dishwasher without losing its platinum and enabled the cook to freeze and cook in the same casserole. Refrigerators came in canary yellow, turquoise, lettuce green and even two-tone blue and white (with a pink interior). Frigidaire observed the 50th anniversary of the Imperial Dishmobile and Mirro introduced a line of electric appliances that had charcoal-blue trim.

Plastic was the "in" material for the kitchen as designers showed how it could be used for countertops, cabinet surfaces, walls and paneling. Cooks could watch time pass on such novelties as the General Electric Teatime Clock that was shaped like a tea kettle and the Pennsylvania Spice Chest Clock of sculptured cherry wood that included a rack for four spice bottles below the clock's face.

The 1970s were boom years for gourmet cooks. Taking advantage of the interest stirred by earlier television cooking shows, many good cooks opened cooking schools or offered cooking classes in their communities. Eager

As celebrity cooks and travel expanded people's culinary horizons, they began experimenting with the cuisines of other countries. They included favorite pots or other cooking utensils as part of their kitchen decor and weren't worried about hiding the kitchen from guests. This kitchen of 1967 had a stove island separating the kitchen's main work areas from the home's dining area. Kitchen collectibles were becoming part of the decor. Courtesy of Armstrong World Industries.

learners absorbed what they had to offer, subscribed to such cooking magazines as *Bon Appetit, Food & Wine,* and *Gourmet,* and browsed the bookshops to select from a huge harvest of new cookbooks.

Carl Sontheimer made it easier for the enthusiastic cooks to try all the new recipes when he introduced the Cuisinart Food Processor in 1973. In 1977, Cuisinart began publishing its own magazine, called *The Pleasures of Cooking.* Its masthead read like a "Who's Who" of the culinary world at the time with such luminaries as James Beard, Jacques Pepin, Barbara Kafka, Abby Mandel and Paula Wolfert.

As in the previous decade, cooks continued to showcase their new-found knowledge by forming gourmet clubs (updated and upscaled versions of the old covered dish suppers) but still were known to take shortcuts on weekdays. After all, they could buy breakfast in easy-to-eat bars and could serve the new Betty Crocker "Snackin' Cake" in the same pan used to mix and bake it. The only utensil required was a fork to mix the batter.

Planters Oil would send a wok to any consumer who enclosed $5.95 and a cap from its 100% peanut oil. The West Bend corn popper's top flipped over and became the serving bowl for popcorn. Mirro was marketing an omelet pan that had two recipes printed on its sides.

A fuel shortage meant people often passed the time by cooking or by doing such home-based crafts as decoupage, block printing and basket weaving.

Kitchen colors were changing from brights to earth tones. The Sears 100% immersible Flavor Fresh percolator came in parsley green, poppy red and curry yellow. Regal Ware Inc. of Kewaskum, Wisc., coaxed: "Hey, American Woman. You like bold colors in your fashions, your car and your

The country look was "in" in the 1970s and with it, came a plethora of country-style collectibles. In this 1970s kitchen, warmth was provided by baskets, stoneware and other cooking equipment that was in full view. Courtesy of the makers of Armstrong Flooring.

furniture, even your bathroom fixtures. Now how about doing something about those pots and pans?" Regal was promoting its Mardi Gras line of cookware in avocado, flame and harvest gold. The porcelain-clad aluminum was coated with nonstick Teflon II.

Armstrong World Industries was showing its Solarian flooring for the kitchen in avocado green and filled in the rest of the picture with chrome and wicker furnishings, live plants on wicker bookcases with glass shelves, butcher-block countertops and clear glass canisters. But the fresh, clean lines of this kitchen were about to give way to the country look that began in earnest late in the 1970s.

The kitchen of the 1980s became a display mecca for every kind of collectible, from fruit jars, yellowware and redware to treenware and pewter. Exposed beams were used to show off basket and copper cookware collections, as well as to hold up the kitchen ceiling. Kitchens also became brighter, thanks to window walls, greenhouse windows and skylights. Regular appliances became inconspicuous.

Despite the beauty and brightness of the kitchens, as well as the cozy touches added by kitchen collectibles, daily cooking was becoming an endangered art. Microwave ovens proliferated and found their way into almost every kitchen by the end of the decade. If family members weren't popping frozen entrees into the microwave, they stopped for takeout food or dined in restaurants. When there was some at-home cooking to be done, men were pitching in and helping out.

Gourmet clubs formed in the 1960s and 1970s were having a harder time scheduling meals because many women had joined the full-time work force. Main course salads and grilled foods became popular because they simplified mealtimes for hurried cooks and reflected growing health concerns that developed during the decade. Claims of "low-salt," "low-calorie" and "high-fiber" helped sell hundreds of convenience foods.

Fancier cooking and meals from scratch were weekend pastimes. Pasta machines and bread machines offered some old-fashioned flavor but cut short the amount of time needed to obtain it. Herb gardens were planted. Cookbooks continued to flood the market, but they became coffeetable decorations and bedtime fare, rather than kitchen manuals.

During the final decade of the 20th century, kitchens will become "great rooms" for every member of the family. Country decor will be scaled back a little bit, to allow some open space in the room. Decor will take different directions, too, as people explore their own history and personalize their surroundings to reflect their roots. Although there are many sleek, contemporary kitchens making the pages of national magazines, Art Deco and 1950's-style kitchens are experiencing revivals, too.

Appliance garages are being used to park equipment not being used, but still other appliances, designed decades ago, are being displayed as part of a kitchen's period decor. Rolling carts pull out of cabinet sections to become work centers that can be moved anywhere in the kitchen. Refrigerators may once more be available in modular units (as they were in the 1950's), and

At the end of the 1980s, the kitchen was compact and organized, although there was still some room for decorative elements. Courtesy of the makers of Armstrong Flooring.

kitchen computers will do everything from retrieving recipes to placing the grocery order.

Small appliances will be user-friendly so that consumers won't have to read detailed instruction booklets before being able to use them. They'll be designed to operate efficiently and conveniently. European styling will continue to be popular. Countertop appliances will take up less and less room so there's more of a chance they'll be left out, rather than tucked into a cabinet or drawer until they're forgotten and, eventually, discarded.

Foods prepared in home kitchens will be lower in fat and fresh and organically grown or raised. Ethnic fare will reflect America's traditional melting pot and go far beyond basic Chinese, Italian or Mexican.

Kitchens designed during the 1990s will continue to "make room for daddy" in formal ways. While men helped occasionally with cooking tasks in the 1980s, dual-income households now have double workstations, with double sinks, double countertop cooking areas and even two microwave ovens. Because both parents will be working together in the kitchen, it follows that children will be there, too. With luck, they'll be learning food preparation and family recipes as well as taking the time to do their homework at the kitchen table or breakfast bar.

While some people will stay home to save money, others will spend more time around the house to be with their families and recapture old values. As the new millennium approaches, the preservation of family traditions will be as comforting as the cooking and comfort foods that warm our kitchens.

Collecting Considerations

The Collector's Kitchen of the 1990s

Before World War II and throughout the 1950s, Early American antiques were the expected norm in decorating a collector's kitchen. But that era is history. Today, defining a collector's kitchen is not nearly so simple and stocking it no longer is limited to 18th or early 19th century antiques. And these kitchens aren't found solely in grand country homes and old, rambling farmhouses. Kitchen collectibles add warmth to the heart of suburban split-levels and are equally at home in urban apartments.

Broadly interpreted, a collector's kitchen of the 1990s is filled with what a person likes, covets and collects. There will surely be some tools or furnishings from the 18th, 19th or early 20th centuries. But today's collectors are quite happy including some gadgets used just a generation or two before their own. They're also beginning to accumulate kitchenware from the 1930s, 1940s, 1950s as well as from the 1960s and 1970s.

Carol Bohn, an organizer of KOOKS (Kollectors Of Old Kitchen Stuff) and a resident of Mifflinburg, Pa., said, "One of the reasons why kitchen collecting is growing is because it still is an affordable field. People can collect kitchenware at any level and from any era. There are great finds out there for everyone. A person can make a collection of it for $30, $300, $3,000 or more." She added, "No matter whether a person is going into a hot category like eggbeaters or rolling pins or a segment that is just beginning to attract collectors like wireware (used to make all kinds of kitchen tools like cream

A sunny green Fiestaware salad fork now is used as a decorative item, but was a useful kitchen utensil in the 1940s.

Iron pie crimper with a round barrel is thought to date from the late 1700s or early 1800s. From the author's collection.

whippers, trivets, flour sieves and pie racks), it's an investment in nostalgia." According to Bohn, filling a kitchen with flea market treasures or antique shop finds is all part of our interest in our roots and what life was like for people who came before us.

THE EVOLUTION OF COUNTRY STYLE

The country style, a new and important phase in acquiring kitchenware and decorating homes that evolved in the 1960s, came about for several reasons. First, not everyone could collect Early American because that translated to East Coast, and mostly, New England. Thus, many of the most desirable antiques were out of range geographically for collectors in the rest of the country. Second, these highly coveted 18th-century antiques became out of range financially for all but the wealthiest of collectors. The country style also owes a debt to the social changes of the 1960s as well as to the Bicentennial. The so-called hippies of the 1960s found beauty in nature and in a return to the old ways that characterized life in an earlier and simpler America. As these hippies became yuppies who joined the mainstream, they still rebelled against living in homes with contrived decor and considered museum-style Early American to be much too stifling. They needed and wanted to be comfortable in a home environment they created for themselves by collecting things they liked and recalled from their own pasts.

The Bicentennial, with its grassroots celebrations that began in every town and hamlet across America and climaxed with enough fireworks to cast a golden glow on the Statue of Liberty, made it clear that America's history was far more than that 150-year period before the American Revolution. The immigrants who came through Ellis Island from Ireland, Italy, Germany, Poland and dozens of other countries had just as much to do with this country's growth and prosperity as those who stepped off the Mayflower. It was time to re-examine all of America's roots. People in each region of the country looked to their past, joyously rediscovering their own cultural heritage. Linking their personal histories to the country's past became part of American kitchen collecting and decorating in its current form. It has become a decorating style that isn't likely to fade as quickly as something like the Memphis design movement because it's right for Americans and for the times. Americans, known the world over for their casual and comfortable lifestyles, can find just as much pleasure in filling their kitchens with Fiestaware or Fire-King as they can in passing the time in a well-worn rocking chair.

Delicate berry baskets like this one were taken on many a country outing in a time when berry-picking provided a day's amusement. Collectors covet them for the memories they evoke, as well as for their simple beauty.

Salt and pepper shakers easily fit into kitchen decorating schemes and can be rotated in and out of storage as seasons change. The bright pink flowers on these Stangl shakers are cheerful harbingers of spring and find their way out of their boxes in time to replace St. Patrick's Day Leprechauns or shamrocks.

Jean LemMon, former editor-in-chief of *Country Home* and now editor-in-chief of *Better Homes & Gardens,* has said, "Country in all its forms is an honest way of decorating, rather than another example of keeping up with the Joneses. It's giving up the high fashion tailored suits for khaki slacks and a flannel shirt or shedding what really isn't you. Assembling the furnishings that connect you with your immediate and more distant past is fulfilling and honest."

It's also comforting. Surrounding yourself with these trappings of the past is something of an emotional security blanket when the world is in a constant state of flux and international crises can emerge at any moment. Old kitchenware that becomes part of a home's decor will endure. After all, anyone who has taken the time and spent the money to assemble a collection of old gadgets is not likely to give them up every year or two, just to remain trendy. It just doesn't make good sense, particularly during tight economic times. At the same time, anyone who assembles a kitchen collection that is true to his or her own heritage (rather than having a decorator assemble it) isn't going to part with these special finds quickly or even in a lifetime.

In the 1970s, Americans approached flea markets, yard and garage sales, as well as antique shops and malls, as if they were off on treasure hunts. Out to buy remnants of their past, they quickly assembled an eclectic array of furnishings for their homes and, particularly, for their kitchens. As collection after collection filled every bit of available space, home interiors began looking like wall-to-wall flea markets.

During the 1980s, the publishing industry began to define and limit kitchen collecting by working certain elements, including stoneware, graniteware and baskets, into various decors with cookie-cutter regularity. Country had become as hot as an old kitchen range on a cold winter's day. But as everyone scrambled to obtain the most popular country trappings, prices for

Ever wonder how dieters could thin-slice bread in the days before bakeries were turning out presliced, thin-cut diet breads? This Slice A Slice gadget, which held the bread securely while it was being sliced, was the answer.

Thomas Stahl redware cup is now a hot collectible and would make an attractive addition on any type of table—either rustic pine or fine cherry.

many of these items skyrocketed in value in a relatively short period of time. As prices rose, so-called country collectors were forced to begin discovering and accumulating items from more recent, and still affordable, eras. Suddenly, electrical appliances and colorful kitchen gadgets from the 1920s, 1930s and 1940s became part of the collecting picture. In the late 1980s and early 1990s collectors calmed down a bit (after all, their homes had only so much room for collections) and prices stabilized. They're still collecting, however. Mindful of space limitations (as well as the time it takes to keep collections clean), they're rotating their displays and choosing new items carefully. They're even justifying some purchases by using what they buy.

As kitchen collecting matures during the 1990s, Americans will explore their roots in other lands. But they'll also look to their more immediate past for their kitchenware. Finally, they'll also be focusing on patent-dated, mass-produced antiques and collectibles. They'll no doubt weave in some pieces made by native Americans as well as simpler Victorian country furnishings that are more comfortable than ornate and decorative. The solid, simple and straightforward furnishings that characterized the turn-of-the-century Arts and Crafts movement will become an increasing presence in decorating. (You've no doubt seen chairs and other pieces associated with the Arts and Crafts movement, but it might have been called Mission or Mission Oak furniture.) Although some Americans may be a bit short on their knowledge of world geography and history, they will undoubtedly cross-pollinate their kitchens with trappings they discover in other countries. They'll also intermingle decades and even centuries as they search for their roots and design a highly personal, but thoroughly comfortable environment.

Raymond Waites, considered a pioneer of the American country movement and cofounder of New York City's Gear, Inc. design firm, sees no end to the dominance of loosely defined country style of decorating. But he points to still another direction it will take during the 1990s. Collectors will take a more formal approach to country. His example: When he used to entertain, he'd put some candles in old glass jelly jars and place them on a rustic pine table. Today, he's more likely to use a baroque-style silver candelabra on the pine table for mood lighting during a party.

Although he readily admits there are some people, such as his mother and mother-in-law, who would say that kind of decorating is all wrong, Waites said, "I love it. The tension makes a room interesting. It's like wearing a T-shirt with a tuxedo or a silk blouse with blue jeans. It's like plunking a display of old, handwoven baskets in the middle of a sleek, black and white and stainless-steel 1990s kitchen."

Kitchen collectors needn't worry about mixing design styles and decorating periods, either, if they follow Waites' simple strategy. He advises that people should decide early in their lives on the colors they love. No matter whether they discover a piece of Stangl pottery or a turquoise toaster, they'll have their color preferences to help make their buying decisions. Color, after all, does an excellent job of unifying a mixture of furnishings from different periods and styles.

What to Save from the 1990s

The faded, denim apron hanging on a hook in my kitchen is a constant reminder that I've carelessly destroyed a collectible. It's an apron like those used by one of the era's most famous chefs. In now-barely legible writing, the trademark apron bears her name—Julia Child. It also is imprinted with the classic words she used to conclude her televised cooking programs—"Bon Appetit!" Mailed out as a promotion when one of Child's books was a new selection for The Book of The Month Club, the apron was a practical giveaway. I pressed it into service at a time when I had no other aprons nor any knowledge of the potential future value of kitchen collectibles. If it were sent to me today, I would treat it far differently. I'd carefully wrap and save it for the future, along with numerous other examples of 1990s kitchenware.

THE "THIRTY YEAR RULE"

Such behavior is a collector's answer to speculating on the stock market because it's done in the hopes that the objects will gain value in future years. But those who speculate in kitchenware also should know about the "Thirty Year Rule" coined by antiques and collectibles expert Harry L. Rinker: for the first 30 years of anything's existence, its value is purely speculative. Accord-

This green Red Wing Pottery teapot, with a handle made to look like wicker and its leaf design, could recall summer days in winter's darkest hours—when a warm cup of tea always hits the spot.

Printed aprons have become a form of advertising, for products, brands, restaurants and cooking schools.

ing to the rule, there has to be time for people to use, destroy and discard many of the identical, mass-produced objects. And it also takes 30 years for a person who grew up with something to miss it and, in a wave of nostalgia, attempt to reacquire it.

My apron fits these requirements. As I demonstrated, some of the aprons will be destroyed or discarded. Also, the endearing "French Chef" who affected many lives by sparking an age of culinary discovery will surely inspire nostalgia about good food and good times in years to come. With all that in mind, I rationalize ruining my apron as doing my part to increase the value of those still held by others. But it just doesn't make me feel any better. The experience has made me all the more determined to buy and stash other examples of today's kitchenware so that I'll have my share of treasures when my era's kitchen equipment shows up 30 to 50 years from now on the tables at antiques and collectibles shows and fairs.

What should be saved? Dealers and collectors laugh when asked and generally say something like, "If I knew answers like that, I'd be rich." But anyone who has spent some time buying and selling kitchen collectibles and antiques can make some guesses and constructive suggestions about the 1990's tools that will be tomorrow's collectibles. Gary Miller and Scotty Mitchell, for example, have saved every attachment Cuisinart ever introduced and also admit to saving gadgets that are amusing.

Marian Gore, of Marian L. Gore Bookseller in San Gabriel, Ca., suggests saving regional charity cookbooks that tell something about the community and contain its special recipes; limited-edition cookbooks or culinary histories; books that contain people's culinary memories and recollections like the tomes produced by the late M.F.K. Fisher: children's cookbooks and celebrity cookbooks.

Teapots in unusual shapes are among the items Kathy Schneider, of Pearl Washington's Kitchenware in Whitman, Mass., is saving. One of her treasures is a limited-edition teapot bearing the likeness of former President Ronald Reagan.

Another dealer suggested buying upscale kitchen utensils and equipment because they will generally be of higher quality and will have more appeal to tomorrow's collectors than run-of-the-mill housewares.

DEVELOPING A SAVINGS PLAN

But with a little thought, any collector who knows the current market for antiques and collectibles can develop a more focused personal savings plan. Design, style, and color are important. The idea is to buy kitchenware that will be in as much demand tomorrow as today's coveted Art Deco or 1950s-era equipment. Consider purchasing equipment or ephemera with connections to recognizable celebrities (like my apron) or cartoon characters. Pick up appliances and kitchenware that reflect the times or might seem curious to later generations. A Salad Shooter that sends chopped and diced veggies flying into a salad bowl or a machine that turns ordinary vegetables into curlicues, could be in this category. How about a coffeemaker for one or a mini food chopper/processor because both were created for today's smaller households?

Kitchenware designed for holidays probably will be good material for a collection. Consider such items as limited-edition Christmas cookie molds and cake pans, special holiday plates and other trimmings like Halloween or Valentine's day cookie cutters.

With these ideas in mind, here's a partial list of the things I'm considering:

❧ Cooking magazines including *Food & Wine, Bon Appetit* and *Cooking Light,* because these publications are logging tomorrow's culinary history today.

❧ Sleek appliances featuring European styling.

❧ Recipe pamphlets produced by food manufacturers in an effort to promote sales for their products.

❧ Commemorative tins, bottles and boxes marking food product anniversaries, special holidays or special events. (I still have the plastic cube containing red, white and blue jelly beans marking Ronald Reagan's inauguration.)

❧ Aprons, canvas bags and other forms of ephemera that bear food company logos or that are connected with famous culinary personalities.

❧ Brightly colored kitchen tools like Swiss vegetable peelers that come in green, yellow, red and blue.

❧ Pretty ceramic spoonrests in vegetable or fruit shapes.

❧ Glass cake pans and reproduction ceramic ware including food-related majolica.

The styling, design and the way it cooks could make American Harvest's Jet Stream Oven a collectible of the future. Courtesy of American Harvest.

Saving the catalogs distributed by the nation's leading kitchen supply and cookware companies, like Williams-Sonoma, is a wise idea because these will also be collectible. Of course, the catalogs also will help to identify various kitchen gadgets and gizmos of their times.

Longaberger Basket Company's Santa cookie mold could have plenty of cross-market appeal in the future. Those who might be interested in it include collectors of Longaberger baskets, Christmas items, Santa Clauses, and cookie molds.

❧ Kitchenware made for use by children.

❧ Cookie jars, sandwich makers and waffle irons with familiar characters such as Mickey or Minnie Mouse, Snoopy, or the Sesame Street gang.

❧ A stylish fondue pot.

❧ Cast-iron muffin pans with unusual shapes like seashells, zoo animals, hearts or teddy bears.

❧ A cast-iron frying pan bearing the image of Cajun Chef Paul Prudhomme, who taught the world to blacken redfish.

Just remember that any kitchenware stashed for future collectors must be in mint condition. All items I've named, or anything anyone else decides to save, must be maintained in the original boxes with still-sealed overwrap. It's the only way to guarantee these future collectibles will bring maximum value.

Upset at the news that you can't use any of it? Too bad. The newer the kitchenware is, the better its condition must be. As Rinker said, "If an object produced in the 1990s is used even once, its long-term collectible value has been jeopardized seriously." There's only one way for an avid cook to cope with this reality and that is to buy two of any item—one to use and one to save or, in other words, one for the kitchen and one for the closet, attic,

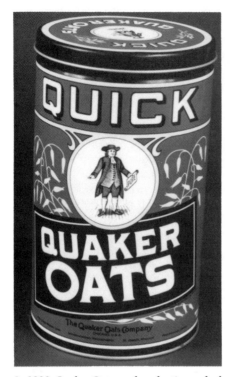

Oreo cookies are hard enough to resist under normal circumstances. But when the packaging makes them doubly appealing, as this Christmas tin does, they become an irresistible temptation.

In 1990, Quaker Oats produced a tin marked to be a replica of its 1922 Quick Quaker Oats label.

The attractive blue tins made to mark the 100th anniversary of Maxwell House 1892 Slow Roasted Coffee could catch the eye of tomorrow's collectors, just as tins of yesteryear are of interest to today's collectors.

garage or crawl space. There will be a 30- to 50-year wait to see if I've been right about the kitchenware to save for future collectors. Wanna meet at your warehouse or mine when the time comes?

It's relatively certain that the kitchen will remain as the heart of the American home. Studies have shown that it's still the place for family conversations, gatherings, study, bill-paying and phone conversations. And unless tomorrow's Americans are radically different, they're still going to want warm and cozy surroundings. Kitchen antiques and collectibles surely will be a part of those settings.

State of the Market

The recession of the late 1980s and early 1990s did its share to pare down the kitchenware market that was booming in the late 1970s and early to mid-1980s. "Some collectors who lost their jobs had to sell their collections. Others had less discretionary income," said Dana DeMore, publisher of *Kitchen Antiques & Collectibles News.*

But the category was no harder hit than any other, according to Joan and Warner Johnson of Kitchen Cupboard Antiques in Randolph, N.J., and Andover, N.Y. The couple, who have been buying and selling kitchen antiques for 32 years, have come to expect their business to go the way of the housing market. "When real estate is slow, the antique business is slow. When the housing market is good, we do well," said Joan Johnson.

Translating this into recession reality meant that a good dry sink that sold in a week or two during good times sometimes sat for a month or more before being bought when the recession was at its worst. The story is the same for early painted furniture. According to Johnson, "Four or five years ago, it sold very quickly. But when times were slow, we had to hold onto it for a while." Once-scorned collectibles from the 1930s and 1940s and even those from the 1950s and 1960s have also begun getting more attention from midlevel buyers who entered the market for more recent collectibles when they were squeezed out of the higher-priced antiques market.

Nevertheless, high-income collectors, who had money before the most recent recession, generally also had full wallets during the toughest years. The Primitive Man of Carmel, N.Y., otherwise known as Bob Cahn, said the recession's effects on his business were marginal. Known for his ability to find almost anything for anyone who has the money to pay for it, Cahn specializes in merchandise that is different and top-of-the-line because, he said, "I need to keep a step ahead of my customers. Their requests for hard-to-find antiques never slowed down during the recession. The only thing I could say, however, is that my list of new customers was slower to grow." A veteran of numerous major shows, he also observed that, "There have been more 'tire kickers and museum-goers' out there than there are acquirers. These are the people who view a trip to an antique show as a vicarious thrill rather than seeing themselves as actual participants."

But there is plenty of action when something good is sought. "Competition for such rarefied items as nutmeg graters, eggbeaters and lemon juicers is so ferocious that when one person puts out a pictorial want list, his competitors photocopy it and put their names on it," Cahn said. An *Antiques Week* Eastern Edition contained an advertisement for an Express Egg beater (characterized by its flyswatter-shaped blade). It sold for $50. Another collector heard about it and offered the first buyer $300. Said DeMore, who offered the example, "There still are plenty of people in the market who can spend $500

This happy-faced china reamer has found it harder to find a happy home since its price climbed to more than $25 and lookers became more cost-conscious and less prone to make spur-of-the-moment purchases.

If you grew up with Fiestaware, you may be so tired of it that you've lost all interest in it—until you see the price a piece like this orange pitcher brings at an antique show or flea market.

on an eggbeater, $700 or more on a nutmeg grater or thousands on a good piece of furniture."

But there is one way in which the last recession seasoned both the small- and the big-time buyer. Just as people at all levels of income now think twice about spending top dollar for dinner in a gourmet restaurant, the buyers of kitchen antiques and collectibles are more careful about what they're buying. At any level, they want value for their money. The free-spending 1980's have been replaced by the tight-fisted 1990's. "Buyers have been very tough negotiators," Johnson said. She added, "They've wanted better deals, no matter how well something has been priced. Profit margins really suffered." But she sees some "lightening up" with an improving economy, because the demand for kitchen antiques and collectibles always exceeds the supply. "The competition is out there for buyers, just as much as it is for sellers. As people's collections advance and items become harder to find, they'll be looking for the item they don't have. When they find it, they're going to want it and will have to pay for it." Competition for kitchen collectibles and antiques in future years will heat up even more, as more and more buyers vie for what is out there.

CURRENT TRENDS

Johnson named some of the market's steadiest categories and some of the changes she has seen in the last 30 years:

Redware was popular among collectors 30 years ago. It still is. Good American redware, particularly Pennsylvania pieces and those that are signed, will continue to hold their value.

Stoneware has peaked out. The pieces that are selling now for remarkable prices are only those that truly are unique. They have one-of-a-kind shapes or very unusual designs.

Baskets have taken a slide. They brought really high prices during the 1980s. But that has slowed down. Also, very good reproductions of painted baskets have scared some people out of the market. There are still plenty of buyers out there who'll pay good prices for specialized baskets like cheese baskets from New England or berry baskets from New Jersey. If I see a specialized basket like a drop-bottom apple basket (a picker fills it in the tree, then carries it to a collection point and then releases the bottom so the apples drop out into a bin), I buy it because I know I'll be able to sell it.

Step-back, corner and other cupboards still sell, particularly if they're good ones without a lot of restoration.

Bob and Kaaren Grossman of B&K Kitchen Primitives and Collectibles in Chester, N.J., expect the markets for tinware and japanned ware to continue growing. They specialize in Kreamerware, including everything from cookie cutters, canisters and spice sets to the company's less well known copper kettles, coffee pots and sugar shakers. Grossman added, "Unusual mechanicals, including various pitters, raisin seeders, marmalade cutters, slicers and grinders are selling well, particularly those with patent dates."

There's still a great demand for cast-iron and wooden apple parers as well as interest in early blacksmith-forged hearth tools, according to Cahn, who specializes in wafer and waffle irons. According to well-known paper dealer Norman Martinus of Nostalgia Gallery in Kitty Hawk, N.C., the market for kitchen advertising, giveaway recipe booklets, seed packets, trade cards, tin and paper containers as well as signs picturing food remained strong even during the height of the recession. "After all, I don't sell anything that anyone has to have. Although my customers might have had less discretionary income, they still bought the collectibles they wanted," he said. Magazine advertisements by famous illustrators such as Maxfield Parrish, memorabilia featuring African-Americans such as Cream of Wheat and Aunt Jemima

In very good condition, this Enterprise #49 vegetable slicer retains much of its original paint.

Mechanical devices, like this cast-iron raisin seeder, always sell well.

advertisements and any kitchen paper with a connection to Rumford Baking Powder are currently moving quickly, according to Martinus.

Graniteware is moving well in the Midwest and the South. Electric toasters and Jadite are hot on the West Coast according to Don Thornton of Sunnyvale, Ca.

Only nutmeg graters come close to matching the national popularity of Thornton's specialty—eggbeaters. One dealer said, "I remember the days when the trade papers and their authors looked down at eggbeaters and chastised operators of shows featuring too many of them. They asked 'After all, how many of these things do people want to look at?' That's certainly not the case anymore. I buy all I can find." Thornton doesn't find the current fascination with eggbeaters to be surprising, though. The expert, currently working on a new book on eggbeaters that'll contain 300 photos and 300 patent drawings plus dozens of old advertisements for eggbeaters said, "They are America's greatest inventions and the best mechanical tools ever made. They have mechanical beauty and simplicity and they are great utilitarian devices. They really beat eggs. And collecting them is a challenge. Every time I think I have or know of them all, another one turns up."

When it comes to more recent kitchenware, Chuck and Kathy McCue Schneider of Pearl Washington's Kitchenware in Whitman, Mass. have seen their field become much more crowded with dealers who have scaled down from higher-end antiques. "Although it's harder for us to find our stock, it's

Eggbeaters, in all their forms, are interesting visually and mechanically. This Handy Maid beater is particularly attractive thanks to its green measuring cup style container.

These experimental eggbeaters were found in the attic of an old home in Saugerties, N.Y., in the summer of 1991. They were fashioned by Ulysses Grant Teetsall and his son Harold between 1915 and 1927 for their Holt Lyon Company. From the collection of Don Thornton.

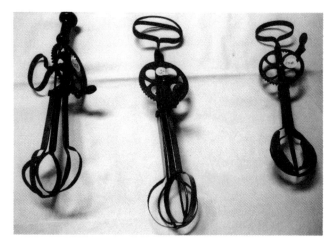

good news for buyers because they can find the collectibles at more places," said Kathy Schneider. Her husband offered an example of what has happened. "Early in our career, we set up at a show with an array of toasters and other kitchen collectibles. Many were in the $10 to $15 range. We were across from a man who specialized in fine antiques that were priced in the hundreds. He watched us sell out of our stock. The next time we attended that biannual show in Boston, he was wearing a luau shirt covered with pineapples and selling toasters, too."

What's hot in collectibles today? Depression era dishes, particularly in solid colors. Fiestaware is always popular. Refrigerator containers, particularly the jadite and sapphire shades made by Fire-King. Sugar shakers. Straw containers. Early 1950s juicers, now that juicing has become popular. Reasonably priced green and red utensils. 1940s and 1950s dinette sets and occasional tables that can hold a microwave oven. Everything from canister and spice sets to racks of utensils in 1950's pink or "almost turquoise." Even the smoked glass and plastic utensils and kitchenware from the 1970s are starting to move. Only the 1960s-era utensils are slow to sell because avocado green and harvest gold just don't fit in with current decorating schemes.

TODAY'S COLLECTOR

Those who enter the antiques and collectibles market today are going into a world that's far different than it was 30 years ago. Collectors and dealers acknowledge that many of the kitchen antiques that were popular when they started still are popular. But their prices are much higher and the competition to possess them is much keener.

A new public awareness that there is potential value in a household's everyday kitchen tools means that it's far less likely that people will discard them or fritter them away for ridiculously low prices. "In earlier decades, people simply didn't know what they had or valued new tools more highly than the old ones," Kaaren Grossman said. "Shortly after my husband and I started collecting kitchen tools and crocks, my mother came to visit us. She looked around and then exclaimed, 'Oh, my goodness. I threw all that junk out when my mother died. It went to the dump.' As soon as she said it, my mother tried to qualify it. But I understood what she was saying. Her attitude was entirely different. Today, we're discarding less and recycling more. I'd love to find that dump."

In other words, the green movement has spread to the antiques and collectibles market, but here it makes financial as well as environmental sense to save yesterday's tools and gadgets. DeMore added, "Today's collector must be really aggressive and spend lots of time on the road (or have a good network) to find top-quality kitchen collectibles and antiques at good prices. These days, much of the great stuff has already gone into collections or museums."

The awareness of the potential value in kitchen antiques has grown for various reasons. Early kitchen collectibles price guides and collectors guides that hit the market in noticeable numbers in the 1970s and 1980s deserve

Although collectors would know that this tool is an egg whip, novices might mistake it for a flyswatter in need of restringing!

This vegetable skimmer had a very ordinary function but its design makes it visually interesting as a metal sculpture of sorts.

Pot scrapers were popular ways for manufacturers to get their message to homemakers day in and day out. Each time a person reached for this one, she or he was reminded of the Sharples Tubular Cream Separator.

some of the credit for educating the public. Articles on kitchen antiques and collectibles in *Country Home and Country Living* brought out-of-mind kitchen items back into focus and boosted their prices considerably. Features in trade papers have helped, too. Finally, stories on the national news and wire services about out-of-this-world prices paid for kitchen equipment have jolted people who once might have been more careless with the possible collectibles and antiques passing through their hands. After all, there probably isn't a person who wouldn't handle a family's old crockery more carefully after hearing stories like the one about a two-gallon, salt-glazed jug that brought $17,050 at auction. The sale was at the Harmer Rooke Galleries in New York City. The jug, c.1840, was inscribed "Barnabus Edmonds & Co., Charlestown" and was decorated with a blue American eagle clutching arrows and a draped, tasseled cord.

THE INTERNATIONAL MARKET

Americans generally specialize in American kitchenware. But they've also ventured into the international market after reading magazine articles featuring everything from French and English country to Scandinavian country antiques or after deciding to incorporate some antiques from countries representing their roots. Small-time buyers have tucked "smalls" into their suitcases. (Antique molds and pie crimpers have frequently found their way into my luggage.) Others have either paid to have larger antiques shipped home or have bought kitchen items from dealers who routinely import container loads of antiques from other countries. Hope-Vere Anderson, of Anderson Antiques, Murfreesboro, Tenn., whose family has specialized in importing Scottish antiques to the United States for the last 25 years said, "People do import their heritage. There's always a demand for Scottish and Welsh dressers (cupboards) with plate racks as well as meat covers (domes), large platters, fire tools, flow blue dinnerware, pewter, copper and brass utensils. They also want mortars and pestles, scales with brass weights and copper bowls, jelly kettles and decorated Victorian glass rolling pins." Anderson said, "Until recently, the attitude of people in Scotland was that they wanted modern things, not old stuff. So they eagerly got rid of the old to make room for the new."

But the tables are turning on Americans. The rest of the world is waking up to the value of American antiques and collectibles, as well as to the value of their own. Canadians are snapping up some American primitives such as apple parers. There are reports that the Dutch and the Germans have been buying small electrical appliances. (Mexicans buy small appliances by the truckload from West Coast flea markets, but they're buying them to use rather than for collections.) The British have begun buying collectibles such as the colorful aluminum drinking glasses from the 1950s.

England's Mike and Tessia McCurdy, of Cooks Books (Rottingdean, Sussex, England), have purchased two major collections of American cookbooks. Some of the books will be sold to customers from the U.K. and Europe, but as Tessia McCurdy indicated, "The great bulk of them probably will go right back to the States since many of our customers are Americans." The British even are buying some small electrical appliances despite the difference in current. Tony Curtis, the Galashiels, Scotland-based publisher of Britain's *Lyle Official Antiques Reviews,* said, "People here are buying popcorn poppers and some other appliances and experimenting with adapters to see if they can get them to work. It's a strange kind of one-upmanship. They also like collectibles that everyone can identify with, like those featuring Disney characters as well as green and red enamelware. "But Britons also are buying some American antiques for souvenirs because they

Butter molds, because they're small, attractive and primitive, are appealing to collectors on both sides of the Atlantic.

British collectors like interesting mechanical devices like this nutcracker that attached to a table or countertop for easy operation. Its long, curved handle reads "St. Louis, USA", and it would be a desirable souvenir of a trip to the States because its origin is clearly marked.

like the homespun look of such tools, as well as quilts. It's exciting to think they have something that might have gone West on a wagon train." According to Curtis, they've carried home American coffee grinders as well as other mechanical implements, salt crocks, butter churns, bread peels, breadboards and baskets that are peculiarly American. They've also paid to have all kinds of American pine furniture shipped to Britain. Curtis explained, "It used to be that the British would spend £10,000 or £15,000 to redo their kitchens. Now they're spending their money to buy decorative items for their current kitchens. They've become interested in everything. Antiques from the Edwardian and Victorian eras. Collectibles from the 1930s and 1940s. The 1950s are good, too, because they make design statements that are just as strong as those from the Art Deco period and because goods from the 1930s are beginning to get out of reach." According to Curtis, Europeans are buying back their own past from the Americans, whenever they can. "Americans shouldn't be surprised when they hear British, Italian, Dutch, German or French accents in the New York auction houses. We're buying the things we sold cheaply in the first container-loads that went from Europe to America 35 years ago."

The international trading of antiques back and forth is governed largely by the strengths of the currencies involved. When the pound and other European currencies are strong, the antiques and collectibles will be traveling from west to east. When the dollar is strong, the antiques and collectibles will move from east to west. It's a circle of trade that promises to keep the antiques and collectibles markets afloat on both sides of the Atlantic for a long time to come.

3

Resources for Collectors

The wisest move a beginning collector can make is to begin collecting information long before he or she starts collecting objects. Two or three months spent studying is a minimum. Some pros even say prospective collectors shouldn't start buying until they have spent six months studying the category of kitchen collectible they want to acquire. It is time well spent. A person who is familiar with the antiques and collectibles marketplace will know what there is to collect, what's common and what's not, and will also have an idea about how much an item should cost. It is the only sane way to get started and ensures that the beginning collector will make the most of his or her money.

"Collecting school" begins with tours of museum collections and scouting trips (no buying yet!) to everything from flea markets and yard sales to antiques and collectibles shops and malls, as well as auction houses and house sales. It continues with subscriptions to trade newspapers on antiques and collectibles as well as buying collector's guides and price guides. It finishes with would-be collectors reading specialized books on the category that interests them, whether it is Fire-King glassware, Red Wing pottery, McCoy cookie jars or Griswold cast-iron cookware. "Graduates" must keep their knowledge current by joining and participating in collectors' clubs, studying the club newsletters and maintaining their subscriptions to the trade newspapers. Publications including the *Maine Antique Digest* (P.O. Box 645, Waldoboro, ME 04572); *The Antique Trader Weekly* (P.O. Box 1050, Dubuque, IA 52004-1050); *Collectors News & The Antique Reporter* (P.O. Box

5 7

The new-found popularity of Fire-King kitchenware, including this casserole, is being discussed in trade papers and in several new books.

156, Grundy Center, IA, 50638) and *Antique Week* (Suite 220, 525-K E. Market St., Leesburg, VA), as well as many other national and regional periodicals play a major role in keeping collectors informed. In addition to articles on specific antiques and collectibles, these publications contain calendars of shows and special events, provide reports of prices paid for various items at auction, and serve as marketplaces for buyers and sellers. For a full list of periodicals available to collectors, consult *Maloney's Antiques & Collectibles Resource Directory, 1994–1995* by David J. Maloney (Wallace-Homestead, 1993, 496 pp.) A sharp collector never stops reading and learning more. Keeping current with collecting trends, crazes and prices, as well as being able to forecast future collecting trends, can make collecting particularly rewarding.

Museums and Archives

Visiting museums is a great first step for collectors seeking an education because the admission price buys a ticket to a world of information. The Smithsonian Institution's various collections certainly are grand enough to provide a picture of what's to be collected when it comes to kitchen equipment. But they're somewhat scattered and may look less inviting in these hurried times than a museum offering the convenience of "one-stop learning" such as the Culinary Archives and Museum of Johnson & Wales University in Providence, R.I. Created largely from the donations of Chef Louis Szathmary, the archives include everything from a goose-feather brush for spreading butter on apple strudel, raisin seeders and nutcrackers to fireless cookers, string bean slicers and examples of what are believed to be the nation's first patented bread slicer and first patented meat grinder. There are also some 9,000 menus, thousands of periodicals, culinary pamphlets and postcards, hundreds of copper, ceramic, tin, pewter and enamel molds and thousands of wooden spoons from all over the world. As a matter of fact, the Szathmary Family Collection has been called "The Smithsonian Institution of the Foodservice Industry."

Barbara Kuck, who has been looking after Chef Louis' collections since 1971 and is now curator of the culinary archives at Johnson & Wales, said,

Chef Louis Szathmary, who operated The Bakery Restaurant in Chicago for many years, also spent much of his time acquiring kitchen treasures of all kinds. His collection, donated to Johnson & Wales University in Providence, R.I., makes up a major portion of the school's Culinary Archives and Museum.

"We say we offer 'one-stop shopping' for culinary researchers because we have the materials that enable them to read about food and equipment of the era they're studying. But we also have some of the actual tools and the manuals and recipes that came with them."

Szathmary, who for 25 years was the proprietor of The Bakery Restaurant in Chicago, can be considered a collector's collector. Before retiring and donating his collections to Johnson & Wales, he invested much of his time and restaurant fortune amassing more than 200,000 culinary antiques and collectibles. Before the collections were shipped to Rhode Island, they filled 35 rooms, from floor to ceiling, above the restaurant. The chef, also a trained psychologist, began collecting almost as soon as he arrived from his native Hungary in 1951. "I had the suit on my back, one change of underwear, $1.10 in my pocket and 14 books in my bag. I didn't speak English and just to survive, I bought clothes and other things I needed at Goodwill and The Salvation Army. I couldn't believe the things people were throwing away. I decided those things would be valuable some day and that I would collect them."

Voracious is the only way to describe Szathmary's appetite for culinary objects. "Perhaps it was because I started with nothing that I had to have everything," he explained during one of his visits to Johnson & Wales. "Besides," he added, " collecting things associated with my profession, like cookbooks or tools, was much more appealing to me than collecting something like stamps that somebody had licked." Of his decision to donate his lifelong collections and of his advice to others to consider doing the same (particularly if prospective heirs to a collector's treasures are likely to treat them as junk), he said, "My restaurant was across from a funeral parlor. For 25 years, I watched very carefully and I saw that no one ever got to take anything with them." Recalling his early days of collecting, he said, "It was

Perhaps because they served such a pleasant treat, ice-cream scoops inspired many designers. This one is Gilchrist's No. 33.

lots of fun. I enjoyed finding things, looking for things and even missing things (those things I couldn't afford anyhow)."

Living history museums such as Colonial Williamsburg in Virginia and Plimoth Plantation and Old Sturbridge Village (both in Massachusetts) add another dimension to collectors' knowledge, as villagers regularly demonstrate just how important various tools were for daily living. Adventurous collectors who sign on for hearth cooking classes at these museums will never forget the fiery red embers gathered on the rimmed lid of a dutch oven, the heat of the flames on their foreheads and cheeks, the weight of the cast-iron kettles, and the taste of the food they helped prepare. Of course, this is also where a little knowledge can become dangerous. A hearth cooking session could spawn a collecting frenzy. Don't be surprised by a sudden urge to accumulate all the necessary hearth antiques and trade the ultramodern split-level house for an old colonial with a walk-in fireplace.

Other, less widely known museums and archives can have special meaning for kitchen collectors. There are museums focusing on a single category like salt and pepper shakers (the Judith Basin Museum in Stanford, Mont.) or cookbooks (some of the major collections can be found at The New York Public Library; The Library of Congress; The Katherine Angell Library of the Culinary Institute of America; the H.B. Meek Library at Cornell University; The Schlesinger Library at Radcliffe College; the Mandevile Library at the University of California at San Diego; the Los Angeles Public Library; the University of Iowa library; Johnson & Wales Culinary Archives and the Michigan State University Library at Ann Arbor.)

There are archives dedicated to specific subjects such as glass. The Leonard S. and Juliet K. Rakow Research Library, within the Corning Glass Center Complex in Corning, N.Y., for example, can provide some trade catalogs, retail catalogs and information on certain glass manufacturers.

Don't overlook the idea of contacting corporate archivists for help. Jane Applegate, manager of Dayton Power & Light Company's room-sized collection (1900 Dryden Rd., Dayton, Ohio) said, "We use the artifacts (both pre-electrical and electrical kitchen appliances) to supplement the company archives." The archives, documenting the early 20th-century marketing of electricity to American consumers by selling them appliances, are open by appointment to serious researchers.

Wilbur Chocolate Company has assembled a treat for chocolate lovers. Its Candy Americana Museum (64 N. Broad St., Lititz, PA) is concentrated in just a few small rooms that are chock-full of candy molds, chocolate advertising and packaging and chocolate pots. It is a delight that is matched only by the aroma of the melted chocolate coming from the nearby candy-making demonstrations in the company's candy shop.

Whenever you're traveling, check local historic sites first for inspiration. Next, look for museums or historical societies in towns where well-known lines of kitchen equipment were made. You might find a special collection or an eye-opening exhibit of the company's history and products. No museum? Check with the town's reference librarian to see if any additional information is available.

Eugene Kosche, curator of history for The Bennington Museum in Bennington, Vermont, described just how much of a find these special museums can be. "Our stoneware collection illustrates the history and production of Bennington's Norton Pottery as well as the neighboring United States Pottery. Some of the pieces we have on display, like a 25-gallon water cooler that's 40 inches high and is decorated with drawings of deer, houses, fences and a two-story building, haven't been found anywhere else."

The Ohio Historical Society's Museum of Ceramics at East Liverpool details the history of some 150 companies (including Hall and Homer Laughlin) in the region that once produced half of America's dinnerware.

Corporate museums are another source of information. Fruit jar collectors, for example, might want to make a pilgrimage to Ball Corporation headquarters in Muncie, Ind. Although the museum is just a single, large room devoted to the history of the fruit jar, it contains some nearly priceless, very rare jars produced by Ball.

When researchers could find no household records detailing the arrangement of Harriet Beecher Stowe's Hartford, Conn. kitchen, they assumed she would have followed the advice she and her sister Catherine gave for planning an efficient kitchen plan in their book, *American Woman's Home* (first printed in 1869 and reprinted by the Stowe-Day Foundation, 77 Forest St., Hartford, CT 06105). The kitchen was restocked with the equipment and furniture these forward-thinking women of the 19th century envisioned as essential to a step-saving kitchen. (See Chapter 1 for a more detailed description of this early "modern" kitchen.)

No matter which museum or historic site a collector visits, the kitchen and its tools are likely to be important because they are essential to most museums' stories of American life. Explained Christopher Bensch, curator of furnishings at the Strong Museum in Rochester, N.Y.: "Kitchen equipment has been crucial throughout the nation's history because so much of home life has involved food preparation, eating and cleaning up. Culinary displays always draw visceral reactions from our visitors because they identify with these tools more readily than anything else." The Strong Museum's collection dates from 1820 to the present and goes beyond the expected historic displays of such items as glass rolling pins, bowls, graters and grinders. Recently, there were special exhibits of Pyrex baking dishes and 20th-century glass refrigerator jars. Still another exhibit will feature early electrical appli-

Chocoholics can indulge more fully in their favorite pleasure by acquiring chocolate collectibles and antiques like this Lowney's Cocoa tin at the same time they're sampling new kinds of chocolate. A tin like this one will appeal both to the chocolate lover as well as the general kitchen collector.

Eye-catching box for Greer's "Moo Girl" Creamery Butter brings country flavor to the kitchen display shelf.

This creamer with a blue, green and brown flint enamel glaze is a fairly common example of Bennington pottery. The Bennington Museum provides an extensive look at the kinds of utilitarian shapes and vessels that were produced.

ances. Bensch added, "We just purchased a microwave oven because we have to carry the culinary story onward."

If you, too, feel the urge to carry culinary stories onward by collecting a few things of your own, the next step is to become familiar with the wealth of references available.

Price Guides, Reference Books, Collector's Clubs and Newsletters

300 Years of Kitchen Collectibles, Third Edition by Linda Campbell Franklin (Books Americana, 1991, 645 pp.) is the premiere book in the field of culinary antiques. Franklin's new and greatly expanded third edition contains nearly everything you need to know, from prices and physical measurements of the objects to warnings about reproductions. It requires careful study because interesting quotations and old-fashioned recipes are mixed in with standard listings. And in a change from previous editions, in which photographs appeared near the category discussed, they are now grouped at the end of each section. This book also includes five mini-chapters on housekeeping collectibles, but those who wish to explore this topic further should consult her book, *300 Years of Housekeeping Collectibles* (Books Americana, 1992, 212 pp.)

Linda Campbell Franklin has also served as contributing editor for *A Price Guide to Victorian Houseware, Hardware and Kitchenware* by Ronald S. Barlow (Windmill Publishing Co., 1992, 375 pp.). Barlow offers a fairly extensive selection of kitchenware including apple corers, butter prints, cake baskets, can openers, cast-iron pots, Dutch ovens, eggbeaters, graniteware, ice-cream freezers, tea kettles, lemon squeezers, milk cans, oyster ladles, potato scoops, pie knives, teapots, toothpick holders and waffle irons. The book features some marvelous catalog illustrations showing the object's original prices. It also includes a modern price guide.

Kitchen Collectibles: An Illustrated Price Guide, by Ellen Plante (Wallace-Homestead, 1991, 164 pp.) provides some prices and pictures, but it is much smaller in scale than Linda Campbell Franklin's book. Plante includes chapters on advertising memorabilia, large and small appliances, cookware, everyday dinnerware, gadgets and utensils, kitchen furniture, pottery, storage containers and woodenware. Within each chapter, she gives the history of each collectible category, along with leading manufacturers and the range of products produced. In the cookware chapter, for example, she offers the history and evolution of iron, copper, tinware, graniteware, aluminum and glass cooking equipment.

Kathryn McNerney's *Kitchen Antiques, 1790–1940* (Collector Books, 1991, 224 pp.) with large pictures and an accompanying price guide, is another possible reference for the collector.

Two books by Jane H. Celehar, although out-of-print, are worth picking up if spotted on a bookseller's shelf because they give the collector some perspective on how the kitchenware market has changed over the years. They are *Kitchens and Gadgets 1920 to 1950* (Wallace-Homestead, 1982, 144 pp.) and *Kitchens and Kitchenware* (Wallace-Homestead, 1985, 208 pp.). The second book covers the period from 1900 to 1950 with a decade-by-decade narrative and documentary illustrations (magazine advertisements and catalog pages) of how the kitchen evolved from a dreary scullery to the colorful and inviting postwar family kitchens of the 1950s.

SPECIALIZED SUBJECT REFERENCES

Collectors will also find an array of specialized books on specific collecting categories. Here is just a sampling of what is available.

It's time to start saving tins like this one for FFV Macaroon Krisps. Its good condition and bright red and green colors add to its desirability and will increase its value in the years to come.

Advertising on food containers   There are a number of books to collect in this category, including the *Antique Advertising Encyclopedia* by Ray Klug (LW Book Sales, 1993, 326 pp.); *Huxford's Collectible Advertising, An Illustrated Value Guide* by Sharon and Bob Huxford (Collector Books, 1993, 173 pp.); *America For Sale, A Collector's Guide to Antique Advertising* by Douglas Congdon-Martin (Schiffer Publishing, 1991, 176 pp.); the *Advertising Identification and Price Guide* by Dawn E. Reno (Avon Books, 1993, 568 pp.) and *Food and Drink Containers and Their Prices* by Al Bergevin, (Wallace-Homestead Book Co., 1988, 269 pp.). Although none of these books focus specifically on food, they touch briefly on many of the popular categories, including containers and tins for baking powder, cocoa, coconut, coffee, crackers, gum and candy, marshmallows, oats, peanut butter, peanuts, popcorn, soups, spices, syrup, tea and miscellaneous items (including everything from Grape Nuts to Cracker Jack). Each book has something to offer, depending on the collector's focus. A few moments skimming several should be all you need to find the right one.

African-Americans   Jan Lindenberger, author of *Black Memorabilia for the Kitchen, a Handbook and Price Guide* (Schiffer, 1992, 144 pp.) wrote, "In the last 15 years, black memorabilia has become an increasingly popular area for collecting." She added, "Many black collectors are buying the stereotyped figures to show their children how blacks were viewed by other races in earlier times."

Baskets   *Wallace-Homestead Price Guide to Baskets*, Second Edition, by Frances Johnson (Wallace-Homestead, 1989, 233 pp.), is a dictionary-style listing of baskets, offering both a history and description of American baskets.

Another book for the shelf is the *Collector's Guide to Country Baskets* by Don and Carol Raycraft (Collector Books, 1985, 1994 value update, 129 pp.), which focuses on working baskets crafted for specific functions; for example, cake and candy baskets, bread-raising or bread-serving baskets, berry baskets, apple baskets and apple drying baskets.

Cookbooks   *Cookbooks Worth Collecting* by Mary Barile (Wallace-Homestead, 1993, 224 pp.) is destined to become an invaluable reference for those who want to collect cookbooks. Its price guide listings are supplemented by a wealth of information. It is a how-to handbook for beginning collectors and also contains detailed information on regional, community and charity cookbooks.

A *Guide to Collecting Cookbooks* by Col. Bob Allen (Collector Books, 1990, with 1993 value update, 213 pp.) contains a full-color section of cookbook and recipe booklet covers that shows just how attractive these early publications were. The volume includes some hardcover and softcover cookbooks, as well as charity, fund-raising and regional cookbooks. It also devotes many pages to various food companies and the recipe booklets they produced to promote their products, such as chocolate, baking powder, raisins, baking soda, yeast, shortening, milk and gelatin.

Linda J. Dickinson also has a newly updated *Price Guide to Cookbooks & Recipe Leaflets* (Collector Books, 1990, with 1993 value update, 190 pp.) but offers little information other than the listings of books and prices.

Cookie cutters   Phyllis Steiss Wetherill, author of several out-of-print books on cookie cutters and molds and the publisher of the newsletter *Cookies,* reports she is getting ready to release an update on her second book, *An Encyclopedia of Cookie Shaping.* For more information, send a self-addressed, stamped envelope to her at 5426 27th St. NW, Washington, DC 20015. In an earlier book, she noted that every household contains at least one kind of cookie cutter, whether or not it ever is used to cut dough: The rim of a glass. She said, "It is available and meets my definition of a cookie cutter, which is 'any tool that can cut rolled dough into a desired shape.' "

Cookie jars   Mike Schneider's book, *The Complete Cookie Jar Book* (Schiffer Publishing, 1991, 312 pp.) includes more than 2,000 colorful illustrations, which makes it an attractive volume to read and own. Don't reach for a cookie jar (unless it is already in your kitchen) until you read Schneider's information on counterfeits, reproductions and fakes. He also provides basic information for collectors, including a history of the category, types of ceramic jars and decoration, prices, condition and problems of collecting. The next section covers the cookie jar giants, McCoy and American Bisque; the third section covers 12 additional manufacturers. Buyers and sellers of cookie jars are listed, and there's also a segment on character cookie jars (shaped like Santa Claus, Disney characters and others).

Another key reference is *The Collector's Encyclopedia of Cookie Jars* by Fred and Joyce Roerig (Collector Books, 1991, with 1993 value update, 391 pp.). The Roerigs' book documents, in full color, row after row of cookie jars with accompanying prices and brief sections of information at the start of various segments. For example, there are brief histories of the Nelson McCoy Company of Roseville, OH and Shawnee Pottery of Zanesville, OH.

Ermagene Westfall has written two books: *An Illustrated Value Guide to Cookie Jars* (Collector Books, 1989, 255 pp.) and *An Illustrated Value Guide to Cookie Jars II* (Collector Books, 1993, 255 pp.). In her second book, she has used different, and generally harder-to-find, jars for illustration. Photographs are full-color and she covers numerous manufacturers as well as grouping jars by topics such as "Walt Disney," "Foreign Jars," and "Plastic Jars."

McCoy collectors will be interested in obtaining *McCoy Cookie Jars: From the First to the Last, Second Edition* (Nichols Publishing, 1991, 197 pp.).

Although neither a price guide nor a collector's guide, *The Cookie Jar Cookbook* by Steffi Berne (Villard Books, 1991, 194 pp.) will appeal to those who collect these special containers. Baking cookies and collecting cookie jars are Berne's twin passions, and she has combined them in a book that can be kept in the living room or taken to the kitchen.

In reading any of these books' prices, remember that the cookie jar market underwent a period of considerable speculation in the late 1980s and has now calmed down a bit.

Dinnerware (See also Pottery)

The Collector's Encyclopedia of American Dinnerware by Jo Cunningham (Collector Books, 1982, prices updated 1992, 320 pp.) gives a brief history of the industry that began in the mid-1600s in the New York and New Jersey area. It covers 48 makers of pottery including Bennington, Canonsburg, Crooksville, Hall, Harker, Hull, Homer Laughlin, Mt. Clemens Pottery, Pfaltzgraff, Red Wing, Salem, Stangl, Steubenville and Western Stoneware. The book contains many full-color illustrations and black-and-white backstamps (markings on plate backs identifying manufacturers) as well as newspaper and magazine advertising. There's also a small section on juvenile or children's pieces by various potters, from Dick Tracy plates to Elsie the Cow and Uncle Wiggily mugs.

(See also *Kovels' Depression Glass & American Dinnerware Price List* by Ralph and Terry Kovel (Crown, 1991, 249 pp.) under the "Glass" category.)

The Collector's Encyclopedia of Fiesta, Revised Seventh Edition by Bob and Sharon Huxford (Collector Books, 1992, 160 pp.) contains full-color illustrations of more than 1,000 pieces of Fiesta, making it a valuable reference for those seeking the original colors (turquoise, light green, ivory, yellow as well as red and dark blue) or the 1950's shades of rose, gray, chartreuse and forest green. In addition, the book includes Harlequin (also made by Homer Laughlin but without a trademark, which was less expensive and sold exclusively by the F.W. Woolworth Company) as well as Riviera, which was even less expensive than Harlequin (and lighter in weight, too). The authors include a discussion of other colored dinnerware lines that are similar in appearance to those produced by Homer Laughlin as well as information on the radioactive red "go-alongs" such as frames, handles, flatware and carriers for pitchers and glasses. Don't miss the interesting chapter on experimentals and trial glazes, as well as Kitchen Kraft and Oven Serve (oven-to-table kitchenware).

The Collector Books series offers a wide assortment of books on various manufacturers' dinnerware. Joanne Jasper's book *The Collector's Encyclopedia*

Stangl pottery sandwich plate could also have done double-duty as a fruit plate, thanks to its colorful design. Harvey Duke's *Stangl Pottery* (Wallace-Homestead, 1992) is a great reference for all who want to learn more about this New Jersey manufacturer.

of Homer Laughlin China, Reference and Value Guide (Collector Books, 1993, 205 pp.) focuses on the company's white tableware, rather than the colorful lines like Fiesta, Harlequin and Riviera. Sharon and Bob Huxford have gone beyond Homer Laughlin to write *The Collector's Encyclopedia of McCoy Pottery* (Collector Books, 1980 with 1993 value update, 239 pp).

Margaret and Kenn Whitmyer have focused on the production of the Hall China Company of East Liverpool, Ohio in their book, *The Collector's Encyclopedia of Hall China* (Collector Books, 1989 with 1992 value update, 240 pp.).

Neva Colbert has written *The Collector's Guide to Harker Pottery, Identifications and Values* (Collector Books, 1993, 127 pp.) while Barbara Loveless Gick-Burke has produced the *Collector's Guide to Hull Pottery: The Dinnerware Lines, Identification and Values* (Collector Books, 1993, 167 pp.). Another reference book for dinnerware collectors is *Debolt's Dictionary of American Pottery Marks: Whiteware & Porcelain,* 1993, 288 pp.) by C. Gerald DeBolt.

Harvey Duke, well-known for his work on Hall Pottery including *Hall: Price Guide Update* (ELO Books, 1992, 35 pp.) and *Hall 2* (ELO Books, 1985, 125 pp.) and the author of the *Official Identification & Price Guide to Pottery & Porcelain, 7th Edition,* (House of Collectibles, 1989, 447 pp.) now has directed his attention to Stangl Pottery. His book, *Stangl Pottery* (Wallace-Homestead, 1993, 150 pp.) gives the company history and offers information on the early, hand-painted Prestige line, stoneware and later lines of dinnerware as well as a segment on children's dinnerware.

Those interested in flow blue, a term that describes a category of blue and white china in which the blue color of the pattern runs into the white background will find *Flow Blue: A Collector's Guide to Pattern, History and Values* by Jeffrey B. Snyder (Schiffer Publishing, 1992, 160 pp.) and the *Collector's Encyclopedia of Flow Blue China* by Mary Frank Gaston (Collector Books, 1983 with 1993 value update, 160 pp.) to be helpful. Gaston, who has researched and documented this style of decorating china that began in Britain some 150 years ago, noted that the United States has become the prime collecting grounds for flow blue because so much was exported during the last century.

Ellen R. Hill has done an impressive job of documenting the patterns, body styles, makers and back stamps for Mulberry Ironstone in her loose-leaf notebook-style text, *Mulberry Ironstone, Flow Blue's Best Kept Little Secret* (Ellen R. Hill, 1993, 500 pp.). This china, made primarily in England from 1840 to 1870, generally was transfer-printed or hand-painted in any of several colorations including dark grays, browns or purplish blacks. As in flow blue, the designs could also flow.

Another reference is Petra Williams' revised edition of *Flow Blue China and Mulberry Ware: Similarity and Value Guide* (Fountain House East, 1993, 209 pp.).

Eggbeaters   Don Thornton's new book called *Beat This: The Eggbeater Chronicles* (Offbeat Books, 1994, 244 pp.) will undoubtably become the definitive work on this category of kitchenware. Thornton is the authority on the subject, and his book will contain 26 chapters on the major manufacturers (from A&J to Dover), the various types of beaters (from water-driven to electric) and contain nearly 300 photos, 300 patent drawings and dozens of old advertisements. For more information, write to Offbeat Books at 1345 Poplar Ave., Sunnyvale, CA 94087.

Electrical appliances   *Price Guide to Collectible Kitchen Appliances, From Aerators to Waffle Irons, 1900–1950* by Gary Miller and K. M. Scotty Mitchell (Wallace-Homestead, 1991, 179 pp.) covers coffeemakers and sets; combination appliances (such as perc-o-toasters that brewed coffee and toasted bread); cooking appliances (from broilers to popcorn poppers); irons; mixers and whippers; toasters; waffle irons and sandwich grills; and novelty appliances (electric flour sifters, coffee grinders, knife sharpeners). The nearly 250 photographs and 90 advertisements from *Ladies' Home Journal, Good Housekeeping* and the *Saturday Evening Post* of the early 1900s make this book an interesting read, even if you have no intention of collecting electrical appliances.

Fruit jars   There are two basic reference volumes that fruit jar collectors must have: *The Standard Fruit Jar Reference* by Dick Roller (Acorn Press, Paris, Ill., 1983 with price update, 475 pp.) and *The Collector's Guide to Old Fruit Jars Red Book #6* by Alice Creswick (Alice Creswick, 1990, 230 pp.).

Creswick offers nearly 5,000 prices in her jar descriptions, which also cover printing, patents, size and glass color. The softcover manual provides definitions of terms and a list of reproduction fruit jars to help beginners avoid a few pitfalls.

Roller, who also is the author of the *Fruit Jar Newsletter*, covers patents and trademarks, fruit jar pioneers like John L. Mason, the Ball Brothers and Alexander Kerr, and gives histories of some of the country's best-known glass houses, including the evolution of the Ball Corporation, Hazel-Atlas and Kerr

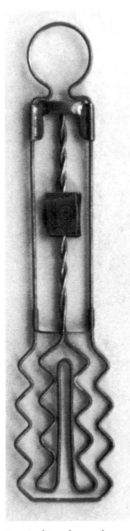

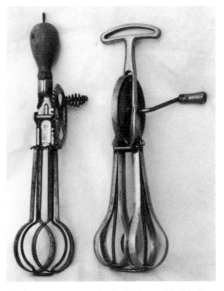

Eggbeaters are particularly hot with kitchen collectors. Don Thornton's new book, *Beat This: The Eggbeater Chronicles,* is the authoritative source on the subject.

This simple, all-wire Archimedes eggbeater made its mark as a promotional item for Horlick's Malted Milk Corporation of Racine, WI. This wavy dasher, 9 1/2-inch model is quite rare, commanding prices of more than $100. It is marked Horlick's on the metal button that moves up and down in the center. Courtesy of Don Thornton.

The Dormeyer Manufacturing Company's Deluxe model of the Dormeyer Mixer was "as beautiful as a piece of silverware with its case of polished aluminum, handles of jet black Bakelite, and all steel parts chromium plated," according to this December 1929 advertisement.

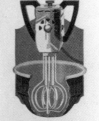

Manufacturing Company. To get the most out of this publication, you'll also need to order a supplementary price guide.

A Collector's Guide to Ball Jars by William F. Brantley (Rosemary Humbert Martin, 1975, 100 pp.) is out-of-date, but if it is still available from the Ball Consumer Affairs Department, it is well worth the $8 or so they charge for it. To see if you still can get a copy, write to the Ball Consumer Affairs Department, P.O. Box 2005, Dept. GB, Muncie, IN 47307-0005). It is a little treasure that gives the reader an appreciation for the industry, defines basic terms like "lightning seal," "wide mouth" and "zinc closures," and offers full-color photographs that give meaning to color terminology like "Ball Blue," amber, blue-green, aqua, and flint (when an older glass jar turns a smoky gray, lavender, pink or honey-amber after exposure to the sun). The booklet also includes a history of the five Ball brothers who founded the company and a detailed outline of the company's production through the years.

Glass   *Kitchen Glassware of the Depression Years* by Gene Florence (Collector Books, 1990 with 1992 value update, 224 pp.) is a general reference that every glass collector should own. One of the many glass sourcebooks written by Florence, this one examines utilitarian pieces designed specifically for kitchen use, such as water bottles, sugar shakers, syrup pitchers, refrigerator containers, rolling pins, salad sets, salt boxes, measuring cups, batter jugs, ice buckets and funnels. The profuse use of color makes this an excellent book for a collector. The author explains which colors are hard to find and includes a detailed chapter on spotting reproductions and newly made items. Two more of Florence's books are *Collectible Glassware from the 1940's, 50's and 60's* (Collector Books, 1992, 144 pp.) and *The Collector's Encyclopedia of Depression Glass. 10th Edition.* (Collector Books, 1992, 244 pp.). Each follows a similar format, with generous use of full-color photographs.

A second must-have reference, *Warman's Glass* by Ellen Tischbein Schroy (Wallace-Homestead, 1993, 171 pp.), offers a broad overview of more than 200 types of European and American glass. Schroy points out that practically any kind of glass, from Fostoria to pattern or milk glass, could end up in the kitchen. Categories covered include fruit jars; ovenware, dinnerware and kitchenware by Fire-King; salt and pepper shakers; pattern and milk glass; Depression glass; advertising glass; and, of course, kitchen glassware.

Kovels' Depression Glass & American Dinnerware Price List by Ralph and Terry Kovel (Crown, 1991, 249 pp.) focuses on companies producing glass, ceramic dinnerware, pottery, porcelain and semi-porcelain, largely along the Ohio River in southern Ohio and West Virginia. It provides information on clubs and publications that will be of interest to Fostoria or Cambridge collectors, as well as to those interested in Candlewick and the broader category of Depression glass, which, the authors explain, has come to mean glass made from 1925 to the 1970s.

Pyrex was greeted as an exciting innovation in cookware when Corning first introduced it. In *Pyrex By Corning, A Collector's Guide* by Susan Tobier Rogrove and Marcia Buan Steinhauer (Antique Publications, 1993, 134 pp.), the authors describe the much-heralded attributes of the Corning invention.

Hazel Atlas Crisscross refrigerator jar in cobalt blue allowed a housewife to see which leftover it contained, without having to open it.

Millions of fruit jars have been produced. Finding out if any in the family's possession are treasures will require research.

A wonderful advertisement the authors feature pictures a woman pouring boiling water over a Pyrex casserole frozen in a block of ice.

The Collector's Guide to Anchor Hocking's Fire-King Glassware by Garry and Dale Kilgo and Jerry and Gail Wilkins (K&W Collectibles, P.O. Box 473, Addison, AL, 1991, 164 pp.) is filled with illustrations from the authors' collections. The book describes the evolution of the Hocking Glass and the Anchor Hocking corporate symbols and provides a brief history of the company that began in 1905. Production of glassware marked "Fire-King" began around 1942 and continued until 1976. The authors claim Fire-King, with its colors like jade-ite, turquoise blue, azure-ite, pink, gray, luster, blue, white and ivory and the accompanying designs (dots, stripes and florals), represents "a large portion of the next generation of collectible glassware."

April M. Tvorak has also focused on Fire-King. Serious collectors may wish to order the *History and Price Guide to Fire-King* (VAL Enterprises, 1992, 30 pp.) and *Fire-King II* (published by the author, 1992, 29 pp.), which is described as a "companion guide to the original history and price guide to Fire-King."

Carol and Gene Markowski's *Tomart's Price Guide to Character & Promotional Glasses Including Pepsi, Coke, Fast Food, Peanut Butter and Jelly Plus Dairy Glasses & Milk Bottles* (Wallace-Homestead, 1990, 152 pp.), discusses how glass is made and also provides a bit of history, such as explaining that Coke glasses were made to give soda fountain attendants a lined guide to how much syrup to use. They conclude, "Any glass marked with an advertising logo, character or design is collected by someone." The book is arranged alphabetically, according to the initial letter, with "D" for Davy Crockett and "S" for Snoopy.

Finding your way around the *Collector's Guide to Cartoon and Promotional Drinking Glasses. Pepsi. McDonald's. Sports. Disney. Coca-Cola and Much More* by John Hervey (L.W. Book Sales, 1990, 180 pp.) requires a little more knowledge because you must know that a particular series of glasses was produced by Pepsi before you can look up that design. Pepsi, according to the author, was the largest sponsor of cartoon glasses in the 1970s.

Graniteware   The *Collector's Encyclopedia of Granite Ware, Colors, Shapes and Values* by Helen Greguire (Collector Books, 1990, with 1992 value update, 414 pp.) and *The Collector's Encyclopedia of Granite Ware: Colors, Shapes, and Values, Book 2* (Collector Books, 1993, 384 pp.) are key references for collectors who want to learn about patterns and color descriptions, enameling types, names and makers, determining age and cleaning and preserving this kitchenware. The market generally follows the values Greguire sets.

Although out-of-print, buy *The Graniteware Collector's Guide with Prices, Book II* by Vernagene Vogelzang and Evelyn Welch (Wallace-Homestead, 1986, 158 pp.) if you can find it. Although the prices are out-of-date, the authors offer additional information on the making and assembling of graniteware, its care and repair, and discuss some of the best-known companies that went out of business once such modern inventions as aluminum, stainless steel and Pyrex ovenware were introduced.

Hoosier cabinets   Hoosier cabinets, and other cabinets made in similar styles, were introduced as step-savers for homemakers in the early years of the 20th century. Their popularity waned in the 1930s when built-in kitchen cabinets were introduced. *Hoosier Cabinets* by Philip D. Kennedy (Kennedy, 9256 Holyoke Court, Indianapolis, IN, 46268, 1989, 168 pp.) includes short histories of the major manufacturers, including Hoosier, Boone, McDougall, Napanee and Sellers. Magazine advertisements provide illustrations of the way the cabinets looked and how they were marketed. The author also provides helpful information on restoration, from cleaning to rebuilding, as well as refinishing and the availability of replacement parts.

Housewares   *The Housewares Story: A History of the American Housewares Industry* by Earl Lifshey (The National Housewares Manufacturers Association, 1973, 384 pp.) devotes numerous chapters to the evolution of kitchens and the equipment they contained, from ice-cream freezers and refrigerators to pots and pans and household scales. Particularly interesting is the author's description of the decision to make housewares colorful but to standardize those colors so that homemakers didn't have 20 different shades of green or blue or any other color in their kitchens. His chapter on the electric age covers everything from coffee grinders and whistling tea kettles to toasters, waffle irons and woks.

Graniteware coffeepots were examples of equipment in use at all hours of the day in many households. But it is hard to find them in good condition. The reason—the colorful coating was easily chipped and damaged during everyday use.

All-metal kitchen cabinets being made by the Kalamazoo Stove Company in 1918 were promoted as "sanitary, easy to keep clean." They also wouldn't warp or wear out, which, probably was a reference aimed at the manufacturers of the popular wooden kitchen cabinets of the day.

Baking powder manufacturers competed heavily for customers. They earned favor and got their name around in many ways, including the creation of cookware items like this cake turner, which promoted "Rumford, The Wholesome, Baking Powder."

See also *300 Years of Housekeeping Collectibles, Identification and Value Guide* and *A Price Guide to Victorian Houseware, Hardware and Kitchenware*. (Full listings for both books can be found on the first page of this chapter.)

Ice-cream dippers In *Ice Cream Dippers, An Illustrated History and Collectors Guide to Early Ice Cream Dippers* by Wayne Smith (Smith, P.O. Box 418, Walkersville, MD 21793, updated in 1991, 183 pp.), the author provides the history of the ice-cream scoop, from William Clewell's first one in the 1870s to those made in the 1940s. He includes photography and documentation of 113 dippers, provides biographical information on the major inventors, lists manufacturers and tells his readers how to clean and display their collection as well as how to date it. The new price guide comes with the book.

Iron *Griswold Cast Iron: A Price Guide* (L-W Book Sales, 1993, 176 pp.) is the newest book on the market for those who collect this best-known and most popular brand of cast iron. Although a Griswold collector did not write the book, L-W Book Sales uses much of the material compiled by collector Steve Stephens of San Anselmo, CA. The book contains numerous photographs of items in the Griswold line and includes illustrations from the 1891, 1920, 1933 and 1937 catalogs. There's also a miscellaneous section containing such items as Griswold pocket calendars, business cards for a Griswold purchasing agent and a griddle display rack. L-W Book Sales has a second volume in the works.

For many years, *Griswold Cast Iron Collectibles, History and Values* by Bill and Denise Harned (PRS-Harned, 1986, 192 pp.) was the only book on the market. Although the prices are outdated, the book still is available to anyone who wants to gather more information on Griswold. It outlines the company history, gives photographs of the product line, describes preservation and restoration techniques and includes some of the circa 1928 recipes from "Aunt Ellen," which were enclosed in boxes of Griswold products. Copies can be ordered from the Harneds. For more information, write PRS-Harned, in care of Denise Harned, P.O. Box 330373, Elmwood, CT 06133-0373. Enclose a self-addressed, stamped envelope.

Antique Iron Identification and Values by Kathryn McNerney (Collector Books, values updated in 1991, 231 pp.) offers an overview of the age of iron and details buying, cleaning and curing it. It contains one chapter devoted to kitchen and pantry iron.

Molds *Chocolate Moulds. A History & Encyclopedia* by Judene Divone (Oakton Hills Publications, Oakton, VA, 1987, 160 pp.) gives a history of chocolate, confectionery firms and "fancy goods" (those special molds that have added to chocolate lovers' enjoyment). The author covers full molds, flat molds, figural molds and holiday molds and describes how to clean them and identify their manufacturers.

Plastics Collecting kitchenware isn't limited to the high-priced antiques of earlier centuries. As Dana DeMore, publisher of the *Kitchen Antiques and Collectibles News,* observed, "There's room for everyone—even those who want to collect modern-day kitchen magnets." *Collecting Plastics, A Handbook and Price Guide* by Jan Lindenberger (Schiffer Publishing, 1991, 160 pp.) provides additional evidence that more modern products are interesting and fun to collect. Nearly a third of the book is devoted to plastics in the kitchen from bowls, breadboxes, butter keepers, cake keepers and canisters to kitchen gadgets, pitchers, refrigerator items, salts and peppers, serving pieces, spatulas, and syrup pitchers.

Pottery *Collector's Guide to Country Stoneware & Pottery, Second Series* by Don and Carol Raycraft (Collector Books, 1990, with 1992 value update, 120 pp.) gives the chronology of the industry beginning with the 1500s when many potters in England and Germany were turning out early household vessels, to 1735 when Pennsylvania's redware potters got their start, to the production of yellowware (in the East Liverpool, OH area from the 1830s to

This rabbit-shaped chocolate mold, in two parts, is fun to display, particularly at Easter time.

Norton crock, made in Bennington, Vermont, has its lid intact and has an attractive decoration that will make it perpetually popular with collectors.

1900). It includes many photographs plus values and complete descriptions of stoneware.

Another general reference is the *Official Price Guide to American Stoneware,* first edition, by George Sullivan (House of Collectibles, 1993, 276 pp.). The author describes the manufacturing processes and the glazes and types of stoneware. He also discusses imported stoneware and provides names of museums and historical societies that can be resources for those seeking more information.

Blue and White Stoneware by Kathryn McNerney (Collector Books, 1981, with 1993 value update, 158 pp.) describes the process used to make blue and white stoneware and some of the many ways in which it was used; for example, coffee and tea pots, measures and holders, mugs, pie plates, roasters and bakers, rolling pins and containers for salt, spices and other food items.

Red Wing Collectibles: An Identification and Value Guide by Dan and Gail DePasquale and Larry Peterson (Collector Books, 1992 update, 166 pp.) is a fascinating look at the stoneware potters located in Red Wing, Minn. For 90 years, from 1877–1967, the town was the self-proclaimed "Pottery Capital of America." The book traces the history and evolution of the stoneware companies of Red Wing, including the Red Wing Stoneware Company, the North Star Stoneware Company, the Union Stoneware Company, the Red Wing Union Stoneware Company, and lastly, the Red Wing Potteries. Scanning the book's sections gives one an appreciation for the role stoneware played as it was shaped into bowls, pitchers, mugs, bean pots, butter crocks and canning jars, as well as crocks, jugs, churns and water coolers. The authors offer investment advice about the quality, decoration, shape and glaze of the stoneware and mention that having the proper lids for various stoneware pieces adds considerable value because so many were broken during daily use.

Redware, America's Folk Art Pottery by Kevin McConnell (Schiffer Publishing, 1988, 96 pp.), covers the first pottery made in colonial America. As McConnell explains, this utilitarian pottery was made from clay containing iron and mineral compounds that fired to a reddish hue in the kiln. The author explains redware terminology, including "sgraffito," which was made by coating the redware with a yellowish slip that was allowed to partially dry before it was scratched, creating artistic designs.

Sturdier than redware, yellowware became popular for kitchen use. *Yellow Ware An Identification and Value Guide* by Lisa S. McAllister and John L. Michel (Collector Books, 1993, 127 pp.) includes manufacturers and their marks as well as prices and photographs of kitchenware including molds, many crocks, rolling pins, custard cups, teapots, colanders and pitchers.

Salt and pepper shakers

Salt and pepper shakers Helen Guarnaccia has turned out the greatest quantity of books on this topic. Her newest is *Salt & Pepper Shakers IV, Identification and Values* (Collector Books, 1993, 239 pp.). In 1993, she also issued value updates on her first two books, first published in 1985 and 1989. *Salt and Pepper Shakers III: Identification and Values* was published in 1991. The author has observed, "Salt and pepper shakers show trends in style and fashion. In 1989, 'country' was in and a vendor came out with a series of black and white cows. In 1990, when the Southwest was in fashion, there were new shakers in the shape of cacti, guns and holsters and vultures. When nostalgia came in, there were 2-piece chrome-look jukebox salt and pepper shakers as well as art-deco toaster shakers." She categorizes shakers according to their design, including, animals, children, feathers and fins, food, holidays, household objects, miniatures, people and series. She also gives her thoughts on tomorrow's collectibles.

Melva Davern, who wrote her first salt and pepper shaker book in 1985, is another well-known name in the category. Davern, first president of the Novelty Salt and Pepper Shakers Club, observed that collecting is achieving recognition because novelty shakers are being listed in general price guides. Her current book, *The Collector's Encyclopedia of Salt and Pepper Shakers, Figural and Novelty* (Collector Books, 1990, with 1993 value update, 213 pp.) covers American-made salts and peppers in much broader categories than Guarnaccia uses.

The World of Salt Shakers, Second Edition by Mildred and Ralph Lechner (Collector Books, 1992, 310 pp.) discusses collecting salt shakers and some outstanding rarities. It then lists the salts by glass house (manufacturer) and pattern name, rather than theme or shape. There's information on pattern details with close-up photography, pattern names, production colors, approximate dates of first manufacture, existence of reproductions and the physical height of each shaker. In *The Complete Salt and Pepper Shaker Book* (Schiffer Publishing, 1993, 280 pp.), author Mike Schneider discusses collecting history, classifying the shakers, and building and maintaining a collection. He covers both figural and nonfigural salt and pepper shakers. On his price guide segment he comments: "My job is to reflect prices, not set them." He suggests that collectors compare his prices with those of Davern and Guarnaccia and then make their own determinations because they vary greatly for some shakers.

Tinware   Several books are available including: *To Cut, Piece and Solder* by Jeanette Lansky (Foxtree Publications, 1982, 80 pp.); *Tinware—Yesterday and Today* by Elmer S. Smith (Applied Arts Publishers, 1974, 40 pp.) and *American Tin & Tole Ware* by Mary Earle Gould (Charles E. Tuttle, 1977, 136 pp.).

OTHER BOOKS YOU'LL ENJOY

The books listed here should provide a few ways to distract yourself if collecting becomes an addiction!

Kitchen Culture, Fifty Years of Food Fads by Gerry Schremp (Pharos Books, 1991, 224 pp.) explores the fads and fashions of haute cuisine and home cooking from the 1940s through the 1980s. Schremp examines the country's ever-changing cooking habits, from the wartime rationing of the 1940s, through the bounty years of the 1950s, the ethnic food explorations of the 1960s and 1970s, to the "lite" years of the 1980s. Along with the foods people served, the author provides a look at the kitchens and the ingredients Americans used during the time period.

Treat yourself to a Christmas present and purchase a copy of *The Christmas Cook, Three Centuries of American Yuletide Sweets* by William Woys Weaver (Harper Perennial, 1990, 268 pp.) anywhere it can be found (the publisher has none to sell; a cookbook dealer will have to find one for you). If there ever was a book that could stimulate a collector to use some of the treasures being hoarded, it is this one. As Weaver said, "I've tried to give readers a cupboard of ideas brimming with pies, cakes, puddings and confections, bonbons and nic-nacs and well-nigh forty thousand sweet things." He has carefully interwoven holiday food traditions, history and old-time recipes (which have been updated) with a collection of beautiful illustrations and photographs of various kitchen antiques.

America Eats, Forms of Edible Folk Art (Harper & Row, 1989, 198 pp.) is another book by William Woys Weaver that blends the history of America's folk cookery with useful recipes and kitchen collectibles. It's for the cook, the collector and anyone else who wants to learn more about the country's culinary history.

Old Sturbridge Village Cookbook edited by Caroline Sloat (The Globe Pequot Press, 1984, 254 pp.) contains authentic Early American recipes for the modern kitchen. Staff members at the village worked with the recipes of Lydia Maria Child in *The American Frugal Housewife* to develop the Old Sturbridge cookbook. The recipes are printed in three ways: in their original form as they appeared in Child's book, in a variation adapted to modern stove cooking, and again with current hearth-cooking instructions. Sloat has included an informative chapter detailing necessary equipment and basic information a person needs to know before undertaking hearth cookery.

American Gourmet, Classic Recipes, Deluxe Delights, Flamboyant Favorites, and Swank "Company" Food from the '50's and '60's by Jane and Michael Stern (HarperCollins, 1991, 286 pp.). The Sterns, with an ironic and affectionate eye for the American dining scene of recent decades, look back at the 1950s and 1960s. They discuss the rise of upscale and international restaurants, television cooking shows, flaming desserts, the mingling of food and sex, brandname cooking and dozens of other cultural phenomena. It's a joy to read because they include recipes from the times, including such foods as "Quiche Lorraine—The Way it Was Meant to Be," "Life Affirming Moussaka," "King for a Day Hot Crabmeat Appetizer" to desserts such as "Babas au Rhum the Hard Way," "Beginners' Crepes Suzette" and "Classic Flaming Baked Alaska." After a few chapters, you'll have the urge to start using your fondue pots again.

REPRINTS AND FACSIMILES OF EARLY COOKBOOKS

Each year, more and more reprints and facsimiles of early cookbooks are created as interest in the nation's culinary history continues to grow. Here are a few I've enjoyed reading for the pictures they present of daily life in earlier times.

American Woman's Home by Catherine E. Beecher and Harriet Beecher Stowe (The Stowe-Day Foundation, 77 Forest St., Hartford, CT 06105, 1991, 500 pp.) is quoted extensively in Chapter 1.

The American Frugal Housewife by Lydia Maria Child, written in 1828 is published in cooperation with Old Sturbridge Village by Applewood Books, 10 Denlar Drive, P.O. Box Q, Chester, CT 06412, (no reprint date given), 130 pp.

The Virginia House-Wife by Mary Randolph, first published in 1824, was one of the most influential cookbooks of the 19th century. Edited by Karen Hess, the facsimile edition is available from the University of South Carolina Press, which has produced numerous other books for those who love to cook and eat and are fascinated by America's culinary history. Other titles of particular interest are *The Kentucky Housewife* by Lettice Bryan (first published in 1839) and *The Carolina Housewife* by Sarah Rutledge (first published in 1847). Send for a catalog by writing to the University of South Carolina Press, 1716 College St., Columbia, SC 29208.

COLLECTOR'S CLUBS AND NEWSLETTERS

Whenever you correspond with someone about newsletters, collectors' clubs or a specific collectible, always remember to include a self-addressed, stamped, legal-sized envelope!

The best overall collectors club for general kitchenware is KOOKS (Kollectors of Old Kitchen Stuff). Sign up for membership and you'll also

Figural salt and pepper shakers have hooked many a collector.

Heavy-duty Bonanza apple parer made by the Goodell Company of Antrim, Vermont, was a key piece of kitchen equipment for a Pennsylvania family who had extensive apple orchards and fewer fruit buyers than they would have liked.

Dana DeMore, publisher of *Kitchen Antiques & Collectibles News* demonstrates a cake mixer he found at a New Jersey estate sale. The enterprising cake baker had to hold the mixer over a bowl with one hand and turn the crank with the other hand.

receive *Kitchen Antiques & Collectibles News,* a bimonthly newsletter covering many categories of collecting. To join the club and obtain subscription information, contact Dana and Darlene DeMore, 4645 Laurel Ridge Dr., Harrisburg, PA 17110.

Advertising *Paper Collector's Marketplace* is a major monthly publication for buyers and sellers of advertising trade cards, magazines and magazine art, and manufacturers' recipe pamphlets, as well as paper items associated with practically any category of collectible from baseball cards and autographs to maps and postcards. Write to PCM at P.O. Box 128, Scandinavia, WI 54977-0128.

The Antique Advertising Association of America has a newsletter called *Past Times.* Write to D. Hirsch, P.O. Box 1121, Morton Grove, IL 60053.

The Ephemera Society of America, P.O. Box 37, Schoharie, NY 12157, focuses on collectibles printed on paper that were not made to last. This group's publication is *Ephemera News.*

The National Association of Paper and Advertising Collectors publishes the *Paper & Advertising Collector (PAC).* Write to P.O. Box 500, Mount Joy, PA 17552.

The Tin Container Collectors Association publishes a newsletter called *Tin Type.* The address is P.O. Box 440101, Aurora, CA 80044.

Apple parers To contact the International Society of Apple Parer Enthusiasts, write to John Lambert, 3911 Morgan Center Rd., Utica, OH 43080.

Bottles, openers and corkscrews The Federation of Historical Bottle Clubs has a newsletter called *Federation Glass Works.* Write to Barbara A. Harms, 14521 Atlanta Ave., Riverdale, IL 60627.

To subscribe to the newsletter, *Antique Bottle & Glass Collector,* write to James Hagenbuch, P.O. Box 87, East Greenville, PA 18041.

Another publication is *Bottles & Extras Magazine* by Scott Grandstaff, P.O. Box 154, Happy Camp, CA 96039.

To obtain more information about *Just for Openers,* club and newsletter, write to John Stanley, 605 Windsong Ln., Durham, NC 27713.

The Figural Bottle Openers Collectors Club publishes a newsletter called *The Opener.* For more information, contact Donna Kitzmiller, 117 Basin Hill Rd., Duncannon, PA 17020.

Cast iron The Griswold and Cast Iron Cookware Association publishes *The Kettles n Cookware Cast Iron Newsletter.* The contact for the Association is Grant Windsor, P.O. Box 3613, Richmond, VA 23235. The contact for the newsletter is David Smith, Postal Drawer B, Perrysburg, NY 14129.

There's also a monthly newsletter called *Griswold Cast Iron Collectors' News & Marketplace* by Jim Haynes, P.O. Box 521, North East, PA 16428.

Cereal collectibles To subscribe to the newsletter *Free Inside,* contact Michael Vollmer, 249 South Highway 101, Solana Beach, CA 92075.

Cookbooks The Cookbook Collectors Club of America, Inc. publishes a newsletter, *Cook Book Gossip.* Write to Bob and Jo Ellen Allen, 231 East James Blvd., St. James, MO 65559.

Simple corkscrew made at BeechDale Farm in Bird-in-Hand, Pa., carried advertising for Brubaker's Creamed Pudding including "The eating of the pudding is the proof" and "U-TRY-ME."

The Cookbook Collectors' Exchange is an excellent national tabloid. To subscribe, contact the publisher, Sue Erwin, P.O. Box 32369, San Jose, CA 95152-2369.

Cookie cutters   To join the Cookie Cutter Collectors Club, contact membership chairwoman, Ruth Capper, 1167 Teal Rd. SW, Dellroy, OH 44620. The club publishes a newsletter, *Cookie Crumbs*. Write to editor Chris Birdsell, Route 3, Box 354, Stanberry, MO 64489.

The newsletter, *Cookies* is published by Phyllis Wetherill, 5426 27th St. NW, Washington, DC 20015.

Corn items   The Corn Items Collectors Association, Inc. publishes a newsletter, *The Bang Board*. Contact the editor, E. Eloise Alton, 613 North Long St., Shelbyville, IL 62565.

Dairy   The newsletter, *Creamers* is published by Lloyd Bindscheattle, P.O. Box 11, LakeVilla, IL 60046.

The Cream Separator Association has a newsletter, *Cream Separator News*. Contact Dr. Paul Dettloff, secretary, Rte 3, Box 189, Arcadia, WI 54612.

The club The Ice Screamers has a newsletter, *The Ice Screamer*. Write to Ed Marks, P.O. Box 5387, Lancaster, PA 17601-0387.

To join the National Association of Milk Bottle Collectors, Inc., contact Thomas Gallagher, 4 Ox Bow Rd., Westport, CT 06880-2602.

Dinnerware   *The American Pottery Journal,* covering pottery, cookie jars, salt and pepper shakers, and dinnerware, is edited by Kathy Lynch. For more information, write to the journal at P.O. Box 14255, Parkville, MO 64152.

The Fiesta Collectors Quarterly covers Fiesta, Epicure, Hall China, Harlequin and Lu-ray dinnerware. To subscribe, write to 19238 Dorchester Cir., Strongsville, OH 44136.

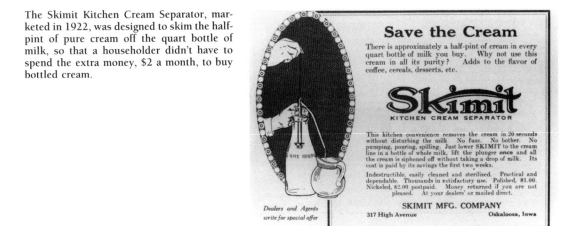

The Skimit Kitchen Cream Separator, marketed in 1922, was designed to skim the half-pint of pure cream off the quart bottle of milk, so that a householder didn't have to spend the extra money, $2 a month, to buy bottled cream.

Save the Cream

There is approximately a half-pint of cream in every quart bottle of milk you buy. Why not use this cream in all its purity? Adds to the flavor of coffee, cereals, desserts, etc.

Skimit
KITCHEN CREAM SEPARATOR

This kitchen convenience removes the cream in 20 seconds without disturbing the milk. No fuss. No bother. No pumping, pouring, spilling. Just lower SKIMIT to the cream line in a bottle of whole milk, lift the plunger once and all the cream is siphoned off without taking a drop of milk. Its cost is paid by its savings the first two weeks.

Indestructible, easily cleaned and sterilized. Practical and dependable. Thousands in satisfactory use. Polished, $1.00. Nickeled, $2.00 postpaid. Money returned if you are not pleased. At your dealers' or mailed direct.

Dealers and Agents write for special offer

SKIMIT MFG. COMPANY
317 High Avenue   Oskaloosa, Iowa

The Flow Blue International Collectors Club publishes a newsletter, *Blueberry Notes.* Write to Don and Larie Hensley, 28 Irene St., Brooksville, FL 34601.

The Hall China Encore newsletter is published four times a year. Contact Kim Boss, 317 N. Pleasant St. #CIC, Oberlin, OH 44074-1113.

Collectors of Tea Leaf Ironstone can join the Tea Leaf Club International and receive the newsletter, *Tea Leaf Readings.* Contact Eleanor Washburn, 222 Powderhorn Dr., Houghton Lake, MI 48629.

To join the International Willow Collectors, write to Harry J. Hall, president, 145 Maple Dr., Springboro, OH 45066.

The National Autumn Leaf Collectors Club publishes the *Autumn Leaf Newsletter.* Contact Beverly Robbins, secretary, 7346 Shamrock Dr., Indianapolis, IN 46217.

To receive the *National Blue Ridge Newsletter,* covering Blue Ridge china produced by Southern Potteries, Inc., contact Norma Lilly, 144 Highland Dr., Blountville, TN 37617-5404. The contact for the Blue Ridge Collector's Club is Phyllis Ledford, Rte. 3, Box 161, Erwin, TN 37650.

The Watt Pottery Collectors Club produces a newsletter, *Spoutings.* Contact Dennis Thompson, P.O. Box 26067, Fairview Park, OH 44126.

Eggs   The club, Pastimes, publishes the *Eggcup Collectors' Corner* newsletter. Write to Dr. Joan M. George, 67 Stevens Ave., Old Bridge, NJ 08857.

Fruit jars   To join the Ball Collectors Club and receive the *Ball Collectors Club Newsletter,* contact Mason Bright, 22203 Doncaster, Riverview, MI 48192.

Dick Roller publishes the *Fruit Jar Newsletter.* Write to him at 364 Gregory Ave., West Orange, NJ 07052-3743.

Glass   To receive the magazine *Antique Bottle & Glass Collector,* contact James Hagenbuch, P.O. Box 187, East Greenville, PA 18041.

For a subscription to *Bottles and Extras* magazine, write to Scott Grandstaff, P.O. Box 154, Happy Camp, CA 96039.

The Collector Glass News newsletter is published by Michael J. Kelly, P.O. Box 308, Slippery Rock, PA 16057.

To subscribe to the magazine, *Glass Collector's Digest,* write to David Richardson, P.O. Box 553, Marietta, OH 45750-0553.

The National Early American Glass Club publishes two newsletters, *Glass Shards* and *Glass Club Bulletin.* For more information, write to P.O. Box 8489, Silver Spring, MD 20907.

The Daze, a newspaper that's billed as "The Nation's Market Place for Glass China and Pottery", is published by Depression Glass Daze, Inc. Contact editor Teri Steele, 275 State Rd., Box 57, Otisville, MI 48463-0057.

Graniteware   The National Graniteware Society publishes the *National Graniteware News.* Write to P.O. Box 10013, Cedar Rapids, IA 52410-0013.

This green glass reamer made quick work of lemons and had plenty of room for juice that could be poured neatly into any recipe-in-the-making.

A collector looking to acquire more Hazel Atlas products like this pitcher in cobalt blue, can watch "for sale" advertisements in *The Daze,* one of the leading publications for Depression-era china and glassware.

Collectors have managed to cover entire walls with simple, hanging spring-balance scales.

Hammered aluminum *The Aluminist* newsletter is published by Dannie Woodard, P.O. Box 1346, Weatherford, TX 76086.

Jelly jars To join the Jelly Jammers Club and receive the newsletter, *Jelly Jammers' Journal,* contact Art Snyder, 110 White Oak Dr., Butler, PA 16001-3446.

Pewter The Pewter Collectors Club of America publishes the *Pewter Collectors Club of America Newsletter.* Write to William Paddock, 29 Chesterfield Rd., Scarsdale, NY 10583.

Piebirds *Piebirds Unlimited* has been produced seven times between 1990 and 1992. Contact Lillian Cole, 14 Harmony School Rd., Flemington, NJ 08822.

Reamers To join the Mid-American Reamer Collectors, write to Winnie Cerbin, 2262 Clay St., Austinburg, OH 44010. The club newsletter, *Juicy Journal* is edited by Karen Maxwell, 222 Cooper Ave., Elgin, IL 60120-2128.

To join the National Reamer Collectors Association and receive the newsletter, *NRCA Quarterly Review,* contact editor Ray Maxwell, Rte. 30., Box 67, Frederic, WI 54837.

Salt and pepper shakers The Antique and Art Glass Salt Shaker Collector's Society has a newsletter called *The Pioneer.* For more information, contact William Avery, 2832 Rapidan Tr., Maitland, FL 32751.

The Novelty Salt & Pepper Shakers Club publishes the *Novelty Salt and Pepper Shakers Club Newsletter.* Write to Irene Thornburg, 581 Joy Rd., Battle Creek, MI 49017.

Scales The International Society of Antique Scale Collectors publishes the Magazine, *Equilibrium.* Write to Bob Stein, Suite 1706, 176 West Adams, Chicago, IL 60603.

Stoneware and pottery *Bottles & Extras Magazine,* produced by Scott Grandstaff (P.O. Box 154, Happy Camp, CA 96039), contains a column on stoneware.

The Blue & White Pottery Club publishes *The Blue and White Pottery Club Newsletter.* Write to 224 12th St. NW, Cedar Rapids, IA 52405.

To join the Majolica International Club and receive the *Majolica International Society Newsletter,* contact Michael G. Strawser, President, Suite 103, 1275 First Ave., New York, NY 10021.

The Red Wing Collectors Society, Inc. produces the *Red Wing Collectors Newsletter.* Write to David Newkirk, 8263 State Highway 25 NE, Monticello, MN 55362. (Newkirk also has written two books on Red Wing Pottery and has them available for sale.)

Tea To subscribe to the newsletter, *Tea Talk,* write to Diana Rosen, 419 North Larchmont Blvd. #225, Los Angeles, CA 90004.

Toothpick holders *Toothpick Bulletin,* the newsletter for the National Toothpick Holders Collectors Society, is produced by Judy Knauer, 1224 Spring Valley Ln., West Chester, PA 19380. The contact for the society is Joyce Ender, Box 246, Sawyer, MI 49125.

4

Factors Influencing Price

Antiques shops, shows and malls, flea markets and auctions do not operate like catalog showrooms. Buying is not a simple matter of paying a preset catalog price. In the world of kitchen antiques and collectibles, anything can happen when buyer and seller negotiate a deal. Final prices might not be anything like the sums listed in a price guide. That's why "going solely by the book," (i.e., a price guide) to determine an object's value is a mistake. A carefully researched price guide that accurately reflects retail market prices at press time is just one of the tools a collector needs to determine the price to pay for a yellowware bowl or a selling price for an Enterprise cast-iron coffee mill.

One could argue that any price a person pays for a special treasure, whether it's a finely carved wooden springerle board, a one-of-a-kind apple parer or a rare basket, is fine if the object makes the collector happy. That's certainly true for the price-is-no-object buyer who does not quibble over prices and can afford anything, no matter what it costs. But the most recent recession made this kind of buyer about as rare as fiddlehead ferns.

Bargain hunters who strive to make a killing each time they work a show or sale and ordinary collectors who have limited funds and want to get the most for their money are the characters more commonly found shopping wherever kitchen antiques and collectibles are sold. These folks need to know more than current price guide figures.

To understand the market, you must learn to identify the factors determining price. This information not only keeps you from spending too much

Those who do not care for anise-flavored cookies might say the nicest thing about springerles are their designs, which are created by wooden boards such as this one containing 12 carved images and measuring 7 3/4 by 4 1/4 inches.

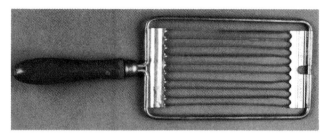

A tomato slicer, an affordable utensil, with its sharp stainless-steel blades, allowed a user to cut a tomato into uniform slices. The hand-held slicer was set at a 45-degree angle to a work surface, and the tomato was cut by sliding it back and forth across the serrated blades.

for a particular item, but also prevents you from passing up the buy of a lifetime. Buying wisely also means there might be a little more money left over to cover the cost of the next find.

The major factors influencing price include: the category's general affordability, collecting crazes, condition, completeness, repair and restoration, scarcity, geographic location and cross-market appeal. In addition, price guides themselves can alter a market's pricing structure.

Affordability of the Category

Clearly, if you seek antiques from the 1600's, 1700's, 1800's and early 1900's you will usually pay more for your collection than a person who is acquiring mass-produced kitchenware from the 1950's, 1960's and 1970's. But no matter whether your interest is in kitchen antiques or collectibles, the sooner you begin acquiring them, the better. As Harry Rinker, a nationally known antiques and collectibles expert, points out: "When a person is in his 30s, items from his childhood are still affordable. When he is in his 40s, the items are starting to become expensive. But when a person becomes 50 or older (the definition of an antique), buying back one's childhood will require substantial investment." Of course, goods from earlier generations can be totally out-of-reach.

Here's how affordability affects pricing throughout a category: When most items are $50 or less, there's a lot of action as people buy collectibles to use and keep. But when prices climb for the top-quality items in a collecting

Foley Food Mills, still sold today, are affordable collectibles that can be used from time to time to process a variety of fruits and vegetables. One wonders, however, about how popular they were as Christmas gifts for homemakers—even if they did come in a bright red Christmas box.

category, prices at the bottom go up, too. When eggbeaters sell for $200, $300, $400 or more and nutmeg graters command $700 or higher, some collectors will have to shift their focus. Dana DeMore, publisher of the *Kitchen Antiques & Collectibles News,* added, "In 5 or 10 years, as more people collect kitchenware and fewer good pieces are coming in, I'm afraid beginners will be priced out. They'll have to look into things like collecting refrigerator magnets."

Collecting Crazes

Collecting crazes can be triggered by something as simple as a feature in *Country Home* or *Country Living.* As they focus on anything from agateware to cookie cutters, the magazines' photographs may stir a fond memory, which, in turn, creates desire to own. But there's no event in the history of collecting kitchenware that did as much to fuel a craze as the sale of Andy Warhol's collection of 134 cookie jars for $240,350—an average price of $1,794 each. A year after the April, 1988 sale, an *Antique Week* article pointed out that if the jars had sold for their price-guide values, they'd have brought an average of under $50 each. News of these fabulous prices created enough excitement to get former cookie jar collectors back into the market and to stimulate newcomers to begin collecting. New York collector Wendy Johnston said, "I don't think there was a major publication in the country that didn't cover the cookie jar portion of the auction in some way."

Condition

Perhaps the most basic factor affecting price (when there's no decorating magazine feature or famous name associated with kitchenware) is general condition. It's a good starting point in determining how much kitchenware collectors will pay for their purchases. When there's a buyer's market, especially during a recessionary period, collectors can afford to be particular about condition. If they're interested in mass-produced kitchen items of the 20th century, this is particularly true. When literally thousands of examples exist, there's no reason to settle for a chipped or cracked Fire-King casserole

This coffee mill has really been through the grinder. Missing the knob on the drawer where the ground coffee was collected, it no doubt saw lengthy service before it became a kitchen decoration.

The shiny finish is gone from the surface of these cookie cutters from the 1920's. Be sure to completely dry the cutters before storing them and don't keep in a damp basement where they can suffer damage from the conditions.

or Pyrex ovenware dish. On the other hand, some allowances are made for the condition of certain antiques—particularly handmade objects that are well over 50 years old. Even if a one-of-a-kind piece of Red Wing stoneware is marred by a chip or a crack, it will still have some value because of its uniqueness.

But there are limits. Culinary historian William Woys Weaver offered an extreme example: "An old cast iron stew pot was brought to me. It had a utilitarian beauty to it. Made by an iron furnace in central Pennsylvania, the pot even was signed. In good condition, it would have been worth $1,000. But the previous owner had ruined it by planting it with petunias and plopping it in her front yard. It was so pitted that there was simply no way I could undo the damage. It was worthless."

Grading standards that rate condition exist for certain categories of kitchen collectibles and play a role in determining an object's selling price. Standards for cookbooks, for example, have been particularly well defined. Naturally, the better a book's condition, the higher a price it will bring. Mary Margaret Barile, author of *Just Cookbooks* and *Cookbooks Worth Collecting* outlined the way cookbooks' conditions are rated:

> A book in fine condition may have been opened a few times but is nearly brand new; a book in "very good" condition shows small traces of use like a page that's slightly bent, a single smudge, or perhaps a minute tear in the cover; a book in "fair condition" (the category into which most cookbooks fall) contains clear signs of wear but is complete; a book in "poor condition"

probably has torn or missing pages that clearly affect its usefulness; a "reading" copy is legible but still in poor condition because it has undergone some abuse. An ex-library copy is one that has been taken from circulation and shows many signs of wear from its brutal shelf life. The library's name often is stamped on one or many of the pages and marks also remain where the library card and pocket were pasted. Finally, a "binding" copy is one which is in bits.

Sadly, many of my favorites are in the "reading" category because their pages have been splotched and spattered by flying ingredients like milk, butter, vanilla, vinegar and oil.

A collector who buys for fun but also sees the collection as a form of long-term investment, is better off acquiring a few "very good" or even better examples rather than purchasing many books in fair or poor condition. In other words, very good cookbooks will go up in value, while ex-library reading or binding copies will be worth far more to the cook who plans to use them in the kitchen than they will be to a collector who expects to keep them on the shelf.

Beginners should not be discouraged to find that the top items in their collecting category are priced in the hundreds or thousands of dollars. The kitchenware field is peppered with stories of collectors who have become small-scale tycoons. They play the market, anticipating trends and buying and selling carefully, so that their investments yield handsome profits. These profits, of course, are plowed back into the collection to buy or trade up for better examples.

Scarcity

Along with condition, collectors must know enough about their particular categories to recognize a certain color or certain trait that makes one collectible more scarce and valuable than another that is nearly identical. Ellen Tischbein Schroy, author of *Warman's Glass,* explained:

Consider a butter dish in a common pattern called 'Crisscross.' This pattern, made by Hazel Atlas Glass Company between 1936 and 1938, was designed to hold a pound of butter in the stick form we now know. The value for the clear version of this butter dish is $15 to $18. The very same butter dish in green or pink would be valued at $30 to $35. However, a person who is lucky enough to find or own a deep blue example, will have a butter dish that's worth $75 to $85.

The Crisscross pattern is plain and went unnoticed for many years by collectors. It was the deep sapphire blue that began to attract buyers and prices reflected this. Now, collectors are beginning to purchase the other colors in the hope that they will grow in value like the blue.

She warned, however, "Beware of 'marriages' between the different colors. Hazel Atlas did not mix or match!"

Is a particular kitchen collectible the first in a long line of products? It's generally worth more than later versions. K. Scotty Mitchell, who cowrote

Having the original box adds to the value of these salt and pepper shakers, which advertised the Westinghouse Laundry Twins, a clothes dryer and a "laundromat" with its exclusive "Weigh to Save Door" and "Water Saver." There could be some limited cross-market appeal to other kinds of collectors, too, if they're after the Westinghouse name or have an interest in smaller-scale depictions of major appliances.

Price Guide to Collectible Kitchen Appliances: From Aerators to Waffle Irons, 1890–1950 with Gary Miller, said, "We have the first General Electric electric toaster. We also have the first Westinghouse toaster. The two came out within months of each other. The Westinghouse has never been used and is still in its original box."

The toaster's box is one example of how original packaging can affect price. But DeMore offered still another example: "I've seen the original box for a nutmeg grater increase the grater's price by 50 percent or more. There have been cases where the box has been valued more highly than the grater because a collector figured he might never see another box but did stand a chance of finding another grater.

Completeness

Having the directions for using various gadgets and appliances influences selling price, too. A collector won't mind paying a little more for an Enterprise vegetable slicer or a cast-iron apple parer if it includes a sheet of operating instructions. (I've read and tried some and have decided to leave heavy-duty slicing and dicing to the food processor. The apple parer, on the other hand, does a pretty good job!)

Completeness counts in every category. A glass rolling pin that's missing the cap to seal chilled water in its center and the coffee mill that's missing its drawer certainly will not command the same prices as complete ones. Mitchell added, "When you go to buy an Armstrong kitchen appliance, make sure the cord is with it. Otherwise, you could spend a lifetime hunting for the right one. The same goes for certain waffle irons that came with two-headed cords for heating top and bottom elements separately."

Repairs and Restoration

Repairs and restoration to improve an object's condition, to make it complete again, or worst of all, to make it look like new, can be as misguided as tinting mashed potatoes blue! The goal of any repair or restoration should be to stabilize the object with every original part preserved. Nothing should be done that can't be undone.

If the kitchen antique or collectible is extremely valuable but damaged, a

Why did someone spray-paint this cornstick pan? It might have been easier than cleaning it. Perhaps the owner thought it would look better with a coat of glossy black paint. No matter what the reason, its value was destroyed.

The Enterprise #5 meat chopper carried a patent date of June 5, 1888, and clamped to a table to do its work.

professionally trained and licensed conservator should be contacted. Local museum officials should be able to supply a collector with the names of these college-trained experts.

Barbara Kuck, curator of the Culinary Archives at Johnson & Wales University, Providence, R.I., is a minimalist when it comes to altering the appearance or operation of a piece of kitchenware: "We have what we think is the earliest patented meatgrinder (August 1859). It's about the color of burnt sienna, but I'm not about to give in to the people who want me to rub it with oil so it will shine a little. I think things should be left as they were found, if at all possible."

I'll confess that I've removed all but the front from a drawer in the top of my pie safe, so that it could be used as a two-shelf liquor cabinet. Tall wine and liquor bottles couldn't be stored upright on the top shelf unless the drawer was removed. But I have carefully saved all of the bits to re-attach the drawer and drawer-front, should I ever want to use the cabinet for something else, or sell it. To my credit, I left the top shelf as it was—deeply scored by the chew marks of some starving rodents who found it in a Midwestern barn before I did. (I did risk cleaning it with soap and water and lots of disinfectant, though!)

Avoid the temptation to spray-paint a balance scale, trivet or cornstick pan. An old oak kitchen cupboard shouldn't be stripped of its original paint (if it truly was original) or be stripped and stained to look like walnut or cherry when it's actually oak. Such acts not only destroy kitchen history, but they also lower the value of the item.

DeMore, writing in an early issue of *Kitchen Antiques & Collectibles News,* warned his readers not to "skin" old tin, a process that can be done in a matter of minutes. He explained, "Skinning refers to the practice of removing the surface finish on an older piece of tin to produce a more lustrous appearance. When a piece of tin is skinned, it loses its historical and monetary value."

Geographic Location

Find a kitchen antique near the place where it was made and it might cost more to buy it. This happens because most collectors like to own objects that

This old bread toaster was an advertising item. Its wooden handle says, "John Schaible Steam Vienna Bakery, South Side, Easton, Pa." The 17 1/2-inch-long tool would be of interest to those who collect toasters and would also attract attention from Easton residents, who either remember the bakery or collect kitchen tools containing advertising.

were made practically in their backyards. They'll want the food-related giveaways imprinted with local merchants' names such as the long-handled, wire bread toaster (to hold one slice over the wood or coal stove) with a bakery's name on it. I wound up paying extra for my round, oak kitchen table made by the Watsontown Table Company of Watsontown, Pa., because the auction I was attending was near Watsontown, and my major bidding opponent, as I learned later, wanted the table because a relative had worked in the factory.

There are instances, however, where finding a collectible in its home territory means it will be cheaper because that's where examples of it will be the most common.

Geography can have still another effect on price. DeMore said he believes the overall market for kitchenware has become much less regional and that prices generally seem much more uniform across the country than they used to be. But there are still exceptions that prove that there can be a right or wrong place to buy. For example, Philip D. Kennedy, the Indianapolis, Ind., author of *Hoosier Cabinets,* said, "Twenty years ago, Hoosiers and similar cabinets produced by other companies could be bought for $5 or $10. About 10 years ago, they became collectors items. Now, prices vary considerably depending on their condition and the area of the country in which they're being sold. Dealers in this part of the country are selling the cabinets, in good condition, for $500 to more than $1,000. In California, they're selling for as much as $2,000."

Of course, no matter where a person is, there's the chance of a once-in-a-lifetime buy, either because the seller doesn't care or doesn't know the value of an object. Kennedy said, "I saw a Hoosier advertised for $100 in the Indianapolis newspaper. I called about it and the people told me they'd sold it within minutes of the paper's hitting the street." No wonder!

Mitchell and Miller developed their guide's price listings for small appliances by averaging prices around the country. But California collectors, into high style and going wild over Toastmaster turquoise, yellow, pink, red and brown toasters from the 1950s, told the authors their prices were off the wall. That's because they were paying as much as 10 times more in a hot market. Instead of scoffing, however, they'd have been smarter to ask Miller and Mitchell for some tips on the best areas in which to buy the toasters and heading east to do their shopping.

Basic setting can influence price, too. Dealers paying high overheads for space in a major city's downtown shopping district need to cover more expenses than a person selling antiques and collectibles in a rundown shed or garage in a small town.

Cross-market Appeal

An item that appeals to more than one kind of collector has cross-market appeal and could bring different prices in different markets. A Mickey Mouse or Donald Duck cookie jar by Hoan will appeal to the general cookie jar collector, to the collectors who specialize in Hoan cookie jars, to Disney collectors as well as to those who specialize in anything to do with Mickey or Donald. In general, the broader the object's appeal and the better its price, the faster it will move.

Cross-market appeal should be remembered when buying or selling. Wise buyers hunt for the object in the market that values it the least; wise sellers know which kinds of collectors pay a premium price for the item they want to sell.

Using Price Guides

Although a well-done price guide provides ballpark figures for retail prices, it isn't meant to tell you how much to pay for an object, any more than it will tell you how to price it for sale. That's because the actual price at which an object will change hands, satisfying both buyer and seller, is subjective and a result of the current market, rather than a single price guide. Nevertheless, there are occasions when a new price guide—particularly the first to document a certain kind of collectible—can have a great impact on market prices. Suddenly, everyone is "going by the book," rather than pricing the objects based on their own ideas.

Valley Farm's Bing Crosby ice-cream container has cross-market appeal to those interested in ice-cream collectibles, ice-cream boxes, celebrity food advertising and those who treasure anything connected with Der Bingle. Speaking of which, have you tucked away containers of Paul Newman's product line like his Newman's Own salad dressing, tomato sauce, salsa, etc.? Just some food for thought . . .

During the Christmas season of 1915, practical gift suggestions included an electric percolator or an electric toaster, along with numerous serving pieces.

When selecting price guides for a personal library, it's a good idea to ask more experienced collectors for the names of the books they use. Don't be surprised if they name several. Different books are likely to picture and price different objects within a category, providing a broader view of the market. Comparison shopping for information in the antiques and collectibles world is similar to soliciting a second or third opinion from doctors or checking newspaper advertisements and catalog listings before buying something like audio equipment. Asking a pro for advice will help a beginner avoid another kind of price guide—those produced by dealers or collectors who are seeking to establish a market or justify the prices they're charging, rather than reflecting the current market correctly. This problem arises when authors have failed to check the right sources or didn't want to.

5
Tips on Buying and Selling

Every kitchen collector can spin a yarn or two about a special find in a relative's attic, basement or kitchen. American culinary historian William Woys Weaver discovered his great-grandmother's redware mold for sponge cake in his grandmother's basement. A cousin's home in New Jersey yielded a handwoven Quaker fruit basket signed and dated (1852) by its maker, Ebeneezer Thompson. My grandmother's *American Cookery* magazines (1913 to 1939), stashed under the eaves in my mother's attic for 30 years, have become my treasure. Marked with my grandmother's handwritten recipe notes, the magazines also give renewed voice to earlier cooks who described their struggles, for example, to open a tin can without bloodshed in the days before electric can openers.

Finding the mold and basket or the *American Cookery* magazines wasn't the end, however, it was the beginning. All it takes is one or two discoveries—no matter whether they're cookware and utensils, appliances, kitchen furniture or cookbooks—to spark enough interest to light a full-scale fire in a collector's soul.

A person has to decide what to spend—time or money—when ready to start a collection. There's always the option of going to the nearest antique shops and buying out their stock or paying whatever it costs to buy an existing collection that's up for sale. But it is stalking the elusive raisin seeder, the finely carved butter mold or intricate Nantucket Lightship basket that provides the thrill of the hunt. In short, a person who bypasses this phase will miss out on one of the biggest joys of collecting.

The writers who filled the pages of *American Cookery* magazines with timely information for cooks of the early 1900s were also logging the era's culinary history, just as today's food magazines are doing the same for the end of the 20th century.

This black enamel Landers, Frary & Clark Family Scale logged as much as 20 pounds on its dial. The company was based in New Britain, Conn.

Scrounging relentlessly in family attics and basements, however, will wear out a collector's welcome quickly. The family cannot and will not be able to satisfy a kitchen habit. A network of sources is needed.

Building a Supply Network

There are broad ways to build a supply network, as well as very focused techniques for reaching specialized sources in certain collecting categories. Begin by talking to friends. Sharing information about kitchen wants produced some unexpected results for Dale Schmidt, a Salem, OR, collector. Digging in his father's basement turned up his grandmother's treasured cookie irons, brought from Romania. They triggered another memory. "I asked my dad if he knew what had happened to my grandfather's sausage stuffer. He didn't. Then I told a long-time family friend that I was trying to find it." A few days later, the elderly friend returned, carrying a burlap sack. He handed it to Schmidt and said, "You ought to have this. Your grandfather gave it to me years ago." The bag contained the missing stuffer.

Talking to neighbors is another tactic that brings results. Cookbook collector Mary-Margaret Barile has spent so much time talking to the people in her New York state neighborhood that they know better than to discard cookbooks or sell them to anyone else before calling her.

Chances are good, however, that even a local network of relatives and friends won't be extensive enough to support a growing kitchen habit. When

Double-barreled cast-iron sausage stuffer was a tool that saw heavy use during autumn butchering time on farms.

you reach this point, you won't need a crystal ball to know that travel figures prominently in the future. But just as you plot the points you want to see when you travel, you must compile a "want list" of specific kitchen items before hitting the road. Your want list is simply a neatly printed listing of the particular kitchenware you want, along with your name, address, and day and evening phone numbers.

Give copies of your list to any collector or dealer whose interests are similar and who are willing to accept it. (Thanks to computers, both collectors and dealers are logging collectors' wants in databases that can be called up when something is found. It's an evolving system that is the antiques and collectibles world's answer to dating services because the computers are matching collectors with objects they'll love.)

Hitting the Road

In addition to a stack of want lists, a collector's car should also contain such essentials as a flashlight and a magnifying glass, a few basic tools (in case you buy something big that needs to be disassembled before it can be transported) and boxes and wrapping material to safely pack smaller purchases. If you're going to spend the day outdoors in hot sun, at a big flea market or antiques show, remember to apply some sunscreen and pack a hat and sunglasses. A good picnic lunch and a jug of ice-water are additional creature comforts for a person who tires quickly of syrupy sodas and overdone hot dogs.

FLEA MARKETS, GARAGE SALES AND SECOND-HAND SHOPS

When the car's packed, it's time to go to local garage sales, yard sales, thrift shops, charity "white elephant" sales and flea markets. Because there are many 20th-century kitchen collectibles still within affordable price ranges, attending these events means a shopper probably won't go home empty-handed.

Shop early for the widest selection, and possibly, for a good buy from a seller who is anxious about how well the day is going to go. Shop late for bargains. Flea market pros say there's a chance of making some good buys

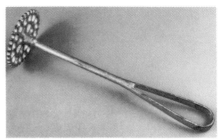

The Jiffy Way egg scale (U.S. patent # 2,205,917) quantified egg-grading technique. Its colors (green body with stripes of orange, green, yellow and red) make it a particularly decorative collectible.

A potato muddler has a totally different look than most other traditional metal potato mashers. Although its three-inch diameter blade did its job, making mashed potatoes by hand for a crowd still must have been slow going.

near the end of the day, because sellers are tired and would rather sell than repack an object and drag it to another sale somewhere else.

Making the rounds of second-hand shops also has its rewards, although many proprietors today are sophisticated enough to know when they have something of value. If I hadn't been visiting the shops near Northwest Circus Place in Edinburgh, Scotland, I'd have never met Mr. Dick. Although he looked the part of one of Charles Dickens' characters, and his shop certainly was a curiosity (so dark and so full that it was impossible to see more than a fraction of the junk piled from floor to ceiling on either side of the single, narrow aisle), he had the uncanny knack for having Victorian china biscuit barrels, old pudding molds and beautiful little ivory and brass pie crimpers at very reasonable prices. (Of course, a Scottish friend did all the talking so that my American accent didn't result in substantial price increases.)

Steve Stephens was touring San Francisco's junk shops to add to his varied collections (few collectors have just one specialty), when he found a Griswold waffle iron that eventually would figure heavily into the way he would spend his collecting time. "It had a $10 price tag. I got it for $5 and have used it ever since. My mother gave me some more skillets when she realized I liked cast iron. Then I found myself wanting more skillets to match the ones I had, and a little popover pan and some muffin pans. . . . " Before Stephens tired of acquiring cast-iron kitchenware, he spent 15 years finding some 2,000 pieces.

Hand-lettered signs along country roads should be enough to bring a collector's car to a halt. When someone wants to unload an accumulation that's cluttering a garage, barn or porch, there's always the chance of making an interesting find. Scotty Mitchell and Gary Miller purchased one of their favorite kitchen appliances after it had languished in a barn for years. It was a 1939 KitchenAid mixer. "It wouldn't work at first, but it wasn't much of a gamble since we only paid a dollar for it," Mitchell said. After cleaning a mud wasp's nest out of it, they took it to a repair shop where the trouble was spotted quickly. The packing grease had frozen so the motor couldn't run.

Straight-sided stoneware crock will have particular appeal to Pennsylvanians because of its clear and attractive markings for the H.J. Heinz Company's Pickling and Preserving Works in Pittsburgh, U.S.A.

The KitchenAid Mixer came with so many attachments that the company also marketed a special storage cabinet for them.

Once the old grease was removed and replaced, the mixer's motor once again could churn its way through all types of batter.

Of course, some kitchen collectibles don't even have to be under cover to be finds. Dick Roller, nationally known fruit jar expert and author of the *Fruit Jar Newsletter* and *The Standard Fruit Jar Reference,* made one of his favorite discoveries in southern Missouri. He said, "It was about 1970 and we were searching for fruit jars when we came to an old junky place where the jars were setting out in the grass in a side lot. I was picking up this and that when I came across a pint jar that was half full of water. It said 'Ball Perfection.' I took it inside and paid about 75 cents for it. A short time later, I visited Ball headquarters in Muncie, IN, and asked them to tell me what I had. They weren't sure, either. I researched it with their help and finally determined that it was produced around 1914 and was made for use with a different type of patent sealing process. But the seal just wasn't good enough and the line of jars was dropped."

AUCTIONS

Studying newspaper classified advertising sections for news of nearby auction listings is a weekly exercise for collectors on the hunt. If a sale sounds interesting, read the listing carefully for preview hours. Consider calling the auctioneer's office to check on accepted methods of payment and on other terms of sale so you know the rules of the game before you start to play.

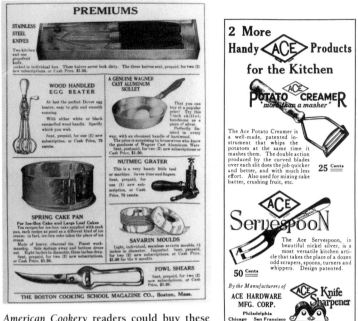

American Cookery readers could buy these kitchen items for cash or were rewarded with some of them for subscribing. Note that the wood-handled Dover eggbeater was advertised as "perfect" because it was easy to grip and smooth running.

Ace products like the Potato Creamer and the classic Servespoon Wire can be found among household goods at auctions and still are useful kitchen tools.

(Reading through the "household goods" or "articles for sale" in the local newspaper is less worthwhile. Focus on the classified sections of more specialized publications in the antiques and collectibles market and the eye strain will pay better dividends.)

Weekly sales of household goods in auction houses and whole-house or so-called "porch" auctions often are excellent sources of close-to-home kitchen collectibles. Attending auctions in certain parts of the country where saving everything is an ingrained trait can be like finding morels on the forest floor. That's the case in my home town in southeastern Pennsylvania. Old-timers here are reluctant to embrace newcomers. But my husband's 80-year-old Pennsylvania Dutch grandmother (who always washed out plastic bags and dried them on the clothesline for reuse) finally gave me a nod of approval when she heard that I still had the first two-slice toaster, popcorn popper, crockery slow-cooker, fondue pot and coffee percolator that were wedding presents nearly 25 years ago. (Stored in their original boxes and with their instruction booklets, they give me a sense of security. Even as I reach for my thoroughly modern toaster that adjusts to everything from a thin slice of diet bread to a thick bagel, I like knowing the old two-slice can still produce golden slices of skinny bread, if I could get anyone to eat them. Although the modern, drip coffeemaker switches on flawlessly before dawn, I like knowing I can still have a cup of "boiled" coffee if it ever lets me down. And even the old popcorn popper, with a plastic top that flipped over to become a serving bowl for the oil-popped popcorn, becomes more of a novelty as fewer people remember anything but the new-fangled air poppers that send kernels flying out dispensing chutes like coins from a slot machine.

Of course, Pennsylvanians aren't the only ones who're preserving the past and creating mother lodes of collectibles for future collectors. Kitchen collectibles can be found wherever people have had to eat. In other words, anywhere. Because few people can afford the money or time it takes to eat out all of the time, they've had to acquire at least basic equipment for home cooking. And if they have been half-serious about making good food, their acquisitions will have gone well beyond refrigerator and stove.

Arrive early and stake your claim

Arrive at an auction during the preview period (several hours before the sale begins) and you'll be able to judge just how advanced the householder was in cookery. You should get a bidding number (before there's a long line), get situated and check out the items you're interested in buying.

Selecting a good spot for a folding chair is as critical as finding a dry campsite because a bidder will literally be camped in that spot for much of the day. The location should provide a clear view of the selling platform and also enable the auctioneer to see the bidder. At porch auctions, early arrivals get the best spots. At auction houses, however, regulars sometimes have earned their front-row seats, which are reserved for them. Even if the seats aren't reserved, the stalwarts who spend week after week will know the routine and arrive early enough to stake their claims to particular seats by covering them with pillows, cardboard boxes, blankets or cushions. Move any of these markers and you're likely to risk a curse that could last a lifetime!

Study the offerings

Once you've gotten a number and picked a location, spend the rest of the presale time by studying goods for possible bidding and purchase. Look closely. See any flaws? If the room is too dark to see objects properly, any potential purchase should be carried carefully to a

A double-bladed chopping knife was rocked back and forth to cut ingredients.

Yellowware bowl trimmed with brown bands added color to the kitchen. With its 6 1/4-inch diameter, it was a nice size for mixing small amounts of batter.

place where it can be examined and then returned to the correct lot. Is an object too big to carry? Get out your flashlight. Take the extra time to check dirty or soiled pieces closely because a blanket of dirt can cover up serious flaws like chips, cracks or crazing.

Rummage through box lots because these helter-skelter assortments sometimes contain the best buys of the day (goods whose value wasn't known by those who threw them into the boxes). Although Dick Roller remembers not even wanting to go to a farm sale his wife spotted in the newspaper, he found a box lot that made the trip worthwhile. "I figured it would be one of those places where 'lots of canning equipment' meant an assortment of old mayonnaise jars." But then he spotted a box with an inverted half-gallon jar sticking out of it and decided to take a closer look. "I usually don't collect half-gallons but this one was special because it also contained a patented pickle pusher (a glass insert that kept fruit or pickles submerged in the jar's liquid)."

Check your bidding selections

Individual items examined during the preview period should be checked again, just before the bidding begins. I learned this the hard way when I assumed a small stoneware pitcher hadn't suffered any damage in the half an hour since I'd looked at it. When I won the bid, I discovered the pitcher's spout had been chipped. (If something like this happens, a buyer can protest the change in condition and an auctioneer might take the object back to re-bid it, but he doesn't have to.) Box lots need to be rechecked, too, shortly before they come up for bid. Frequently, unscrupulous auction-goers will switch items from box lot to box lot so that everything they want is in a single box. That means an unsuspecting bidder could wind up "holding the bag" on what is no longer a good box.

The Milwaukee, Wisconsin, firm marketing Cream City Ware was generous in singing the praises of its enamelware, which went well beyond stove-top basics. Good Christmas gifts in 1930 were the roaster, cake cover and handled tray, bread cover, and an easy-pour pitcher for waffle and pancake batter as well as iced tea.

Gamblers who don't mind spending some of the week's grocery money on junk might bid on something they didn't examine during the preview period. But a wise collector won't do it. I learned this lesson very early in my auction-going career. When the auctioneer called for bids on a cupboard that had been concealed by other furniture during the preview period, I was on the opposite side of the room. It looked good to me. I heard a bid for $5; another for $10. The cupboard was going to go for $15. I couldn't believe it. My hand shot into the air to catch the auctioneer's eye. It was mine! But the exhilaration quickly faded when I examined my purchase more closely. It turned out to be little more than heavy-grade cardboard with wood veneering on the fronts of the doors. I wanted to get rid of it the next day, but my husband insisted we save it. It is still in the basement, piled with canned goods. But as its cardboard sides warp a little more each time water seeps into the basement, I pray for its eventual collapse and disintegration.

Ins and outs of bidding   Finding a gold mine of kitchen collectibles at an auction can be exhilarating, but be a careful collector and don't lose your head in a sudden bidding frenzy. To avoid being burned, decide in advance on the amount you will spend for a piece of kitchenware and drop out if bidding goes beyond that preset limit. (It goes without saying that you already know an object's worth because of careful research and knowledge of the collectibles market.) Because auction-going and bidding can be addictive, you must be careful not to spend more than you can afford.

Paying attention to the bidding at all times is also vital. You are in for a real shock if you think you have just bid $15 when, in fact, you bid $1,500!

Knowing which people are dealers can be helpful, too. It's knowledge gleaned from attending a number of auctions and getting to know the other bidders. Watching how a dealer bids can give some extra hints about the current market value of a particular piece. A dealer will generally drop out when the bidding reaches 30% to 50% of the current market value (unless the item is something the dealer wants for a personal collection, rather than for resale). After all, a dealer has to double the price he or she pays to break even, and triple the price to make a profit. When you're squared off in a bid against a dealer and he or she drops out, this also tells you that you can multiply the last bid by two or three to get a very rough idea of the object's price tag, or its current book value if it were being sold in an antique shop. As you attend more and more auctions and become familiar with specific auctioneers' styles as well as the bidding habits of competitors (many of the same people turn up at sale after sale), you will develop a strategy for bidding success.

But for those who haven't developed this expertise yet, some bidding advice was offered by Harry Rinker, a nationally known antiques and collectibles expert. Beginners, he suggested, should get into the bidding as soon as it starts on items they want. Pros know how to get into bidding later, but it is risky if a person is unfamiliar with an auctioneer's selling pattern. Rinker explained, "The theory behind waiting to get into the bidding until the

Food press could put the squeeze on fruits, separating pulp and seeds from juice. This one, which was 22 inches high when the handle was fully extended, had a 4-quart capacity.

A fruit jar collector might be interested in related items, such as this advertising box for Bulldog Jar Rubbers, which were used to make the seal between fruit jar and canning lid.

last minute is that a person who thought he was going to get the item is discouraged by the entrance of a 'fresh' bidder and gives up."

Rinker also advised that you increase your odds of winning a bid if you stick to odd numbers. In other words, when setting your personal bidding limits, the figure should be something other than usual thresholds like $50, $75, $100, $250 or $500. "Going just one bid over that, like $70, $90, $110, $260 or $510, can get you the object," Rinker counseled.

Other logistics Auction-goers shouldn't buy something that's really big unless they've made arrangements, in advance, for getting the purchase home. Auctioneers generally won't warehouse goods for bidders. Although this sounds like common sense, a friend of mine made a spur-of-the-moment whimsical bid of a quarter on an old piece of office equipment. She got it and it weighed a ton. Luckily, she was able to get to a phone, enlist four friends to help lift it and find a truck to haul it. To this day, however, the mechanical monster remains on her back porch.

Keeping an eye on anything purchased at an auction is essential, until it can be loaded in the car, van or truck. Goods should be removed immediately, if possible. Because there's always so much activity around the auction area, with people carrying things off, it's hard to tell who has paid for what. And there's no one to police the action. Recording purchases and prices paid as the sale goes along is also a good idea, in case there are discrepancies when it is time to pay for the goods.

Focusing in on Your Treasure

At the same time you are attending house auctions, flea markets and yard sales, you should also be developing the more focused segment of the supply network. This means finding specialized dealers and collectors who share similar kitchenware interests. Although some attend general auctions and sales, far more can be found in other ways. If you are a new collector, join a club if there is one in your area of interest. The membership fee pays for itself by supplying the names of many other collectors, specialized dealers and calendar listings of specialized shows a collector won't want to miss. This information usually comes in club newsletters (see the listings in Chapter 3) as well as from studying the classified sections of the most widely read trade papers in the antiques and collectibles world. One look at *The Cookbook Collectors' Exchange,* for example, will be exhilarating for a fledgling collector who will instantly have names and addresses of people buying and selling cookbooks as well as a bulletin board where his or her own needs can be advertised.

As the new *Kitchen Antiques & Collectibles News,* published in Harrisburg, Pa., by Dana and Darlene DeMore becomes more widely circulated, it, too, will be an excellent source of names of specialized dealers and collectors. (Already, the newsletter provides an interesting digest of current prices paid for kitchen collectibles and has in its classified section, advertisements from people seeking anything from apple parers and advertising tinware to food labels and flour sifters.)

Subscribe to major trade newspapers including *Antique Week* (P.O. Box 90, Knightstown, IN 46148) and the *Maine Antique Digest* (P.O. Box 645, Waldoboro, ME 04572) for information about major auctions around the country. Their classified sections also contain news of major shows as well as advertisements from dealers with goods to sell. (Those advertising the items that interest you should be sent your current want list. Send one off whenever a new name is found.)

DEALER CONTACTS

If you purchase several items from a particular dealer, you may begin receiving the dealer's specialized catalog or be able to get it for a nominal fee, if one is published. This is particularly true in the cookbook segment of the market. But dealers in other fields, such as fruit jars, will also supply photocopied or printed lists of their current stocks upon request and payment, perhaps, of a nominal fee.

Because far more is sold through the mail and on the telephone than ever changes hands at antiques and collectibles shows, there's more to attending a show than simply buying for a collection. Spend time developing contacts with dealers and other collectors with similar interests. Sometimes, collectors establish relationships that enable them to trade with one another for the pieces they want. "That's how I acquired fully a third of my collection," said

Steve Stephens about his cast-iron cookware acquisitions. "The important thing in trading is to remember that exchanges have to be fair. I've always saved the duplicates I have of rare pieces for trading, because to get good stuff you have to trade good stuff." Talking and distributing want lists at special events is another good use of time for a collector who's searching for some particularly elusive kitchenware.

EFFECTIVE BUYING

As a collector works a show, his or her primary interest is seeing what can be bought to add to a collection. At an auction, an auctioneer pits a number of bidders against one another to get the best price for the seller and increase his commission. But more often, when a person is at a show, a flea market, in an antique shop, or in a farmer's barn full of junk, buying ultimately boils down to the interaction between a buyer and a seller. And it is this interpersonal relationship that really makes the hunt for antiques and collectibles interesting.

A person who has something to sell has the responsibility of determining what the object is worth by doing some research. Attending many shows and auctions will provide a feeling for the market. Checking a current price guide gives retail values (or inflated values if the author hasn't been careful about the way prices were determined). Of course, if you're trying to sell something to a dealer, he or she isn't going to pay the price published in the price guide. To make a profit and stay in business, figure on the dealer paying about 30 to 50 cents on the dollar of this value. Fellow collectors may be willing to pay somewhat more, about half the book value or more, if it is an object they covet.

As a buyer, you must also do your homework so that you know when the price is right for an item found at a show, sale or shop. And if the price is right, rein in any outward signs of excitement because your expression and level of enthusiasm can have a profound effect on price. Do your best not to let the dealer know how much you want a particular chocolate mold. Or how you can already picture a spice cabinet in your kitchen. Remember: The best way to make sure a dealer's price isn't set in stone is to keep a stone-face.

If you succeed in driving a hard bargain and making a good buy, you will have a story that can be told for a lifetime. But should you misjudge your opponent (the seller), you could lose a chance at something good. Wendy Johnston, a Brooklyn, N.Y., collector of cookie jars, said, "I never tell a person what they should or shouldn't spend on an item. But if you don't buy it, someone else will. The worst thing is to walk away and regret it. Decide what is best for you and make a decision you are sure you can live with."

Because she has become so particular about the cookie jars she collects, she has "pickers" (people watching for the things she wants) all over the country. But, occasionally, she allows herself the time to attend one of the three annual flea market weeks at Brimfield, Mass. "I won't forget that morning seven years ago. It was 4 a.m. when we left Brooklyn and as I was driving along Route 20 through Brimfield, the sun was just coming up. My

The above cut illustrates the Hamilton nut-cracker. This nut-cracker is made of malleable iron, is nickel plated and will not break. Good for a lifetime. One of the best on the market for pecans and can also be used for cracking other nuts.

PRICE, $1.00 PREPAID

Remit by money order, express order, or bank draft to KRAUTH & BENNINGHOFEN, Hamilton, O., and we will deliver the nut-cracker by Parcel Post to the buyer's address.

The Hamilton Nut-Cracker was designed for a lifetime of use and was particularly good for breaking the shells of pecans, according to the Hamilton, OH company selling it for $1.

This McCoy cookie jar was made in the shape of a box-style coffee mill, perhaps to suggest the beverage that makes the best accompaniment for fresh-baked cookies.

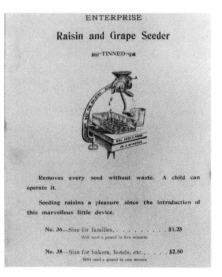

The tinned Enterprise Raisin and Grape Seeder supposedly removed every seed without waste and was so simple to operate that even a child could do it. "Seeding raisins is a pleasure since the introduction of this marvelous little device," boasted the catalog.

son spotted some cookie jars in the market. I stopped the van practically in the middle of the road and ran down the hill to the stand. They had an American Bisque Mohawk Indian (originally intended to promote Mohawk carpets) and a Brush "Little Angel" cookie jar. I wanted them badly. They were marked $350 each. I said 'I'm going to take both. What is the best price you can do?' The dealer answered, '$350 on each.' The jars were rare. They were wonderful. I said okay and handed over seven $100 bills. I'd gone through almost all the money I'd saved for the show in a minute, but I didn't mind. I couldn't wait to get home and unpack them and hold them."

Steve Stephens drove his share of hard bargains when he was adding to his cast-iron collection, but he has had his share of anxious moments that season his advice. "I usually try to bargain for things but when I see that someone is literally giving away a rare piece because it is priced so low, I now know better than to turn them off by offering them an even lower price."

He described one sale when he found a Griswold loaf pan with a cover. "I had never known that a cover existed for the pan, so I knew that it was a rare piece. The lady was asking $35 for the pan." Stephens asked her if she'd take $30. She told him she couldn't because it belonged to her husband and he hadn't returned to the stand. "I walked away for a while and then returned. She had pulled it off the display but her husband still hadn't reappeared. When I was ready to leave, I came back and finally offered her the $35," Stephens said. The woman's husband still hadn't returned and Stephens' interest made her anxious about accepting even the $35. But she finally sold it to him.

Another time, Stephens encountered a country farmer at a flea market who was selling a box of fancy rosette irons for $10. "I offered him $5, even though $10 really was low enough. It was worth about $30 at the time. The man refused me then and when I tried to buy it for $10 later, he refused to sell it at all. I had alienated him and shouldn't have."

Collectors should treat good dealers with respect, because they, too, could wind up being dealers. It can't happen? Oh, yes it can. Frequently. Even most of the time. Collectors often become at least part-time dealers when they want to sell off duplicates or less-valuable pieces to raise the cash to build and refine their own collections.

6

Using Your Kitchen Collectibles

Inspiration from the Past

Why struggle to make pie dough from scratch using your grandmother's recipe and rolling pin when there are ready-made crusts waiting on the grocer's shelf?

Why take the time to make homemade waffles or pancakes when the frozen versions can go from box-to-microwave-to-breakfast-plate before you've poured the first batter onto the griddle or waffle iron?

Why fuss with bread from scratch when you can drive to the grocery store and do a week's worth of shopping in the time it takes to get the dough to rise?

Taste the homemade versions, side by side with the convenience foods, and you'll understand why collecting kitchen utensils and learning to use them is worthwhile and fun. It's easy to lose sight of just how good from-scratch foods taste when homogenized, bland convenience foods have become staples of most families' everyday diets. The rewards of making foods are multiplied if you have the chance to use the very same tools your mother or grandmother used, or ones just like them. You'll be mixing in the best flavor enhancer of all—your very own past.

Betty Groff, who has written numerous cookbooks based on her family's Pennsylvania Dutch food traditions, always uses her mother's rolling pin and cooking forks. And when she reaches for a recipe, it comes from her mother's large wooden recipe box. "The minute I use a tool that has been passed along

The sharp tines of old-fashioned cooking forks make them ideal for a myriad of kitchen uses, whether it's poking a stalk of broccoli or a baked potato to check for doneness or pricking a pie crust to vent steam as the filling bakes.

The Household Liberty Coal and Gas Range was "Built to Bake," thanks to its two gas ovens and one coal oven. The only question was whether or not the cook could keep track of what was happening in all three without having something burn!

to me, I start remembering the good times. You get used to the feel of certain tools, too, like my mother's rolling pin. It's what I expect. It's comfortable, as comfortable as putting on a pair of old slippers after I've been on my feet all day," Groff said.

Maria Cavallo, chef and owner of Cavallo's Country Cottage in Easton, Pa., works in a modern, streamlined restaurant kitchen but has made room for her grandmother's polenta pot, an uncle's General Electric monitor-top refrigerator and her mother's coffee grinder in the work area. She said, "As I work with them, or see them while I'm doing other things, they give me the energy to go on and to excel in what I'm doing."

Not all tools from the past are worth using. In the best-forgotten category is one particular cherry pitter my mother purchased. The family joke had always been that if there was a single pit to be found in a cherry pie, it always turned up in my father's slice. But after we used the cherry pitter on the sour cherry crop, his single slice contained a record 17 pits and the rest of us came up with four, five or six pits per person.

Of course, as any good cook knows, there are certain cooking utensils from the past that are unmatched and just as useful today as they were when they first appeared. Each Christmas, my mother gets out my grandmother's long, slender metal spatula. The wonderfully flexible blade makes easy work of lifting paper-thin roll-out cookies from the pastry cloth to baking sheets. I covet it, but mom isn't parting with it. At other times, however, she has shared the special wealth of her old utensils and equipment. Not long after I had set up housekeeping, I baked a batch of medium-size chocolate-chip cookies. But the still-warm cookies kept sagging and falling through the spaces between the wires of my modern-day cake racks, leaving them broken or misshapen. I had been spoiled by the cooling racks my mother and grandmother used—the ones with enough wires to prevent even the daintiest of cookies from falling through. I found a few of these racks at an auction and

Enterprise cherry stoner could make quick work of a bucket of cherries. But because this model lacked an adjustment to compensate for different-sized cherries, it sometimes left in as many pits as it extracted.

Note the difference in the amount of space between the wires of an older cooling rack (on the bottom) and the newer one that's on top. Although cooling racks might not be a popular collecting category, most good cooks appreciate the value of the old ones and save them to use.

Dexter metal spatula is so flexible it can be used to pick up and transfer very thin roll-out cookies from pastry cloth to cookie sheet.

dropped a hint to my mother that I was looking for more. Once she knew I was ready to appreciate them, she gave me some of her extras. Although the racks stand little chance of ever becoming the focus of a collecting craze, their design and resulting good performance give me a great deal of pleasure. That's what collecting is all about.

Groff said she feels the same way about her time-worn cooking forks. "Modern companies have tried to make them but the new versions' tines are much too wide. My mother's forks, with their very thin and very sharp tines, allow me to prick baked potatoes or test a chicken or turkey breast for doneness without leaving giant, tell-tale holes in the food."

Julia Child treasures two special wooden rolling pins that have seen her through miles of dough.

Groff always reaches for her grandmother's cast-iron frying pan when she's making raw-fried potatoes that are so brown and crisp that they need to be cut with a knife. (The secret to getting the potatoes just browned, rather than blackened, and cooked in the middle, she says, is turning the potatoes after they've browned on one side and then splashing some water into the frying pan. Cover the pan for a few minutes to steam the potatoes in the center. Then uncover and finish crisping the other side.)

Culinary historian William Woys Weaver said, "I don't think there's anything I'd rather use than a cast-iron skillet when I'm frying ham or bacon. Sheet-iron roasting pans are wonderful for meats as well as goose and duck. Spit-roasted meats have a totally different taste and texture than foods that have been 'roasted,' baked really, in the oven. And you haven't had a piece of toast until you've tasted a slice of homemade bread toasted to an orangey-yellow on the prongs of a toasting fork."

Betty Groff, Pennsylvania's best-known Pennsylvania Dutch cook, shows off her grandmother's heart-shaped mold for making egg cheese—an old-time treat that was served on bread, along with Golden Syrup or molasses or more simply, with a sprinkling of nutmeg.

Here's a closeup of a similar, footed egg cheese mold that had holes to allow the moisture to separate from the curds and form the cheese.

A well-seasoned, properly cared for cast-iron frying pan can endure several lifetimes of cooking duties.

Listening to those who have cooked with kitchen collectibles surely will work up an appetite for the foods, as well as the collectibles. What it spells for you is fun—the fun of finding and using the tools and the fun of sharing the foods you've made with family and friends.

IDEAS FROM OLD COOKBOOKS AND MAGAZINES

Examine old cookbooks and magazines to see what earlier cooks managed to make in their kitchens with the equipment they had and you'll be amazed. They made timbales, tarts and tzimmes, to say nothing of all sorts of puddings, pies and pastries. The level of sophistication they achieved is impressive, given their lack of conveniences and their difficulty in getting some raw ingredients.

Country cooks often had to put in extra effort to accomplish some culinary feats. As Judith Snyder of the Philadelphia, PA-based Victorian

Society commented, "The reality for the Victorian housewife wasn't always pleasant. If she lived miles away from the nearest town and butcher shop, she was the one who had to chase the chicken around the backyard, kill it and pluck it before she ever got around to cooking it."

The frenzy of creativity that greeted new cooking equipment and new ingredients sometimes tempted old-time cooks to get just as carried away as modern ones who have made such concoctions as squash-blossom fritters with red pepper puree.

Scanning the pages of *American Cookery* magazine from 1910 to 1940, was enlightening. There were recipes for Mexican and Chinese foods (and you thought yours was the first generation of home cooks to try making foods like enchiladas and steamed dumplings!) as well as detailed instructions for elaborate desserts and all kinds of hearty meat and poultry dishes.

But it's more fun to recall some of the off-the-kitchen-wall recipes these folks attempted as they explored the culinary world. There were recipes for chocolate popcorn pudding; a hot dog crown roast (a mound of bread filling encircled by split hot dogs standing on end and secured by toothpicks and strips of bacon); Cincinnati chickens (pork tenderloins that were stuffed, rolled and tied to resemble the shape of roasting chickens, garnished with "wings" of preserved cherries, and served on a bed of sauerkraut); peanut brittle sandwiches (the brittle was crushed with a rolling pin or by running it through a meat chopper and then combined with butter to make a pasty spread for bread); spaghetti rabbit (pasta in tomato sauce spooned over toast), pigs ears with apple puree and french-fried bacon (an artery-clogging idea without equal).

Although some of the earlier experiments might sound funny, there's another lesson to be learned from old-time cooks. They worked without such conveniences as food processors, convection and microwave ovens and electric can openers, but still approached new recipes and new equipment with an enthusiasm that was nothing short of pioneer spirit. Imagine making the change from a coal range to an electric stove! And all the while these cooks were adjusting to the new ways, they never lost sight of the idea that making food could be fun. No matter whether they were preparing food for a box social or coming up with recipes for a waffle supper, they put their hearts into it. Consider what Bob Brown had to say in a summer, 1938, issue of *American Cookery*:

Cooking is not only on the air, it's in the air. Everybody's doing it. Everybody's talking about it. Just listen in on the liveliest group at any party these days and you will find the subject that calls forth real enthusiasm and attracts the brightest-eyed attention is not art, politics, books or plain gossip, but cooking. And it will be no matronly huddle of housewives, either, swapping recipes to fill the family bread-basket. There will be plenty of young things quoting Savarin, with men epicures and amateur chefs steaming like their own casseroles, each waxing eloquent about his pet Three-Day Punch, Beef Stroganoff, or the proper use of his favorite liqueur in Eggs Benedictine. Amateur cheffing, indeed, though not yet as popular as golf, has ping-pong beat by a mile and is fast developing into cooking competitions

With a 7-inch or 8 1/2-inch diameter, these brown-glazed stoneware milk bowls make attractive containers today for fresh whole fruit or fresh rolls when setting up a buffet featuring kitchen collectibles as serving dishes.

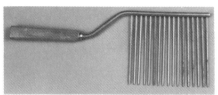

During the 1920s, a cake breaker was advertised as "a remarkable new table accessory that breaks cake in even, beautiful portions, free from crumbs, leaving the most delicate frosting or filling intact."

where goodly prizes are hung up. It is the best indoor sport we know, giving the tired business man a chance to relax, have a little fun in the kitchen and wine cellar, forget workaday affairs by exercising a genius for hospitality and showing off hidden talents.

He advocated cook-off parties and cooking clubs. But there were a host of other sociable ideas for having fun with food. There were suggestions for box socials. (In case you don't date back to iceboxes and Hoosier cabinets, these were old-time money makers for church or civic groups. The women prepared the boxes of food, which were auctioned off to the men. Proceeds went to the treasury of the organization and the boxes, containing enough food for two, were shared by the purchaser of the box and the woman who prepared it.) Covered dish suppers already were recognized as informal and social ways to have a meal. Then, as now, they were recognized as great ways to simplify getting together with friends because cooks shared the expense and trouble of advance food preparation.

Kitchen parties were popular, too. Guests, warned in advance that they'd be preparing food, donned paper chef's hats (to get the crowd into the proper cooking spirit) and tackled their assignments from the hosts—no matter whether they were to create a salad or make a vegetable casserole like scalloped tomatoes. Guests also cooked their own entrees like steaks or chops, either on the range or on an electric grill or two. If there was a shortage of space for cooking, one enthusiastic author noted that several guests could be sent to the laundry to cook on a three-burner hot plate. Kitchen party guests also ate their meals in the kitchen, either on kitchen cabinet counters or drain boards. Again, if there wasn't enough room, the author encouraged readers to use the portable ironing board for an additional, impromptu table. (With luck, the guests who had to cook on the laundry-room hot plate finished their tasks early enough to press for a better dinner table than the ironing board.)

Sunday breakfasts were another favorite way to entertain, and authors detailed hearty down-on-the-farm menus that would no doubt be popular once more, in this time when comfort foods are being rediscovered and enjoyed.

Finding a 1937 April Fool's Day menu and recipes in *American Cookery* stirred memories of my own grandmother's pranks. I'll never forget her story about how she tricked her candy-loving friends by hand-dipping a special box of chocolates with fillings that ranged from cubes of soap and cotton balls to cocktail onions.

Although candy wasn't part of the magazine's menu, "pears" were fashioned from lightly colored mashed potatoes; "carrots" were shaped from mashed hubbard squash; cherries were baby beets that had been carefully trimmed and a slice of pie that looked like dessert was the main-course meat pie. A tray of sandwiches (slices of cake with buttercream filling in the middle) were dessert in disguise. Although it certainly took a good deal of effort to assemble such a meal, cooks apparently were willing to take the time to have fun with food.

As the 20th century progressed, there were the all-pink parties (all foods had to be pink) as well as gatherings that focused on a buffet's chafing dishes. But perhaps the most frequent and entertaining event during the first half of the 20th century was the waffle supper. From the number of articles written about such events, it sounds as if they were about as popular as the fondue parties of the 1960s and 1970s.

Hostesses who planned and successfully executed such suppers were as popular as the parties they organized. There were pitfalls, however, particularly if the would-be waffle supper hostess didn't have the right kind of waffle iron. Women of the day looked for well-known, reliable makes that had clean lines and a minimum of seams and cracks to complicate the cleaning process. According to one *American Cookery* writer, better models were chromium plated in the early 1930's and didn't discolor or tarnish at ordinary cooking temperatures. They didn't scratch easily, either. Colored handles made some of the contemporary models very popular but these, she claimed, were not as durable as those with black handles. Finally, the wise housewife was to choose an iron with a flexible cord (rather than a stiff one) covered with glazed cotton (rather than Rayon) for durability. Grids were made of cast aluminum that didn't have to be washed between uses, or even before the first use, since the first waffle on an iron was the "cleaner." It was baked and discarded. After each waffle-making session, the grids were to be wiped clean with a dry cloth.

With new iron poised for action, the waffle supper hostess could make the waffles at the table or on a serving cart and pass them to guests when the waffles were still warm enough to melt and capture the butter and real maple syrup in all the nooks and crannies. The hostess could show some extra culinary flair by adding a square or two of melted chocolate to the batter and serving the waffles with ice cream. Following the example of a famous tearoom specializing in nut waffles, she could chop pecans or English walnuts and stir them into the batter. She could add sliced apples to the batter and serve these fruity waffles with powdered sugar and vanilla sauce. Plain waffles could be further embellished by strawberries and whipped cream for a different kind of shortcake. The variations seemed limitless and enabled the dedicated waffle party hostess to make everything from main course to dessert. One Sunday night waffle supper menu, guaranteed to appeal to the average taste, included small link sausages, plain waffles with butter, fruit salad and coffee and a dessert of nut waffles with maple syrup. An alternative, for those who didn't want breakfast foods in the evening, was creamed chicken on waffles, hors d'oeuvres of raw vegetables (today's crudites) and chocolate waffles with ice cream and whipped cream.

If you've been stirred to mix up some waffle batter or begin other festive culinary experiments with your collectibles, read on for a few more minutes to learn a little more.

Considerations for Use

Will you buy the tools solely for display, to obscure the truth that little else goes on in your kitchen than opening bags and boxes of convenience foods and punching numbers into a microwave oven's control pad? Or will you use your collection to enrich your family's lives, by making real foods with old equipment and providing a true taste of the past?

This is the crossroads for a kitchen collector, much like opening a cookbook and then deciding if it contains any recipes that will be made. As Weaver explains it, "There's a romance about the past, particularly because we've lost some of the qualities of life provided by the old agricultural lifestyle. When was the last time you smelled freshly mowed wheat or a loaf of bread baking in the oven?" Weaver continued, "Working with the foods and old recipes gives you a connectedness with the past."

Actually, most collectors take a middle road. They opt to use some items. Others are saved for display, either because they're too valuable to use, unsafe or not terribly useful on a daily basis. Have you reached for a cream separator, raisin seeder or mayonnaise mixer recently?

KNOW THE ITEM'S VALUE

If you're ready to take on the culinary challenge presented by collectibles, there are several points to consider. Ask yourself if you, and the collectible you want to use, can take the heat. If the item breaks or is ruined, can it be replaced easily? How much will it cost, if it is easily found? Rolling pins and cooking forks are among the collectibles that still are plentiful and relatively inexpensive.

If you treasure an item's sentimental value as much or more than its material value, think carefully before proceeding. A year ago, my mother found my grandmother's white pottery Christmas pudding bucket in her attic, where it had been subjected to severe temperature extremes for the better part of 30 years. Made in Germany in the 1890s, it had survived the attic ordeal beautifully. But did I have the courage to fill it with a lumpy batter of nutmeats and candied fruits and sit it in a pan of hot water in the oven for several hours? No way. I wound up scouring flea markets until I found an all-metal pudding mold that I can use with complete peace of mind. Brian Howard, a Carlisle, Pa.-based conservator, said, "If the antique or collectible

White ceramic pudding bucket or mold dates from the 1890s. In excellent condition, it belonged to my grandmother. But I couldn't bring myself to use it and wound up buying several all-metal molds at flea markets for making our steamed Christmas puddings.

is good enough to be a museum artifact, it should not be used. And collectors should be aware that the more an item is used, the more chance there is for damage or additional wear which will reduce the item's value."

SAFETY FIRST

I cannot emphasize this point enough: Don't use your collectibles until you've made sure they're safe. Also make sure you know enough about seasoning or cleaning them to avoid ruining them. The best advice I have about using collectibles is that if you have any doubt about the safety of the material used in the collectible, leave it on the display shelf. Experiment with something else until you're able to get more information. An excellent source of information is a museum conservator, particularly at those historic properties offering cooking demonstrations. Call the American Institute of Conservation in Washington, D.C. at 202-452-9545 to obtain the name of a conservator near you.

Metal collectibles

COPPER AND BRASS. Weaver, one of the nation's leading experts on food history, has worked with more kinds of antique culinary equipment than most collectors ever will accumulate. He warns that **antique copper pots and pans should not be used.** The copper, reacting with the food, produces verdigris, which is a virulent poison. One early cookbook author noted that an entire family died as a result of this poisoning.

Weaver added, "There's lots of copper equipment from the Balkans and Turkey being sold on the antiques market right now, because it looks very primitive and there's a decorative quality to it. But it is best left hanging on the wall. Don't cook with it." Even if an antique copper vessel's tin lining appears to be in good condition, tin melts easily and is easily scratched. Knowledgeable cooks knew that wooden spoons are the only utensils that should ever be used in these pots.

Julia Child, who acquired numerous antique copper pots when she and her husband Paul were living in Paris, mounted them in a geometric design on a blue wall in her Cambridge, Mass., kitchen. She said, as she talked on the phone about her kitchen equipment, "They're beautiful to look at but I don't use them. It costs as much to have them re-tinned as it does to buy them."

The interiors of brass kettles (which generally were used for making preserves, rather than for everyday cooking) also pose dangers as Mrs. Cornelius mentioned in her 1859 book, The *Young Housekeeper's Friend*. To preserve fruit and make jellies, she said, "A kettle should be kept on purpose. Brass, if very bright, will do. If acid fruit is preserved in a brass kettle which is not bright, it becomes poisonous. Bell-metal is better than brass, and the iron ware lined with porcelain, best of all."

Clearly, it is much safer to enjoy the sight of these antiques and collectibles, rather than risk using them. Admire them from a distance, too. If you must handle kitchen treasures made of metal, wear clean, cotton gloves because acids and salts that form on the skin can lead to corrosion on copper, brass and cast iron. It's true for old tinware, too, according to Dana DeMore, publisher of *Kitchen Antiques & Collectibles News*. He said, "I learned my lesson the day I spotted one of my fingerprints forever etched into the side of a treasured tinware coffee pot."

Tidy collectors shouldn't be too quick to polish their brass and copperware. "Each time an item is polished, additional metal is removed," said Howard. If a person really believes an object needs to be polished, the conservator suggests using a commercial product such as Never Dull on brass and copper, rather than polishes that contain ammonia. Residue from ammonia-containing polishes can be reactivated by humidity and can cause

Old-time cooks were well aware that brass kettles needed to be scrupulously cleaned and prepared before they could be used for cooking jellies and jams.

Copper pans like this 19th century saucepan with an iron handle make nice decorative elements in a kitchen if you have the time to keep the copper polished. Copper pots and molds are best used for decoration rather than cooking because they pose serious health risks if their protective linings aren't in perfect condition.

continual corrosion of the metal, according to Howard. Do not use mixtures of lemon juice and salt because they're too abrasive and salt is the worst thing to put in contact with the metals. Howard said, "Chloride contamination causes corrosion." Don't use toothpaste, because it is too abrasive, too.

Moisture and humidity are the enemies of most metals. Those that are on display should be dusted frequently with a dry, lint-free cloth or with a soft brush because dust attracts humidity and can allow corrosion to get a start.

LEAD. Lead molds, like those used for ice cream, should be used for display only. Said Weaver, "The Victorians developed molds for ice cream and candy from alloys that looked like lead. Most of these were patented alloys and, often, those patent marks are on the mold. The presence of a patent mark on the mold probably means it is safe to use. But if you have any doubts, don't use it."

CAST IRON. Julia McNair Wright, in her 1881 book, *The Complete Home,* was fond of field grasses for household purposes. She noted that a cook could get the iron taste out of new kettles by boiling a handful of hay in water in the kettles—a process that could be repeated if necessary. She also sweetened stoneware (like crocks or firkins used to store butter) by boiling them in straw water. She added, "Hay water is a great sweetener of tin, wooden and ironware."

That's not the only advice available about cast iron. Experts differ on the way in which it should be seasoned, but do agree that it must be seasoned and reseasoned to develop a nonstick surface. Ask a conservator or other collectors for advice and decide on the method that sounds best to you.

Howard said, "If the object is a heavily corroded piece of cast iron, using a wire brush to remove some of the loose corrosion should not adversely harm it. If it is not going to be used for cooking, it can be coated with stove black after it is cleaned." The conservator added, "If there is a black, sticky buildup on the cast iron, there's a chance someone made the mistake of coating it with linseed oil." He recommends removing it with acetone, which is available in hardware stores. Just work with it in a well-ventilated area and be sure to follow the manufacturer's instructions for use.

If you are planning to cook with cast iron you have collected, you will want to wash it and dry it thoroughly, as well as season it, before storing it in a dry place. Steve Stephens, a California cast-iron collector, sometimes goes further than Howard because he wire brushes the surface of cast-iron cookware with cleanser to remove soil. He then rinses it and dries it and puts it in an oven heated to 450 degrees to darken it. Then, after it cools down a bit

Cast-iron griddle needs a good deal of attention to restore its usability. But once completed, it could turn out Paul Bunyan sized pancakes.

but is still warm, he wipes the surface with a thin layer of solid Crisco and wipes any excess off. Stephens warned, "Do not heat or cool a piece suddenly, like putting a large, cold pan on a red hot burner or you will crack it." He added that sand blasting a piece of cast-iron cookware with any kind of material can destroy its value.

If it's possible to reseason cast iron and bring it back to life, Weaver will do it, too. Once remnants of burned-on food have been removed from a salvageable piece, he rubs the cookware with a bacon rind and then puts it in the oven at 450 degrees for 30 minutes until it smokes. Once he has used a frying pan or pot, he wipes it out and rinses it, but does not scour it. Then he puts it back in the oven at 270 to 300 degrees and leaves it there until it is completely dry. "If you've been baking, just turn the oven off and put the pot in for a while. It's very hard on old iron to leave water on it. You don't want rust spots," Weaver said.

England's Mrs. Beeton warned that even after the pans have been thoroughly dried, they need to be stored in a dry place to prevent rust. Never pour cold water into a hot pot, either, she advised, or you could crack it.

To avoid destroying the seasoned surface you've worked so hard to create, one household guide advised that liquids shouldn't be boiled in ironware and such acid-containing foods as wine or citrus juices should not be poured into the pan.

The Women's Institute Library of Cookery volume called *Essentials of Cookery,* in 1917, advised, "Before a new steel or iron griddle is used, it must be tempered so as to prevent the food that is to be baked on it from sticking. If it is not tempered, much time will be consumed before its surface will be in the right condition to permit baking to proceed without difficulty, and this, of course, will result in wasting considerable food material. Tempering may be done by covering the griddle with a quantity of fat, placing it over a flame or in a very hot oven, and then allowing it to heat thoroughly to such a temperature that the fat will burn onto the surface. This same precaution should be observed with new waffle irons and frying pans made of steel or iron if the best results from such utensils are desired."

To use a waffle iron on the coal range, a stove lid was removed from one of the openings and the waffle iron was set in the opening, which allowed the actual griddle part to be turned. The gas range's waffle iron had a griddle part that rested on a base that was high enough to allow it to be turned without lifting it off the range. "In using a waffle iron of either kind," advised the Institute, "it should be heated while the waffle mixture is being prepared; then it should be thoroughly greased on both sides. No excess fat, however, should be used, as it will run out when the griddle is turned over."

TIN UTENSILS. Tin utensils that aren't too valuable to be used, like some very common cookie cutters, should be thoroughly dried after they are washed. When Pennsylvania Dutch cooking expert Betty Groff washes some of her old all-metal graters, she pops them in a warm oven for a few minutes to get rid of moisture.

Howard suggested a different method to dry tin—with a blow dryer—so that the solder joints won't be damaged by the excess heat of an oven.

Coffin-style nutmeg grater can be cleaned by
brushing it with a soft, dry paint brush.

Groff still uses a nutmeg grater that has been handed down through the
family. When she has obtained the amount of nutmeg she needs, she simply
brushes the residue out of the surface grid with a small, soft-bristled paint
brush and then stores the grater in a dry place until she is ready to use it
again. (A word of caution: Don't risk using the nutmeg graters you've
collected until you know their values. Because they are very popular with
collectors, rare ones can be worth hundreds of dollars.)

DeMore, a dedicated tinware collector, advised, "The best thing to do for
tinware is maintain a stable environment (avoiding dampness) and the worst
thing people can do is 'skin it,' that is, remove the surface finish of an older
piece of tin to produce a more lustrous appearance."

ALUMINUM. Scrubbing an aluminum pan with a soap pad can remove
surface markings; if it is badly discolored, a few easy ways to brighten it up
include filling the pan with water and adding a few teaspoons of lemon juice,
vinegar or cream of tartar to the water or cooking some tomatoes or rhubarb
in it.

ENAMELWARE. Enamelware should be treated like glass, according to
an article in the May, 1924, issue of *American Cookery.* The author explained
that most enamelware consists of a coating of glasslike material over a thin
steel foundation. And she cautioned that if it is heated too quickly or to a high
temperature using dry heat, the outer glassy coating will chip off and make
the utensil dangerous to use.

If you're still tempted to use your enamelware pieces, consider the tale of
woe of one New Jersey antiques dealer (who wished to remain nameless). She
said, "I was serving up lemonade at a summer picnic, using a yellow and
white graniteware dipper. A little while later, I noticed the dipper was no
longer yellow and white. Just white."

Imported or antique dinnerware

Dishes, pitchers and other
serving pieces such as platters and bowls from other countries can sometimes
pose health problems if the dishes are unglazed or have been improperly
glazed. Glazes can contain unhealthy concentrations of lead as can some
painted decorations or decals. Some antique dishes and dishes made earlier
in this century in America can also be a problem. Handcrafted or homemade
china also should be checked. Although, there is no simple visual test that
enables a collector to detect lead content, prudent collectors can take several
steps to protect themselves and their families. If there is any doubt about

dishes to be used as well as displayed, order a test kit. Two common ones are Leadcheck Swabs (HybriVet Systems, Inc., P.O. Box 1210, Framingham, MA 01701) and Frandon Lead Alert Kit (Frandon Enterprises, P.O. Box 300321, Seattle, WA 98103). HybriVet's toll-free number is 800-262-LEAD and the number for Frandon is 800-634-2341).

In addition to being certain about the glaze, all designs should be under the glaze and, preferably, only around the rim of the plate, rather than on the surface where food is placed. At the very least, don't serve high-acid foods or beverages in questionable ceramic pieces. For example, orange juice, tea or coffee, carbonated beverages, tomato-based sauces, applesauce, citrus fruits, pickled products and salad dressings containing vinegar are all acidic and can penetrate the glaze and make the lead leach into food.

Never put foods in questionable ceramic pieces when warming them up in an oven! Heat speeds the leaching of lead. Also, don't use dishes with damaged glazes (cracked, scratched by the cutting action of knives or excessive scrubbing, or those with a glaze that is chalky after they're washed). Food should never be stored in these dishes, either. Use proper glass refrigerator containers or plastic containers instead.

Also use your lead test kits to check for the presence of lead in some painted glassware, especially those 1950's style tumblers with black and gold ornamentation. Just as chalking is a sign of potential trouble in glazing on dishes, it's another clue on glasses.

REDWARE.   Lead in the glaze of old redware, along with its fragility, are two reasons why Weaver refrains from using the antique pieces in his collection. They're also the reasons why you shouldn't use old redware either. Catherine Beecher, author of *The American Woman's Home,* offered a similar warning in 1869 when she wrote: "Acids should never be put into red earthen ware, as there is a poisonous ingredient in the glazing which the acid takes off."

Weaver uses modern, nonleaded redware that is made according to old designs. First, however, he seasons it to help keep the clay bodies from cracking and to prevent the glaze from crackling. His method: "I check the size of the piece and then add water to the boiler I'm going to use. If I'm using 5 gallons of water, I'll put in at least 3 to 4 quarts of rye bran or whole wheat bran and boil it. Once the mixture looks like a glutinous soup, I submerge the new redware in the 'soup,' one piece at a time. I use a gentle boil and keep

Lead in the glaze of antique redware, as well as its fragility, makes it unwise to use it for anything but display.

each piece in for at least 30 minutes. Then I take it out of the pot and wipe it off. When it has cooled completely, I'll rinse it with lukewarm water to remove the remainder of the bran from the surface."

His procedure sounds similar to the advice offered by Lydia Maria Francis Child in her 1829 book, *The Frugal Housewife*. She wrote, "Put new earthenware in cold water and let it heat gradually until it boils. Then cool it again slowly. Brown earthenware, in particular, may be toughened this way. A handful of rye, wheat or bran thrown in the water while it is boiling will preserve the glazing so it will not be destroyed by acids or salt."

A potter demonstrating the production of redware at Pennsylvania's Landis Valley Museum near Lancaster also warned that uneven heating can shatter his newly made pieces. He said, "Bake a whole pie and it will be alright. But put the pie plate back in the oven to reheat the only remaining piece and you'll probably wind up with a broken plate."

Wooden utensils and molds Wooden utensils and molds can pose challenges and dilemmas. Weaver generally uses a buttery, top-quality Spanish olive oil to condition wooden molds for cookie prints and rolling pins that are going to be used, as well as the surface of his kitchen worktable. "If the utensil makes your fingers greasy two days after you've applied the olive oil, you've used too much," Weaver said. But he doesn't use this treatment on just anything. "If I have a rare butter mold, I treat it like an old book with its original binding. That is, I leave it as close to its original condition as possible. If you are not going to use the wooden utensil, don't oil it. Put it where it won't be damaged but be prepared for a tragedy or two. Sometimes, if the butter mold is bought from a shop or mall that's not well heated and then is taken home by a collector, the heat and dryness in the air will split the wood. I know because it has happened to me."

Lollipop-style butter mold has a rabbit design in its center.

But that's not the only danger to old wood. In summer, if you're living in an old house that is humid, wooden objects that have been oiled can become moldy. Bugs and mice also are inclined to give wooden utensils and bowls a few nibbles. Weaver solves the bug and mold problem by popping the antiques in the freezer. He said, "The technique works well but don't make the mistake of sending a friend to get something out of your freezer. After all, finding rolling pins in the freezer basket next to the ice cream could cause a friend to question your sanity."

Howard advised, "If you are not going to use the woodenware, a coating of microcrystalline wax can be used to help preserve the wood without risking mold growth."

Many wooden rolling pins, still available for $5, $8 or $10 aren't too valuable to be used. But they do need to be cleaned properly before and after use in this time when eggs in raw dough can be contaminated with salmonella. Just wiping them off after use is not going to solve the problem. Wash the rolling pin quickly in hot, soapy water. But never leave it soak in the water or the wood could soften, absorb water and crack.

Baskets   Expect baskets to darken if you leave them hanging from the rafters in the kitchen—dust and grease will surely collect on them. It is simply the price a collector pays for wanting to be able to see the baskets. Special ones should be stored carefully in chests or some other roomy, covered containers. But care must be taken not to pack them too tightly or they'll warp.

"I was told I could use warm water to wash my rye straw bread baskets that were powdery from old flour. I did it once, with great trepidation," Weaver said. "It worked but I told myself I'd never do that again!"

Howard mentioned two conservative treatments for soiled baskets: "Spit cleaning" spots using a little saliva on a cotton swab or using a rag very slightly dampened with water.

Electrical appliances   Before an old kitchen appliance is plugged in, its safety should be checked. See Chapter 9 "Electrical Appliances" for detailed safety tips.

This 21-inch diameter, Pennsylvania Dutch style split hickory basket makes an attractive decoration in any kitchen.

Authors Gary Miller and K. M. Scotty Mitchell suggest using aluminum mag-wheel polish from auto parts stores and soft rags to clean exteriors of chrome and nickel-plated appliances. Nonabrasive kitchen cleansers and oven cleaners are in their cleaning arsenal but they warn collectors to proceed carefully. They've learned from experience that overzealous efforts can remove more than grimey buildups: On some of the appliances, they've accidentally obliterated a few manufacturers' names.

So, depending on your mood and the season, consider getting out the waffle iron for a waffle supper or excavating until you find the right pot to hold a luscious, chocolate dessert fondue. Give yeast dough another try if you want to work off tension and be rewarded for it. Or, recreate a fancy Jell-O mold. It's time to get cooking! But always remember: Safety first.

7

Decorating with Kitchen Collectibles

Making a home for your kitchen collectibles begins in the kitchen. It's the natural place for them to be—whether you choose simply to display them "just-for-nice," as the Pennsylvania Germans say, or whether you plan to put them to use. Over the centuries, no other room of the house has inspired so

Cookie jars, like this Shawnee Pottery Puss N'Boots, are not only hot with decorators, but are popular with practically everyone. The memory of freshly baked cookies and a glass of cold milk will strike a chord with anyone who has ever needed a midnight snack.

This high-gloss orange Fiesta teapot is an example of how pottery can be used to add splashes of color to a kitchen.

many tools or types of equipment, from rolling pins and cookie cutters to sausage stuffers, bread mixers and apple parers. The ones you choose for your kitchen will add something that wallpaper and paint can't supply— memories. No matter whether your nearest neighbor is three miles away, or at an arm's length on the other side of a brick wall, kitchen collectibles can be a part of your home.

The most comfortable country decorating schemes pull from all generations of a person's past. But those who choose to focus on a specific decorating period in history will be able to find kitchen collectibles to reinforce the look.

Art Deco cries out for the rounded, graceful lines of a shiny, chrome toaster, a chrome and plastic breakfast set and the colors of Fiestaware. A Victorian home's kitchen is enhanced with molds for puddings and cakes and cast-iron pots and pans that look like they've just come off the range.

A home with a more modern look, fashioned largely from furnishings of the 1960s or 1970s, ought to contain at least one fondue pot and a crockery slow-cooker on the shelf.

Country Decor

No matter what style home you have, from Cape Code cottage to one-story rancher, the kitchen often is the first, and perhaps the only, room to go "country." It and the adjoining family room also are where family members spend most of their waking hours. That means the kitchen should be comfortable and casual, no matter how sophisticated and sleek the rest of the house appears. After all, the kitchen is the room that invites people to be natural. It tempts them to let down their guards and be children again, if only long enough to reach into the cookie jar for a freshly baked oatmeal bar. It tempts them to sneak down for a midnight snack or compose an impromptu sandwich at the kitchen counter.

Hang a cast-iron griddle in the kitchen because you like remembering stacks of steaming buckwheat cakes with maple syrup trickling down the sides, like a slow-motion waterfall. Display your mother's rolling pins because they recall lattice-topped cherry pies or Christmas roll-out cookies so thin that it took a dozen to make one mouthful. Line up the yellowware mixing bowls if they bring back special thoughts of a rich devil's food cake or gooey brownies. Save a spot on the shelf for your grandmother's coffee grinder if the smell of fresh-brewed coffee, mingling with the aroma of frying bacon, always roused you from a night's sleep at her house. It's a much more comforting memory than a jangling alarm clock.

Kitchen collectibles are practically to be expected in country homes, of course, where families have had the space to save the tools and equipment used by each generation. They're often so taken for granted that they simply become part of the woodwork. But they're equally pleasing in the heart of the city. For that matter, peppering the city kitchen with collectibles can make the room a specially welcome retreat from street noises and crowds. Take the time to watch the dough rise and knead it by hand, and the day's tensions,

This box-type Parker's National Coffee Mill that was produced by the Chas. Parker Company of Meriden, Conn., has an attractive design with its domed hopper, top crank and dovetailed corners and drawer. It contained a list of patents inside the drawer that began with Feb. 7, 1860. The last legible date was June 12, 1883 or 1885.

This wooden sugar bucket no longer collects sweet, sticky sap, but it does help hide clutter in any part of the house.

from commuting to meeting deadlines, will fade as the yeasty aroma permeates the apartment.

Making your own kitchen as cozy and warm as your mother's or grandmother's kitchen will make memories for your own children. That's reason enough to begin a collecting binge.

AVOIDING COUNTRY CLUTTER

As you collect, however, be mindful of a newspaper cartoon that pictured a massive fireplace decorated with a wooden duck. It was surrounded by the rubble of collapsed brick walls, windows and doors. The caption indicated that the collapse had resulted from the weight of one too many collectibles. It is worth at least a chuckle from collectors who have been successful in their pursuits. The flea market or yard sale look in decorating, with table after table and shelf after shelf filled with items too numerous to count, can be visually and physically overwhelming if the collector has the unhappy task of keeping his or her own treasures clean.

If you can't stop collecting, and you've run out of room for new displays, it's time to consider a new game plan. It might not be a bad idea to clean up your country look a bit. Don't panic. I wouldn't think of telling you to pack up your treasures and sell them. And I certainly wouldn't tell you to stop collecting. Just begin rotating your collectibles in and out of storage. Another

Victorian homemakers were masters of molding foods. This one created a side dish with an attractive ear of corn as a decoration.

Another wonderful Victorian tradition, making molded ice-cream desserts, created a demand for intricate molds like this pewter one for a Christmas tree. This mold has plenty of cross-market appeal to kitchen and ice-cream collectors as well as Christmas collectors.

A toleware creamer could fill a pleasant spot in the family room or on the mantle if kitchen display areas are limited or filled.

strategy is finding room for more by spreading the kitchen collectibles throughout the house.

When displaying your collectibles, avoid the temptation to plop them throughout the house in perfectly symmetrical displays. Learn to group things, to create focal points and use negative space, rather than having things everywhere.

DISPLAYING WITH STYLE

There are certain kitchen collectibles that have become synonymous with country decorating, including granitewear, stoneware, baskets, yellowware and redware. But even when these similar elements are used by many people the results never look prefabricated. Each country kitchen becomes a personal statement about the past a person is trying to preserve because there are so many shapes and designs within each category of kitchen collectibles and so many ways of displaying them.

Small collections fit easily onto open shelves, fireplace mantles, walls and splashbacks between counters and wall cabinets. Some will fill plate racks and kitchen cabinets with glass doors. Still more treasures can be perched

Wall space begs to be filled with kitchen collectibles. A wooden slaw cutter like this one would be a great piece to hang since a spot high on a wall will also keep little fingers away from its sharp blade.

atop floating, soffitless kitchen cabinets, which have become fashionable perches for extra country collectibles.

Additional treasures can be stacked or lined up side by side in anything from the massive step-back cupboards to classic corner cupboards.

Assorted crocks can hold anything from floral bouquets to cooking utensils.

Baskets hung from kitchen rafters serve active duty holding vegetables, fruits or bunches of fresh flowers, hold towels and toiletries in the bathroom or contain selections of magazines, books or videotapes in the family room.

A vintage coal or wood stove provides the right setting for cast-iron equipment, from tea kettles to frying pans, as well as enamelware. Ice tongs hang from rafters or from the side of the old icebox (that you had to have to go with the tongs).

Brass buckets hold pine cones and copper ham boilers contain logs for use in the fireplace.

Redware can add color and contrasting shapes to bookshelves in the den or living room.

Wire egg baskets can hold far more than eggs.

Cookie cutters, eggbeaters, wooden cooking utensils and nutmeg graters make interesting wall displays.

A jelly cupboard with doors left open adds color to a room because it can become display space for anything from fruit jars to a collection of old-time food containers.

Creating a Personal Statement

Getting the idea that using your collectibles isn't a style for which you need to call a decorator? Creating an environment that says something about you and your past and ensures that you are comfortable is something that *you* have to do. You can't call in a decorator and say, "I like earthtones. I'll be away for a month. Call me when you're through." You've got to get involved in the display possibilities because that can be almost as much fun as the search for the collectibles themselves.

At a New York City antiques and collectibles show, a dealer who was offering a stock of tall, broad cupboards and large country tables was asked about demand for these big-ticket, big-space items in Manhattan. He responded, "People can make room for anything, if they have a use for it." He hit the nail on the head. If you want a kitchen collectible as small as a cooking fork or as big as a pie safe you'll think long and hard about a way to use it.

That's how Hoosier cabinets have become furnishings for home offices (where better to store paper, books and other office supplies and still have room to collate papers?). They're also convenient as a temporary bar during parties. One collector even thought of using one in a nursery to organize baby paraphernalia. Dry sinks have become entertainment centers or plant stands in living rooms. Old-fashioned iceboxes have returned to limited service as beverage coolers. Dough trays can contain home baking equipment but they also can hide assorted clutter when friends drop in unexpectedly and there's no time to clean properly.

Some kitchen collectibles provide even more of a challenge. Have you ever debated about where to keep the sausage stuffer or the right place for a cherry pitter? You could simply sit the stuffer on a shelf and fasten the cherry

An old counter scale still can be used to weigh items, but it also can be part of a room's decoration, particularly when its pretty brass scoop is filled with an arrangement of fresh, colorful fruit like apples and oranges.

Careful use of nicely decorated stoneware pieces in varying shapes and sizes, such as this two-gallon crock with a feather design and imprinted with "Richard C. Remmey, Phila.," allows kitchen collectors to enjoy their treasures in different ways.

Have some fun with a durable kitchen collectible like this apple parer. Fasten it to a table, and after letting guests peel the apples, turn them into a quick apple crisp or cobbler.

pitter to the shelf beside it. But that's taking the easy way out. How about lining up some of these conversation pieces on a recessed shelf under a kitchen worktable? Betty Groff, probably America's best-known Pennsylvania Dutch cook, keeps her cherry pitter mounted on her fireplace mantle when she's not using it. "People tell me it looks like a spider when they see it from the other side of the room," she said. No worktable or fireplace mantle handy? Then consider rotating some of your prizes for specific decorating assignments.

During the holiday season, ironstone pitchers look great filled with greens and holly branches. Build a pyramid of oranges and applies in the brass scoop of a counter scale and tuck sprigs of pine in between the fruits.

Put out an old wooden bowl filled with mixed nuts and invite guests to test their mettle at using any one of the assembled figural or animal nut-crackers.

A sausage stuffer, if it's the type that looks like machinery rather than a gun, could become a table's centerpiece during a sausage and pancake supper.

Take a page from my father's book (used whenever mom wasn't around at mealtime) and serve foods right in the cooking pans. But make your table presentation a bit classier than dad's (since he simply used old gray aluminum saucepans). Use cast-iron pots and pans and fill them with hearty, old-fashioned foods like beef stew and cornbread.

Set up an ice-cream sundae bar with a few of your less valuable ice-cream scoops and dishes and serve the assorted sauces in old cream pitchers.

Set up a buffet using stoneware crocks as serving bowls and ice buckets for wine.

Stack fresh rolls on top of a bread machine (the bucket type with the hand lever, not the modern electric ones) and fill the inside with still more.

Fill wide-mouthed fruit jars with shelled nuts or even pickled beets and eggs.

Fasten an apple parer, with apple on it, onto the dessert table containing apple pies, cobblers or dumplings and let guests give it a whirl.

Is your mind spinning with possibilities for your own collectibles? Notice that not one of these suggested uses does anything to destroy the integrity of the collectibles themselves.

8

Cookbooks, Culinary Ephemera and Advertising

Cookbooks

During the early days of the woman's movement, the mere mention of cookbooks was considered by some to be demeaning. Few wanted to hear about the hardships women had to endure to test their ovens in the days before thermostats. They didn't want to know how a woman coped if her husband brought an unexpected guest home for dinner and she had to whip something up on short notice, without the help of a microwave oven, convenience foods or takeout food stores.

These early activists, sadly, didn't care about Amelia Simmons who, 20 years after the American Revolution, penned *American Cookery, or The Art of Dressing Viands, Fish, Poultry and Vegetables, and the Best Modes of Making Pastes, Puffs, Pies, Tarts, Puddings, Custards and Preserves, and All Kinds of Cakes . . . Adapted to This Country, and All Grades of Life.* But this cookbook, thought to be the first written by an American, was also the first to include recipes for truly American foods like johnnycakes.

Neither were they interested in Mary Randolph who wrote *The Virginia House-Wife* in 1824, Lydia Maria Child who wrote *The Frugal Housewife* in 1829, Catherine Esther Beecher who designed and wrote about organizing a step-saving, efficient kitchen in 1869 in *American Woman's Home* or Eliza Leslie, the most widely published cookbook author of the first half of the 19th century. They didn't feel the need to learn more about Mary Lincoln,

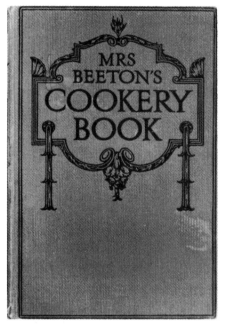

A reprint of the *American Woman's Home* by Catherine E. Beecher and Harriet Beecher Stowe enables students of the past to read what the women had to say without having to pay a high price for an original copy. Courtesy of the Stowe-Day Foundation, Hartford, Conn.

Mrs. Beeton, who served up plenty of kitchen advice in her *Cookery Book*, was a household name on both sides of the Atlantic.

principal of the Boston Cooking School, and successor, Fannie Merritt Farmer who would write the country's most popular cookbook of all time—*The Boston Cooking-School Cookbook.*

But ignoring the culinary history recorded by these women, and many others like them, belittles their pivotal contribution to civilization.

A GLIMPSE OF HISTORY

Karen Hess, a culinary historian who has edited several well-respected facsimile editions of early cookbooks including *The Virginia House-Wife* (University of South Carolina Press, $24.95), said, "I agree that women shouldn't have to cook. They should be doing whatever they want to do. But having said that, women invented cooking. We must recognize that for centuries, this was the only place where women were allowed to shine."

And shine they did. They had answers to practically every question an early housewife could ask. What about oven temperatures? Lydia Maria Child advised: "If you are afraid your oven is too hot (for baking flour bread), throw in a little flour, and shut it up for a minute. If it scorches black immediately, the heat is too furious; it if merely browns, it is right." She added, "Some people wet an old broom two or three times, and turn it round near the top of the oven till it dries; this prevents pies and cake from scorching on top." (Let's just hope the old broom hadn't spent years sweeping the floor before it was twirled above the baked goods!)

She also had the perfect solution for a fast dessert. In her 1832 edition of *The American Frugal Housewife* (available as a facsimile edition from Applewood Books, Boston), she advised: "If your husband brings home company when you are unprepared, rennet pudding may be made at five minutes' notice; provided you keep a piece of calf's rennet ready prepared soaking in a bottle of wine. One glass of the wine to a quart of milk will make a sort of cold custard. Sweetened with white sugar, and spiced with nutmeg, it is very good." It's also enough to make a modern reader grateful for simpler desserts like yogurt.

"These authors were some of the great women of the 19th century and among the first in America to become famous. Their names became household words as they sold millions of cookery books, offered cooking lessons and used their influence to achieve reforms in practically all aspects of daily life," according to Jan Longone, an antiquarian bookseller who owns The Wine and Food Library in Ann Arbor, MI, and is the author of an accurate and detailed monograph called *American Cookbooks and Wine Books 1797–1950*.

Today, as these stars of Early American cuisine are being rediscovered, collectors are paying hundreds, if not thousands of dollars, for original copies of some of their books. According to Longone, "Gems of the 18th century from America and Britain, like first editions of Amelia Simmons' book or the first edition of Hannah Glass' second book on confections, are selling for more than $5,000." Even a fine copy of a 20th century first edition like Erma

Cake Secrets, produced in 1928, contained the history of Swans Down Cake Flour and provided homemakers with recipes for butter and sponge cakes, as well as quick bread and pastry ideas.

Rombauer's *The Joy of Cooking,* can be worth more than $1,000. Recipe pamphlets from the late 19th and early 20th centuries can be worth at least $4 to $8 apiece and often, $25 or more (particularly if the illustrations were done by famous artists like Maxfield Parrish or Rose O'Neill).

"The most exciting trend in cookbook collecting today is the acknowledgment by academicians that culinary history is at least as important, if not more important, than other types of history in understanding our country and its past," Longone said. It is about time, according to Julia Child, America's culinary grand dame. Working tirelessly to establish college degree programs in gastronomy (without requiring students to cook a thing or exchange a recipe), she declared, "The study of food involves anthropology, history, sociology, science and nutrition. Great civilizations have risen and fallen based on the need for food."

REPRINTS AND FACSIMILES

But valuing cookbooks for the versions of history they present is not the only cookbook collecting trend Longone sees. Each year, more individuals, organizations and libraries begin working to establish cookbook collections, increasing the demand and sending prices higher and higher for these treasures of American culinary history. She added, "University presses are producing more reprints or facsimiles of the early works, increasing the supply of volumes of culinary history at affordable prices." Although some

Kate Smith worked with Ann Pillsbury to select 55 of her favorite Ann Pillsbury Cake Recipes.

The Good Shepherd Home "Benefit" Cook Book was promoted as a "valuable publication for a worthwhile cause" when it was printed in 1945.

can be fairly expensive if they have been redone on rag paper with full-leather bindings, Longone advises her customers to buy the reprints or facsimiles. They're invaluable when it comes to saving wear and tear on originals.

The facsimile editions of the early cookbooks are helping to put an end to what Karen Hess calls "The terrible hiatus between us and our past in matters of cooking." Hess advised that taking the time to read Mary Randolph's writings in *The Virginia House-Wife,* for example, reveals that Early American cuisine was enriched by the skilled use of wine and herbs. "For that matter," said Hess, "You'll discover there is really very little that is new. Randolph thickened her sauces with egg yolk and whipped in butter, something the chefs who were into nouvelle cuisine 'rediscovered.' She added, "That wonderful Early American cuisine underwent terrible upheaval and today, we've mistakenly judged the cuisine based on what has been totally changed by industrialization and a break with our past."

Books like Randolph's went out of vogue when cookstoves came into use. Skilled cooks abandoned their kitchen jobs for higher paying positions in the factories and left housewives to muddle through with the assistance of untrained help. Ingredients changed, too. Hess said, "Flour behaved differently because it was milled differently. Maria Parloa, in her 1887 book *Miss Parloa's Kitchen Companion,* bemoaned the inability to get the wonderful old-fashioned cornmeal."

ETHNIC, REGIONAL, COMMUNITY AND CHARITY BOOKS

Ethnic cookbooks are becoming more than mere collections of recipes, according to Longone. "Now they're telling us how their communities came to be, as well as more about their culinary customs. We learn what various foods mean to the culture of others and how that culture fits into our own." For armchair travelers, ethnic cookbooks provide tastes of places and foods they may never experience any other way. On the other hand, jet setters buy them for souvenirs and use them to recall and create the foods of places they've visited.

Regional cookbooks, another popular category among today's collectors, must be saved. "These books tell us what is really happening on local plates. In New Orleans, for example, there are wonderful foods like gumbo. We need to collect the books that tell us how to make those specialties," Child said.

Mary-Margaret Barile, author of *Cookbooks Worth Collecting* (Wallace-Homestead, 1993, 224 pp.), an excellent, how-to handbook for beginning collectors, added that the regional, community and charity cookbooks should not be discounted by collectors. "Charity cookbooks, with a history that dates to the Civil War, are far more interesting than most people realize. They let you see a small town that is no longer there. You learn who operated a glove shop in Madison, WI, in 1923 or who belonged to the Presbyterian Church in Glens Falls, NY, in 1875. Sure, some of the information could be found in a courthouse but it is more fun to read it in a cookbook." Barile added, "Community cookbooks also provide a rare glimpse into the daily lives of women and families in the average middle class. It's much easier to find out what Teddy Roosevelt ate on the Fourth of July or what foods were served at Lincoln's inauguration than it is to find out what the average American was doing in her kitchen."

Longone also values charity and community cookbooks highly. She serves as a judge for the annual Walter McIlhenny Community Cookbook Hall of Fame Awards, sponsored by the makers of Tabasco sauce. "I'm very fond of people who have used their kitchen talents to raise money for good causes," Longone said.

COOKBOOKS MAKE GOOD READING

New cookbooks have captured 25 percent of the publishing industry's special interest market. Each year, 800 to 1,000 new ones are printed. "Cookbooks always have been good sellers but now they are unbelievably popular," Longone said. "When I read the Sunday edition of *The New York Times* or visit two or three book shops selling the newest ones, my heart drops to my toes. I worry that I'll never be able to keep up with it all."

Paradoxically old cookbooks are equally popular with buyers according to Longone and other antiquarian booksellers. In a time when many people claim there's simply "no time to cook," this is good news indeed for cookbook dealers and authors, to say nothing of the publishing houses. That's because cookbooks, if they're not cut-and-paste compilations of standard recipes, make good reading. Memories, recollections, anecdotes and tales of meals, cooks and restaurants offer far more than simple measurements and ingredient lists. Despite the academic world's recognition of cookbooks' historic significance, some people still haven't gotten the word that it is acceptable to simply read, rather than cook from, cookbooks. No apologies are necessary for curling up to read a cookbook on a rainy Saturday afternoon or for choosing a cookbook, rather than a detective story or Gothic romance, for bedtime reading.

Longone, who admitted she once was a snob and thought herself too intelligent to spend time with cookbooks and cooking, discovered the need for both when she and her husband moved to Ann Arbor. "It was a dry city so good restaurants were scarce and everyone was a good cook. People invited us to their homes and served us wonderful food. I decided I had to learn to cook. To my astonishment, I turned out to be fairly good at it."

One thing led to another. She began offering cooking classes that grew out of her travels and did some catering, too. Then, she taught a course on gastronomy at the University of Michigan. In researching the course, she realized what could be found in old cookbooks and decided she would make it her business to supply those hard-to-find cookbooks to people who wanted them. She took the money she earned from teaching the course to buy two cookbook collections, and those 1,500 books became the start of her shop, which today contains more than 15,000 culinary titles specializing in Early American cookbooks. "There isn't a day when someone doesn't call me and

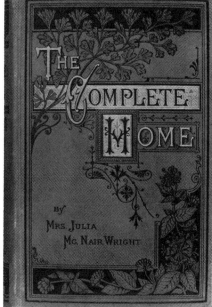

The Pennsylvania Dutch regional cookbooks produced by Betty Groff contain the standards like shoo-fly pie, chicken pot pie, potato filling and corn pie but also are peppered with memories and recollections of Lancaster County life.

Mrs. Julia McNair Wright's book, *The Complete Home*, was copyrighted in 1879 and makes for interesting reading on a quiet afternoon. Wise old Aunt Sophronia offered advice on everything a housewife would ever want to know.

say, with a funny laugh, 'I know you won't believe this but I don't use cookbooks. I read them like novels.'"

Longone believes. It has been 20 years since she began buying and selling out-of-print food and wine books.

Confessions from cookbook readers come as no surprise to John Bantock of Classic Books, Sarasota, Fla.: "Many of my customers have no intentions of actually cooking from the books. Sometimes they tell me they buy out of wishful thinking. They tell themselves they'll get around to using the books 'one of these days.'" Some of his most avid cookbook readers are non-cooks who have trouble even managing to warm frozen dinners in microwave ovens.

WHO COLLECTS COOKBOOKS?

Both men and women collect, although the field is dominated by women. (Men collect more wine books.) Some spend hundreds or thousands to acquire the finest first editions of the most important cookbooks.

Others, like many of the readers of Sue Erwin's bimonthly tabloid, the *Cookbook Collectors Exchange*, enjoy learning more about classics like the Pillsbury Bake-Off editions or the Farm Journal cookbooks, but buy for their collections on a much smaller scale. Sometimes, they're not as concerned about the edition, condition or quality of a book's binding as they are about obtaining some useful recipes. There's even a listing of swappers who prefer to trade each other for cookbooks or pamphlets they're seeking. Erwin commented, "Our circulation has just taken off. We have readers in all 50 states and subscriptions have quadrupled in the three years since we've started." Collectors who would like to buy or swap certain cookbooks are given free listings, which means this well-done publication is brimming with advertisements that help collectors find cookbooks or pamphlets they want and sell what they no longer need. Cookbook dealers pay a commercial rate for advertising.

Erwin's readers often collect for nostalgic reasons. So do some of Nahum Waxman's customers at Kitchen Arts and Letters (1435 Lexington Ave., New York, NY 10128). "I keep a picnic hamper of old cooking pamphlets near my cash register. Customers who go through them will make comments like, 'I have a million of these things at home.' But then they'll spot something that relates to a specific memory. 'My mother had this Royal Baking Powder cookbook when I was a child' . . . 'My mother always used this Spry cookbook but my sister-in-law got it when we broke up the household' . . . 'I had a copy of this but it fell apart.'" Waxman has heard many reasons but they all add up to one thing: A certain booklet, no matter whether it is for Bakers Chocolate or Washburn Crosby flour (forerunner of Gold Medal) will ring the right bells and a customer will buy it.

Scholars use cookbooks to search out material relating to their studies.

Waxman estimated 70% of his customers are in the food business. There are chefs who seek old cookbooks for "new" ideas. Caterers check out his collection when they have to construct a party around a certain theme. Restaurateurs seek books in his out-of-print section when they want to recreate the atmosphere of a certain time period, using the foods, drinks, menu styles and decor described in cookbooks of the era.

Waxman can even forecast what's about to happen in the New York restaurant scene (phenomena like the resurgence of supper clubs and grill restaurants) by restaurateurs' cookbook purchases. "Those who look to the old cookbooks to understand and evoke a certain atmosphere are looking for more than comfort food. They're after a comforting environment."

Some people collect cookbooks for the fun of it. And there are collectors who don't even know they are collectors. Longone explained, "There are people who own hundreds of cookbooks. Whenever they or their spouses travel for business or pleasure, they buy a few cookbooks to remember their trips. Friends give them cookbooks for birthday or holiday gifts. They can't resist buying an occasional cookbook at a yard sale or flea market because they spot a recipe they'd like to try. And they've saved all the cookbooks and recipe pamphlets their mothers and other relatives have treasured and passed along.

"Asked if they are collectors, they'd say 'No.' But a count of the cookbooks and cooking pamphlets would be in the hundreds. That's a collection, all right!" Longone said. All they need to do is make the transition between simply amassing and serious collecting. "A beginning collector wants to buy everything in sight until the person realizes that neither he nor any other person will ever be able to collect every cookbook," Longone said.

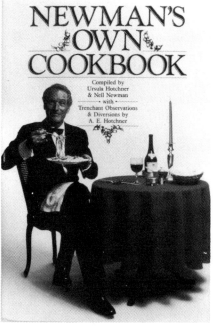

The 1945 Crisco booklet *Recipes for Good Eating*, depicted a mother and daughter preparing a batch of cut-out cookies.

Celebrity cookbooks are perennial favorites with collectors. This one, featuring Paul Newman, should have shelf appeal for decades. It's also special because the income from the cookbook's sales, as well as the profits from the Newman's Own line of food products, are donated to charity.

William Woys Weaver, a culinary historian who lives in Devon, Pa., admitted, "I still find myself wanting to buy everything I don't have, but I know that could be bankrupting. You can't collect the world. You have to find a focus to keep your sanity and keep your expenses within reason."

When Weaver was asked to estimate the number of cookbooks and pamphlets in his home collection, he answered, "Well over 5,000. No, make that 10,000. I'm just not sure how many I have. I need an archivist. At least that would prevent me from buying duplicates."

SPECIALTY COLLECTIONS

The potential for specialization is as great as the number of cookbook subjects. "Many people want cookbooks featuring restaurants, inns and taverns. Some love chocolate and desserts and buy those books. Geographically oriented collectors will buy cookbooks from the county, region or state they live in. Collectors could go after Long Island cookbooks or cookbooks produced in the parishes around New Orleans. Southerners are known for their fervor when it comes to southern cookbooks. Few good collections of this region's treasures can be found outside the South," according to Longone.

Celebrity cookbooks are also popular. Fans of Marjorie Kinnan Rawlings' *The Yearling* want her book *Cross Creek Cookery*.

Cookbooks for children are a particularly appealing category for collectors. (One couple Longone knows has managed to amass more than 1,200, including some in French and Japanese.)

"Herb and spice people are fanatic collectors. There's interest in Western Americana as well as Pacific Rim cookery and Southwestern cookery," Longone said.

Still other areas for specialization include books on markets and marketing, pastry, cake decorating, bread making, candy, cheese and game. Skim the categories within a dealer's catalog like Longone's, and you'll see even more possibilities.

Another ironic twist, according to Longone, is that students of the women's movement are now focusing on the New England schools of cookery and the women who ran them because they were active in abolition, social welfare and educational reform as well as in the development of recipes and cooking techniques. Eliza Leslie is a particular favorite of hers, thanks to the early author's "unbelievable interest in the quality of ingredients and the diversity of food." Longone added, "Leslie lectured and wrote books even beyond the United States. One of her little books was on cornmeal. Until recently, people thought it had just been published here in 1847. But the same pamphlet was published in 1846 in London. Its purpose was teaching the Irish to use cornmeal during the devastating Irish potato famine." She said the New York Public Library (widely known for its collection of cookbooks and culinary ephemera) has one of the very few known copies of this edition.

Authors Jane and Michael Stern, who are credited with starting the comfort food movement in the United States with their books *GoodFood, RoadFood, Square Meals* and *American Gourmet* collect with a lack of focus that almost becomes a specialization all its own. Jane Stern explained:

> We never go to antiquarian shows or first edition auctions. The books we like to collect are other people's complete and utter junk. We get them for 10 cents apiece at flea markets and garage sales. We think people haven't caught up with this. They're so busy collecting Victoriana and Early American that they haven't figured out that the stuff we're buying will be what they want in another 30 years. I don't think we've ever paid more than $10 for a book. If there's a big book sale, we go the last day and buy the books for $1 a box.
>
> The cookbooks we like are the ones from the 1940s through the present. We probably have 10,000 cooking pamphlets that provide recipes for new products and foods. Booklets like "10,000 Things to Do With Prunes," or "Have a Banana Festival," "The Delights of Jell-O," and "Cooking with Tapioca" are fun to read.
>
> We also have four boxes of manuals and recipe booklets for weird appliances. We have directions and recipes for things like sausage stuffers, vegetable slicers and nut crushers as well as an in-the-egg scrambler.
>
> They're part of pop culture that falls below the line of importance in most culinary historian's minds, but they're much more fun than dry culinary histories describing how Squanto planted corn. Reading about how big business, housewives and home chefs interacted with each other is fascinating. We like to ponder such questions as what buying an in-the-egg scrambler tells about its buyer.

TIPS FOR COLLECTORS

Books, catalogs and price lists No matter whether you're interested in Early American hearth cookery or food trends since the 1950s,
there's a whole world to discover. But like explorers headed for the Poles,
never leave home without preparing properly for your expedition. Buy a copy
of Barile's *Cookbooks Worth Collecting* and you'll have an instant guide to
collecting that covers everything from general advice on collecting to, history
and lore of notable cookbooks to an up-to-date price guide and information
on charity and fundraising cookbooks.

Written originally to accompany a cookbook exhibition at the University
of Michigan, Longone's monograph, *American Cookbooks and Wine Books
1792–1950,* should be required reading for serious collectors. It covers 19th
century reformers, teachers and culinary authorities, additional 19th-century
American classics, regional and ethnic traditions in cookbooks as well as
America's charitable cookbooks. (Order it for $18.50 by writing to Longone
at The Wine and Food Library, 1207 W. Madison, Ann Arbor, MI 48103.)

You might also want to pick up a price guide for cookbooks. Col. Bob
Allen's *A Guide to Collecting Cookbooks* (Collector Books, $14.95, 213 pp.) is
noteworthy for its collection of full-color photographs of cookbook covers
and its listings of softcover cookbooks and recipe pamphlets produced by
manufacturers. He also produces a monthly newsletter ($20 per year for
those who join the Cookbook Collectors Club of America, Inc., P.O. Box 56,
St. James, MO 65559).

Ordering catalogs from several cookbook dealers provides an up-to-date
picture of selling prices and enables you to establish something of a price
guide in your mind for books you'd like to obtain. Write to Barile and she'll
put you on her mailing list (Heritage Publications, P.O. Box 335, Church St.,

Just Cookbooks by Mary-Margaret Barile has a
humble title, but it is an invaluable handbook
for aspiring cookbook collectors. Barile has
just completed *Cookbooks Worth Collecting*
(Wallace-Homestead, 1993), a must for anyone interested in cookbooks of all eras.

Arkville, NY 12406). Longone will send one of her regular catalogs for $3; her rare books catalog is $5. Marian L. Gore Booksellers' catalog is $3.50 (P.O. Box 433, San Gabriel, CA 91778). Phyllis King, of MCL Associates (P.O. Box 26, McLean, VA 22101-0026), produces a number of different catalogs each year. Describe your cookbook collecting interests and send $3.50 with your list and she'll send you the catalog that best matches your interests.

Subscribe to Erwin's newsletter by sending $12 to *Cookbook Collectors' Exchange,* P.O. Box 32369, San Jose, CA 95152-2369. Just reading the advertisements and swap columns will give you a touch of collecting fever. You'll also find information on all kinds of out-of-print cookbooks as well as new regional and community cookbook releases.

You can also purchase auction catalogs and request a listing of prices paid at the auction.

Longone suggests buying cookbook bibliographies. "Although they're expensive, ugly and don't look interesting, there is no way of understanding what you have unless you have the bibliographies. If major library cookbook collections don't have the book and if it is not listed in the bibliographies, it could be a rare book and, therefore, more valuable. "Bibliographies also help you sort between a book's various editions. If the book you have is the 5th edition, you'll be able to tell how that edition differed from the first edition," she added.

Working with dealers   Serious collectors also need to develop a good relationship with dealers they can trust. "I'm not saying you shouldn't go to garage sales and auctions and find a book for 25 cents rather than $25. But if you're trying to find specific titles, volumes or editions, it helps to have another person looking for you. It increases your chances of finding something you want," Longone advised. (Some dealers offering search services charge a small fee in addition to the price of the book. Others do the search for free.)

But try not to be the original ugly cookbook collector—the one who tells a dealer that he has been searching for a certain book for 10 years and has to have a copy, only to protest the price and refuse it when the dealer manages to find it. Said one, "He'll protest the $10 asking price by saying something like "it only cost $1.95 when it was new." Warned Longone, "If you finally find a pamphlet you've been looking for, but it is priced at more than you expected, think twice before walking away. You might pass it up, figuring you could buy several other pamphlets or cookbooks for its purchase price. But you also might spend the rest of your life looking for another copy. It's the cookbook collectors' version of 'a bird in the hand is worth two in the bush.'"

Cookbook speculators aren't popular, either. Longone said, "If you want to collect only with the idea of being able to sell at a profit, please collect something else." Still, Longone acknowledged, "There are books once bought for $25 that could be sold again for hundreds of dollars. A rare cookbook in very good condition is a rare find and a wonderful investment."

Factors influencing value Scarcity is a major factor affecting price, but there are other considerations, too. Condition is primary, and Barile does a good job of explaining everything from "fine condition" to "poor" (with torn or missing pages).

Completeness of a collection is also important. Having 10 of the first 20 Pillsbury Bake-Off cookbooks is interesting, but having the complete run is far more impressive. So is having all 10 volumes of a 10-volume set, according to Longone.

Having the original dust jacket adds to value, as does printing by a famous press or illustrations by a famous artist. "If the book belonged to someone famous or has a special inscription, it could be more valuable," according to Longone.

Finding what you want Where do collectors find their cookbooks and recipe pamphlets? Sometimes these little treasures are already in your kitchen drawers. If they're not, go to any book sales to benefit charities. Barile said, "I've noticed that unless someone on the committee is a cookbook addict, cookbooks generally are the most underpriced books to be offered." Although she haunts jumble sales, book sales and flea markets, she said good cookbooks at reasonable prices are becoming harder to find. There are fewer and fewer stories of rare cookbooks being bought for 50 cents and sold for

Pillsbury Bake-Off cookbooks are quite popular with collectors who spend their time trying to acquire a full run of these booklets that have featured the winning recipes of each year's contest since the late 1940's.

"The 'Junket' Folks" produced this pamphlet of *121 Tested Recipes* by Mary Mason (director of Junket's domestic science department) for the 1940 World's Fair. This, of course, gives the pamphlet cross-market appeal to cookbook, Junket, and World's Fair collectors.

hundreds. Sometimes, however, an old food pamphlet tucked into a cookbook by a previous owner becomes a find when it turns out to be worth as much or more than the hardbound cookbook.

Booksellers are wise to the market, too, and are pricing cookbooks accordingly. "If you know there's a house sale at the home of a woman who was a good cook, chances are she had some cookbooks and her family won't want them all. You might get some good buys if there aren't many other collectors in the auction crowd," Barile said.

One of her most fundamental strategies, however, is simply getting the word out to friends and neighbors that she is interested in cookbooks. "I tell them, 'please don't throw them out. I'm willing to pay something for them.'" She has been so successful in spreading the word that the post office staff in her home town of Arkville, NY know what mail is intended for her, even if it is addressed only to "The Cookbook Lady."

Protecting your collection   Once you have begun collecting cookbooks, it is necessary to protect your investment. Although it seems obvious, Barile said some collectors fail to take proper precautions. If you know you have a valuable book, or a book that is valuable to you, consult a conservator (your local librarian should be able to give you a name or two.)

Barile, who keeps her cookbook collection in a temperature- and humidity-controlled 50-degree room year round, said books should be standing upright rather than laying flat and also should be away from direct sunlight. Barile added, "Tell people not to go at cookbooks in their collections with vacuum cleaners (putting a piece of hosiery over the suction wand doesn't make it alright). They shouldn't use staples or duct tape to repair them, either. It's also an absolute mistake to 'dog-ear' pages, bend their spines or mark pages with paper clips."

"Never mend pages with ordinary tape. It's death to a book," said Hess who uses a special library tape made for use on good books. "It actually can be peeled off without causing damage to the paper. I use it on pages to prevent little tears from becoming bigger."

Splashing a cookbook's pages as you cook might endear the volume to you, but it often isn't a plus to another buyer. To avoid having his cookbooks' pages covered with cookie dough or cake batter, Weaver always copies recipes from cookbooks on legal pads and takes the sheets of paper to the kitchen.

Damp basements or garages aren't good for cookbooks either, said Barile. However, she pointed to the grease and sunlight found in most kitchens and offered a final irony, "The kitchen is probably the worst room in the house for storing your cookbook collection."

Culinary Ephemera

Although they were made to be thrown away, many examples of culinary ephemera are highly coveted today. Booklets that you, your mother or grandmother had stuffed away in a kitchen drawer could be valuable for

FOREWORD

Wᴛʜ a General Electric Refrigerator, many of your family food problems and your perplexities about entertaining can easily be solved. The suggestions listed and the recipes which have been tested and compiled are intended to serve as a guidebook for you.

In the main, I have given basic recipes planned for four to six people. These foundation recipes have been adapted particularly for the General Electric Refrigerator. By varying flavors and colorings and garnishes, you may provide an endless number of tempting dishes.

Electric Refrigerator Recipes and Menus was specially prepared for the General Electric refrigerators of the 1920s. Author Miss Alice Bradley, in her introduction, wrote, "To many people electric refrigeration is still such a novelty that they scarcely realize the range of its possibilities. It is almost like having an Aladdin's lamp and not knowing the right way to rub it."

more than the recipes they contain. For example, the makers of Jell-O called on top illustrators, including Norman Rockwell, Maxfield Parrish and Rose O'Neill, to produce illustrations for their booklets. The result is that various Jell-O publications are sought by collectors who want the recipe booklets as well as those who focus on the works of certain illustrators.

Longone said, "Finding a 1925 book on the introduction of a new refrigerator is remarkable. There might have been 500,000 copies, but most will have disappeared by now. The information it contains may not exist anywhere else. The same goes for sales catalogs produced by manufacturers of appliances and cookware." She continued, "Culinary ephemera like recipe pamphlets promoting various companies' food products (everything from Jell-O, baking soda, chocolate and flour) and products (pots and pans, mixers, ice cream makers, stoves and refrigerators) can be worth more than a great big book.

Advertising

Magazine advertisements from the 1920s to the 1940s, (when they were full of color but much less commercial looking) are popular with Nahum Waxman's customers at Kitchen Arts and Letters (1435 Lexington Ave., New York, NY 10128). There are people who collect nothing but Cream of Wheat ads, for example. He added, "Advertising trade cards produced from the 1870s to the 1890s are very much a part of social history. We sell a great many of them, both framed and unframed. They're popular on different levels. They are a fascinating chapter in the history of American commerce. They were a naive approach to advertising without subliminal hoohahs or

Cream of Wheat advertisements have been a popular focus for collectors of magazine advertising.

An advertising trade card for Pillsbury Flour makes its point, thanks to the three women standing on a spinning top.

Among the 12 pies that husbands liked best in 1952, according to Spry's "Aunt Jenny," were chocolate cream, lemon meringue, deep-dish blueberry and cherry.

fancy notions. The fronts of the cards contained colorful illustrations while the backs delivered messages like, 'Buy Horsford's Baking Powder because it is the best' or 'Buy our flour because it's free of beetle grubs and roaches.' The same cards may have been full of lies but each assured you that, unlike competing products, this particular one was the best."

Because full-color printing was a new and fascinating phenomena at the time, the trade cards were collected and mounted in albums (it's tough to find them without glue spots) by consumers who got them from grocers and salesmen and in products they purchased. The cards contain at least four-color printing. But some feature 10 and 12-color printing (no longer done today because it is too labor-intensive). Besides the beauty of the printing, the other beauty of these cards is that a collection takes up very little room!

9

Electrical Appliances

Americans have plugged into a new category of kitchen collectibles in recent years—electrical appliances. These mini-monuments to American ingenuity, designed to simplify or eliminate culinary tasks, are being recognized for their classic lines and solid construction.

Retrieved from attics, basements, garages and closets, they're being polished and placed on kitchen counters and shelves, both for display and use. They're turning up frequently in photo layouts on feature pages of decorating magazines as finishing touches or accent pieces in country-style or retro-style

Today, manufacturers are going back to some of their popular and classic designs. Here is a Proctor Silex new classic toaster, which uses yesterday's styling but contains up-to-the-minute technology inside. Courtesy of Proctor-Silex.

General Electric Toaster Model D-12 toasted bread in full view of breakfast table but required cautious use because the red-hot elements were exposed.

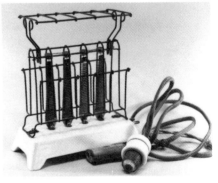

kitchens. They're even being reproduced by several major appliance manufacturers who have decided to go after a share of this growing nostalgia market.

Toasters are the hottest items in the appliance category, according to Gary Miller and K. M. Scotty Mitchell, authors of *Price Guide to Collectible Kitchen Appliances: From Aerators to Waffle Irons 1900–1950* (Wallace-Homestead, 1991, 180 pp.). Collectors are also going after coffee sets (pot, creamer, sugar and matching tray), mixers (the little ones with glass bottoms as well as Sunbeam Mixmasters, KitchenAids and a host of other makes), milkshake and malt makers, popcorn poppers, waffle irons, tabletop stoves and slow cookers.

Electrical appliances make up a populist category, inviting collectors at all financial levels. Except in a few geographic locations, even the most desirable of small kitchen appliances are priced in the hundreds, rather than the thousands of dollars. Why collect older appliances at all, when so many modern ones are around to perform kitchen tasks? Mitchell answered, "There's a certain feel and weight to them. They weren't feather-light. When you feel their weight and hold them in your hands, you know these appliances were designed to last a lifetime (the very reason why some manufacturers put themselves out of business)." Mitchell added, "There's also a certain charm and value to old appliances' offbeat designs, even though they were mass-produced."

Bandleader Fred Waring prepared one of his famous health drinks in the original model of the Waring Blendor.

The reader was invited to figure out what was wrong with this picture of a 1930 kitchen that contained such modern conveniences as an electric refrigerator and electric dishwasher. The KitchenAid and its attachments, of course, could replace all the antiquated kitchen utensils and equipment displayed on the work table.

It's easy to find proof of just how sturdy these earlier appliances were. Members of your own family may have some of these ancients around. I know my father swears by his mother's KitchenAid mixer, dating from the 1920s, when he is mixing yeast dough for breads.

When Waring tried to find the 50 oldest Blendor units in America, to celebrate the company's 50th anniversary in 1985, consumers swamped the company with 20,000 letters and photographs of early units. When it was over, a gentleman from Houston was judged the winner with his unit that was purchased for $35 in 1937 and was originally used to make malteds and milkshakes at his family's drive-in restaurant. He still uses it to mix up the same recipe for banana milkshakes that bandleader Fred Waring popularized when he was promoting the Blendor in the 1930s.

Starting Your Collection

Although you may initially have no intention of collecting electrical appliances, all it takes is a few minutes and a single purchase or an unexpected gift. Mitchell and Miller, for example, were at a garage sale when they saw a solution to a problem. They spotted an old Edison hot plate that would provide them with an extra cooking surface when they were entertaining and bought it.

Not long after that, they bought an old coffeepot and decided it made excellent coffee. Before long, relatives gave them some vintage toasters to go along with the coffeepot and hot plate. They were on their way. Today, their collection of well over 1,500 appliances takes up an entire room of their home. And although they may have stopped counting all their new acquisitions, they haven't stopped collecting. Said Miller, "We don't collect the commonplace. We don't need 29 of one kind of toaster and 42 of another. We do use discretion."

Well-heeled collectors seek appliance firsts as well as those with the best designs. But a fledgling collector with just a small amount of cash shouldn't be discouraged, because even a little money can buy plenty of amusement in this category. The first toasters produced by Westinghouse (the Type C Toaster Stove) and General Electric (the X2 and D12 models) are highly collectible and command more than $100 each. In their original packages, their value easily doubles. And if these toasters are found in their original packaging on either the East or the West coast, expect selling prices closer to stratospheric levels. The thrifty collector will plan a vacation to the Midwest or the South to search for more affordable electrical appliances.

But even if you can't afford to travel farther than the streets of your hometown, you can accumulate appliances like popcorn poppers and egg cookers. "They're cheap and they're fascinating to collect and use. Popcorn poppers can be found from $5 to $25 at flea markets and yard sales while egg cookers sell for even less ($2 to $15)," according to Mitchell.

Low-budget collectors could try speculating in this category—paying rock-bottom prices for electrical appliances that have yet to capture the imaginations of other collectors. What's in this "nobody wants them" cate-

Farberware's Broiler Robot had ebonized handles and trim. Made of heavy-gauge brass that was heavily nickel- and chrome-plated, it was equipped with a two-heat unit and broiled, cooked, stewed or toasted.

The Coffee Robot was a Farberware first—its original completely automatic coffeemaker, which was introduced in 1930. This Silex model made three to eight cups of coffee and had a patented bowl release. Courtesy of Farberware.

gory? Appliances like toaster ovens, fondue pots and electric roasters. Mitchell, who has collected four full-sized roasters so far, commented, "I'm confident that cooks eventually will realize the value of the roasters, particularly if they do a lot of entertaining. After all, they're well built and increase your oven capacity. They're still being manufactured, but the new ones sell for more than $100 while 1940s and 1950s versions sell for $20 or less." He uses his roaster for everything from cooking a turkey to making a Texas-sized batch of chili.

Accumulating items like electric fondue pots is something of an exercise in faith. Once enough people get rid of the ones in their homes, they'll wish they had them back. It's not an idea to be discounted or laughed at, particularly if you plan to be around for a number of decades in the next century. Miller said, "The 'gadgety' kinds of appliances that are introduced or promoted at Christmas time are the sorts of things that will be collectible 20, 30, or 40 years from now." Miller and Mitchell admit to buying and storing a brand new Presto Tater Twister as a future collectible. Miller also makes a point of purchasing every attachment Cuisinart introduces for its food processors.

No matter what a collector's financial means, the category demands a narrower focus. Few people would have the money, let alone the display space, to collect every electrical kitchen appliance ever made. Collect a certain kind of appliance, whether that means an assortment of coffeepots or sandwich grills. Consider waffle irons with pretty porcelain insets, although some collectors are tempted to pay more than they should for these, according to Miller and Mitchell. (Prices for these distinctive waffle irons are listed between $50 and $60 in their price guide.)

Collect by manufacturer. White Cross was selling a two-burner hot plate ($5.50), a nickel-finished two-slice toaster with automatic reversing ($4.80), and a brand new seven-cup percolator with a heat-proof glass top ($5.80) in July, 1930. In 1955, General Electric's Christmas line of appliances included an automatic coffeemaker, an all-purpose mixer, an automatic skillet, a speed

Some collectors of electrical appliances for the kitchen are betting that Presto's Tater Twister will be a future collectible. Courtesy of National Presto Industries, Inc.

Apparently, people were also in a hurry in earlier decades as some scrambled to buy Farberware's Super Speed coffeepot that promised "True Coffee faster than you can boil water." It was billed as the "World's Fastest Coffeemaker." Courtesy of Farberware.

In 1955, General Electric's kitchen appliances that were suggested as Christmas gifts, included an automatic coffeemaker, an all-purpose mixer, an automatic skillet, a speed kettle, automatic toaster and automatic grill and waffle baker.

kettle for boiling water, an automatic toaster and an automatic grill and waffle iron. Perhaps you'd like to amass all the styles of toasters Toastmaster ever produced. In 1955 alone, the company offered a Toast N Jam Set (with toaster, "rich walnut tray inlaid with brown simulated leather, a Gay Melmac toast plate and two jam jars in a smart black metal holder") as well as one-, two- and three-slice toasters and a B16 Powermatic that automatically lowered bread into the toaster, toasted it, and served it up, "all by itself."

Collect by the decade. Miller said:

The 1920s were wonderful years for innovations. There was ample money available for companies to go wild with appliances and they did. They were almost as bad as the Victorians were. They had 49 pieces of silverware in one place setting or a special utensil for every kind of food. In the 1920s, there was an appliance for almost everything.

As we got into this, we realized the only piece of equipment that had not been invented in some form in the first 50 years of the century was the microwave oven. The early cooks had coffee grinders, a version of a food processor and electric flour sifters.

There were engineering advances in the 1920s, including tabletop stoves that could cook eggs, bacon and pancakes at the same time.

There were refinements like heat indicators on waffle irons to show when they were at the right temperature, toaster timers and coffeemakers that shut off once they were finished perking.

The 1930s were interesting from a design standpoint, too. The Art Deco movement that influenced so much of American life was reflected in the appliances. Miller said, "There were companies producing appliances with designs that were absolutely special." An example? "The Coleman Lamp & Stove Company of Wichita, Kansas, produced a round waffle iron on an oval base. The black and white enameled insert on the top pictured a leaping gazelle."

Collect all the attachments for a particular appliance, just as Miller buys those for Cuisinarts. Depending on the unit you select, it could be quite a project. Sunbeam Mixmasters and KitchenAid mixers had so many attach-

The front cover of the Sunbeam Mixmaster manual shows happy cooks showing off all kinds of foods made in their mixers.

Perhaps Sunbeam Mixmaster owners were particularly happy with their mixers because there were attachments to do almost anything from sharpening knives, paring apples and turning an ice-cream maker to opening cans, shelling peas and churning butter.

ments in their lines that the manufacturers also sold cabinets in which to store them. (Naturally, if you decide to collect all attachments for these mixers, you too, will need to find and buy one of those cabinets!)

Factors Influencing Value

No matter what focus you bring to your collection, there are certain factors that contribute to various appliances' value. Remember that electrical appliance collecting is still in its infancy, so there is a great deal of price speculation, price manipulation and just plain price testing going on. No one knows how many appliances survive. Think for a minute about how many old appliances your mother or aunts saved, whether or not they used them.

Design is another factor that has a major influence on an appliance's desirability and selling price. Design variations within each category are enormous. Some early toasters resemble miniature electrical generating stations, complete with exposed elements. Those of the Art Deco period, on the other hand, conceal their contents within stylish, well-rounded sides. The Porcelier Toaster, for example, is a beauty. Made in the 1930s by a company in Greensburg, PA, its body is basket-weave porcelain, with floral transfers on the sides. Miller and Mitchell said, "We think these were the only toasters ever made in pottery. We talked to a man who worked in the factory and he told us that the company scrapped 11 toasters for every one that was placed on the market. That means these toasters were horribly expensive to make and those that were sold were of top quality." Although they value the Porcelier toaster at $75 in their price guide, Miller and Mitchell have been

The Sunbeam waffle iron turned out four waffles at a time, a boon when family members were hungry and in a hurry.

offered $600 for one in their collection. "It's just not worth that much because there are more out there," said Mitchell. "I'd have felt guilty accepting that much money for it." His collector's blood prevented him from selling it, too. He said, "I just couldn't part with it, anyway."

One can't discuss the variations in toaster design without talking about the 1918 PERC-O-TOASTER. Armstrong, the manufacturer, promoted this appliance that could make coffee and toast at the breakfast table at the same time, thanks to a hot plate that radiated heat both up and down. According to their advertisement, this heating unit made "delicious coffee, always steaming hot," at the same time it toasted bread flat, with "both sides being done to a golden brown at once, to insure crisp, tender toast." Should you come across one of these contraptions, Miller and Mitchell list its price at $60.

Uniqueness of function, another pricing influence along with basic design, is illustrated by the 1938 Toast-O-Later. Miller and Mitchell like it because the toast "walks" through the machine on a tooth-like conveyor and drops out on the other side. This breakfast table conversation piece still can be purchased for less than $100.

Color shouldn't be discounted, either. Californians, for example, are eager to acquire Toastmasters in such 1950's shades as yellow, turquoise, pink, red, brown and black. Hankscraft Egg Cookers made in the Fiesta colors of the 1940s, command a higher price than some of the other models.

Buying Tips

Armed with pricing information, where are you going to find the treasures you'll want to buy? Spread the word about what you want among friends, relatives and neighbors. Don't worry about what they'll think. They probably already regard you as a bit eccentric—most collectors are.

Don't overlook your own attic or closet. After all, that harvest-gold electric fondue pot you received as a wedding present in the 1970s may be just a few years away from becoming a desirable collectible.

If a household search and word-of-mouth advertising yields nothing, or not enough, keep looking. Electrical collectibles finally have earned a little space in antique shops, but many are still to be found in less expensive locations. Saturdays spent at yard sales, garage sales and flea markets are bound to turn up some treasures. Make the rounds of thrift and charity shops. Estate sales also are good places to build a collection. Most folks who lived through the Depression were savers—not only saving every electrical appliance they ever bought but also stashing the original packaging and directions for the equipment.

Collectors in the field shouldn't worry too much about external soil, according to Mitchell and Miller, although the underlying finish should be intact. They've discovered that aluminum mag-wheel cleaner, available in auto stores, does a good job on nickel and chrome surfaces. Nonabrasive kitchen cleaners sometimes work, too. As a last resort, to remove a heavy accumulation of grease and dirt, they advise trying oven cleaner on an

Presto introduced its first electric pressure cooker in 1954. In 1956, the unit had a removable control. By 1971, the electric unit pictured was available in harvest gold, burnt orange and avocado, which were popular colors at the time.

This advertisement from a 1958 issue of *The Saturday Evening Post*, showed General Electric's introduction of the forerunner of the company's Toast-R-Oven toasters. In addition to the conventional toaster on top, it featured a baking drawer along the bottom.

appliance's surface. Apply it with care, in a well-ventilated area, and according to package directions. Proceed carefully because it is easy to obliterate a manufacturer's name with such heavy-duty chemicals.

Unless you plan to start an appliance parts salvage yard, don't buy rusted or obviously broken appliances. On the other hand, if you find a really clean appliance, grab it. Although its near-mint condition indicates it wasn't terribly useful to previous owners, it still could be fun to have.

Be sure there's nothing "foreign" inside the unit. Mitchell and Miller have found everything from kitchen forks to dead rodents in equipment they've examined.

Try to determine if the appliance works before buying it. But examine the unit carefully, before doing anything. Mitchell advised, "Use common sense. An appliance with a frayed or cracked cord shouldn't be plugged in until the cord is replaced." It is fairly simple to remove a machine's bottom plate and replace the old cord. Detachable cords generally come in two or three standard sizes that still are in stock at older hardware stores. However, some appliances required a single cord with two heads. If the two-headed cord isn't with the appliance, don't buy it because you might never find the cord you need.

Because there's always a danger of a short or shock from an appliance, they suggest, "Ask the person who wants to sell you the appliance to plug it in." At the very least, a collector who is checking out an appliance at home, should always use insulated pliers, rather than taking plug in hand, the first time it is tested in an outlet. The elements should be intact around the mica in the old flip-flop toasters. Very early hot plates, whose elements were sealed in heavy clay under an iron top, can't be repaired.

Front cover of the manual for the Everhot Electric Roasterette, *How to Cook Happy-Family Meals,* depicted a family eagerly awaiting the dinner about to be dished from the depths of the appliance.

The New "Classics"

Although some consumers might be tempted to buy the new classic appliances being reintroduced and marketed by major manufacturers, Mitchell doesn't view this as a threat to his hobby. "I think these new lines will drive the price of the older appliances up. In the first place, they'll make people aware of the old and beautiful high-design pieces. As a collector, I'd like to have the new and the old and display them side by side on the counter.

Milk-shakes have been popular for decades. Here is the Cyclone #1 model shown side by side with the model Hamilton Beach is making today.

On the other hand, the new appliances might even stimulate the sales of the older ones because they'll probably be cheaper at yard and garage sales than the new ones on department store shelves," Mitchell said.

"People remember the classic styling. They think of those products as simpler and remember that they worked," according to one company spokesman. Among new classics currently on the market are the Hamilton Beach Classic Blender and Classic Drinkmaster, Proctor Silex's Classic Toaster and Classic Mixer, the Oster Beehive Blender and Farberware's classic electric percolators. It's an unabashed appeal to the sense of nostalgia in all of us. The literature with the Hamilton Beach Drinkmaster says it all: "In 1911, drugstores across the country began using the Hamilton Beach soda fountain mixer to make thick, rich milkshakes and malteds. Today, the Hamilton Beach classic Drinkmaster brings home the same old-fashioned goodness."

Of course, true nostalgia buffs believe the old-fashioned goodness will be even better if it is prepared in the real thing, no matter whether it's a milkshake from the drink mixer or a piece of slightly blackened toast that has just been launched from a toaster and caught in midair.

✳ **10** ✳
Modern Reproductions

A stroll through a thriving wholesale warehouse or gift shop that is brimming with reproductions is an eye-opening experience for a person who wants to begin collecting kitchen antiques. What's inside? A sampling: stoneware crocks; pitchers and bean pots with all kinds of primitive designs; graniteware; coffee mills; cookie jars; cookie boards and cookie cutters; spongeware; depression glass in all shapes and sizes from butter dishes and glass rolling pins to measuring cups, reamers and salt and pepper shakers; hearth tools; cast iron; and brass and copper kitchenware. The wholesalers advertise in major antiques and collectibles trade papers. If their massive warehouses (often as large as 30,000 or 40,000 square feet or more) are too far away to visit, call for catalogs. If there's a charge, pay it willingly. Consider it an educational expense.

Kitchenware catalogs have their share of reproductions, too, because some timeless tools always are part of a good cook's equipment. Consider these descriptions, plucked from some of the latest catalogs:

"New antique chocolate molds" that are "identical to costly antique versions used by professional chocolate makers in Europe."

Stoneware bowls for those who "weren't fortunate enough to inherit bowls like these."

"A throwback to another era before non stick coatings and aerosol baking sprays, this 10-inch round, tin-plate cake pan with a flat blade that swivels around the edge and bottom, releasing the cake, has survived the test of time."

Two and three-tine kitchen forks that were "grandma's favorites."

"Back again is the classic white enamel steel bread box. Yes, the one that was on the kitchen counter when you were a child."

"Old-fashioned bread bucket enables people to knead dough easily by hand (suitable for 18 cups of flour or six loaves). Turn the crank and within minutes your dough is ready. These hard-to-find buckets were popular in most homes a hundred years ago."

Browse the giftware catalogs that supply gift shops and you will find antique wire reproductions including fruit-jar sterilizing baskets, egg baskets and pie-cooling racks. They will also list old-fashioned stew forks, trivets, ladles, skimmers, hooks, tin-plated spice and kitchen graters, cookie cutters and baskets. On a larger scale, there will be pie safes, corner cupboards, dry sinks and ice boxes to be found. All of these items are clearly marked and priced as reproductions. But once they leave a warehouse, gift shop or store, the confusion begins. "People who sell clearly identified reproductions are not breaking the law or doing anything unethical. But we all know what happens with the products once they reach the field. Someone, somewhere, will misrepresent them," said Bill Mergenthal, president of the American Antique Association, which was founded to stop the manufacture of reproductions that are not permanently marked. He stressed, "We have no problems with reproductions. But we want them identified forever with a mark that can't be removed. Mergenthal figures that about 95% of reproductions are marked simply with tags or labels that are easily removed—making it difficult, or nearly impossible, to distinguish them from the originals.

Why worry about unmarked reproductions in the antiques and collectibles market that always has been known for its caveat emptor (let the buyer beware) attitude? In times when a sluggish economy thins the number of potential buyers, there's concern about turning off still more buyers with bad experiences. Novices, who have trouble distinguishing between something old and something new old might stop buying because they don't want to get burned on a reproduction. Consider also future generations of collectors who will really be in a muddle. After all, if a good quality reproduction hangs on someone's wall, sits in a kitchen or gets used for 20 or 30 years, it'll be even harder to distinguish between it and the original.

Some Basic Definitions

Reproductions are mass-produced, exact copies of an original piece (or at least, an attempt has been made to duplicate the original as closely as possible).

Copycats are stylistic copies of an object, also mass-produced, that have enough features to make them resemble something real and confuse the person who is unfamiliar with the original.

Fakes, on the other hand, generally are one-of-a-kind attempts to make something that looks old. The same tools and techniques are used as those to make the original, and then, signs of aging are added, too.

Separating old from new is further complicated by the issue of today's skilled craftsmen who have learned time-honored techniques to faithfully reproduce the tools of earlier times and by *reissues*, which have been made in original molds and so are identical to earlier antiques and collectibles. Craftsmen, at work at national and state historic sites, or in studios, sometimes permanently sign their work so it is easily identified. Sometimes they don't.

Reissues are a particular problem in the world of glass. Gene Florence, in his book *Kitchen Glassware of the Depression Years,* notes that the demise of the Westmoreland Glass Company and the resulting sale of its glass molds to other glass companies means the market now has many pieces that are identical in nearly every way, to the original Westmoreland pieces. Unless the reproductions are made in colors other than those of the originals, telling them apart could be nearly impossible.

The same thing happened with the Federal Glass Company's Madrid pattern, according to Ellen Tischbein Schroy, author of *Warman's Glass.* She noted that Federal produced Madrid from 1932 to 1939 (in green, pink, amber, crystal and Madonna blue) and also revived the pattern for the Bicentennial in 1976. But Bicentennial pieces were clearly marked with the addition of the date to the molds. When Federal went bankrupt, however, Indiana Glass purchased the molds, including that of Madrid. They renamed the pattern "Recollection," removed the Bicentennial markings, and have continued making it in colors including blue, pink and crystal. To identify the glassware as a Federal or Indiana product, a collector has to be knowledgeable enough to know the subtle differences.

As interest in the past grows, more and more of it will be reintroduced to the present. In other words, it's not going to get any easier for collectors.

Small-appliance manufacturers have jumped on the bandwagon with their new versions of classics like early toasters, blenders and milk-shake machines.

University presses, as well as other publishers are releasing facsimiles of early cookbooks.

Chuck Williams, founder of the nationally known cookware chain Williams-Sonoma, said, "Occasionally, we have gotten special requests from customers for old-fashioned tools. They remember something their mothers used and want it. Sometimes, the manufacturer is in business. But other times, it is impossible to find a substitute."

The interest in earlier hand tools is understandable to Williams who said, "A person who wants to learn cooking basics like making cakes or loaves of bread will have a much better understanding of consistency from hand-mixing the batter or kneading the dough. It's a good idea to get the feel of cooking so that a person understands what the batter or dough should be like, before turning to professional equipment like electric mixers and food processors."

He recalled one woman who inherited a potato masher that her mother had used all her life. She liked it so much, according to Williams, that she had it reproduced and called it "My grandmother's potato masher." "It was a good one that we decided to carry in the stores," according to the cookware chain's founder.

Cumberland Country Store, whose catalog illustrations and contents gives it a turn-of-the-century look, specializes in old-fashioned tools and equipment for homeowners and farmers who yearn for simpler days. "Kitchen items are among our biggest sellers. Our customers like cast-iron pieces like the cornstick pans, small skillets, blue-speckled graniteware, stoneware bowls, coffee mills, rolling pins, and wooden tongs and wooden biscuit cutters. They like the idea of going back to days before electricity, or at least back to the tools they remember from their childhood," said a spokesman for the store and mail-order business based in Crossville, Tenn.

Reproduction Market

There are many markets for the reproductions or they wouldn't be sold. In addition to cooks who like the look and feel of tools modeled after those of earlier years, there are decorators who simply like the look of antiques or collectibles but don't want to pay the price for originals. Gary Miller, who sees the new lines of classic electrical appliances driving up the price of the older ones because they create a new awareness and desire for older styles, likes to display the new versions next to the old versions. There are the collectors who buy and display antiques and collectibles and the reproductions. William Woys Weaver, culinary historian, commented, "Certain things are too precious to use. I try to get viable working copies like the redware that's made for me by a person in New Jersey. Many people would enjoy cooking with earthenware cooking equipment that is safe and useful (the antique versions have too much lead in their glazes)."

Jan Longone, owner of The Wine and Food Library in Ann Arbor, Mich., said, "I always encourage cookbook collectors to buy facsimiles, even when they have original editions. That way, they can read and work from the newer ones and save the old ones."

There are times however, when a collector really doesn't want a reproduction but ends up with one. Steve Stephens named a few problem areas in cast iron: "Cornstick pans, rabbit and Santa Claus molds are common reproductions sold at flea markets. The repros of the Griswold rabbit mold are particularly good and have fooled some major collectors. Wagner toy waffle irons and tea kettles were made and also were reproduced. The small Griswold crispy cornstick pan has been reproduced many times. One particularly poor version is mismarked the 'Criswold cornsnic' pan. The manufacturer was so careless that basic words were misspelled and, to top it off, they got the number wrong, too. The real Griswold version is No. 262, rather than 252." Stephens added, "A person who looks closely at some of the cornstick pan reproductions will see that their surfaces are more grainy and that the kernels are not as well defined."

The Keen Kutter No. 8 waffle iron also has been reproduced and a novice would have a very difficult time telling the difference, according to the San Francisco cast-iron collector. Other copycats he has seen include a toy Keen Kutter waffle iron and a toy Griswold heart and star waffle iron. Stephens said, "Keen Kutter made a waffle iron but not a toy one. Griswold made a toy waffle iron, too, but it didn't contain hearts and star."

Cookie jar collectors have their challenges, too. "Major reproductions are being made of the better jars in various collectible series," according to collector Wendy Johnston of Brooklyn, N.Y. "Some new jars are being made from original molds. In other cases, molds are being made right from the jars."

Johnston figures from 30 to 50 jars have been handled this way. A novice who doesn't know that the new ones are slightly smaller than the originals could wind up paying top dollar for a reproduction. Colors can be a key, too. The collector commented, "New jars will have brighter primary colors than those on the originals."

Hearth items and punched tin coffeepots are being made in Indonesia, according to *Kitchen Antiques & Collectibles News* publisher Dana DeMore who also warned, "Watch out for reproduction pantry boxes."

Copper cooking equipment is coming into the antique market from the Balkans and Turkey, according to Weaver who said, "It looks primitive and has a decorative quality to it. A person can hang it up but shouldn't cook with it."

Collectors in other fields have their stories, too, but all of this should simply serve to alert a novice to be careful until you're aware of the reproductions in your field.

Avoiding Pitfalls

Awareness doesn't come without effort, however. Keeping track of reproductions requires correspondence, bookkeeping and reading. If you encounter a new reproduction you should bring it to the attention of a newsletter for collectors, if there is one for your specialty. (It goes without saying that subscriptions to appropriate newsletters are necessary, too.)

Always order warehouse catalogs and giftware catalogs as well as mail-order catalogs from kitchen supply shops. Clip and save photographs and descriptions of the products related to the category. Send away for the catalogs of craftsmen and their studios. Double check to see if there are any others advertised at the back of decorating magazines and send for those, too.

Be familiar with relevant price guides—good ones often contain information on reproductions. The glassware books by Gene Florence, *The Collector's Encyclopedia of Depression Glass* and *Kitchen Glassware of the Depression Years,* are good examples. Alice Creswick includes a listing of reproduction fruit jars in her book, *The Collector's Guide to Old Fruit Jars. The Collector's Encyclopedia of Fiesta, plus Harlequin, Riviera and Kitchen Kraft,* by Bob and Sharon Huxford includes a section called "A Word to the Wise." In it, they warn, "Styles, designs, decorations and even glazes were flagrantly copied from one pottery to another. Whole lines were stolen from pottery dumps!" They also mention other manufacturers and contemporary dinnerware companies whose lines are similar enough to confuse beginners.

The *Antique & Collectors Reproduction News* is a relatively new publication (first published in April, 1992, by Antiques Coast to Coast, P.O. Box 71174, Des Moines, IA 50325), which promises to provide a "monthly report of fakes, frauds and facts." The American Antique Association (702 W. 76th St.,

Davenport, IA) provides a quarterly newsletter about reproductions and also provides members with a Reproduction Hotline for reporting those they've spotted, getting help with disputes over purchases of unmarked reproductions and getting the latest news about a specific type of reproduction or retailers. *Collectors News* (P.O. Box 156, Grundy Center, IA 50638), a monthly tabloid, publishes "Reproduction Alerts" from the American Antique Association.

In the field, there are additional precautions a collector can take. Stephens advised collectors to be cautious and examine potential purchases as closely as possible. "Look at them in daylight. Ask questions of the seller concerning the age, origin and any history of the piece he knows." He added, "Look for legitimate signs of wear and use (in the case of cast iron there often is a buildup of baked-on grease and carbon and signs of wear on the bottom of a pan from being slid on a stove top or moved in and out of the oven.) If a pan has been rusted chemically, it will have a reddish orange look to it."

Because anyone can become a dealer (there are no licensing or education requirements that must be met), the collector should work with dealers who've been fair and honest in their past dealings. And, warns William Woys Weaver, "Because there are some unscrupulous dealers mixed in with lots of nice ones, it is important to take what they tell you with a grain of salt. If it turns out to be true, fine. But don't believe automatically. A dealer can say, 'I bought that in Boyertown, Pa., two days ago.' But it could have been shipped into the states recently from a place like southern Italy. Buying it in Boyertown doesn't mean that it was used by several generations of Pennsylvania Germans who lived in Boyertown all their lives."

From Stephens and numerous other collectors comes the advice to handle as many examples of items in a category as possible. "After you've held and examined 500 Griswold products, you'll know its look and feel pretty well," Stephens concluded.

Too-good-to-be true items probably are, according to Wendy Johnston. "There aren't a whole lot of bargains anymore. Falling into things is happening less and less because there are more collectors. If a Brush Hillbilly frog, American Bisque Casper the Ghost or McCoy Leprechaun cookie jar is at an unrealistically low price, it's probably a reproduction."

PART TWO

Kitchen
Collectibles
Price Guide

❧ A
ADVERTISING
Ashtray, Power's Coffee Shop, Fargo, ND, Bakelite **40.00**
Bank
    California Raisin, vinyl, figural raisin and Sun–Maid Raisin box, orange sunglasses, 1987 copyright, 6½" h **25.00**
    Chicken Delight Chef, bank, 6" h, vinyl, figural, 1960s **25.00**
    Kleek–O Eskimo, Cliquot Club, plaster, holding Ginger Ale bottle, silvered base, 1930s, 7" h **200.00**
    Kool Aid Man, plastic, mechanical, 1970s, 7" h **25.00**
    Magic Chef, vinyl, 1950–60, 7½" h **30.00**
    Pillsbury Doughboy, cylinder, cardboard, metal caps, blue and white, 1980s, 7" h **10.00**
    Rutter Bros. Dairy Products, dairy truck, plastic, white, red decal, c1960 **40.00**
    Tony the Tiger, plastic, figural, 1970s, 8½" h **40.00**
Beach Bag, Maxwell House Coffee, figural, coffee can **25.00**
Camera, Kraft Velveeta Shells & Cheese Dinner, hard plastic, yellow, illus instruction leaflet, 1950–60 **12.00**
Creamer
    American Dairy Foods **12.00**
    Anthony's Cream **13.00**
    Casey's Dairy **12.00**
    Progressive **10.00**
    Rosebud Dairy **9.00**
    Swaner's, original cap **16.00**
    Velvet, Owensboro, KY **17.50**
Display, Whitman's Chocolates, painted wood, movable hand, blue dress, c1930 **120.00**

Display Cabinet, Coleman's Mustard, tin, red and black lettering, yellow ground, three int. shelves, 10" w, 7¼" d, 16" h **70.00**
Fan, cardboard, diecut, full color adv
    Elsie The Borden Cow, wood handle, c1910 **35.00**
    Lebel's Dairy, girl in highchair, spilled milk from her cup on front, Compliments of Lebel's Dairy, 145 E Hollis Street, Nashua, NH, on back **10.00**
Flour Sacks, Pillsbury's Best XXX Flour, c1930–40, original box, 3¼" h **25.00**
Hanger, 9¾" h, Gridley Dairy, assorted colors, Little Miss Curleylocks pictured in various outfits, price for set of five **45.00**
Ink Blotter
    Arm & Hammer Baking Soda, cardboard, 1920s, 4 × 9¼" **10.00**
    Morton's Salt, black and white photo, c1930s, 3¼ × 6¼" **5.00**
    Universal Super Strength Milk Bottles, picture of plant in Parkersburg, WV, address of NE representative in Hartford, CT, white and orange lettering, white ground **9.00**
Letter Opener
    Armour Meats, celluloid, rooster head **55.00**
    Uneeda Biscuits, metal, c1920, 8¼" l **50.00**
Measuring Tape, Cass Dairy Farm, Inc., Jersey & Ayshire Milk on front, You Can Whip Our Cream But You Can't Beat Our Milk, Try Our Cream on reverse, celluloid container **30.00**
Mirror
    Angelus Marshmallows, oval, multicolored illus, blonde cherub, green background, rim inscription "Mirror Free With Package Angelus Marshmallows Or Mailed For 3–2 ct. Stamps.

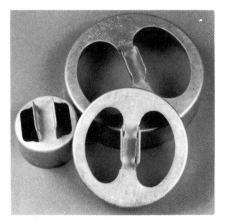

Set of three interlocking biscuit cutters that advertised Calumet Baking Powder could be displayed or used.

Ask Your Dealer, Rueckheim Bros &
Eckstein, Chicago," 2¾" l   **75.00**
Beeman Gum, pocket   **150.00**
Big Jo Flour, red, white, and blue flour
bag, early 1900s, 2¼" d   **50.00**
CD Kenny Co, Teas, Coffees, Sugars,
paper over metal, red and white,
c1900   **30.00**
Ceresota Flour, Prize Bread Flour of
the World, celluloid, c1920,
2⅛" d   **50.00**
Checkers Popcorn, "Eat Eat Eat," celluloid, red, white, and blue, c1920,
2⅛" d   **100.00**
Ceresota Flour, celluloid, multicolored
illus, dark brown rim, early 1900s,
2⅛" d   **50.00**
Garland Stoves and Ranges, tin, emb
logo, inscription "Sold Everywhere/The
Worlds' Best," early 1900s,
1¾" d   **25.00**
Horlick's Malted Milk, The Nutritious
Food–Drink For All Ages, celluloid,
c1900   **75.00**
Monitor Stoves and Ranges, celluloid,
black and white, logo design,
1¾" d   **20.00**
Morton's Salt, celluloid, 1940s   **35.00**
Robin Hood Flour, aluminum, emb
Robin Hood image, inscription "None
So Good As Robin Hood," 1930s,
1½" d   **20.00**
Stacey Chocolates, sunset over wa-
ter   **35.00**
Thea–Nectar Pure Chinese Tea, emb
brass shell back, Chinese symbols with

entwined honeybee and "T," 1870s,
1½" d   **50.00**
White House Coffee, The Flavor is
Roasted In, red, white, and blue,
1920s, 2¼" d   **25.00**
White Rock Spring Water, "The
World's Best Table Water," tin rim,
multicolored illus of kneeling woman,
2" d   **150.00**
Note Hook, Breakfast Cheer Coffee, inserted rigid wire, full color coffee can
illus, celluloid, green ground, early
1900s   **65.00**
Pencil Clip, celluloid
    Christopher Milk, "Builds Champions,"
    white lettering, blue ground, 1930s,
    ⅞" d   **15.00**
    Diamond Crystal Salt, salt box, 1930s,
    ⅞" d   **18.00**
    Ziegler's Clean Milk, milk bottle and
    flowers, early 1900s, ⅞" d   **25.00**
Pinback Button
    Borden's Fern Butter, red, white, and
    blue design, 1901–12, ⅞" d   **15.00**
    Bowman Milk, Bud Bowman character,
    1940s, 1" d   **12.00**
    Charlie The Tuna, "Charlie For Presi-
    dent," red, white, and blue,
    1960s   **30.00**
    Cherry Smash Soft Drinks, multi-
    colored, portrait of George Washing-
    ton, dark red shaded to olive green
    ground, black advertising inscription,
    c1912, 1¼" d   **40.00**
    Columbian Stoves and Ranges, red,
    white, and blue, c1913, 2⅛" d   **35.00**

Pratt's apple segmenter reduced a peeled or
unpeeled apple to 22 neat, wedge-shaped
sections with 11 revolutions. Only the core
was left on the fork. Patented in 1856, this is
the two-arm model. There also was a one-
arm style. Courtesy of Phyllis and Jim Moffet of Modesto, Ill.

This rare Bergner apple parer and segmenter
was made by Geo. Bergner of Washington,
MO. Patented in 1872, it is thought to be the
only parer made west of the Mississippi
River and is coveted by collectors. Courtesy
of Phyllis and Jim Moffet of Modesto, Ill.

Davis OK Baking Powder, red, yellow, black, and white, c1896, $\frac{7}{8}$″ d **25.00**

Drink Satisfaction Coffee, blue and white, diecut flag, 1900–01, $\frac{5}{8}$″ d **18.00**

Fisher's Blend Flour, red, white, and blue flour sack, early 1900s, $1\frac{1}{2}$″ d **30.00**

Fleischmann's Yeast, "John Dough Raised on Fleischmann's Yeast," oval, full color, baker with bread loaf body parts, c1915, $1\frac{1}{2}$″ l **40.00**

Frisbee's Alfalfa Clover Honey, multi-colored design with three honey bees, 1901–12, $1\frac{1}{4}$″ d **50.00**

Garland Stoves and Ranges, red and white, list of company products, early 1900s, $1\frac{3}{4}$″ d **25.00**

Gold Dust Washing Powder, multi-colored, black youngsters seated in tub, white background, black lettering, 1890–1900, $\frac{7}{8}$″ d **55.00**

Heinz Tomato Soup, full color, c1896, $\frac{7}{8}$″ d **35.00**

King Arthur Flour, multicolored design, c1896, $\frac{7}{8}$″ d **40.00**

Krug's Bread, red and white, 1930s, 1″ d **12.00**

Limetta/The Drink of Drinks, youngster riding St Bernard, $1\frac{1}{4}$″ d **75.00**

Lion Coffee, inscribed "Millions Drink It," coffee cup illus, early 1900s, $\frac{7}{8}$″ d **25.00**

Nabisco Shredded Wheat, Top O' The Morning, red on white, c1940, $1\frac{1}{4}$″ d **20.00**

Oscar Mayer Yellow Band Weiners, full color litho, 1930s, $1\frac{3}{8}$″ d **10.00**

Pillsbury's Flour, The Flour That Sells Around The World, c1910, $1\frac{1}{4}$″ d **50.00**

Quaker Rolled White Oats, full color, red rim, c1920, 2″ d **75.00**

Red Cross Macaroni, red, white, and blue, 1930s, $1\frac{1}{4}$″ d **25.00**

Square Deal Bread/Safety Club, silvered brass, black incised inscription, 1930s, $1\frac{1}{4}$″ d **20.00**

Time To Drink White House Coffee, full color, 1910, $1\frac{1}{4}$″ d **50.00**

Towle's Log Cabin Maple Sugar, full color, c1896, $\frac{7}{8}$″ d **20.00**

Pitcher, glass, clear, Esso tiger illustrations and slogan in eight languages, late 1960s, $9\frac{1}{2}$″ h **25.00**

Pocket Knife, HJ Heinz Co, silvered metal, two steel blades, text one side, "57" symbol other side, Meriden Knife Co, early 1900s, 3″ l **25.00**

Puzzle

Calumet Baking Powder, cardboard, 9 pcs, early 1900s **20.00**

Frito–Lay Inc, character symbol, 84 pcs, 1970s **15.00**

Sewing Kit, Borden's Mitchell Dairy, Elsie pictured on cov, Milk's Good Anytime, Better still Make It Borden's slogan **8.00**

Sherbet Glass, Jell-O Brand Dessert, fluted edge, red lettering, c1930, $3\frac{1}{2}$″ d, 4″ h **28.00**

Stickpin

Empire Cream Separator **20.00**

Gold Dust Washing Powder, full color celluloid, brass rim, c1896 **75.00**

Grande Andes Kitchen Ranges, patriotic decoration **12.00**

National Cream Separator, Quaker **10.00**

Sharples Separator **25.00**

Thermometer

Cocoa Flavored Sambo Dairy Drink, wood, 1937 patent date, $5\frac{1}{4}$ x 12″h **50.00**

Drink Dr Pepper, full color litho tin, c1930, 17″ h **150.00**

Moxie, tin, bottle and man pointing, "Good At Any Temperature," $25\frac{1}{2}$″ h **550.00**

Pepsi–Cola, emb metal, red, white, and blue, c1932, 27″ h **100.00**

Puritan Ice Cream, cardboard, c1923, $12\frac{1}{2}$″ h **35.00**

Thimble, NuMaid Margarine, plastic **2.50**

Trade Cards

Adams' Pepsin Tutti Frutti, c1890, $4\frac{1}{2}$ × $6\frac{1}{2}$″ **25.00**

Borden's Condensed Milk, three children hugging each other and holding a can of Borden's Condensed Milk, directions for use, New York city address on back, copyright 1889 **10.00**

Chase & Sanborn Coffee, full color illus, 1886, 3 × 5″ **15.00**

Conqueror Wringer, Baking Day, Donaldson Bros **10.00**

Crosse and Blackwells' Pickles, Sauces & Condiments, girl showing man pickle jar, color **15.00**

Glendale Coffee, child with googly eyes, color **8.00**

Gold Dust Washing Powder, diecut, full color, c1890, 3 × $3\frac{1}{2}$″ **35.00**

Granite Iron Ware, color **12.00**

Heinz, full color, diecut, pickle shape, girl holding can of baked beans, c1890, 2 × 5″ **15.00**

Hires Root Beer, full color, c1900, 3 × 5″ **20.00**

Hood's Sarsaparilla, full color, titled "First Lesson," dog capturing rat, c1890, 3¼ × 4¾" 10.00

Lake Superior Mills Wonder Flour, Forbes Litho 12.00

Lightning Blizzard Ice Cream Freezers, two sided, window cutout 20.00

Lion Coffee, full color portrait, free pocket knife premium offer, 3½ × 5½" 10.00

Quaker White Oats, full color, c1900, 2¾ × 5½" 20.00

Red Cross Stoves & Ranges, The Crusaders Return, color 6.00

Tray

Baker Cocoa, tip 125.00

Best on Record Flour 25.00

Fairy Soap, girl sitting on soap bar, holding flowers, orange center, brown rim, tip, c1936, 4¼" d 75.00

Goebel's Malt Extract, girl and chalkboard, tip 90.00

Murray Co Sodawater Flavors, "Fresh Sodas Sundaes," two colonial men seated on benches, tapping sodas, 1930–50, 12" d 130.00

Stollwerck Chocolate, tip 25.00

Teaberry & Beech Nut Gum, tip, glass, green, decals 38.00

Whistles

Cap'n Crunch 5.00

Checkers Popcorn, litho tin, red, white, and blue, c1920 40.00

Cracker Jack/Angellus Marshmallows, cardboard, red, white, and blue, Jack one side, marshmallow box other side, 1930s, 2½" l 28.00

Oscar Mayer Weiner, plastic, red, 1950s 8.00

Zig Zag the Food Confection, litho tin cylinder, siren, red, white, and blue, Germany, 1920s, ½" d, 1⅜" l 50.00

APPLE BUTTER JAR

Redware, dark brown glaze, wear and minor hairline, 6¾" h 90.00

Stoneware, interior with dark brown Albany slip glaze, applied mug type handle, impressed "F. H. Cowden, Harrisburg, PA," 7" h 125.00

APPLE CORER

Boye Needle Co, tin, wood handle, patent 1916 12.00

Gem Apple Corer, patented by James Fallows, Philadelphia, Jan 2, 1877, tin tubular corer, wooden knob handle 15.00

Grayline Housewares, Inc., Chicago, IL, steel, 5" l 10.00

APPLE PARER

Clover, gears 75.00

Goodall, Antrim, NH, 1893, cast iron, original box 40.00

Keen Kutter, E. C. Simmons Hardware

The Davis apple slicer was patented in 1834. From the collection of Chuck and Bonnie Badger.

Very scarce Tripp Bros. apple slicer was mounted on a board that had a hole in it. The slicer was placed over a suitable container. A peeled or nonpeeled apple, with the core removed, was placed in the hopper. An arm, with seven blades that were approximately 3/8-inches apart, was passed through the apple. Beautiful apple rings fell into the container. The device was patented in 1883. Photo courtesy of Phyllis and Jim Moffet, Modesto, Ill.

Co, St. Louis, MO, cast iron, patent May 24, 1898 **95.00**
Lightning **135.00**
Reading Hardware Co, Reading, PA, cast iron, patent dates: May 5, 1868, May 3, 1875, Oct 19, 1875, Nov 14, 1875, May 22, 1988 **80.00**
Sinclair Scott, Baltimore, MD, Top Gear, cast iron, late 19th C **50.00**
Wood, bird's eye maple, forged iron fork and handle, clamps to table **175.00**

APRON
Cotton
  Hand sewn
    Green and white check **40.00**
    Patchwork design, waist length, ties **25.00**
  Machine sewn
  Print, floral, blue and white, front pockets, fits over shoulder, ties in back, c1940 **20.00**
  White, embroidered flowers **45.00**
Crocheted **15.00**
Linen, long, tatted hem decoration **35.00**

❧ B
BAKING PANS
Angel Food Cake Pan, dark tin, faceted sides, Star of David shaped **30.00**
Baking Pan
  Graniteware
    Blue and White, large swirl, small **95.00**
    Chrysolite, swirl **125.00**
    Iris, swirl **195.00**

Pie pans from bakeries that bear the bakery names and designs can make an interesting and decorative collection.

Robin's egg blue, round **20.00**
Bread Pan, Ideal, tin, double loaf, two tubes **30.00**
Bundt Pan, Graniteware, gray **15.00**
Corn Stick Pan
  Griswold Mfg Co, Erie, PA, cast iron
    No. 262, well defined ear of corn design **75.00**
    No. 954, plain, two rolled handles **50.00**
  Wagner Ware Krusty Korn Kobs, PatentJuly 6, 1920, cast iron **75.00**
Danish Pan, Griswold Mfg Co, Erie, PA, No. 32 **60.00**
French Roll Pan, cast iron, rect, 2 rows of 6, No. 11, 6½ × 12½″ **15.00**
Jelly Roll Pan, Graniteware, blue and white, large swirl **40.00**
Muffin Pan
  Cast Iron
    G F Filley, No. 3 **100.00**
    G F Filley, No. 4, eye bars **120.00**
    Griswold Mfg Co., Erie, PA, No. 946, eight flat sections **45.00**
    Unknown maker
      Round, open handles, patent date April 5, 1856 **140.00**
      Party Shapes, heart shapes, stars, plain, and fluted edge round shapes, embossed patent date July 10, 1871 on handles **185.00**
  Graniteware
    Cobalt and white, eight muffins, large swirl **225.00**
    Gray, six muffins **20.00**
Popover Pan, Griswold Mfg, Erie, PA, No. 10, cast iron, eleven sections, finger grip handles, c1890, 11″ l, 7½″ w, 1¾″ d **60.00**
Vienna Roll Pan, Griswold Mfg Co, Erie, PA, No. 26, cast iron **85.00**
Wheat Stick Pan, Griswold Mfg Co, Erie, PA, No. 639, cast iron, well defined wheat design **135.00**

BASKET, DECORATIVE
Aluminum, hand wrought
  Canterbury Arts, floral spray design, twisted center handle, helmet mark faces left, 12″ d **28.00**
  Continental Hand Wrought Silverlook, Chrysanthemum pattern, marked "No. 1088," 7¾″ l **18.00**
  Farber & Shlevin, china insert with Indian Tree pattern and gold border, aluminum frame and handle **20.00**
  Hand Forged/Everlast Metal, Harvest pattern, flared sides, scalloped handle, 12″ l **12.00**
McCoy Pottery
  Basketweave, green and white ext.,

white int., marked "McCoy USA,"
1957 **25.00**
Oak Leaves and Acorns, marked "Mc-
Coy USA," 1952 **30.00**
Noritake China, Tree in the Meadow pat-
tern, 4⅜" l, 4" h **110.00**
Roseville Pottery
Columbine, blue, 376–10,
1/123 **175.00**
Florane, 10" d **135.00**
Peony, pink, 378–10, 1/119 **135.00**
Snowberry, blue, 1BK–10,
1/133 **145.00**
White Rose, pink, 363–10,
1/112 **115.00**
Stangl Pottery, Terra Rose, No. 3251, 11
× 9" **75.00**

BASKET, UTILITARIAN

Berry, 6" h, woven splint, handmade **50.00**
Buttocks, woven splint, weathered gray
finish, some damage
12 × 14", 7½" h plus bentwood handle **50.00**
14 × 15", 7" h plus bentwood handle,
square, some age and wear **85.00**
14 × 18", 8" h plus bentwood handle **95.00**
17½ × 20", 11" h plus bentwood
handle, stripped surface, traces of white
paint and some damage **60.00**
21 × 21", 11" h plus bentwood handle, some age and damage **72.00**
Cheese, woven splint, round
15" d **125.00**
21" d, 7" h, good age and color, minor
damage **275.00**
Egg, 3½ × 6 × 7", buttocks bottom **80.00**
Field
Splint, wooden bottom, old natural patina, "H.S.B." painted in red, 15" d,
11½"h **60.00**
Woven splint, round, good color, bentwood rim handles, minor damage,
18" d, 12¾" h **85.00**
Gathering
Rye straw, rim handles, wear and one
handle partially restored, 18" d,
9" h **105.00**
Woven splint
Oval
Flared sides, traces of old red
paint, some damage, 10½ ×
13½", 5" h plus bentwood handle **85.00**
Radiating ribs, old varnish, 15 ×
16", 6½" h plus bentwod handle **210.00**
Weathered gray finish, 11 × 16",

8½" h plus bentwood han-
dle **60.00**
Round
Scrubbed finish, 17" d, 7¼" h
plus bentwood handle **115.00**
Weathered gray finish, minor
damage, 15" d, 8½" h plus well
shaped bentwood handle **105.00**
Goosefeather, woven splint, dome lid,
good color, bentwood handles covered by
lid, rim of lid broken, minor damage,
25" h **80.00**
Herb Drying, woven splint, open weave
base, minor damage, 16" d, 6¾" h plus
bentwood rim handles **240.00**

BATTER JUG

Bauer Pottery, Ring, extensive line intro-
duced in 1931, cov, Dark Blue **95.00**
Franciscan, Apple Pattern **200.00**
Hull Pottery, Little Red Riding Hood,
Hull Pottery **425.00**
McKee Glassware, chrome handle and
cover
Cobalt blue **125.00**
Ruby **95.00**

BEAN POT

Hall China
Chinese Red Pattern, #5 **150.00**
Orange Poppy Pattern **60.00**
Pastel Morning Glory Pattern (a.k.a.
Pink Morning Glory) **150.00**
Red Dot Pattern (a.k.a. Eggshell Polka
Dot), #2, one handle **125.00**
Wild Poppy Pattern (a.k.a. Poppy and
Wheat), #5, one handle **175.00**
Stangl Pottery, Colonial Pattern, #1388,
individual, Persian Yellow **18.00**
Stoneware, blue and white, molded dec
and figures, emb "Boston Baked Beans,"
int. crazing, 6⅜" h **185.00**

BEAN SLICER

Bean–X, Orange, NJ, blued steel blade,
springs, 6½" l **12.00**
Vaughn's, Chicago, IL, cast iron, green
wood handle, clamps to table,
12" h **40.00**

BELL

Ceramic
Chef holding wine bottle and glass,
marked "Occupied Japan," 3" h **24.00**
Mammy, plaid dress **50.00**
Wood, cow, 7" h, handmade **40.00**

BOWL

Aluminum, hand wrought
Arthur Armour
8" d, pine and mountains, anodized
gold trim **18.00**
11½" d, sundial and zodiac signs,
inscribed "Grow Old With Me, The
Best Is Yet To Be" **55.00**

Bright yellow Fiesta 9 1/2-inch salad bowl provided a splash of color to greens before any other ingredients were added and tossed.

Rodney Kent, tulip, flower ribbon handles, marked "Hand Wrought Rodney Kent, No. 450," 10″ d   **20.00**
11¼″ d, Chrysanthemum pattern, applied leaves, Continental Hand Wrought Silverlook, marked "No. 715"   **15.00**
American Art Pottery
    5″ d, 3″ h, inverted umbrella shape, gold bisque, bronze spatter   **10.00**
    10 × 4 × 2″, octagonal, elongated, green, yellow int.   **8.00**
Bauer Pottery, Ring pattern, 14″ d, Green   **165.00**
Blue Ridge, Sungold #1 Pattern, Candlewick shape, 9½″ d   **20.00**
Depression Era Glassware
    Crisscross pattern, cobalt blue
       7¾″ d   **70.00**
       9¾″ d   **120.00**
Fire King, Tulip pattern
    7½″ d   **12.00**
    8½″ d   **16.00**
    9½″ d   **16.00**
Hall China
    Pastel Morning Glory Pattern (a.k.a. Pink Morning Glory), oval   **35.00**
    Red Dot Pattern (a.k.a. Eggshell Polka Dot), 8¾″ d   **25.00**
    Wildfire Pattern, oval, 9″ l   **28.50**
Harker Pottery, Mallow Pattern, 10″ d   **30.00**
Homer Laughlin, Harlequin Pattern, 5½″
    Maroon   **10.00**
    Red   **7.50**
McKee Glass
    4″ d, 2¾″ h, French Ivory   **3.50**
    4¼″ d, custard   **6.00**
    6″ d, Skokie Green, double scallop   **13.00**
Metlox Pottery
    Aztec Pattern, Poppytrail line, 9½″ d   **18.00**

California Ivy Pattern, Poppytrail line
    5¼″ d   **6.50**
    9″ d   **25.00**
Provincial Fruit Pattern, Poppytrail line
    5″ d, tab handle   **4.00**
    6″ d   **4.00**
    7″ d, deep   **8.00**
    10″ d   **18.00**
Plastic, gray, multicolored speckles, marked "Texas Ware"   **15.00**
Redware
    Cream colored slip, brown spots, flakes, 6½″ d   **80.00**
    Yellow slip, worn interior, 5½″ d   **75.00**
Rockingham, mottled brown sponging
    9½″ d, 4¼″ h, exterior tan and white stripes under brown sponging   **135.00**
    11½″ d, 3¼″ h, shallow   **125.00**
    12½″ d, 3¼″ h, shallow, wear, minor hairlines, small edge flakes   **85.00**
Roseville Pottery
    Carnelian I, pedestal, blue   **55.00**
    Clematis, blue, 12″ d   **145.00**
    Fuschia, green, 847–8   **95.00**
    Pine Cone, blue, 179–9   **150.00**
Shawnee Pottery
    Corn King
       No. 5   **25.00**
       No. 6, 6½″ d   **30.00**
       No. 92, 6″ d   **25.00**
    Corn Queen, No. 5   **25.00**
Tinware, decorated, 7¾″ w, 12¾″ l, 3⅝″ h, oval, original dark brown japanning, red, yellow, and white floral dec, minor wear   **350.00**
Woodenware, burl
    Oblong
       13″ w, 24½″ l, 4″ h, simple cut out handles, old metal repair on age crack along one side, refinished birch, traces of old red paint   **110.00**
       15½″ w, 15¾″ l, 5″ h, ash, good figure, old wear with soft finish   **1,250.00**
       17¼″ w, 25″ l, 7½″ h, ash, excellent figure, good old worn dark brown patina, deep bowl, small protruding end handles, short rim cracks, old puttied repair in bottom   **2,550.00**
    Oval
       13½″ w, 17½″ l, 5″ h, ash burl, good figure, old worn finish, simple hollow carved rim handles   **1,425.00**
       11¼″ w, 13¾″ l, 9¼″ h, double animal head handles, simple relief, chip carving, old worn finish with dark stain in center, carved initials "K.S.J." on bottom   **1,400.00**
    Round
       5½″ d, 2½″ h, ash, hand carved, ir-

1924 *McCall's* magazine advertisement showed the variety of baked goods produced by Uneeda Bakers (Nabisco).

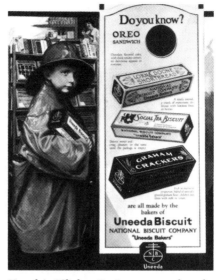

Uneeda's "Slicker Boy" was created at the turn of the 20th century to promote Nabisco's moisture-proof package for its crackers and cookies. This advertisement was printed in 1923.

regular shape, old brown finish, minor wear **150.00**

6⅝" d, 2¾" h, ash, old brown finish, good turned detail on exterior **325.00**

8½" d, 3" h, ash, gold figure, old brown finish, good turned detail on exterior, minor age cracks in bottom **375.00**

10½" d, 3½" h, ash, good scrubbed and worn surface, age crack at rim **440.00**

13½" d, 5" h, turned lip, old red exterior, good wear, old color, age cracks **700.00**

21¾" d, 4" h, decorated, worn red and black stripes, age cracks **110.00**

27" d, 9" h, poplar, turned, worn and scrubbed interior, age cracks, wire repair on rim **110.00**

BOX AND/OR PACKAGE
Aunt Jemima Pancake Flour, cardboard, 13" w, 9" d, 14" h **55.00**
Bakers Chocolatiere, Art Deco design **25.00**
Blue River Butter, cows on all four sides, blue, green, and yellow, unused **2.50**
Bossie's Best Brand Butter, four color picture of Jersey cow, Aberdeen Creamery Co, folded **5.00**
Castile Soap, Oletyme Products, Indianapolis, IN, pictures castle, "Made in Accordance with the Fair Labor Standards Act of

1933," three bars, 7¼ × 3½ × 1" **7.00**
Fun–To–Wash, 3¼" h, full color illustrations of black Mammy wearing red bandanna, early 1900s **25.00**
Hill Country Butter, yellow, black, white, stylized floral border, half pound size, unused **1.00**
Quaker Oats, wood, 26 × 18 × 11" **65.00**
Wilson's Clearbrook Butter, farm scene on one side, eight cows, red roofed barn, fields, home, yellow, black, white, and red, one pound size, unused **2.00**
BREAD BOARD
Hardwood, round, carved motto, 9½" d
   Give Us This Day Our Daily
   Bread **50.00**
   Speed the Plough **55.00**
   Staff of Life **50.00**
   Waste Not Want Not **45.00**
Pine, one board wide, applied ends, wear, old red paint on back, 17½ × 23½" **50.00**
BREADBOX
Chrome, rectangular, black trim, wood handle **10.00**
Graniteware
   Rectangular, green and white, hinged lid, c1920, 19" l **95.00**
   Square, gray, raised red handles and letters **25.00**
Metal
   Betsy Ross Moderne pattern, white, red

trim, marked "Roll–A–Way, E M
Meder Co," 1930s **15.00**
Painted, yellow, fruit decal **15.00**
Plastic, red and white **20.00**
Tin, white, red enameled top, 12″ l **12.00**
Wood, carved, "Give Us This Day,"
12½″ h **80.00**
BREAD KNIFE
American
Climax, plain wooden handle, carbon
steel blade, truncated tip, 13¼″ l **15.00**
Comet, Christy, Fremont, OH, carbon
steel, iron loop handle, patent Nov 12,
1890, 12″ l **15.00**
Tip Top Boy, wood handle, pointed
carbon steel blade, trademark of boy's
head, 15″ l **20.00**
Victoria, wood handle, carbon steel
blade, truncated tip, American Cutlery
Co, 14¾″ l **20.00**
English
"Bread" carved on wooden handle, steel
blade, marked "Sheffield,"
19th C **35.00**
Wheat sheaf carved handle, blade
marked "Alexander E. Foulis" **45.00**
BREAD MAKER
Universal, Landers, Frary, Clark, tin and
iron, impressed "Awarded Gold Medal St.
Louis Exposition" **70.00**
White House Bread Maker, tin, cast iron
gears, table mount, 1902 **125.00**
BREAD PLATE
Aluminum, hand wrought
Chrysanthemum decoration, ornate
handles **20.00**
Flying geese decoration **15.00**
China
Bavarian, hand painted spring scene,
pastel colors, gold band, artist signed,
14″ l, 7″ w **90.00**
Metlox Pottery
California Provincial Pattern,
Poppytrail line **40.00**
Homestead Provincial, Poppytrail
line **25.00**
Nippon, pink asters, green leaves, gold
trim **225.00**
Noritake, gold handles
Azalea Pattern, 12″ l **40.00**
Hand painted scene in center, wide
border, hand painted stylized flow-
ers, maroon wreath **65.00**
Pale green and gold floral border,
white background, open handles,
14″ l, 6¼″ w **24.00**
Cut Glass, brilliant cut, signed "Libbey,"
13½″ l **175.00**
Glass
Actress pattern, HMS Pinafore,
12″ l **90.00**

Aurora pattern, ruby stained, large star
in center, 10″ d **35.00**
Beaded Grape pattern, square **30.00**
Be Industrious, oval, clear, handles, 12
× 8¼″ l **50.00**
Canadian pattern, clear, 10″ d **45.00**
Cupid and Venus pattern, amber **75.00**
Give Us This Day, clear, rosette center
and border, round **65.00**
Liberty Bell pattern, clear, Constitution
signers' names, emb 1776–1876 **80.00**
Maple Leaf pattern, vaseline, oval, 13
× 9½″ **50.00**
Old State House, sapphire blue **175.00**
Tennessee pattern, colored jewels **75.00**
Waste Not Want Not, lattice border,
clear, 11½″ l **35.00**
Wheat and Barley pattern, milk
glass **60.00**
Wildflower pattern, square, clear **30.00**
Majolica, Oak Leaf with Acorns pattern,
12¼″ l **120.00**
Silverplated, grape clusters on self han-
dles **65.00**
Tinware, decorated, brown ground,
painted fruit, leaf motif border, 19th C,
12¾″ l **3,025.00**
Wooden
Flemish Art, hand painted florals,
motto, artist signed **50.00**
Round, "Bread" embossed on rim, hand
rubbed oil finish **15.00**
BROCHURES
Alpha–New England Salad Cream, pre-
miums, 24 pages, black and white, 1902,
6½ × 4½″ **10.00**
Chase & Sanborn Tea & Coffee, 48
pages, black and white illus, 1889,
color **15.00**
Gold Standard Coffee, nursery rhymes,
figural package, 4 pages, color **12.00**
Hires Un–Natural History, diecut strip
pages, c1914 **25.00**
H–O Cereal Sunny Jim Denslow, 1910,
32 pages **55.00**
Jell-O Girl Gives a Party, The, Rose
O'Neill illus, 16 pages, color, 5¼ ×
7″ **25.00**
Jewel Stoves, Cooking with Gas Jewel
Stoves and Ranges, 32 pages, illus, two
tone, 5 × 7″ **10.00**
Kellogg's Rice Krispies, six flaps create
different pictures, artist sgd Vernon
Grant, color **20.00**
Magic Yeast, 12 pages, color **8.00**
Maxwell House Coffee Co, Secrets of Cof-
fee Flavor, 20 pages, color, 1927 **10.00**
Old Grist Mill Flour, recipes, 16 pages,
Gies Litho, color **8.00**
Quick Meal Steel Ranges, Ringen Stove
Co, c1904, 3 × 5″ **35.00**

Ralston Recipes, Nursery Rhymes, 23
pages, color **15.00**
Reliable Flour Co, Reliable Primer, 14
pages, color, 3½ × 3¾" **6.00**
Sinclairs Fidelity Meats, 6 pages, color,
1902 **12.00**
Teddy Bears Baking School, 1906 **50.00**
WD Sager Stoves, Chicago, 1915 **6.00**
We Pull for Windsor, picture of Windsor
Farm Dairy, Denver, CO, on front, picture of horses on back, pictures of plant
and workers inside, 18 pages, early
1930s **15.00**
Wrigley's, Mother Goose, 1930s, 4 ×
6" **25.00**

BUTTER CHURN
Glass, Dazey, 4 quart **125.00**
Clay, red, green ash glaze, worn wood lid
and dasher, 16½" h **60.00**
Stoneware, New Geneva, tan clay, tooling,
two tone amber and brown slip with
stenciled design, wear and chips,
18¾" h **150.00**
Tin, flower decal, wood dasher, rust damage, bottom holes, 19" h **55.00**
Wooden, stave construction, table top,
handle **110.00**

BUTTER CROCK
Rockingham, brown glazed pottery, original lid, 8½" d **80.00**
Stoneware, impressed "1½," brushed cobalt blue floral decoration, hairline in

**The Dazey Churn #20, made in St. Louis,
spent many an hour turning cream into butter the old fashioned way.**

base and minor chip on inside of lid
flange, 12" d **420.00**

BUTTER DISH, COV
Aluminum, hand wrought, round, domed
cov, double loop finial, glass insert,
Buenilum Hand Wrought **20.00**
Depression Era Glassware, Crisscross pat-
tern, cobalt blue, quarter pound **95.00**
Franciscan Ware
  Apple Pattern **45.00**
  Desert Rose Pattern, ¼ lb **40.00**
  Duet Pattern **25.00**
  Ivy Pattern, ¼ lb **30.00**
  Starburst Pattern **30.00**
Graniteware, cobalt and white, mot-
tled **195.00**
Hall China
  Autumn Leaf
    ¼ lb, wing knob **450.00**
    1 lb, regular knob **180.00**
  Chinese Red Pattern, Zephyr **185.00**
Homer Laughlin, Harlequin Pattern, Ma-
roon **95.00**
Hull Pottery, Little Red Riding
Hood **350.00**
Knowles, Edwin, Deanna Pattern, open,
dark blue **10.00**
  Navajo Pattern, Poppytrail line **30.00**
  Provincial Fruit Pattern, Poppytrail
  line **25.00**
  Red Rooster, Poppytrail line **30.00**
McKee Glass
  Chalaine Blue, rectangular **75.00**
  Clear top, custard base, rectangu-
  lar **20.00**
  Custard, rectangular **45.00**
  Delphite, quarter pound **285.00**
  Seville Yellow, rectangular **65.00**
  White, plain, rectangular **38.00**
Noritake China, Azalea pattern,
6¼" d **78.00**

BUTTER MOLD
Cast Aluminum, R Hall, Burlington, NC,
star shape, ½ lb, c1940, 3¾" d **20.00**
Wood
  Compote with fruit, foliage, and vegetables, rect, old varnish, one foot replaced, 4 × 5" **250.00**
  Fish, round, scrubbed finish, cracked
  case, 3¾" d **350.00**
  Roses and cherries, rect, old patina, age
  cracks, 4 × 7" **95.00**

BUTTER PADDLE
Woodenware
  5½" l, 4¾" w, oval, old patina **150.00**
  7¼" l, flat, cutout and tooled handle,
  old patina **45.00**
  7¾" l, carved lines and initials
  "M.A.A," dark patina **35.00**
  8½" l, curly maple, old worn finish,
  edge of bowl worn **50.00**

9″ l, ash burl, superb figure through-out, old finish **475.00**

9¼″ l, burl, bird head handle, ash burl, old refinishing **550.00**

9¾″ l, maple, some curl, old finish, age crack in bowl **65.00**

10½″ l, maple, light natural patina **75.00**

BUTTER PRINT, WOOD

Acorn and oak leaf, round, one piece turned handle, old worn patina, 3¾″ d **220.00**

Bird and flowers, bird looking backwards, rect, chip carved edge, old patina, dark stains, 1¾″ w, 4¾″ l, 2½″ h **225.00**

Cow, round, turned threaded handle, scrubbed finish, 3⅞ d **125.00**

Cow with fence and grain, round, carved edge, turned handle, old patina, 4¾″ d **325.00**

Eagle, foliage, and banner "J Richardson," round, turned handle, old patina, age cracks, 3¾″ d **325.00**

Eagle, foliage, and star flowers, round, turned handle, old patina, 4¼″ d **175.00**

Four hearts and compass star, rect, poplar, good dark patina, 3½ × 5″ **165.00**

Leaf design, round, turned handle, 3¾″ d **60.00**

Paddle, carved sheaf, late, 8½″ l **30.00**

Peacock and branch, round, turned threaded handle, old dark finish, 4¾″ d **725.00**

Pineapple design, semicircular, turned inverted handle, old patina, 3⅜ × 7″ **200.00**

Pinwheel, deeply cut, round, turned inserted handle, scrubbed white, 4⅜″ d **300.00**

Rose and thistle, round, one pc turned handle, scrubbed white, 3⅞″ d **85.00**

Stylized floral design

  Lollipop Style, chip carved edge, initials, natural patina, 6⅝″ l **375.00**

  Round

    Double, deeply carved, old dark patina, wear, some edge damage, 4¼ × 4½″ **250.00**

    Finely detailed carved lines, simple turned handle, old patina, age cracks, 4″ d **65.00**

Stylized tulip design, round, turned handle, old patina, wear, edge damage, 4¼″ d **225.00**

Stylized tulip and star design, rect, dark patina, wear, edge damage, and age cracks, 3¼ × 4⅞″ **185.00**

Tulip

  Boldly carved, wedge shaped, old patina, 6¾″ l **400.00**

  Primitive carved, round, pine, old worn patina, 4¾″ d **100.00**

Wheel, floral design, scrubbed, 5½″ l **65.00**

❧ C

CABBAGE CUTTER

Brady, Lancaster, PA, walnut, one adjustable steel blade, cast iron handle, patent March 9, 1880, 25″ l **90.00**

Disston & Morss, Philadelphia, PA, walnut, three steel blades, 24″ l **45.00**

Ideal, graniteware, gray, steel blade **196.00**

Indianapolis Kraut Kutter, Tucker & Dorsey Mfg Co, Indianapolis, IN, wood, two steel blades, patent 1905 **50.00**

Wood, hand made

  Pine, plain **30.00**

  Walnut

    22½″ l, 7¼″ w, heart cutout, old finish **170.00**

    26½″ l, sliding hopper, refinished **30.00**

CAKE DECORATIONS

Bride and Groom

  Bisque, signed "Wilton," c1960, 6″ h **15.00**

  Plaster of Paris, molded, painted black, white, pink, and pearlized white headdress and bodice, 5″ h **12.00**

Candle Holders, stamped tin flowers, price for set of ten **15.00**

Howdy Doody and Friends, seven figural candleholders, unopened on original card **35.00**

CAKE DECORATING SET

Aluminum, tube, six decorating tips, mint in original box **10.00**

Aluminum and copper, eight design attachments **10.00**

Metal, stencil

  Individual, German, c1904

    Flower **15.00**

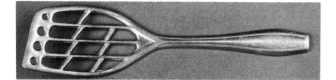

Cast-aluminum cake turner, marked D.R.G.M., Germany, was made early in the 20th century.

Palm Leaves	12.00
Star	10.00
Round, 10″ d, late 19th C	20.00

CAKE MOLD
Heart, cast iron, Griswold Mfg Co., Erie, No. 2 — 25.00
Lamb, cast iron — 55.00
Rabbit, cast iron, Griswold Mfg Co., Erie, PA, two part — 225.00
Santa
  Aluminum, Santa Shape–A–Cake, original instructions and box — 8.00
  Cast Iron, Griswold Mfg Co, Erie, PA, two part — 525.00

CAKE PLATE
Bauer Pottery, Monterey Pattern, pedestal base, Orange–red — 100.00
Ceramic, center color portraits of Dionne Quintuplets, titled "Dionne Quintuplets, Born May 28, 1934, Callander, Ontario, Canada," white ground, gold maple leaf at top, red rim, 11½″ d — 135.00
Hall China
  Orange Poppy Pattern — 15.00
  Pastel Morning Glory Pattern (a.k.a. Pink Morning Glory) — 55.00
Harker Pottery, Colonial Lady Pattern — 22.00
Nippon China, hand painted floral dec, gold and cobalt blue border, green Maple Leaf mark, 10½″ w handle to handle — 275.00
Noritake China
  Azalea pattern, 9¾″ d — 40.00
  Tree in the Meadow pattern — 32.00
Pennsbury Pottery, Amish decoration — 75.00
Stangl Pottery, Apple Delight Pattern, #5161 — 20.00

CAKE SAFE
Bakelite, green handle — 5.00
China, hand painted floral design, English registry marks — 18.00
Plastic, Art Deco styling — 32.00

CAKE TIN
Autumn Leaf pattern — 5.00
Manhattan Island scenes, multicolored litho, c1915, 11 × 12 × 6″ — 25.00

CALENDAR
1903, A & P Tea Co, 19 × 15″ — 180.00
1906, Fleischmann's, July pad, 14 × 10″ — 110.00
1915, Magic Yeast, barefoot boy, 18 × 10″ — 225.00
1922, Sharples Tubular Cream Separators, January pad — 110.00
1927, Broad View Farm, pure milk from our accredited herd, Rochester, NH, little girl climbs steps of house and reaches for giant bottle of Broad View Farm's milk, sheet for each month with saying about milk — 15.00
1930, A C Stram Groceries–URMA Brand–Green Bay, Dawn of Day print, full pad — 20.00
1932, American Stores, 31 × 18″, full pad, framed — 120.00
1933, Coca–Cola, The Village Blacksmith, full pad — 325.00
1943, full color Elsie The Borden Cow cartoon, full pad — 50.00
1944
  Pepsi–Cola, lady on rocker and two men — 60.00
1955, Coca–Cola, original wrapper, home type — 25.00

CANDLE HOLDER
Graniteware, red, leaf shape — 55.00
Roseville Pottery
  Fuschia, green, 1133–5 — 165.00
  Rosecraft, blue, 8″ h — 80.00
  Zephyr Lily, green, 1163–4½ — 75.00

CANDLE MOLD
Tin
  Six tubes, strap handle, arched bracket base, 10½″ h — 110.00
  Eight tubes, handle, 11″ h — 105.00

CANISTER
Franciscan, Duet Pattern, 10″ h — 95.00
Jeannette Glass, Delphite
  Coffee, 40 oz — 475.00
  Tea, 20 oz — 250.00
McKee Glassware
  Custard, 10 oz, round — 16.00
  Delphite, glass cover, 48 oz — 150.00
  Jadite, cov
    Cereal, dark, 10 oz — 98.00
    Coffee, dark, 10 oz — 98.00
    Tea, 48 oz — 90.00

CANISTER SET
Czechoslovakain, opalescent peach luster, matching spice set, vinegar bottle, and salt box — 325.00
Graniteware, cobalt and white, veined, price for six piece set — 195.00
Hall China, Wild Poppy Pattern (a.k.a. Poppy and Wheat), covered set of four — 600.00
Hull Pottery, Little Red Riding Hood
  Coffee — 650.00
  Flour — 650.00
  Salt — 1,000.00
  Sugar — 650.00
Pennsbury Pottery, black rooster decoration, 9″ h flour and sugar, 8″ h tea and coffee canisters — 400.00
Plastic, red sq container, white name, white lid, price for set of four — 15.00

Purinton Pottery
    Apple Pattern, four, sugar, coffee, and
    tea   **90.00**
    Pennsylvania Dutch Pattern, flour, cof-
    fee, sugar, tea   **175.00**

CANNER
Iron Horse Cold Pack, Rochester Can Co,
tin, wood handles, wire rack and lifter,
1930s, 13¾" d, 9" h   **65.00**
Rack, wire, rectangular   **15.00**

CAN OPENER
Riswell, combination can and bottle
opener   **12.00**
Sharp Easy, Premier Mfg Co., Detroit, MI,
patent 1922, combination can and bottle
opener, knife sharpener, wood handle,
iron top   **15.00**
Universal Dazey, cast iron, patent pend-
ing   **87.00**

CASSEROLE, COVERED
Aluminum, hand wrought, Crowmell,
hammered finish, glass liner, ftd   **12.00**
Bauer Pottery, Ring
    4¾" d, individual, Green   **35.00**
    7½" d, Ivory   **50.00**
Fiesta
    Cobalt Blue   **125.00**
    Light Green, 8½" d, Kitchen
    Kraft   **40.00**
    Yellow   **200.00**
Franciscan, Apple Pattern
    1 qt   **125.00**
    1½ qt   **85.00**
    Starburst Pattern, small   **35.00**
Hall China
    Carrot Pattern, (a.k.a. Carrot and Beet)
    Radiance   **55.00**
    Thick Rim, 10½" l   **125.00**
    Chinese Red Pattern, #1,
    Sundial   **55.00**
    Fantasy Pattern
        Sundial
            #1   **95.00**
            #4   **45.00**
        Thick Rim, 9" d   **35.00**
    Mulberry Pattern, 2 qt   **45.00**

Tools enlisted in the battle to open cans.
From the collection of Lyle Krug, Cedar
Rapids, Iowa.

Orange Poppy Pattern
    Oval, small   **45.00**
    Round, 8" d, cov   **42.00**
Red Dot Pattern (a.k.a. Eggshell Polka
Dot)
    Oval   **25.00**
    Round, 9" d   **25.00**
Serenade Pattern, (a.k.a. Eureka Sere-
nade)   **30.00**
Wild Poppy Pattern (a.k.a. Poppy and
Wheat)
    Oval
        9" l   **55.00**
        13" l, cov   **165.00**
    Radiance   **35.00**
Homer Laughlin
    Epicure Pattern, turquoise   **45.00**
    Harlequin Pattern, Maroon   **135.00**
    Kitchen Kraft, 8½" d, metal
    stand   **65.00**
    Riveria Pattern, Mauve Blue   **60.00**
Knowles, Edwin, Yorktown Pattern, yel-
low   **35.00**
Metlox Pottery, Homestead Provincial,
Poppytrail line, 10" d   **25.00**
Purinton Pottery, Apple Pattern,
oval   **24.00**
Shawnee Pottery
    Corn King, No. 74, large   **50.00**
    Lobster, French style, 2 qt   **30.00**

CASSEROLE, OPEN, (BAKER)
Hall China
    Autumn Leaf, French type   **8.00**
    Carrot Pattern, (a.k.a. Carrot and Beet),
    oval, 12½" l   **85.00**
    Red Dot Pattern (a.k.a. Eggshell Polka
    Dot), individual, handled   **30.00**
Harker Pottery, Deco–Dahlia Pattern, cov,
individual, set of four on rotating
rack   **50.00**
Homer Laughlin, Mexicana Pattern,
oval   **25.00**
McKee Glass, oval, Skokie Green, 7" l,
5" w   **16.00**
Morton Pottery, brown Rockingham mottled glaze, 5½" d, 1¾" h   **35.00**

CATALOGS
Albert Jordan Co, NY, 1929, 32 pages,
Agents for "Dick" and "Wusthof" brand of
butcher's and cook's cutlery, diamond
steels, steel hand forged cleavers, splitters,
knives, 8 × 11"   **28.00**
American China Co, Toronto, OH, illustrated price list of white granite and
semi–vitreous porcelain, dinnerware, teapots, bowls, etc., 26 pages, 6½ ×
8"   **40.00**
American Range Corp, Shakopee, MA,
c1930, 26 pages, Sanico Ranges Presents
Their "Tu–Tone" Ranges, 7½ ×
10½"   **18.00**

Apex Rotarex Electric Appliances, Cleveland, OH, vacuum cleaners, wringer and wringerless washers, ironers, folder binder, gilt embellishments, printed in green ink on coated stock, 1929, 18 pages, 9 x 11¼″ **32.00**

Ayer Antique China Co, Ayer, MA, Catalogue of Old Dark Blue Crockery & Old China, Delft, and Other Ware, 24 pages, 5¾ × 8¾″ **20.00**

Brecht Co, St Louis, MO, 1918, sausage making equipment, 78 pages, 7½ × 10½″ **40.00**

Brownell & Field Co, Providence, RI, lists of premiums given in exchange for coupons from Town & Country, Autocrat and Star Coffees and Teas, china services, glassware, silverware, miscellaneous kitchen wares, 1920, 30 pages, 5¼ × 8″ **15.00**

Butler Bros, Santa Claus Edition, 1922, 240 pages **110.00**

Crandall–Bennette Porter Co, 1907, 35 pages, oak dining room tables **48.00**

Dangler Stove Co, Cleveland, OH, 1904, High Grade Vapor Stoves and Ranges, The Klean, Kool Kitchen Ovens, Waffle Irons, Broilers, Toasters, Sad Iron Heaters, etc., 32 pages, 6¾ × 9″ **30.00**

D Eddy & Sons Co, Boston, MA, Eddy Refrigerators, 1925, 36 pages, 6 x 9¼″ **22.00**

Dent Hardware Co, Fullerton, A, 1911, Catalogue of Refrigerator Hardware & Hardware Specialties, Volume B, red and black leather binder **125.00**

Eppelsheimer & Co, New York, NY, c1928, chocolate molds, double sided rabbits, chickens, turkeys, cats, and other animals, Easter plaques, egg boxes, figures, crosses, hats, hearts, bottles, etc., 34 pages, 7 × 11¼″ **50.00**

Estate Stove Co, Hamilton, OH, Catalog No. 138, large half tones of white porcelain enameled ranges, two color coated stock, letter to dealer, retail price sheet, 1941, 24 pages, 8½ × 11 **42.00**

Excelsior Stove Mfg Co, Quincy, IL, c1924, Supplement No. 1 to Catalog 41 of National Stove & Ranges For Gas and Electric, 8 × 10½″ **24.00**

Farwell, Ozmun, Kirk & Co, St Paul, MN, Catalog No. B40, ice tools, meat grinders, sausage stuffers, notebook bound, hard cover, 1940, 242 pages, 9½ × 10½″ **25.00**

Frigidaire Div, General Motors Corp, Dayton, OH, presenting new series of Frigidaire Refrigerators, four color illustrations, coated stock, 1948, 16 pages, 8½ × 11″ **18.00**

General Electric Co, Schenectady, NY, 1933, Freedom, The Joy Of Living Electrically, The Health Kitchen, Refrigerators, Stoves, Dishwashers, etc., color illustrations, 28 pages, 5½ × 8″ **25.00**

General Electric Refrigerator, 1939, 8½ × 11″, black and white photos **15.00**

JC Penney 1972 Christmas, 472 pages **15.00**

James McCutheon & Co, New York, NY, c1929, Housekeeping linens, fancy table linens, hemstitched damask, Empire border, Italian library table scarfs, Mindanao embroidery, napkins, tea clothes, etc., 16 pages, 7½ × 10½″ **20.00**

Kalamazoo Stove Co, Kalamazoo, MI, 1931, 36 pages, Kalamazoo Sales Book, color illus of stones, ranges, etc., 8½ × 11″ **20.00**

Landers, Frary & Clark, New Britain, CT, Universal Vacuum Cleaners Catalog, inserts and brochures of small appliances, announcements, 1940, 25 pages, 8½ × 11½″ **80.00**

L Boardman & Son, Haddam, CT, Special Net Price List, Catalog D, flat table ware patterns, julep strainers, orange spoons, etc., 36 pages, 8¾ × 5¾″ **70.00**

Montgomery Ward
Christmas, 1947 **35.00**
Fall/Winter, 1953 **37.50**

Perfection Stove Co, Cleveland, OH, High Power Oil Burning Ranges and Cook Stoves, 60th Anniversary Catalogue, coated stock, c1940, 5¾ × 8¾ **24.00**

Pittston Stove Co, Pittston, PA, stoves and ranges, 1921, 43 pages, 7½ × 10½″ **21.00**

Richardson & Boynton, Philadelphia, PA, stoves and ranges, 1921, 62 pages, 7¾ × 10½″ **25.00**

Roberts & Mander Stove Co, Philadelphia, PA, electric ranges, half tones, heavy coated stock, silver trimmed pages and cover, wire bound stiff covers, 1935, 34 pages, 9 × 11″ **62.00**

Rock Island Stove Co, Rock Island, IL, No. 35, Riverside Stoves, heavy emb two color covers, coated stock, vignette illustrations of coal and wood ranges, gas combos, heaters, 1923, 80 pages, 5½ × 9¾″ **110.00**

Sears, Roebuck & Co, Christmas, 1933, 88 pages **200.00**

S & H Green Stamp Premiums, 1928 **25.00**

Spiegel, Fall/Winter, 1952 **37.50**

Sprague–Sells Corp, Chicago, IL, canning equipment, 1917, 351 pages, 8¾ × 11″ **44.00**

Spring Time At Woolworth's, 1953, 36 pages **25.00**

Sunray Stove Co, Delaware, OH, Catalog D, gas ranges and heaters, stiff two color covers, coated stock pages, c1910–15, 48 pages, 7 × 10¼″ **90.00**

Tappan Stove Co, Mansfield, OH, two color textured folder, coated stock pages, price sheet, 1935, 49 pages, 8½ × 11″ **42.00**

Thayer & Chandler Co, Chicago, IL, February Supplement No. 55, Bargain Sale, bowls, dishes, vases, etc., 1924, 16 pages, 8½ × 11″ **16.00**

Truman E Clark, Edella, PA, Birthday Spoons, illustrations with verse for zodiac signs, illustrations of actual size coffee spoons, 1907, 16 pages, 3¼ × 6¼″ **28.00**

Turner & Seymour Mfg Co, Torrington, CT, upholstery, hardware, curtain rods, Dover egg beaters, c1930, 92 pages, 9¼ × 11½″, $35.00

Universal Catalog Bureau, Dubuque, IA, Imperial Sash & Door Co, Universal Millwork Design Book No. 20, ceilings, breakfast nooks, furniture, flooring,

doors, windows, 1920, 396 pages, 6¾ × 10″, hard cover **45.00**

Vermont Farm Machine Co, Bellow Falls, VT, dairy and creamery supplies, sugar making apparatus, butter printers, 1883, 22 pages, 6 × 9″ **45.00**

W E Beckmann Bakers & Confectioners Supply Company, St Louis, MO, 1934, 34 pages, 8 × 10½″ **36.00**

Westinghouse All Electric Kitchens, 1936, 20 pages, 8½ × 11″ **100.00**

W F Dougherty & Sons, Philadelphia, PA, food service equipment, punch bowls, jars, ice cream and soda fountain accessories, 1926, 210 pages, 8¼ × 11″ **45.00**

Wincroft Stove Works, Middletown, PA, coal ranges, color illustrations of ten cast iron stoves showing two enameled color selections, chrome or nickel trim, c1932, 20 pages, 7¾ × 10¾″ **65.00**

Zanol Products Co, Cincinnati, OH, Pure Food Products, flavorings, desserts, soft drinks, 1930, 56 pages, 11 × 14″ **40.00**

Zero Refrigerator Co, Zero refrigerators, ice chests, etc., 1896, 32 pages, 3½ × 6″ **22.00**

CEREAL BOWL

China, Dionne Quintuplet, Marie sitting in high chair illustration, 1935, 5½″ d **20.00**

Plastic, advertising, Tony the Tiger, plastic, large orange paw base, 1981, 5″ d **15.00**

Roseville Pottery, sitting puppy decoration **45.00**

CHARGER

Redware, coggled rim, wear and glaze flakes, faint hairline **85.00**

CHEESE PRESS

Primitive, handmade
    Pine and hardwood, old patina, age cracks, 45¾″ h **90.00**
    Tin cylinder, three short conical legs, ring handle, 7⅛″ h **125.00**

CHEESE SIEVE

Basket, weave creating pointed star design, 15″ d, 19th C **225.00**

Copper, pierced, heart shape, three short feet **200.00**

Tin, cylindrical, punched design, feet and handles, 4″ d **100.00**

CHEESE SLICER

Cut–Rite, Wagner Ware, OH, No. 300, aluminum, 7″ l, 3⅛″ w **35.00**

Hacksaw shape, plated wire, loop handle, 6⅝″ l **5.00**

CHERRY PITTER

Enterprise No. 2, Enterprise Mfg Co, Philadelphia, PA, cast iron, tinned finish, adjustable **50.00**

Enterprise cherry stoners were either japanned or tinned (with tin commanding the higher price). The No. 12 stoner was intended to stone cherries with the least possible cutting or disfiguring. The most satisfactory results were obtained by dropping the cherries, one at a time, into the hopper immediately after the sweeper has passed the hole. According to the manufacturer, "with practice, one can become expert."

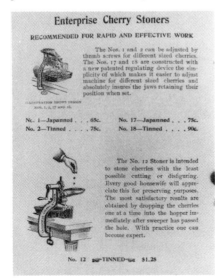

Enterprise Cherry Stoners
RECOMMENDED FOR RAPID AND EFFECTIVE WORK

New Brighton, Logan & Strobridge, cast iron, deep spout, turned wood handle **25.00**

Scott Mfg Co, Baltimore, MD, cast iron, three legs, mounted to wood board, 12″ l **50.00**

Watt No. 15 **60.00**

CHOCOLATE MOLD

Clamp type, two pieces, tin

Basket, 1½ × 4″ **35.00**

Cat, sitting, No. 14, 2¼ × 3″ **20.00**

Rabbit, standing, Germany, 6¼″ h **18.00**

Snowman with hat **45.00**

Teddy Bear **125.00**

Frame or book type

Christmas scene, 4½ × 8″ **30.00**

Hearts, two cavities, 6½ × 6″ **60.00**

Pencil, two cavities, 8½″ **20.00**

Turkey, two cavities, 4½ × 3½″ **50.00**

Tray type

Chickens and rabbits, six different rows, 11 × 17″ **95.00**

Hershey Bar, each section marked "Hershey" **20.00**

CHILDREN'S FEEDING DISH

Nippon China, girl and dog illustration, blue mark, 8″ d **75.00**

Roseville Pottery, sitting rabbit decoration **120.00**

COASTERS

Set of six coasters, papier mâché box, floral dec, marked "Occupied Japan" **18.00**

Set of eight coasters, Autumn Leaf Pattern accessory **45.00**

Single

Aluminum, hand wrought, Edison Institute Museum Entrance, Wendell August Forge, 3¼″ d **4.00**

Metlox Pottery

California Ivy Pattern, Poppytrail line **10.00**

California Provincial Pattern, Poppytrail line **12.00**

Nippon China, floral decoration, blue mark, 3¼″ d **28.00**

Stangl Pottery, Country Garden Pattern **10.00**

COFFEE BOILER

Graniteware

Chrysolite, swirl **175.00**

Gray **25.00**

Iris, swirl **285.00**

Red, swirl **650.00**

COFFEE DISPENSER

Depression Era Glassware, green glass container, wooden wall mounting bracket, black cover and dispenser **465.00**

COFFEE GRINDER

German, sheet and wrought steel, brass finials, tin hopper, wide flat handle with engraved foliage, marked "Zur Erinnerung," 10″ h **105.00**

Golden Rule Coffee, wall mounted, iron and wood, glass insert, 5½ × 4 × 17″ **115.00**

Landers, Frary & Clark, clamp on, metal **65.00**

Attractively decorated box-style iron and wood coffee mill carried the name, "American Logan and Robridge Franco" around the grinding chamber.

Very rare Duke cherry seeder with fancy hopper was made by the Reading Hardware Company of Reading, Pa. Courtesy of Phyllis and Jim Moffet of Modesto, Ill.

Unknown Maker, wooden
  Cylindrical, cast iron handle and
  grinder arm, well made replacement
  drawer, 11¼" h   135.00
  Dovetailed, poplar, pewter hopper, old
  soft finish, 9¼" h   125.00
COFFEEPOT
Fiesta
  Ivory   90.00
  Red   180.00
  Turquoise   135.00
  Yellow   135.00
Franciscan
  Apple Pattern   125.00
  Desert Rose Pattern   125.00
Graniteware
  Blue and White, large swirl   95.00
  Cobalt and White, chicken wire   95.00
  Gray, Columbian label   85.00
Hall China
  Deca Flip, Chinese red and
  white   55.00
  Floral Lattice (a.k.a. Flowerpot)   30.00
  Meltdown, green and ivory   40.00
  Panel   30.00
  Queen, Chinese red   75.00
  Red Poppy, Daniel   55.00
  Rounded Terrace, Rose White   30.00
  Terrace, Gold Label line   37.00
  Tulip   35.00
  Waverly (a.k.a. Crest), large   45.00
Knowles, Edwin, Deanna Pattern, red and
blue stripes   40.00
Metal, Autumn Leaf Pattern acces-
sory   75.00
Metlox Pottery
  Homestead Provincial, Poppytrail 30.00
  Provincial Fruit Pattern, Poppytrail
  line   45.00
  Red Rooster, Poppytrail line   40.00
Morton Pottery
  Rockingham brown glaze, ornate emb
  top and bottom   90.00

**Coffee roaster was placed over an open "eye"
on the stove, after a stove lid was removed
from the range. The crank was turned con-
tinuously until the beans were roasted.
Photo courtesy of Phyllis and Jim Moffet,
Modesto, Ill.**

Woodland Glaze, yellow ware, brown
  and green spatter over transparent
  glaze, 8 cup   85.00
Purinton Pottery, Apple Pattern   25.00
Tin, removable drip top, black wood han-
dle, pewter finial, 9¾" h   75.00
Tinware, decorated, 10½" h, original dark
brown japanning, floral dec, yellow, two
shades of red, white, and green, minor
wear, 10½" h   3,100.00
COFFEE URN
Copper, nickeled finish, barrel shape, two
gallon capacity   200.00
Tin, brass spigot, 15½" h   115.00
COLANDER
Graniteware
  Blue, swirl   125.00
  Blue and Gray, swirl   75.00
  Emerald, swirl   150.00
Tin, heart shape, circle feet,
4¼" h   130.00
CONDIMENT SET
Black Memorabilia
  Mammy and Mose, syrup, salt, and
  pepper, F & F   85.00
  Pickaninny, ketchup and mustard,
  matching holder, ceramic   65.00
COOKBOOKS
Adams, Ron and T. Wilmoth, *And For
Dessert,* WA, 1974, 129 pages   25.00
Alberson, Sarah, *The Blue Sea Cookbook,*
NY, 1968, 290 pages, seafood recipes and
methods   17.50
Allen, Ida Bailey, *Around The World Cook
Book,* Nucoa, Best Foods, 1934, 96
pages   17.50
Ashley, Roberta, *Cool Cooking,* NY, 1972,
176 pages, first printing, color card
covers, photos and biographies of rock
stars and their recipes   55.00
Bailey, Adrian, *The Blessings of Bread,* NY,
1975, 287 pages   45.00
Bartlett, Jonathan, *The Peasant Gourmet,*
NY, 1975, 146 pages   16.50
Batterberry, A. & M., *Bloomingdale's Book
of Entertaining,* NY, 1976, 208
pages   25.00
Bauer, Fred, *Cake–Art–Craft, Cake Decorating, Designs, and Instructions,* Chicago,
1924, 140 pages, first edition, folding
color plate, numerous black and white illustrations, color pictorial cloth
covers   100.00
Blankensteen, Jane, *Nothing Beets Borscht,*
NY, 1974, 242 pages, Russian reci-
pes   25.00
Brown, Helen Evans, et al, *The Virginia
City Cook Book,* LA, Ward Ritchie Press,
1961, 148 pages, illustrations and recipes   25.00
Brown, Nellie, *Recipes From Old Hundred,*

200 Years of New England Cooking, NY, 1939, 236 pages **20.00**

Butler, Cleora, *Cleora's Kitchens; Eight Decades of Great American Food,* OK, 1986, 213 pages **45.00**

Claiborne, Craig and Pierre Franey, *Veal Cookery,* NY, 1978, 229 pages **25.00**

Cobb, Vicki, *Arts and Crafts You Can Eat,* PA, 1974, 127 pages **15.00**

Dalsass, Diana, *Miss Mary's Down Home Cooking,* NY, 1984, 208 pages **19.00**

D'Ermo, Dominique, *The Modern Pastry Chef's Guide To Professional Baking,* NY, 1962, 302 pages **85.00**

Diggs, L. J., *Vinegar,* SF, 1988, history, lore, production methods and uses **25.00**

Dunne, Ida Lee, *The American Hostess Cook Book,* NY, 1949, 544 pages, recipes, menus, biographical sketches of famous hostesses **45.00**

Ellis, Audrey and M. Cavaiani, *Farmhouse Kitchen,* Chicago, 1973, 250 pages **20.00**

Friedman, Sara Ann, *Celebrating The Wild Mushroom,* NY, 1986, 265 pages, first edition, heavily illustrated **20.00**

Gibbons, Barbara, *Slim Gourmet Sweets and Treats,* NY, 1982, 264 pages **17.00**

Hansen, Marilyn, *Cooking By The Calendar, A Family Weekly Cook Book,* NY, 1978, 308 pages **18.00**

Heath, Ambrose
    From Creel to Kitchen, 1939, 110 pages, 175 recipes for fresh water fish **25.00**
    Good Sweets and Ices, 1947, 124 pages **22.00**
    Soups and Soup Garnishes, 1957, 93 pages **20.00**

Hood, H. P. and Sons, *The New Hood Cook Book,* 1941, 394 pages, color illustrations **35.00**

Kite, Dorothy Jackson, *The Firehouse Cookbook,* NY, 1975, 209 pages **25.00**

Langdon, Amelie, *Just For Two,* Minneapolis, 1903, 224 pages, illustrated, stained cover **28.00**

MacDonald, Duncan and R. Sagendorph, *Rain, Hail, and Baked Beans,* NY, 1958, 214 pages, authentic New England recipes **22.00**

MacFadden, Bernard, *Physical Culture Cook Book,* NY, 1929, 372 pages, original dust jacket **30.00**

Matson, Ruth, *Cooking By The Garden Calendar,* NY, 1955, 258 pages, first edition **20.00**

McBride, Mary Margaret, *Encyclopedia of Cooking,* IL, 1938, twelve volumes, 3,006 pages, hard cover **65.00**

McCracken, Mary Lou, *Deep South Natural Foods Cookbook,* PA, 1975, 214 pages **19.00**

Murphy, Margaret, *Fondue, Chafing Dish & Casserole Cookery,* NY, 1969, 290 pages **15.00**

Parker, Dorothy, *The Wonderful World of Yogurt,* NY, 1972, 145 pages **10.00**

Payne, Alma, *Jingle Bells and Pastry Shells,* OH, 1968, 318 pages **25.00**

Penrose, Virginia, *Chester County Cookery,* PA, 1950, 259 pages **25.00**

Pitkin, Mrs. Eliza, *Invalid Cookery,* Chicago, 1880, 127 pages **65.00**

Read, Jean, *McCall's Book of Entertaining,* NY, 1979, 291 pages, first edition, recipes by Mary Eckley, Food Editor of *McCall's,* helpful entertaining hints **20.00**

Rushing, Lilith and Ruth Voss, *The Cake Cook Book,* PA, 1965, 200 pages **20.00**

Ryder, Elmira, *A Cook Book for Nurses,* Worcester, MA, 1901, 83 pages, original gilt stamped cloth **55.00**

Smith, Dawn, *Tried and True Grit Recipes,* 1980, card covers **25.00**

Standard, Stella, *The Art of Fruit Cookery,* NY, 1964, 276 pages, 500 classic and original recipes **22.00**

Stapleton, Daisy Mae, *Daisy Mae's Favorite Recipes,* NY, 1958, 150 pages, Tennessee cook, state fair winners **25.00**

Stewart, Katie, *The Joy of Eating,* MD, 1977, 288 pages, historic color plates and illustrations from ancient Greece to Victorian era **30.00**

Turgeon, Charlotte, *Cooking For Christmas,* NY, 1950, 116 pages **15.00**

Waldo, Myra, *The Diners' Club Cookbook, NY, 1959, 241 pages* **15.00**

Wason, Betty, *Bride In The Kitchen,* NY, 1964, 352 pages **20.00**

Whymper, Robert, *The Manufacture of Confectionery,* NY, 1923, 257 pages **45.00**

Wihlfart, Julius, *A Treatise On Baking,* NY, 1953, 468 pages **85.00**

Wilford, Charles, *Adventures In Sourdough Cooking and Baking,* SF, 1971, 210 pages, card covers **17.50**

Worth, Helen, *Hostess Without Help,* VA, 1971, 217 pages **20.00**

Zavin, Theodora and Freda Stuart, *The Working Wives' Cook Book,* NY, 1963, 164 pages **15.00**

COOKBOOK BOOKLETS

A Calendar of Desserts, 48 pgs, 1940 **5.00**

All About Home Baking, General Foods, 144 pgs, 1933 **6.00**

Arm & Hammer Baking Soda, Good Things to Eat–Tested Recipes, 32 pgs, 1936 **10.00**

Aunt Ellen, Griswold, 1928 **15.00**

Betty Crocker
    Dinner In A Dish, 152 pgs, 1965 **7.00**

1950s booklet for Spry listed Chocolate Rapture Cake and Fudge Frosted Square Layer Cake among the 10 cakes that husbands liked best.

Let's Eat Outdoors, 27 pgs, 1969 **3.00**
Bewley's Best Bakes Better, 8 × 6" **10.00**
Calumet Baking Powder Baking Book, 1931 **4.00**
Ceresota Flour, 32 pgs, 9 × 5", 1930s **18.00**
Certo Recipes For Making Jams & Jellies, 31 pgs, 1937 **4.00**
Chiquita Banana Presents 18 Recipes, 18 pgs, 1951 **6.00**
Cottolene Shortening Recipes, 1905 **15.00**
Cox's Delicious Recipes, 30 pgs, 1933 **4.00**
Crisco Better Baking, 16 pgs, 9 × 11", 1967 **5.00**
Dr King's New Discovery Electric Bitters Prize Cookbook, 1900 **15.00**
Eline's Old Style Cocoa, c1910 **5.00**
Gold Medal Flour Cook Book, 1917, 74 pgs **10.00**
Grand National, 1928 **10.00**
Heinz Book of Salads, 95 pgs, 1925 **10.00**
Jell-O The Dainty Dessert, 4½ × 4½", c1915 **25.00**
Karo Syrup, 1910, 47 pgs, Leyendecker cov **25.00**
Kellogg's, 1978 **6.00**
Knox Dainty Desserts For Dainty People, 41 pgs, 1915 **12.00**
Magic Baking Powder, 32 pages **15.75**
Mary Dunbar's New Cook Book, 1933, Jewel Tea Co **15.00**

Maxwell House Coffee, 22 pgs, 1927 **7.00**
Occident's Baking Made Easy, 1931 **5.00**
Out of Alaska's Kitchens **15.00**
Pillsbury Silver Anniversary Bake-Off, 92 pgs, 1974 **7.00**
Pure Food Cookbook, Mary J Lincoln, 77 pages **45.00**
Pyrex Prize Recipes, 128 pgs, 1953 **5.00**
Rival Crock-Pot Cooking, 208 pgs, 1975 **7.00**
Royal Cookbook, 65 pages **27.50**
Spry Shortening Cookbook, Aunt Jenny's Favorite Recipes, color illus, 50 pgs, 1930s **12.00**
Standard Brands Cookbook, 65 pages **27.50**
Sunkist Recipes For Everyday, 35 pgs, 1933 **3.00**
The Gold Medal Sandwich Book Dedicated to the Earl of Sandwich **4.00**
Walter Baker Choice Recipes, 1923, 64 pgs **10.00**
Wrought Iron Range Co, St Louis, MO, Home Comfort Cook Book, general instructions, canning, 1,000 recipes, first 24 pages are catalog of ranges and heaters, 1925, 221 pgs, 6 × 8 ½" **20.00**

COMPOTE
Aluminum, hand wrought, Wild Rose pattern, 5" h, Continental Hand Wrought Silverlook, marked "No. 1083" **15.00**
American Art Pottery, ftd, dark green bisque, high gloss spatter, 10" d, 6" h **15.00**
Cliftwood Art Pottery, four dolphins support bowl, old rose glaze, 8½" d, 6" h **75.00**
McCoy Pottery, Garden Club, coral, marked "McCoy USA," 1957 **12.00**
Woodenware
   7½" h, 8½ × 8½" sq, worn brown finish, blue stripes, late **40.00**
   12" d, 5¾" h, treen, old worn red, black, and greenish exterior paint, gray scrubbed interior finish **550.00**

COOKIE BOARD
Cast Iron
   Bird design, oval, 3¼ × 5¼" **150.00**
   Cornucopia and fruit design, oblong, 4¼ × 5¾" **75.00**
   Pineapple design, oblong, 4 × 5½" **225.00**
Wood
   Cat on one side, equestrian figure on other, worn, age cracks are scarred by old iron repairs on ends, 6½ × 10" **80.00**
   Four part design, rect, old finish, 3¼" w, 4¼" h **40.00**
   Man, full figure, carved beech, metal edging, old patina, minor age cracks, 6¾" w, 18" h **360.00**

Medallion, almond shaped medallion with roses, cornucopias, and equestrian figure, banner "Genl. Jackson, New Orleans," attributed to Conger, weathered walnut board, old dark finish, full length glued crack, 14½″ h, 26″ h **1,100.00**

Mermaid, primitive relief carving, 9″ w, 9½″ h **45.00**

Seahorse design, 8 × 12½″ **50.00**

Simple relief carved animal, refinished, round, 14½″ d **50.00**

COOKIE CUTTER

Eagle, tin
  4½″ h, exceptionally fine detail, skinny **55.00**
  5¼″ h, crimped wings and tail **40.00**
  6½″ l **85.00**
  9⅜″ l, good detail **85.00**
Goat, tin, exceptionally fine detail, 4¾″ h **90.00**
Heart, crimped diamond, tin, 4″ h **30.00**
Horse, tin
  4¾″ h, running, exceptionally fine detail **90.00**
  12¾″ h **225.00**
Lady, tin, wearing hat and long dress, strap handle with rolled edges, 5¼″ h **35.00**
Man and Woman, tin, exceptionally fine detail, 5½″ h, price for pair **2,050.00**
Peacock, tin, exceptionally fine detail, 4½″ h **60.00**
Rabbit, 7½″ l, tin, good detail **85.00**
Roller, Guirier, tin, wire, three rollers, c1930, original box **40.00**
Squirrel, tin, large crimped edge tail, loose seams, light rust, 5½″ l **105.00**

COOKIE JAR

ABC Pottery
  Cat **65.00**
  Chick, yellow **65.00**
  Churn Boy **225.00**
  Cookie Truck **65.00**
  Kittens on Yarn **65.00**
  Pig-in-Poke **65.00**
  Pig, strawberries **95.00**
  Poodle, maroon **95.00**
  Recipe Jar **135.00**
Abingdon Pottery
  Granny
    Green **135.00**
    White **225.00**
  Hobby Horse **250.00**
  Humpty Dumpty, No. 163 **185.00**
  Jack In Box, 11″ h, No. 611 **295.00**
  Jack-o'-lantern **265.00**
  Little Bo Peep **375.00**
  Little Miss Muffet **295.00**
  Money Sack, No. 588 **80.00**
  Pineapple, No. 664 **75.00**

Three Bears **65.00**
Windmill **225.00**
Applause, 57 Chevy **60.00**
Bauer Pottery, Ring pattern, orange-red **125.00**
Brayton Laguna, Mammy, blue **700.00**
Brush
  Davy Crockett **250.00**
  Hen on Nest **120.00**
  Squirrel on Log **85.00**
F & F
  Aunt Jemima, figural, 1950s, 11½″ h **300.00**
  Keebler Elf **125.00**
Franciscan, Apple Pattern **190.00**
Hall China
  Carrot Pattern, (a.k.a. Carrot and Beet), Zeisel **150.00**
  Chinese Red Pattern, Sundial **225.00**
  Fantasy Pattern, Five Band **225.00**
  Wild Poppy Pattern (a.k.a. Poppy and Wheat), Five Band **225.00**
Hull Pottery, Little Red Riding Hood
  Closed basket **300.00**
  Open basket, gold stars on apron, pink flowers on skirt **325.00**
  Round basket, poinsettias on apron **350.00**
Lefton, Santa **75.00**
McCoy Pottery
  Apple, red **42.00**
  Cat on black coal bucket **275.00**
  Coke Jug **75.00**
  Cookie Stove, black **22.00**
  Dalmatian **425.00**
  Duck, yellow, shortbill, 1976 **60.00**
  Happy Face, original box **45.00**
  Hocus Rabbit **45.00**
  Indian Head, commemorative issue **195.00**
  Koala Bear **85.00**
  Lamb, basketweave base **45.00**
  Little Miss Muffet **65.00**
  Mammy, white **125.00**
  Mother Goose **98.00**
  Mr & Mrs Owl **160.00**
  Nabisco **125.00**
  Nursery Rhymes **65.00**
  Pineapple **90.00**
  Puppy with Sign **85.00**
  Raggedy Ann **90.00**
  Stump, frog finial **38.00**
  Tepee **195.00**
  Touring Car **75.00**
Metlox
  Lion **350.00**
  Scottie
    Black **150.00**
    White **275.00**
Morton, hen with chick **50.00**
Mosaic Tile, Mammy, blue **450.00**
National Silver, Mammy **325.00**

Pearl China, Cooky and Mammy, price
for pair   1,300.00
Purinton Pottery, Apple Pattern   38.00
Ransburg, Davy Crockett   125.00
Red Wing, Chef, yellow   60.00
RRP
  Hootie Owl   75.00
  Sheriff Pig   125.00
Shawnee Pottery
  Basket of Fruit   85.00
  Clown, seal   225.00
  Dutch Boy, gold trim, minor wear to
  gold   255.00
  Owl, gold trim   275.00
  Puss N' Boots   150.00
  Sailor Boy, blue stars, black collar and
  tie, slight paint wear   115.00
  Smiley Pig
    Chrysanthemums   225.00
    Shamrocks   175.00
    Tulips   185.00
Treasure Craft
  Cookie Chef   65.00
  Hobo   65.00
  Stagecoach   95.00

COOKIE PRESS
Aluminum, metal plunger, interchange-
able tips, original box   10.00

The Goodell Manufacturing Company of
Antrim, N.H. produced this very rare machine for cutting green corn from the cob. It
has a quick release to reset the cutter head
and very effectively removes the kernels
from the cob. Marked on the main frame,
"Keystone Corn Cutter," the device was patented in 1883. Courtesy of Phyllis and Jim
Moffet of Modesto, Ill.

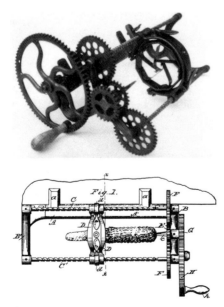

Tin, wood plunger
  Star shape, 10½" l   35.00

COOLER
Stoneware
  21½" h, ovoid, applied shoulder handles, high neck, wheel turned ridges,
  remains of applied decorative detail on
  shoulder between handles, cobalt blue
  quill work flourishes, old chips and fir-
  ing cracks   350.00
  23½" h, ovoid, stenciled cobalt blue label "Alderman and Scott, Belpre,
  Ohio," and "16" in wreath, double ear
  handles, applied tooled ornaments
  around bung hole, hairlines and repair   825.00
  26½" h, cobalt blue slip simple flower
  and flourish, imp screw head design at
  double ear handles and bung hole,
  chips, hairline on one handle   200.00

CORN COB HOLDERS
Bakelite handles, original box   30.00
Plastic handles shaped like ears of corn,
yellow, metal fork type holder, price for
pair   1.00
Wooden handles, metal fork type holder,
price for pair   1.00

CORN CUTTER
Tin, half cylinder, some damage to sharp
teeth   18.00
Wood, hand forged blade, carved wood
handle   12.00

CORNUCOPIA
Roseville Pottery
  Columbine, 7" h   65.00
  Foxglove, blue, 166–6, 2/135   45.00
  Snowberry, 6" h   45.00
  White Rose, blue, double, 145–8,
  1/113   85.00

CRAB BAKING SET
McCoy Pottery, set of six dishes, original
box   30.00

CREAM BUCKET
Graniteware, gray, mottled, tin lid, original label   100.00
Tin, original domed lid, slightly
battered   80.00

CREAMER
Blue Ridge
  Crab Apple Pattern, Colonial shape, in-
  dividual   20.00
  French Peasant Pattern, pedestal
  base   70.00
  Sungold #1 Pattern, Candlewick
  shape   12.00
Ceramic, figural, cow, marked "Occupied
Japan"   25.00
Cliftwood Art Pottery, chocolate drip
glaze, 3" d, 4" h   35.00

Fiesta
  Stick
    Cobalt Blue 30.00
    Red 16.00
  Table
    Cobalt Blue 25.00
    Ivory 14.00
    Turquoise 14.00
Franciscan
  Apple Pattern 25.00
  Coronado Swirl Pattern, gray,
  satin 22.00
Homer Laughlin
  Epicure Pattern, turquoise 15.00
  Harlequin Pattern
    Individual
      Maroon 22.00
      Turquoise 10.00
      Yellow 10.00
    Large, Medium Green 40.00
  Mexicana Pattern 20.00
Hull Pottery, Little Red Riding Hood,
pour through head 275.00
McCoy Pottery, sitting dog, green,
1950s 28.00
Metlox Pottery
  Aztec Pattern, Poppytrail line 18.00
  California Provincial Pattern, Poppytrail
  line 6.00
  Provincial Fruit Pattern, Poppytrail
  line 7.00
Pennsbury Pottery
  Amish Woman's Head, 2″ h 13.00
  Red Rooster, 2″ h 15.00
Shawnee Pottery
  Corn King 20.00
  Tulips 30.00
Tinware, decorated, 4⅛″ h, worn dark
brown japanning, red, green, and yellow
floral dec, 4⅛″ h 450.00
CREAMER AND SUGAR, COV
Aluminum, hand wrought, cup shape,
matching tray, World Hand Forge, price
for three piece set 12.00
American Art Pottery, stylized flowers,
blue, peach spray glaze, 3″ h 18.00
Bauer Pottery
  Monterey Pattern, dinnerware line pro-
  duced from 1936 until 1945, individ-
  ual, Ivory 38.00
  Ring, extensive line introduced in
  1931, Light Blue 35.00
Blue Ridge
  Rose Marie Pattern, pedestal 90.00
  Rustic Plaid Pattern, Skyline shape 7.00
Franciscan
  Apple Pattern, individual size 50.00
  Desert Rose Pattern 50.00
  Duet Pattern 18.00
  Starburst Pattern 30.00

Hall China
  Autumn Leaf, ruffled–D 26.00
  Chinese Red Pattern
    Daniel 75.00
    Morning 95.00
  Fantasy Pattern, Morning 75.00
  Pastel Morning Glory Pattern (a.k.a.
  Pink Morning Glory), D–style 55.00
  Serenade Pattern, (a.k.a. Eureka Sere-
  nade) 29.00
  Wildfire Pattern, D–style 38.50
  Wild Poppy Pattern (a.k.a. Poppy and
  Wheat), New York 110.00
Harker Pottery, Colonial Lady Pat-
tern 20.00
Homer Laughlin
  Dogwood Pattern 10.00
  Riveria Pattern, Light Green 14.00
Hull Pottery, Little Red Riding Hood, side
pour 325.00
Knowles, Edwin, Deanna Pattern, cov,
light blue 25.00
Metlox Pottery
  California Ivy Pattern, Poppytrail
  line 15.00
  Homestead Provincial, Poppytrail
  line 25.00
  Navajo Pattern, Poppytrail line 30.00
Stangl Pottery, Country Garden Pat-
tern 25.00
CREAM SIPHON
Aluminum, Marvel, fits in bottle and si-
phons cream into cream pitcher or other
vessel 6.00
CREAM TOP SPOON
Fritchett Bros Dairy, Pat Applied For,
used with cream top bottle 12.00
CROCK, STONEWARE
10½″ h, brushed cobalt blue floral deco-
ration and "3", stains 160.00

**This stoneware crock, with a decorative blue
bird on a branch, was made by J. Norton &
Company, Bennington, Vermont 1858–61.**

11¼″ h, imp label "Ottman Bros. Fort Edwards, NY 4," cobalt blue slip dec of bird on branch, crack in back   **200.00**

22½″ h, cobalt blue quill work design with leaves and "20," Red Wing Pottery   **165.00**

CRUMBER AND BRUSH

Aluminum, hand wrought

   Hand Wrought Rodney Kent, No. 444   **30.00**

   Wendell August Forge, zinnia design, No. 705   **28.00**

CUSTARD CUP

Graniteware, cobalt and white, large swirl   **65.00**

Hall China

   Carrot Pattern, (a.k.a. Carrot and Beet), thick rim   **20.00**

   Fantasy Pattern, Thick Rim   **20.00**

   No. 488 Pattern   **20.00**

   Orange Poppy Pattern   **5.25**

   Red Dot Pattern (a.k.a. Eggshell Polka Dot)   **18.00**

   Red Poppy Pattern, Radiance   **16.50**

   Wild Poppy Pattern (a.k.a. Poppy and Wheat), Radiance   **20.00**

Harker Pottery, Red Apple Pattern   **6.00**

Sponge spatter, blue and white, rim chip, 2¾″ h   **50.00**

CUTTING BOARD

Cherry, figural, elephant, 8 × 13″   **85.00**

Hardwood, figural, fish, 12″ l   **40.00**

Maple, figural, pig, c1930, 9 × 19″   **15.00**

❧ D

DEEP FRYER

Cast Iron, hook type handle to hold frying basket, patent date July 8, 1879 embossed on side   **100.00**

Cast Iron, Griswold Mfg Co, Erie, PA, basket, No. 1003   **90.00**

DEMITASSE CREAMER AND SUGAR

Franciscan Ware, Coronado Swirl Pattern

   Gray, satin   **15.00**

   Turquoise, glossy   **15.00**

DEMITASSE CUP AND SAUCER

American Art Pottery, stylized flower on cup, flat blossom on saucer, gray, pink spray glaze, 3″ h   **14.00**

Fiesta, Cobalt Blue   **50.00**

Franciscan

   Apple Pattern   **42.00**

   Coronado Swirl Pattern

      Coral, glossy   **35.00**

      White, satin   **35.00**

      Yellow, satin   **15.00**

   Desert Rose Pattern   **35.00**

Occupied Japan, white, yellow and red flowers   **10.00**

DEMITASSE POT

Fiesta Ware, Red   **275.00**

Franciscan Ware, Coronado Swirl Pattern, turquoise, glossy   **75.00**

DINNERWARE

BAUER POTTERY

La Linda Pattern, dinnerware line produced from 1939 until 1959

   Cup and Saucer, Green   **20.00**

   Custard, Turquoise   **8.00**

   Plate

      6″ d, bread and butter, Ivory   **6.00**

      7½″ d, salad, Green   **10.00**

      9″ d, dinner, Chartreuse   **15.00**

Monterey Pattern, dinnerware line produced from 1936 until 1945

   Plate

      6″ d, bread and butter, Turquoise Blue   **10.00**

      10½″ d, dinner, Orange–red   **30.00**

Ring Pattern, extensive line introduced in 1931

   Berry Bowl, Yellow   **12.00**

   Cereal Bowl, Dark Blue   **15.00**

   Cup and Saucer, Burgundy   **20.00**

   Custard Cup, Black   **20.00**

   Plate

      6″ d, bread and butter, Yellow   **10.00**

      7½″ d, salad, Light Blue   **15.00**

      10″ d, dinner, Orange–red   **25.00**

   Soup Bowl, 7½″ d, Burgundy   **25.00**

BLUE RIDGE DINNERWARE

Carnival Pattern, Candlewick shape

   Soup Bowl   **10.00**

   Vegetable Bowl   **12.00**

Christmas Tree Pattern, Colonial shape, plate   **55.00**

Chrysanthemum Pattern

   Cup and Saucer   **9.00**

   Plate

      7″ d, salad   **4.00**

      9¾″ d, dinner   **10.00**

   Soup, flat, 8″ d   **10.00**

Corsage Pattern, Astor shape, soup bowl   **16.00**

County Fair Pattern, Colonial shape, salad plate   **15.00**

Muriel Pattern, demitasse cup and saucer   **32.00**

Normandie Pattern, Skyline shape, cereal bowl   **18.00**

Pembrooke Pattern, Colonial shape

   Bowl, 5½″ d   **3.25**

   Plate, 9″ d   **4.75**

Red Rooster Pattern, Skyline shape

   Cup   **20.00**

   Plate

      6″ d   **8.00**

9″ d	25.00
Platter, 11″ l	22.00
Saucer	6.00

Rock Rose Pattern, Colonial shape, eggcup 18.00

Sunflower Pattern, Colonial shape, plate, 10″ d 8.50

Sungold #1 Pattern, Candlewick shape

Cup and Saucer	12.00
Fruit Bowl	4.00
Plate, 10″ d, dinner	10.00
Soup, flat, 8″ d	10.00

Sunny Spray Pattern, Skyline shape

Cup and Saucer	3.00
Juice	7.00
Water	12.00

Waltz Time Pattern

Bowl, 6″ d	8.00
Cup and Saucer	10.00
Plate	
7½″ sq	15.00
10½″ d, dinner	15.00

Yellow Nocturne Pattern, Colonial shape

Bowl, 5½″ d	8.00
Cup and Saucer	6.00
Plate	
6″ d, bread and butter	3.50
9¼″ d, luncheon	8.00
10″ d, dinner	9.00
Salad Bowl, 9¼″ d	17.00
Soup, flat	10.00

FIESTA

Bowl

4¾″ d	
Cobalt Blue	25.00
Dark Green	20.00
Light Green	15.00
5½″ d, fruit	
Cobalt Blue	20.00
Light Green	15.00
Red	20.00
Yellow	18.00
6″ d, dessert	
Chartreuse	50.00
Gray	50.00
Light Green	22.00
Rose	50.00
Turquoise	50.00
8½″ d, Cobalt Blue	30.00

Cream Soup

Cobalt Blue	40.00
Green	30.00
Rose	65.00

Cup

Chartreuse	18.00
Cobalt Blue	20.00
Dark Green	18.00
Gray	24.00
Turquoise	18.00
Yellow	18.00

Deep Plate

Dark Green	35.00
Gray	35.00
Light Green	24.00
Medium Green	75.00
Red	27.00
Turquoise	22.00
Yellow	22.00

Demitasse Cup and Saucer

Rose	350.00
Yellow	55.00

Egg Cup

Cobalt Blue	35.00
Dark Green	100.00
Gray	140.00
Light Green	30.00
Yellow	30.00

Juice Tumbler

Cobalt Blue	30.00
Green	20.00
Ivory	25.00
Turquoise	20.00

Mug

Cobalt Blue	60.00
Gray	70.00
Ivory, gold letters, hairline	15.00
Medium Green	80.00
Red	65.00

Onion Soup, cov, Ivory 450.00

Plate

6″ d	
Cobalt Blue	5.00
Ivory	6.00
Medium Green	15.00
Red	4.50
Rose	9.00
Turquoise	5.00
7″ d	
Gray	10.00
Medium Green	25.00
Rose	10.00
Turquoise	6.00
Yellow	7.00
9″ d	
Chartreuse	10.00
Cobalt Blue	18.00
Dark Green	10.00
Gray	19.00
Ivory	18.00
Light Green	10.00
Medium Green	35.00
Red	12.50
Rose	18.00
Turquoise	10.00
Yellow	10.00
10″ d	
Light Green	20.00
Medium Green	80.00
Red	25.00
Turquoise	20.00

10½″ d, grill, Cobalt Blue	40.00
Saucer	
Chartreuse	4.00
Cobalt Blue	4.00
Ivory	3.00
Red	4.00
Turquoise	2.00
Yellow	3.00
Sugar, cov, Cobalt Blue	25.00
Syrup, Ivory	195.00
Water Tumbler	
Cobalt Blue	40.00
Green	40.00
Ivory	50.00
Red	55.00
Turquoise	50.00
Yellow	40.00

FRANCISCAN

Apple Pattern, introduced in 1940.

Casserole, cov, individual	45.00
Cereal Bowl, 6″ d	12.00
Cup and Saucer	20.00
Fruit Bowl, 5″ d	10.00
Eggcup	15.00
Mug, 7 oz	95.00
Plate	
6″ d, bread and butter	6.00
8″ d, salad	12.00
9½″ d, dinner	16.00
10½″ d	18.00
Soup Bowl, 5½″ d, ftd	25.00
Tumbler, 6 oz	40.00
Wine Glass	18.00

Coronado Swirl Pattern, produced from 1936 until 1956

Cream Soup, coral, satin	22.00
Cup and Saucer, maroon, glossy	18.00
Plate	
6″ d, turquoise, glossy	3.00
7½″ d, coral, satin	5.00
10″ d, turquoise, glossy	8.00
Teacup, maroon, glossy	9.00

Desert Rose Pattern, introduced in 1941

Cereal Bowl, 6″ d	20.00
Cup and Saucer	15.00
Fruit Bowl, 5″ d	10.00
Mug, 12 oz	45.00
Plate	
6½″ d, bread and butter	6.00
8″ d, salad	11.00
9½″ d, luncheon	12.00
10½″ d, dinner	15.00
Sherbet, ftd	15.00
Soup, flat	14.00
Tumbler, 10 oz	40.00
Wine Glass	18.00

Duet Pattern, introduced in 1956

Cup and Saucer	7.00
Plate	
6″ d, bread and butter	5.00

7¼″ d, salad	9.00
10″ d, dinner	12.00
13″ d, chop	18.00

Ivy Pattern, introduced in 1948

Cereal Bowl, 7½″ d	25.00
Cup and Saucer, jumbo	65.00
Fruit Bowl, 5″ d	8.00
Mug, 4¼″ h	22.00
Plate, 6″ d, bread and butter	6.00
Sherbet	12.00
Soup Bowl, flat	30.00
Tumbler, Libbey, hp dec	14.00

Starburst Pattern, introduced in 1954

Cup and Saucer	18.00
Fruit Bowl	12.00
Plate	
6″ d, bread and butter	8.00
7½″ d, salad	10.00
10″ d, dinner	15.00
Salad Bowl	45.00
Soup Bowl, 7¼″ d	15.00

Trio Pattern

Cup and Saucer	12.50
Fruit Bowl	9.00
Plate	
6″ d, bread and butter	6.00
8″ d, salad	10.00
10″ d, dinner	15.00

HALL CHINA

Autumn Leaf, premium for the Jewel Tea Company, produced 1933 until 1978

Berry Bowl, 5½″ d	4.00
Cereal Bowl, 6½″ d	8.50
Cream Soup	18.00
Cup and Saucer	8.00
Custard Cup, Radiance	5.50
Mug, footed	75.00
Plate	
6″ d, bread and butter	5.00
8″ d, salad	8.50
9″ d, dinner	6.00
Salad Bowl	14.00
Soup Bowl, 8½″ d	10.00

Mulberry Pattern

Berry Bowl, 5¾″ l	6.50
Cereal Bowl, 6″ l	15.00
Cup and Saucer	12.00
Plate	
6″ l, bread and butter	5.00
8″ l, salad	7.50
11″ l, dinner	12.00

Pastel Morning Glory Pattern (a.k.a. Pink Morning Glory), produced in the late 1930s

Berry Bowl, 5½″ d	8.50
Cereal Bowl, 6″ d	20.00
Cup and Saucer	15.00
Custard Cup	20.00
Plate	
6″ d, bread and butter	6.00

7″ d, salad	14.00
9″ d, dinner	15.00
Soup, flat	20.00

Red Poppy Pattern, premium for Grand Union Tea Company, produced from mid 1930s until mid 1950s

Cereal Bowl, 6″ d	16.50
Cup and Saucer	13.50
Plate, dinner, 10″ d	13.50
Soup, flat	20.00

Serenade Pattern, (a.k.a. Eureka Serenade), premium for the Eureka Tea Company, Chicago

Berry Bowl, 5½″ d	5.50
Cup and Saucer	13.50
Plate, dinner, 9″ d	13.50
Soup, flat	13.50

Wildfire Pattern, premium for Great American Tea Company premium, 1950s

Cereal Bowl, straight sided, 5″ d	18.00
Plate	
7″ d, salad	11.00
9″ d, dinner	13.00

HARKER POTTERY

Colonial Lady Pattern

Cereal Bowl	10.00
Cup and Saucer	12.00
Dessert Bowl	7.00
Plate	
Bread and Butter	4.00
Salad	6.00
Soup Bowl	18.00

Mallow Pattern

Bowl, 5″ d	15.00
Plate, 8″ d	10.00

Pansy Pattern

Cereal Bowl	10.00
Cup	10.00
Plate, dinner	10.00

HOMER LAUGHLIN

Dogwood Pattern, c1950

Bowl, 5¾″ d	3.00
Plate, 9″ d	5.00
Soup	6.00

Harlequin Pattern

Cereal Bowl, Yellow	7.00
Cream Soup, Turquoise	15.00
Cup, Maroon	7.50
Cup and Saucer, Gray	9.50
Demitasse Cup and Saucer, Turquoise	40.00
Eggcup	
Double	
Gray	28.00
Turquoise	14.00
Individual	
Gray	21.00
Mauve Blue	20.00
Spruce Green	30.00
Turquoise	20.00

Plate	
6″ d, Maroon	6.00
Chartreuse	6.50
Gray	6.50
Maroon	9.00
Rose	9.00
9¼″ d, Rose	6.00
10″ d, Gray	25.00
Salad Bowl, individual, Yellow	20.00
Soup, flat, Rose	14.00
Teacup, Mauve Blue	16.00

Jubliee Pattern, introduced in 1948

Plate, dinner	
Cream Beige	5.00
Mist Gray	5.00
Saucer	
Celadon Green	3.00
Shell Pink	3.00

Mexicana Pattern, introduced in 1937

Bowl, 5″ d	10.00
Cup and Saucer	12.00
Plate	
7″ d	10.00
9″ d	15.00
Soup, flat	22.00

Rhythm Pattern, c1950 to 1960

Bowl, 5″ d, Maroon	4.00
Plate	
7″ d	
Gray	3.00
Maroon	3.00
9″ d, Chartreuse	6.00
Platter, 11½″ l, Forest Green	13.00
Saucer, Gray	3.00
Soup Bowl, 8″ d	
Chartreuse	8.00
Forest Green	8.00
Harlequin Yellow	8.00

Riveria Pattern, introduced in 1938

Cream Soup, Yellow	30.00
Cup	
Light Green	7.50
Mauve Blue	7.50
Plate, 7″ d, Dark Blue	20.00

Virginia Rose, introducced in 1929 continued until early 1970s

Cup and Saucer	3.50
Fruit Bowl, 5½″ d	4.50
Plate, 9″ d, dinner	6.00
Soup	7.00

KNOWLES, EDWIN

Deanna, introduced in 1938

Cup and Saucer, yellow	10.00
Eggcup, double, turquoise	12.00
Plate	
6″ d, bread and butter, yellow	4.00
8″ d, salad, orange–red	6.00
10″ d, dinner, dark blue	10.00

Esquire, dinnerware line designed by Russel Wright, made from 1956 until 1962

Cereal Bowl, cereal, Queen Anne's
Lace, white background, 6¼" d   **10.00**
Cup and Saucer, Snowflower, pink
background   **18.00**
Fruit Bowl, Snowflower, pink back-
ground, 5½" d   **8.00**
Plate
    6¼" d, bread and butter, Botanica,
    beige background   **6.00**
    8¼" d, salad, Seeds, yellow back-
    ground   **9.00**
    10¾" d, dinner, Grass, blue back-
    ground   **12.00**
Yorktown, introduced in 1936
    Cereal Bowl, 6" d, green   **6.00**
    Cup and Saucer, orange–red   **8.00**
    Custard Cup, green   **6.00**
    Plate
        6" d, bread and butter, yellow   **5.00**
        8" d, salad, cadet blue   **10.00**
        10" d, dinner, orange–red   **12.00**

METLOX

California Ivy Pattern, Poppytrail line
    Cup and Saucer   **5.40**
    Demitasse Cup and Saucer   **18.00**
    Plate, 6" d   **3.00**
California Provincial Pattern, Poppytrail
line
    Cereal Bowl   **3.50**
    Cup and Saucer   **8.00**
    Fruit Bowl, 6" d   **6.00**
    Mug, large   **25.00**
    Plate
        6" d, bread and butter   **4.00**
        8" d, salad   **8.00**
        10" d, dinner   **10.00**
    Soup, flat, 8½" d   **7.00**
Free Form, Poppytrail line
    Berry Bowl   **9.50**
    Cup   **10.50**
    Plate
        6" d   **4.50**
        8" d   **7.50**
        10" d   **10.50**
    Platter   **28.00**
    Soup Bowl, lug handle   **14.00**
Homestead Provincial, Poppytrail line
    Cereal Bowl, handle   **10.00**
    Cup and Saucer   **8.00**
    Mug   **20.00**
    Plate, 10" d, dinner   **8.00**
Provincial Fruit Pattern, Poppytrail line
    Cup and Saucer   **8.00**
    Plate
        6½" d, bread and butter   **4.00**
        7¾" d, salad   **8.00**
        10½" d, dinner   **9.00**
    Soup, 8½" d   **8.00**
Red Rooster, Poppytrail line
    Cereal Bowl, 7" d   **12.00**

Cup   **8.00**
Plate
    7½" d, salad   **6.00**
    10" d, dinner   **10.00**
Strawberry Pattern, Poppytrail line
    Cup and Saucer   **15.00**
    Plate
        8" d   **10.00**
        10" d   **15.00**
Vineyard Pattern, Vernon Ware
    Cereal Bowl, 7½" d   **5.00**
    Cup and Saucer   **7.00**
    Plate
        6¼" d   **4.00**
        7½" d   **6.00**
        10½" d   **7.00**
    Soup, flat, 8½" d   **6.00**

PENNSBURY POTTERY

Cup and Saucer
    Black Rooster   **12.00**
    Red Rooster   **15.00**
Mug
    Eagle   **20.00**
    Sweet Adeline   **20.00**
Plate
    Black Rooster decoration, 10" d   **13.00**
    Hex Sign decoration
        8" d   **18.00**
        10" d   **20.00**
    Red Rooster decoration, 10" d   **18.00**

ROYAL CHINA COMPANY

Colonial Homestead Pattern, Heritage Series, introduced 1950–1952, sold by
Sears
    Cereal Bowl, 6¼" d   **5.00**
    Cup and Saucer   **4.00**
    Fruit Bowl, 5½" d   **3.00**
    Plate
        6" d, bread and butter   **1.50**
        7" d, salad   **2.50**
        10" d, dinner   **3.50**
Currier & Ives Pattern, blue and white
scenic design, Cavalier Ironstone, intro-
duced 1949–1950, part of the Heritage
Series
    Cereal Bowl, 6" d   **9.00**
    Cup and Saucer   **3.50**
    Fruit Bowl, 5½" d   **3.00**
    Mug   **10.00**
    Plate
        6" d, bread and butter   **2.00**
        10¼" d, dinner   **4.00**
    Soup, flat   **6.00**
Memory Lane Pattern
    Berry Bowl   **4.00**
    Creamer   **5.00**
    Cup and Saucer   **3.00**
    Plate
        6" d, bread and butter   **4.00**
        10" d, dinner   **5.00**

Soup, flat	4.50
Sugar, open	5.00

Old Curiosity Shop Pattern, Cavalier shape, 1950s

Cup and Saucer	4.00
Plate	
6″ d, bread and butter	2.00
10″ d, dinner	4.00
Soup, flat, 8½″ d	6.00

STANGL POTTERY

Apple Delight Pattern, #5161, 1965

Cereal Bowl	12.00
Plate	
8″ d, salad	10.00
10″ d, dinner	15.00

Bella Rosa Pattern, 1960

Cup and Saucer	12.50
Fruit Dish, 5½″ d	10.00
Plate, 6″ d, bread and butter	5.00

Colonial Pattern, #1388

Eggcup, Colonial Blue	8.00
Plate, 10″ d, dinner, Colonial Blue	12.00

Country Garden Pattern

Cup and Saucer	15.00
Soup Bowl, lug handle	15.00

Dahlia Pattern

Cereal Bowl	15.00
Plate	
6″ d, bread and butter	4.50
8″ d, salad	8.00
Platter, oval, 14¾″ l	35.00
Server, center handle	10.00
Tile, 6″ sq	20.00

Fruit Pattern, #3697, 1942

Plate	
7″ d	10.00
10″ d	18.00
Sherbet	24.00

Garden Flower Pattern

Cup and Saucer, Rose cup, Leaves saucer	15.00
Fruit Bowl, Calendula, 5½″ d	12.00
Plate	
8″ d, Bleeding Heart	12.00
9″ d, Tiger Lily	12.00

Golden Harvest Pattern, #3887, 1953

Coffee Mug, 2 cup	25.00
Cup and Saucer	10.00
Plate	
8″ d	12.00
11″ d	20.00
Salt and Pepper Shakers, pr	24.00
Vegetable Bowl, divided	35.00

TAYLOR, SMITH, AND TAYLOR

Lu-Ray Pattern, produced from the late 1930s until the early 1950s

Berry Bowl, Chatham Gray	12.00
Bowl	
Surf Green	25.00

Windsor Blue	25.00
Cup and Saucer, Chatham Gray	20.00
Demitasse Cup and Saucer	
Sharon Pink	20.00
Windsor Blue	20.00
Eggcup	
Persian Cream	14.00
Sharon Pink	18.00
Windsor Blue	18.00
Plate	
6½″ d, Sharon Pink	4.00
8″ d	
Chatham Gray	20.00
Sharon Pink	14.00
Surf Green	15.00
Windsor Blue	12.00
9″ d	
Chatham Gray	15.00
Sharon Pink	7.00
10″ d, dinner	
Persian Cream	12.00
Windsor Blue	12.00
Soup	
Flat	
Chatham Gray	30.00
Persian Cream	15.00
Surf Green	15.00
Windsor Blue	12.00
Tab Handles	
Sharon Pink	18.00
Surf Green	18.00
Windsor Blue	18.00
Starter Set, Surf Green, 29 pcs	55.00
Tumbler	
Juice	
Persian Cream	37.00
Sharon Pink	35.00
Windsor Blue	32.00
Water, Chatham Gray	45.00

UNIVERSAL POTTERY

Calico Fruit Pattern

Custard Cup, 5 oz	4.00
Plate, 6″ d	4.00
Soup Bowl, tab handle	6.00

Largo Pattern

Bowl, small	3.50
Plate	
Dessert, 6″ d	3.00
Luncheon, square	4.00

Woodvine Pattern

Cup and Saucer	7.50
Plate, 9″ d	4.00

VERNON KILNS

Brown-Eyed Susan Pattern, Montecito shape, 1946–1958

Mug	28.00
Plate, 6″ d	3.00
Tumbler, 4 oz	18.00

Early California Pattern, Montecito shape, 1935–1947

Demitasse Creamer, orange 20.00
Demitasse Cup and Saucer, dark
blue 25.00
Eggcup, ivory 9.50
Gingham Pattern, Montecito shape,
1949–1958
Cup 5.00
Plate, 10½" d, dinner 5.00
Soup Bowl, 8½" d 12.00
Hawaiian Flowers Pattern, Ultra shape,
1938
Cup, maroon 20.00
Dinner Service, maroon, 91 pcs 850.00
Plate
6" d, bread and butter, maroon 7.50
8" d, luncheon, maroon 18.00
9" d, dinner, blue 30.00
Saucer, maroon 9.00
Homespun Pattern, Montecito shape,
1949–1958
Bowl, 5½" d 4.00
Cup and Saucer 5.00
Plate
7" d, salad 3.50
10" d, dinner 9.00
Tumbler 25.00
Moby Dick Pattern, Ultra shape, 1939
Bowl, tab handle, brown 15.00
Creamer, brown 15.00
Cup and Saucer, brown 18.00
Fruit Bowl, 5½" d, brown 10.00
Plate, 7" d, brown 2.00
Salt and Pepper Shakers, pr,
brown 40.00
Sauce Boat, brown 24.00
Soup Bowl, brown 18.00
Sugar, cov, brown 28.00
Modern California Pattern, Montecito
shape, 1937–1947
Bowl
5½" d, straw yellow 8.00
6" d, straw yellow, handled 12.00
9" d, pistachio 35.00
Cup, straw yellow 10.00
Cup and Saucer, azure 15.00
Mug, pistachio, no handle 28.00
Plate
6¼" d , orchid 6.00
9¾" d, pistachio 12.00
Platter, 12½" l, pistachio 18.00
Saucer, pistachio 3.00
Vegetable Bowl, oval, 9½" l,
azure 20.00
Organdie Pattern, Montecito shape,
1940–1958
Bowl
7¼" d 5.00
9" d 6.00
Cup and Saucer 7.00
Eggcup 24.00

Mug, 9 oz 15.00
Plate
6½" d, bread and butter 2.00
10½" d, dinner 10.00
Soup, lug handle 48.00
Tweed Pattern, Montecito shape, 1950–
1954
Plate
7" d, salad 4.50
9½" d, luncheon 6.00
Saucer 1.25
Soup, flat 8.00

DINNERWARE ACCESSORY PIECES
BABY DISH
Franciscan
Desert Rose Pattern 85.00
Starburst Pattern 75.00
BALL JUG
Bauer Pottery
La Linda Pattern, dinnerware line pro-
duced from 1939 until 1959
Gray 45.00
Ring, extensive line introduced in
1931, Orange–red 75.00
Hall China
Carrot Pattern, (a.k.a. Carrot and Beet),
#4 125.00
Chinese Red Pattern 35.00
Fantasy Pattern
#1 95.00
#3 110.00
Donut 200.00
Homer Laughlin, Harlequin Pattern, 22
oz
Gray 54.00
Maroon 60.00
Stangl Pottery, Colonial Pattern, #1388,
ice lip, Silver Green 35.00
BATTER BOWL
Bauer Pottery, Gloss Pastel Kitchenware,
introduced in 1942, 2 quart, Ivory 40.00

When it came to streamlining, Hall China
had the styling down to an art when the
company made this Westinghouse blue water jug.

Hall China
    Chinese Red Pattern, Five Band **75.00**
    Fantasy Pattern, Sundial   **350.00**

BONBON
Blue Ridge, Nove Rose Pattern, flat shell
shape   **65.00**

BONE DISH
Franciscan
    Desert Rose Pattern, crescent
    shape   **27.00**
    Starburst Pattern, crescent shape **25.00**

CAKE LIFTER
Harker Pottery, Deco–Dahlia Pattern   **28.00**

CANDLESTICKS, PR
Fiesta, tripod, Yellow   **415.00**
Homer Laughlin, Harlequin Pattern, Turquoise, pr   **75.00**
Pennsbury Pottery, roosters, 4″ h **75.00**

CANDY BOX
Blue Ridge, Nove Rose Pattern,   **175.00**

CARAFE
Fiesta
    Cobalt Blue   **225.00**
    Red   **225.00**
    Yellow   **115.00**

CELERY DISH
Blue Ridge
    French Peasant Pattern, leafy   **45.00**
    Nove Rose Pattern, leafy   **35.00**
    Serenade Pattern   **35.00**
    Summertime Pattern, leafy   **30.00**
Franciscan, Coronado Swirl Pattern, yellow, satin   **15.00**
Hall China, Mulberry Pattern, oval,
11″ l   **22.00**

CHOCOLATE POT
Blue Ridge, Rose Marie Pattern **150.00**

CHOP PLATE
Bauer Pottery, Monterey Pattern, dinnerware line produced from 1936 until
1945, 13″ d, Monterey Blue   **35.00**
Fiesta, 13″ d
    Chartreuse   **75.00**
    Cobalt Blue   **50.00**
    Light Green   **20.00**
    Turquoise   **20.00**
    Yellow   **35.00**
Franciscan
    Coronado Swirl Pattern, yellow,
    satin   **25.00**
    Desert Rose Pattern, 12″ d   **45.00**
    Ivy Pattern, 14″ d   **85.00**
Knowles, Edwin, Yorktown Pattern,
10¾″ d, burgundy   **15.00**
Metlox Pottery
    California Ivy Pattern, Poppytrail line,
    15″ d   **25.00**
    California Provincial Pattern, Poppytrail
    line, 12″ d   **15.00**

    Homestead Provincial, Poppytrail line,
    12″ d   **12.00**
    Navajo Pattern, Poppytrail line,
    12″ d   **30.00**
    Red Rooster, Poppytrail line,
    12″ d   **13.00**
Stangl Pottery
    Colonial Pattern, #1388, 12½″ d Colonial Blue   **20.00**
    Garden Flower Pattern, Tiger Lily,
    12½″ d   **40.00**

COFFEE SERVER
Hall China, Chinese Red Pattern,
Sundial   **250.00**
Homer Laughlin, Jubliee Pattern, Shell
Pink   **35.00**

COMPOTE
Franciscan
    Apple Pattern, large   **65.00**
    Desert Rose Pattern   **195.00**
    Ivy Pattern   **95.00**

FORK
Fiesta, Light Green, Kitchen Kraft **65.00**

MARMALADE
Franciscan
    Apple Pattern, cov   **95.00**
    Desert Rose Pattern   **125.00**

MUSTARD JAR, COV
Bauer Pottery, Ring, extensive line introduced in 1931, Ivory   **75.00**
Franciscan, Starburst Pattern   **85.00**

NAPPY
Fiesta
    8½″ d
        Gray   **40.00**
        Red   **32.00**
        Rose   **45.00**
    9½″ d, Cobalt Blue   **60.00**
Homer Laughlin
    Harlequin Pattern, Yellow   **30.00**
    Mexicana Pattern   **25.00**
    Riveria Pattern
        Red   **18.00**
        Yellow   **18.00**

OIL AND VINEGAR CRUETS, PR
Franciscan, Starburst Pattern   **100.00**
Metlox Pottery, Red Rooster, Poppytrail
line   **22.00**
Pennsbury Pottery, jug shape, Amish man
and woman, pr   **135.00**
Purinton Pottery, Pennsylvania Dutch Pattern   **45.00**

PICKLE DISH
Franciscan, Ivy Pattern, 10½″ l   **35.00**
Stangl Pottery, Country Garden Pattern   **20.00**

PIE SERVER
Harker Pottery
    Colonial Lady Pattern   **10.00**
    Red Apple Pattern   **20.00**

PRETZEL JAR
Hall China
    Chinese Red Pattern, cov, hairline
    crack in bottom   95.00
    Pastel Morning Glory Pattern (a.k.a.
    Pink Morning Glory)   150.00
Pennsbury Pottery, eagle decoration, 8 ×
11″   50.00

PUNCH BOWL SET
Hall China, Red Dot Pattern (a.k.a. Eggshell Polka Dot), ftd punch bowl and 12
cups   350.00

RAMEKIN
Hall China
    Chinese Red Pattern, #1   50.00
Salad Bowl
    Orange Poppy Pattern   11.00
    Serenade Pattern, (a.k.a. Eureka Serenade), 9″ d   20.00
    Wildfire Pattern, 9″ d   22.50

SALAD BOWL
Blue Ridge, Wrinkled Rose Pattern, Colonial shape, 10″ d   40.00
Fiesta, ftd, Ivory   150.00
Franciscan
    Apple Pattern serving   95.00
    Ivy Pattern, 11¼″ d   85.00
    Starburst Pattern, serving   85.00
Metlox Pottery, Homestead Provincial,
Poppytrail line, 11″ d   22.00

SAUCE BOAT
Fiesta
    Chartreuse   55.00
    Gray   80.00

SHIRRED EGG DISH
Hall China
    Red Dot Pattern (a.k.a. Eggshell Polka
    Dot)   25.00
    Wild Poppy Pattern (a.k.a. Poppy and
    Wheat)
        5½″ l   22.50
        6½″ l   25.00

SPOON
Fiesta, Cobalt Blue, Kitchen Kraft   65.00
Harker Pottery
    Mallow Pattern, hairline crack   10.00
    Red Apple Pattern   25.00

STACK SET, COV
Bauer Pottery, Ring, extensive line introduced in 1931, set of three, Orange–red,
Green, and Yellow   100.00
Hall China
    Autumn Leaf   75.00
    Red Popppy Pattern   65.00
    Wild Poppy Pattern (a.k.a. Poppy and
    Wheat), Radiance   165.00

UTILITY PLATE
Harker Pottery
    Deco–Dahlia Pattern, 12″ d   15.00
    Red Apple Pattern   20.00

VASE
Bauer Pottery, Ring, extensive line introduced in 1931 6″ h, Green   35.00
Fiesta
    8″ h
        Green   295.00
        Ivory   250.00
        Turquoise   300.00
    10″ h, Cobalt Blue   500.00
Franciscan, Desert Rose Pattern,
bud   195.00

WATER BOTTLE
Hall China, Chinese Red Pattern, Zephyr,
missing stopper   70.00

DIPPER
Cast Iron, hand forged   125.00
Graniteware
    Gray, tubular handle, chocolate
    type   155.00
    Gray and white   20.00
    Red and white   15.00
Wood
    Burl, long handle, old dark finish, edge
    chip on bowl, hairline, 35″ l   185.00
    Maple, slight curl, 9¼″ l   100.00
    Treen, thin bowl, minor edge damage,
    11¾″ l   115.00
Wrought Iron
    Large brass bowl, 21¼″ l   75.00
    Small brass bowl, 15¼″ l   65.00

DISH, COV
Aluminum, hand wrought, 5 × 12 × 8″,
bakelite handle, marked "Cellini Hand
Wrought Aluminum, Chicago"   135.00

DISH, OPEN
Abingdon Pottery, oblong, pink, two
geese dec   35.00
Blue Ridge, Tussie Mussie Pattern, deep
shell shape   50.00
Occupied Japan, ceramic, fish shape,
marked "Occupied Japan"   10.00

DOLL
Blue Bonnet Sue, hard plastic, original
dress, 8″ h   8.00
C & H Sugar, cloth, price for pair   12.00
Chiquita Banana, 10″ h, 1944   70.00
Choo Choo Charlie, 10″ h, Hasbro,
1972   30.00
Elsie the Cow, plush, vinyl head, 1950s,
15″ h   60.00
Green Giant
    Jolly Green Giant, 16″ h, cloth, stuffed, 1966   50.00
    Little Sprout, 6½″ h, vinyl, early
    1970s   25.00
    Keebler Bakery Elf, vinyl, movable
    head, copyright 1974, 6½″ h   25.00
Magic Chef, 7½″ h   12.50

Miss Sunbeam, vinyl, Horsman, 1970,
14″ h **100.00**
Mr Peanut, 8½″ h, wood, 1930s **50.00**
Pillsbury Doughboy, cloth, 1971,
16″ h **10.00**
Pillsbury Poppie Fresh, molded soft vinyl,
6″ h **10.00**
Sailor Jack, Cracker Jack, cloth, Mattel,
1974, 15″ h **30.00**
Swiss Miss, cloth, 17″ h **15.00**
Trix Rabbit, vinyl, 1977 **30.00**
Vermont Maid Syrup, vinyl, 15″ h **30.00**

DOORSTOP
Campbell Kids with dog, cast iron worn
polychrome paint, 8½″ h **160.00**
Cottage, cast iron, blue roof, flowers,
fenced garden, signed "Eastern Specialty
Mfg Co. 14," 8⅝″ l **135.00**
Kitten, cast iron, three kittens in basket,
signed "M. Rosenstein, Lancaster, PA,"
c1932, 7″ h **335.00**
Rooster, cast iron, full figure, black, red
comb, yellow claws and beak,
12″ h **345.00**
Zinnias, cast iron, multicolored flowers,
blue and black vase, detailed casting, two
rubber stoppers, signed "B & H"
11⅝″ h **175.00**

DOUBLE BOILER
Graniteware
Blue **115.00**
Cobalt and White, large swirl, Brilliant
Belle **295.00**
Red, blue trim **45.00**
Tin **60.00**

DOUGH BOX
Cherry, dovetailed, turned feet, white
porcelain knobs, name scratched on
base **265.00**
Maple, dovetailed, old replacement lid,
traces of old red paint, 38 x 19¼ ×
28¾″ **450.00**
Painted, dovetailed, canted sides, paneled
flat cover with center knob, painted blue,
16″ w, 26″ l, 9″ h **160.00**

**Pine dough box with slanting sides no doubt
gave a good start to many a loaf of bread.**

DOUGH SCRAPER
3½″ l, wrought iron, short conical rattle
handle **30.00**
4″ l, wrought iron, heart cutout in blade,
minor damage to iron handle **110.00**
4½″ w, wrought iron, simple tooled
snake head **110.00**

DRIPPINGS JAR
Jeannette Glass, Delphite, round, covered,
"Drippings" in black letters **95.00**
Hall China
Chinese Red Pattern, open,
#1188 **35.00**
Pastel Morning Glory Pattern (a.k.a.
Pink Morning Glory), #1188 **55.00**
Purinton Pottery, Apple Pattern **20.00**

DRYING RACK
Wood
Mahogany, old finish, two part folding
rack, good turnings, 22¼″ w,
32¼″ h **220.00**
Pine
20″ w, 33″ h, two mortised and
pinned bars, block feet with some
damage, old dark green repaint **150.00**
47″ w, 64″ h, old dark patina, shoe
feet, chamfered posts with tapered
finials, three mortised and pinned
bars **200.00**
Wood and Metal, 27 × 6″ folded size, 12
retractable arms, three legs **40.00**

DUST PAN
Graniteware, gray, speckled **100.00**
Wooden, pine, lollipop handle, tapered
lip, gray–blue paint, c1840, 4 × 6 ×
14″ **130.00**

DUTCH OVEN
Griswold Mfg Co, Erie, PA, cast iron,
original cover
No. 6, large emblem **40.00**
No. 8
Large emblem **40.00**
Small emblem **45.00**
No. 10, trivet, large emblem **80.00**
Wagner Ware, cast iron, No. 9 **40.00**

❖ E
EGGBEATER
Androck, red bakelite trim **22.00**
Full Vision, metal, two piece, Art Deco
style **35.00**
Holt, patented Aug 22, 1899 **65.00**
EGG BEATER BOWL
McKee Glass, Skokie Green **10.00**
EGG CALCULATOR
Fite's Peerless Calculator, c1900 **95.00**
EGG CUP
Graniteware, blue, cobalt and white
checkerboard trim, price for pair **95.00**

This early Dover eggbeater, patented on May 31st, 1870, was sturdy enough for heavy duty in the kitchen. From the collection of Chuck and Bonnie Badger.

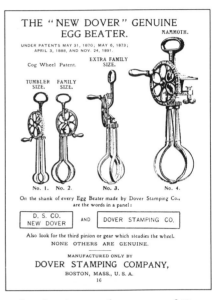

Early advertisement for a range of Dover eggbeaters, from the "tumbler size" to the "mammoth" mixer. Courtesy of Don Thornton, Sunnyvale, Ca.

McKee Glass, Skokie Green, ftd	**12.00**

EGG LIFTER

Spring wire, curled egg shaped scoops, squeeze together handle, 12½" l	**15.00**
Wire, spoon type	**6.00**

EGG SCALE

Metal egg cup, arm and weight	**8.00**
Oakes Mfg Co, painted tin, 7" h	**25.00**

EGG SEPARATOR

Depression Era Glassware, clam-broth	**55.00**
Plastic, Tupperware, yellow	**.50**

EGG SLICER

Aluminum, hinged top, ten cutting blades, c1930, 5" l	**8.00**
Copper, tinned, perforated blades, iron handle, 6" d	**25.00**
Wood, painted frame, ten slicing wires, 4⅛" l	**15.00**

EGG TIMER

Alarm Whistle, aluminum insert, original box and instructions	**15.00**
Chef, Black Memorabilia	**110.00**

EGG WHISK

Spiral	**10.00**
Wire	**6.00**
Wood handle, red, dated 1906	**12.00**

ELECTRICAL APPLIANCES

BLENDERS

Drink Master Mixall, Chronmaster, NY, Chicago, Art Deco design, black metal stand, chrome motor housing, chrome knob on top, front switch, single shaft, clear glass with silver bands, mixes drinks, whips cream, 1934 patent, 14" h   **30.00**

Home Malt Mixer, A C Gilbert, chrome, domed motor housing, crinkle green painted base, 1930s, 13" h   **65.00**

Silex, Philadelphia, PA, #D2606, cream sq metal base housing one speed motor, push button switch, four cup sq tapered glass top, Art Deco center vertical design and measure, soft black plastic lid, early 1940s   **12.00**

CHAFING DISHES

American Beauty, American Electrical Heater Co, Detroit, MI, nickel, 3 pcs, two plugs marked "fast" and "slow," black wood knob and handles, 1910   **50.00**

Manning Bowman, cat. #601, ser. #K–601, high style Art Deco design, chrome, round tray/hot plate, hot water dish, bowl, and lid, black bakelite handles, three prong hi–lo plug, 1925   **45.00**

Universal, Landers, Frary & Clark, #E–940, two quart copper body, hot water pan and lid, faceted base and lid, nickel plated, flat prongs, black wooden handles and knob, 1908–14   50.00

COFFEE MAKERS AND SETS

Farberware, SW Farber, Brooklyn, NY
   Coffee Robot, chrome body with glass top bowl, thermostat keeps coffee warm, stirs, 1937   **35.00**
   Model #208, chrome with garland drape, black wooden handles, late 1930s, 12½″ h   **15.00**

General Electric Dining Room Set, nickel bodies, wooden handles, paw feet, 1918–19
   Chafing Dish   **50.00**
   Hot Plate   **25.00**
   Percolator, glass top   **45.00**
   Water Kettle   **50.00**

Manning Bowman, Meriden, CT
   Coffee Urn Set, cat. #C474–8, ser. #10–30, 15″ h urn, creamer, sugar, and tray, nickel chrome tapered faceted body, ivory bakelite swing handles, short cabriole legs, 1910–25   **60.00**
   Percolator, cat. #381/9, chrome Art Deco body, reeded band at neck and above stepped base, part of dining room set consisting of chafing dish and waffle maker, 1920s, 12″ h   **35.00**

Porcelier Breakfast Service, dining room type, Porcelier Mfg Co, Greensburg, PA, cream colored porcelain bodies and handles, basketweave texture, multicolored floral transfer designs, 1930–40
   Creamer and Sugar, cov   **30.00**
   Percolator, #5007   **55.00**
   Sandwich Grill, #5004   **45.00**
   Toaster, #5002   **75.00**
   Waffle Iron   **45.00**
   Complete Set   **250.00**

Royal Rochester Percolator, Rochester, NY, #366 B–29, nickel body over copper, black wooden handles, 1920s, 10″ h   **15.00**

Silex Dripolator, #550 EC–8, rounded chrome and bakelite hot plate, two piece all glass pot and top, bakelite handle and stand, glass center, rubber connection center, 3 pcs, mid 1930s, 13″ h   **18.00**

Sunbeam Dripolator, Coffee Master, Chicago Flexible Shaft Co, chrome, Art Deco design on side, bakelite, 2 pcs, 1935–44, 12½″ h   **20.00**

United Metal Goods Mfg Inc
   Coffee Maker/Server, model 750, chrome pot with pierced tulip design, clear glass liner lights up when coffee is made, black wooden handle and feet, 1930s, 11½″ h   **45.00**

Percolator, cat. #760, urn shaped body and pierced tilting frame, dec mid body band, emb spout base, ornate handle, indicator light, 1940s, 17″ w   **65.00**

Universal, Landers, Frary & Clark, New Britain, CT
   Breakfast Set, porcelain, cream china bodies, blue and orange floral transfers, 1920–30s
     Creamer and Sugar, cov   **25.00**
     Percolator, chrome mounted, #E–6927   **60.00**
     Syrup, chrome mounted   **20.00**
     Waffle Iron, chrome, pierced stand, drop handle, china lid insert, #E–6324   **60.00**
     Complete Set   **200.00**
   Coffee Service, 4 pcs
     E–9119, nickel chrome, 16½″ h classical urn on flared base, creamer, cov sugar, and tray, open handles with flat tops, large glass insert, black wooden handled spigot, 1912–24   **125.00**
     E–9189, nickel chrome, 14″ h urn on flattened base, tri–form applied legs, drop reverse bail handles, creamer and cov sugar, rect tray with rounded corners, applied leaf banding, glass insert with etched leaf design, 1912   **50.00**
     E–9239, 11″ h classical squatty urn, nickel, upturned open scrolled handles, tall flared base on short feet, smaller top flared with wide opening, green depression glass insert, footed creamer, cov sugar, large oval tray, 1912–24   **195.00**
   Urn, classical design, nickel, cabriole legs, tall curved handles, flat top, lid with large swirled glass insert, 15½″ h   **35.00**

Westinghouse Dripolator, Mansfield, OH, cat. #CM–81, black bakelite handles, 2 pcs, 1940s, 14″ h   **20.00**

EGG COOKERS

Hankscraft, model 599, yellow ceramic, chrome lid, large yellow ceramic knob, instructions on base and cord tag, 1930s   **15.00**

The Rochester, Rochester, NY, egg shaped nickel body, flared base, flat prongs, domed lid, int. fitted skillet/pan, sealed element in base, 4 pcs, 1912   **35.00**

FOOD COOKERS

Betty Crocker Deep Fryer, General Mills, model 9–A, chrome body, rounded corners, black bakelite base with red control, chrome lid, aluminum basket, late 1940s, 11 × 7″   **25.00**

Breakfaster, Calkins Appliance Co, Niles, MI, hot plate/toaster, model #T–2, Art Deco design, louvered, round corners on sq aluminum body, bakelite base and handles, small rect door in side for toast tray, hot plate on top, 1930s **35.00**

Broiler Robot, Farberware, SW Farber, Brooklyn, NY, broiler/grill, round nickel body, two part with internal rack, domed lid with element and three top feet to reverse and turn from broiler to grill, heat indicated, 1938, 11″ d **30.00**

Electric Range, Eureka Vacuum Cleaner Co, Detroit, MI, Art Deco, cream painted body, black porcelainized trim, chamfered top, emb design with "Eureka" across at angle, black bakelite handle, int. racks, fold down sides with chrome surfaces and round hot plates, large red indicator light on lower front panel, black bakelite oven controls, hi–med–lo for hotplates and pre–warm and hi–med–lo control for oven, short feet made into sides of body, top carrying handle, restored, 1930s, 15 × 13 × 19″ h **80.00**

Everhot Cooker, cat. #EC–JR–10, cylindrical body, chrome middle with emb "Everhot" and Art Deco design, black top and base, aluminum lock–on lid, fitted int. with three pans and lids, 1925 patent date, 9½″ d, 13″ h **50.00**

Hotpoint Table Top Stove, General Electric, nickel pierced base and frame holds elements, slots for poacher, broiler, griddle pan, late 1910s, 7″ sq **75.00**

Table Top Stove
> Armstrong Mfg Co, porcelain and nickel body, toaster rack, broiler pan and liner, waffle iron, skillet, four egg poacher with lid, black wooden handles, original cord, 1917 **95.00**
> Lander, Frary & Clark, model #E–988, large control with white china selector, chrome and aluminum frame, pierced holder, broiler and rack, four egg poacher, skillet, lid, black wooden handles, 1924, 7″ sq **150.00**
> Westinghouse, Mansfield, OH
> Frying Pan, steel, cord in wooden handle, six legged iron detachable base, inverts to make hot plate, first electric frying pan, 1911, 6″ d **150.00**
> Roaster Oven, white metal painted body, aluminum top with window and gray plastic handle, lift–out gray graniteware pan, griddle, three lids and marked glass baking dishes, matching stand with clock timer and storage, late 1940s **50.00**

Toaster Stove, type "O" ser. #198158–B, low rect nickel body, removable cabriole legs, top with dark metal strip, serving tray and rack, coiled wire handles, original box, paper guarantee, first Westinghouse toaster, unused, dated June 1904 and 1914, 9 × 5″ **125.00**

HOT PLATES

Disk Stove, General Electric, cat #40101, heavy round iron top on chrome, three tall triangular pierced legs, lower shelf, wooden bun feet, 1920s, 6″ d **30.00**

Westinghouse, Mansfield, OH, cat. #PH–103, round plate, round green porcelainized metal top, hexagonal nickel base, three faceted legs, 1920s, 7″ d **20.00**

MISCELLANEOUS

Baby Bottle Warmer, Universal, Landers, Frary & Clark, #E–9930, cylindrical body, nickel, wooden side handle, bun feet, lid, 1912–14, 4¾″ d **8.00**

Bun Warmer, unmarked, 1930s, 10″ d bowl, Art Deco style, chrome, domed cov, red, yellow, and green wood ball feet and finial, removable fitted wire basket, 1930s **25.00**

Can Opener, Kitchen Pal, Union Die Casting, Whittier, CA, model #58, ser. #7–2031, bright yellow metal body, chrome trim, original booklet, first electric can opener, unused, 1956 **25.00**

Clock Timer, Montgomery Ward & Co, cream body, flat swivel base, windup, electric plug in back, silver and red, 1940s **15.00**

Coffee Mill, KitchenAid, Hobart, model A–9, cream metal motor base, sloped sides, adjustment ring at top, clear glass top, open both ends, threaded black metal lid, first home coffee grinder, 1936, 13½″ h **60.00**

Flour Sifter, Miracle Electric Co, Chicago, IL, ivory metal body, push button above blue wooden handle, decal label, unused, 1930s **35.00**

Home Motor, Hamilton Beach, #29650192, 1910s **30.00**

Knife Sharpener, Handy Hannah, cat. #4950, red and cream body, low flat base, 1930s, 4½″ d **10.00**

Marshmallow Toaster, Campfire Bar–B–Q, Angelus, 2 pc lightweight metal body, sq base, pierced flattened pyramid top, loop wire legs with rubber encased cushion feet, three small metal 2–prong forks, 3″ sq **55.00**

Percolator and Toaster Combination,

Perc–O–Toaster, Armstrong Mfg Co, model PT, nickel, two plug, sq base, cabriole legs, slip–out toast rack in base, 1918 **60.00**

Tea Kettle

Mirro, domed shape, flat bottom, polished aluminum, whistle cover, bakelite handle, 1930–40s, 4 qt **20.00**

Universal, Landers, Frary & Clark, #E–973, low teapot shape, flared base, flattened top with tall handle and shaped, black wooden holder, top knob, 1910–20 **45.00**

MIXERS

General Electric, cat. #149 M8, ser. #10–A, cream colored metal, black bakelite handle, work light in top, three beaters in row, white bowls, head folds down, 1938 **30.00**

Hamilton Beach, 1930–40s, model G, ser. #366839, cream colored metal body, slip–off base, beaters in one unit, bakelite handle, white bowls **25.00**

Handy Hanna, Standard Products, Whitman, MA, cat. #495, natural wooden handle, single shaft, quart jar base, late 1930s **22.00**

Handymix, Mary Dunbar, Chicago Elect Mfg Co, #D–121124, stand, push button, two beaters, late 1930s, 11½" h **16.00**

KitchenAid, Hobart Corp, Troy, OH, rounded cream colored body with heavy aluminum trim and handle, screw–down aluminum bowl, wire whisk beater, aluminum meat grinder, dough hook, 1939, 14 × 12" **50.00**

Knapp–Monarch, St Louis, MO, cat. #6–501, white metal motor housing, louvered sides, red plastic handle, three cup white glass measuring base, mid 1930s, 9½" l **20.00**

Mixmaster, Sunbeam, Chicago Flexible Shaft Co, model K, cream colored metal body, folding handle on stand, green glass bowl/juicer, 1930 **40.00**

Polar Cub, A C Gilbert, hand mixer, #B–89, gray, blue wooden handle, single shaft, original box, 1929, 9½" l **75.00**

Portable Hand Mixer, Sears Kenmore, Model 322–8220, cream colored plastic body, single shaft, original box and booklet, early 1940s, 5" l **25.00**

Unmarked, small, green metal encased motor, metal handle, green depression glass measured Vidrio cup, mid 1930s, 8" l **25.00**

Vidrio, green, original green glass base **18.00**

POPCORN POPPERS

Dominion Elect Mfg Co, model #75, cylindrical, pierced nickel body, cabriole legs, hand crank, red wooden handles and knob, 1920s **24.00**

Knapp–Monarch, St Louis, MO, cat. #12A–500B, oil, aluminum body, wire base, domed glass lid with vented sides, walnut handles, measuring cup, 1930–40 **20.00**

Unmarked, mesh wire basket set in tin, hand crank, black wooden handle and knob, sets atop tin "can" which holds element, attached cord **25.00**

US Mfg Co

Dry, #1, two pc heater in base, lid, hand crank, silver painted metal body with red lid, three red wood vertical dowel legs, 1920–30s **18.00**

Oil, model #10, 3 pcs, heater, pad, and lid, bakelite handles and knobs, hand crank, 1920–30s **36.00**

TOASTERS

Edison Electric Appliance Co, NY

Cat. #214 T–5, nickel base, open sides, separate warming rack, tab holders, 1910 **45.00**

Cat. #E125 T22, flip–flop type, pierced geometric warming top and doors, large black wooden knobs, 1910–14 **35.00**

Estate Stove Co, Hamilton, OH, model 177, nickel, sq body, canted, pierced door rack on four sides turn simultaneously with one button movement, 1922 **75.00**

General Electric

Model D–12, white china base, open wire frame, lift–off warming rack,

Toaster was made by The Nelson Machine & Mfg. Company, Cleveland, Ohio, catalog #94.

screw–in china plug, first marketed
toaster, 1908 **125.00**
Radio Toggle, two slice flip–over type,
pierced nickel body, doors, and top,
large radio knob on side to reverse
toast, 1933 **95.00**
Knapp–Monarch, cat. #21–501, rounded
chrome Art Deco body, flip–flop type,
bakelite handles, mechanical opening device, mid 1930s **20.00**
Manning Bowman, Meriden, CT
#1225, nickel body, double wire me-
chanical turnover doors, bakelite
knobs, pierced top, flat prongs,
1926 **35.00**
Ser. #11–27, Meriden Homelectrics,
flip–flop type, thin pierced doors and
top, tab feet, flat prongs, 1930s **25.00**
Merit Made Inc, Buffalo, NY, ser.
#024146, unusual rounded design, Art
Deco flip–flop type, painted silver gray
body, black metal base, plunger opener
on top, both sides open simultaneously,
never used, 1930s **30.00**
Montgomery Ward & Co, model 9–4KW
2298– B, flip–flop type, sq body,
rounded corners, chrome, bakelite handles, mechanical open, dec sides, mid
1930s **18.00**

**The Sunbeam toaster either popped the
toast up or kept it warm. And it also came
with a "stunning" tray set or buffet set for
informal dining occasions.**

Sears Kenmore, model #307–6323–1,
two slice automatic pop–up, mechanical
clock timing mechanism, rounded
chrome body and base, bakelite handles
and knobs, early 1940s **15.00**
Sunbeam, Chicago Flexible Shaft Co
#4, rect bed 5 × 9″ on flat L–shaped
feet, chrome body, horizontal flip–flop
cage, black handles, 1924 **45.00**
#T–1E, Art Deco design, two slice top
load automatic, chrome body, concen-
tric lines, indicator light, bakelite base
and handles, large rect glass divided
relish tray with toaster compartment **65.00**
#T–9, Art Deco design, two slice top
load automatic, rounded chrome body,
bakelite handles, rect liner and four
glass trays, 1932–40 **65.00**
Toastmaster, Waters Genter Co, Minneapolis, MN
Model 1–A–1, single slice, mechanical
clock mechanism, chrome, Art Deco
style, thin sq body, one top rounded
corner, louvered sides, slightly large
base, bakelite controls, first automatic
pop–up, 1927 **80.00**
Model 1–A–3, Art Deco style, sq
chrome body, one chamfered top end,
vertically fluted design on sides, third
pop–up model, 1929 **35.00**
Toast–O–Lator, Long Island, NY, model
J, ser. #49, Art Deco style, chrome, tall
rectangle with flat sides and top, rounded
vertical ends, bakelite base, slot in each
end, toast "walks" through past small
round window, double mechanical track,
on–off switch, 1938 **40.00**
Universal, Landers, Frary & Clark
#E–7542, single slice automatic, me-
chanical clock mechanism, pop–out
rack, slender sq chrome body, circle
dec on sides, late 1920–early
1930s **50.00**
Flat, pierced top, concave sides, vertically hinged mechanical reversible wire
doors, flat base, small wooden handle,
1912–20 **60.00**
Trademark "LMP" in diamond, pat.
1905, pierced design on spring doors,
slender chrome body, flat base, tab
feet, curved warming rack, 1913–
15 **40.00**
Westinghouse, Mansfield, OH, style
#231570, flip–flop type, nickel body,
wire doors, pierced warmer top, cord
with china plug, 1910s **35.00**

WAFFLE IRONS & SANDWICH GRILLS

Armstrong Mfg Co, waffle iron, model W,
metal tag, black wooden handles, first

heat indicator, early 1920s, 7" d plates **25.00**

Coleman Lamp & Stove Co, Wichita, KA, waffle iron, model 17, round chrome body, 14" oval base, Art Deco style, small china insert on lid, black and white gazelle motif, black bakelite handles, 7½" d plates **30.00**

General Electric, waffle iron, solid iron, three short legs, coiled wire, heat dissipating handles, separate screw–in plugs for top and bottom, 1900 **95.00**

Hostess, sandwich toaster, All Rite Co, IN, sq, ftd, heavy aluminum body with screw–off black wooden handle, original Art Deco orange and black box with "Suggestions" book, 1930, 5 × 5 × 4½" **40.00**

Knapp–Monarch, waffle iron, dessert size, low body, black wooden knobs, dec top, 1930s, 6" d plates **15.00**

Landers, Frary & Clark

Pat. 1916, horizontal type, rect, nickel, round tapered legs, attached tray, black wooden handles, two–headed cord, 8 × 4¼" **75.00**

Universal Sandwich Grill/Waffle Iron, #EA–8601, two waffles, attached tray with bakelite handles, wheat dec on top, reusable plates, 1940s, 10 × 5½" plates **25.00**

Majestic Electric Appliance Corp, San Francisco, CA, hotcake/waffle iron, reversible plates, knob on top acts as foot for open two part grill, makes two cakes at once, nickel body, black wood knobs, 1923, 8" d plates **45.00**

Manning Bowman, waffle iron

Cat. #1646, Ser. #11–55, Art Deco style, chrome, stepped bakelite feet,

---

The popcorn popper manufactured by Quincy Hardware and Manufacturing Company of Quincy, IL was patented in 1892. It had a unique drive mechanism that kept the hopper in motion when the crank wheel was turned. Courtesy of Phyllis and Jim Moffet of Modesto, Ill.

drop handles, reeded edges and top, booklet, 1930s, 7" d plates, 9½" sq base **30.00**

Ser. #24, Art. 1605, 7" round plates, nickel body, domed faceted lid, cabriole legs and attached tray, 1920s **25.00**

Twin–O–Matic, ser. #6060, double, Art Deco style, chrome, round flip–over, chrome, bakelite cradle, heat indicator in middle top, original booklet, 1924–40 **65.00**

Unmarked

Sandwich Grill, triple, nickel body, angled legs, tab feet, black wooden handles, 1920s, 6 × 17" **25.00**

Waffle Iron, child's, green handle, slender, tall legs, 1930s, 4" sq **25.00**

Westinghouse, Mansfield, OH, waffle iron, heavy nickel body, straight legs, mechanical open, front handle, first electric waffle iron found to date, 1905–21, 9 × 5¼" plates **75.00**

➻ F

FIRE SIDE COOKING IMPLEMENTS

Fireside Broiler, wrought iron, tripod base, penny feet, adjustable heart shaped rack with five sets of tines to hold small game, decorative diamond shaped rivet on sprint, 28" h **1,100.00**

Fireplace Crane, wrought iron, 26" l **100.00**

Griddle, cast iron

Free standing, three small legs, round eye handle, c1810 **225.00**

Hanging, heavy bail handle, sturdy legs to set on hearth, c1800 **165.00**

Kettle Shelf, hanging type, wrought iron, very pitted, 16½" h **65.00**

Lighting Stand, wrought iron, primitive, tripod base, adjustable octagonal pan with candle socket, hanger finial, corner spouts, one foot old replacement, 20½" h **385.00**

Skewer, wrought iron, four twisted skewers, 11½" l **150.00**

Spit Rack, wrought iron, spike end, three hooks to adjust end of spit, good detail, 13½ × 19½" **55.00**

Stove Plate, cast iron, from H. W. Stiegel Foundry, stylized floral designs with hearts in double arch, emb "Henrich Wilhelm, Elisabeth Furnace," very pitted, crack in right side, 25½" w, 23½" h **225.00**

Toaster, wrought iron, double jaws end in scrollwork, turned wooden handle, 26" l **140.00**

Toasting Fork, adjustable, brass, weighted conical base, stamped "Patent No. '97," dents in base **165.00**

Although its prime purpose was tenderizing meat, Tyler's Ideal Fiber Cutter also could be used as a food chopper, nut crumbler, mince knife, fish scaler, ice tool and cleaver, according to an advertisement in *American Cookery*. The Muncie, Ind. firm, looking for agents to sell it, claimed the fiber cutter made "any steak so deliciously tender you can cut it with a fork." The nickel-plated tool could be sold direct to homes by Tyler representatives or could be purchased through the mail for $1.50.

Rotary mincing knife was a handy tool for chopping parsley, mint and onions, according to an advertisement from the 1930s.

Trammel, sawtooth
 Brass, simple detail, adjusts from
 18″ l   305.00
 Wrought Iron
  With grease lamp with four spouts,
  15″ h   330.00
  With three prong hook at end, ad-
  justs from 23″ l   115.00
Trivet
 Brass, octagonal, four short feet, en-
 graved star design, 6½″ d   60.00
 Wrought Iron, primitive, fork rest, pit-
 ted   95.00
FISH SCALER
C. D. Kenney, cast iron, 9″ l   20.00
Champion, cast iron   12.00
FLATWARE
Bakelite handles, yellow handles, six place
setting   45.00
Steel, wooden handles, set of four knives
and five forks   12.00
FLOUR SIFTER
Tin
 Kwik, 5 cup, double ended, yellow
 wooden handle   18.00
 New Standard, side crank, c1918,
 7″ h   15.00
Wood, metal crank, bin shape, marked
"Tilden's Patent, 1865"   150.00
FOOD CHOPPER
Enterprise No. 501, cast iron, tinned,
four discs   30.00
Keen Kutter, Simmons Hardware, Model
K110, cast iron, tinned   25.00

Kitchmaster, Chicago Flexible Shaft Co,
plated metal, table mount, three discs,
c1934   25.00
Universal L.F.C., patent date 1897   35.00
Wrought iron
 8″ w, wood handles, one blade signed,
 primitive, price for pair   80.00
 9″ w, crescent blade, turned double
 handles, original maker's label   60.00
FOOD LABEL
Apple Butter, Mt Vernon, white mansion,
7 lbs, 6½ × 8½″   1.00
Baking Powder, Little Fairies, illustration
of Dr Blumer, yellow, red, and black,
11¼ × 5″   1.00
Beans, Old Black Joe, elderly black man
and cabin, speckled butter beans   1.00
Biscuits, Shredded Wheat, four leaf clover
shape, gummed   6.00
Blackberries, Home Canners, 1920s scene
of woman in kitchen ladling fruit from
large open tin can into her own canning
jars, background shows shelves of filled
canning jars, descriptive message describing qualities of Home Canners on both
sides of the image, gilt border, 6½ ×
10″   6.00
Clams, Sportman's Pride, Moclips minced
razor clams, dam, 1¾ x 11″   .50
Coffee, Zodiac, New Orleans, LA, gold
zodiac designs, aqua background, 14 ×
5¾″   1.00
Corn, Arcadia Beauty, Sweet Corn, two
big ears of white corn   1.00

A sampling of chopping knives used by housewives in the days long before food processors. From the collection of Jack and Barbara Butt Anchorage, Alaska.

Cranberry Sauce, Unity, molded cranberry sauce in glass dish, gilt border, 2¾ × 2¼″ .50
Egg Crate, portrait of Chief Sleepy Eye, colorful sunburst, 9¼ × 11¼″ **2.00**
Oysters, Tide Rim, Markham, WA, two oysters and waves **2.00**
Peanut Butter, Verhampshire Brand, rectangular **5.00**
Peas, Tropic Peas, Philadelphia, roaring lion's head, fruits, navy blue design, white background **2.00**
Pickles, H J Heinz Co, pickle shape, gummed, 3¾″ l **15.00**
Pumpkin, Butterfly, golden pumpkin, large butterfly .50
Salmon, Maple Leaf, Ilwaco, WA, salmon steak on plate, red, gold maple leaf, gilt trim, 1¾ × 11″ **1.00**
Skim Milk, Country Maid, blue and white milk maid standing beside cow, carrying milk pail, blue and red background **2.00**
Strawberries, Joe De Marco, juicy berries, leaves, light blue background, 6″ sq .75
Syrup, Longwood Plantation's Syrup, smiling black lady, red bandanna, 8 × 6½″ **1.00**
Tomatoes, Barefoot Boy, little barefoot boy in rolled up pants **2.50**
Yam, Gene–O, man in top hat and tails holding diamond studded cane and big yam .75

FOOD MOLD
Copper, turk's head, decorative detail, dovetailed seams, dents, 10″ d **125.00**
Redware, turk's head, Rockingham glaze **145.00**
Tin, scalloped crown design, 6½″ d **40.00**

FORK
Wrought Iron, three tine, tooling, brass handle, slightly battered, 23″ l **160.00**
Wrought Iron, brass and copper inlay, tooled design, 16½″ l **210.00**

FRUIT BALLER
Metal, hinged cutting ring, red handle, 1920s, 5¼″ l **5.00**

FRUIT CRATE LABELS
Apple, 10½ × 9″
Blue Winner, cowboy in arena on horseback, reaching down to pick up apple **2.00**
Don't Worry, little boy holding apple, black background **1.00**
Merry Christmas, Santa in sleigh, six reindeer in sky, red apple **1.00**
Red Diamond, red and yellow apples, red diamond, blue background **1.00**
Snow Line, colorful orchard scene, snowy mountains, big red apple **2.00**
Tell, red apple pierced by arrow, gray background **1.00**
Wilko, red apple, red border, yellow background **1.00**
Grapefruit
Better N Ever, half sliced grapefruit, blue background .50
Desert Bloom, Redlands, desert scene, white blooming yucca, blue sky **2.00**
Grapes, 13 × 4″
Barlo, smiling boy holding big bunch of grapes .50
CR Van Buskirk, green, red, and blue grapes, gilt and white background .25
Fresno Bella, glamorous girl with big basket of grapes, red background .50
L–Z, smiling boy holding green grapes .50
Our Josie, happy little girl seated beside basket of grapes, big wine glass, blue, yellow background .75
State Center, gilt map of CA, poppies, grapes, red banner, gilt border .50
Lemons, 12½ × 8¾″
Basket, Lemon Cove, golden basket holding five lemons, blue background **1.00**
Cutter, Oxnard, cutter going full speed ahead through choppy seas, brilliant orange and gold sky, dated 1937 **3.00**
Kaweah Maid, Lemon Cove, Indian girl wearing turquoise beads, brown background **4.00**
King Tut, Santa Barbara, Art Nouveau style glass of lemonade, sliced and whole lemons, sugar bowl, blossoms **4.00**
Morning Smile, lemon on opened Sunkist wrapper, blue background **1.00**
Perfection, Ivanhoe, orchard scene, purple mountains, huge lemons and leaves, blossoms in lower left corner, aqua shading to dark blue background **2.00**

Sea Coast, Ventura, two lemons, blue triangle, brown background **2.00**

Sunkist California Lemons, lemons on black background, yellow letters **1.00**

Wave, Santa Paula, two lemons, blossoms, leaves, red background **1.00**

Oranges, 10 × 11″

Airship, Fillmore, old four propeller commercial airplane, royal blue background **12.00**

Caledonia, Placential, thistle spray, tartan plaid background **1.00**

Eat One, Lindsay, arrow pointing to juicy orange, aqua background **2.00**

Golden Trout, Orange Cove, huge trout leaping out of water, slight damage **30.00**

Green Mill, Placentia, avocado green Dutch windmill, yellow skies, white clouds, red background **2.00**

Great Valley, Orange Cove, scenic, orange orchard **1.00**

Have One, Lemon Cove, hand holding a partially peeled orange, royal blue background **2.00**

Homer, Corona, flying homing pigeon, orange, blue, black background **1.00**

Lincoln, Riverside, colorful portrait of Abraham Lincoln, orange, leaves **2.00**

Majorette, Woodlake, vivacious majorette, red, white, and maroon, green background **2.00**

Orange Circle, Orange Cove, large orange circle, two oranges, black and blue background **1.00**

Poinsettia, Fillmore, red poinsettia, green leaves, black background **5.00**

Royal Knight, Redlands, brave knight in armor on horseback, castle, yellow background **2.00**

Strathmore, Scottish bagpiper in kilts, thistles, deep blue background, red plaid border **2.00**

Treetop, Lemon Cove, giant twin Sequoia tree, yellow lettering, blue background **1.00**

Western Queen, Rialto, pretty Indian lady, green sunburst **10.00**

Pears, 10¾ × 7¼″

American Maid, navy blue silhouette of lady wearing floppy hat, orange background **1.00**

Blue Parrot, large aqua parrot on flowering branch **1.00**

Duckwall, colorful wood duck standing by brick wall **2.00**

Forever First, plump juice pears, red holly berries, greens, blue background **2.00**

Littlerock, bunch of pears, orchard **1.00**

Piggy Pears, pink cartoon pig, wearing clothes and bonnet, carrying green basket full of pears, maroon background **2.00**

Snow Owl, fierce snowy owl, blue background **2.00**

Violet, big bunch of purple violets, black background **4.00**

FRUIT JARS

All Right, aqua, qt, metal disc, wire clamp **75.00**

Anderson Preserving Co, clear, qt, metal lid **12.00**

Atlas E–2, seal, half pint, wire, glass lid **10.00**

Ball

Eclipse, Wide Mouth, clear, qt, glass lid, wire bail **2.50**

Ideal, aqua, pt, glass lid, wire bail **2.00**

Mason, aqua, qt, emb backwards "s," zinc lid **4.00**

Perfection, aqua, qt, glass lid, zinc band, handmade **18.50**

Bamberger's Mason Jar, blue, qt, glass lid, wire bail **10.00**

Brockway Clear–Vu Mason, clear ½ pt, metal lid **2.50**

Calcutt's, clear, qt, glass screw lid, handmade **35.00**

Clarks Peerless, aqua, pt, glass lid **8.00**

Crown Mason, clear, qt, zinc lid **1.50**

Cunningham & Ihmsen, aqua, qt, wax seal **15.00**

Dillon, aqua, qt, wax seal **12.00**

Dunkley, clear, qt, hinged glass lid **5.00**

Easy Vacuum Jar, clear, qt, glass lid, wire clamp **25.00**

Everlasting Jar, Improved, clear, qt, glass lid, toggles **15.00**

Franklin Fruit Jar, aqua, qt, glass lid **35.00**

Gem, Wallaceburg, clear, pt, glass lid, screw band **5.00**

Globe, green, pt, glass lid, lever bail **30.00**

Hansee's Palace Home Jar, clear, qt, glass lid **50.00**

Hazel Preserve Jar, clear, qt, glass lid **8.50**

I G Co, aqua, qt, wax seal **25.00**

Independent Jar, clear, qt, glass lid **35.00**

Jewell Jar, clear, ½ gallon, glass lid, screw band **8.00**

Johnson & Johnson, NJ, amber, qt, glass lid **20.00**

Keystone, clear, pt, zinc lid **10.00**

Knox Mason, clear, qt, zinc lid **4.00**

Leotric, aqua, ½ gallon, glass lid, wire bail **10.00**

Lustre, aqua, pt, glass lid, wire bail **8.00**
Mallinger, clear, qt, zinc lid **4.00**
Mason
    Improved, green, qt, glass lid, screw
    band **2.00**
    Iron Cross, quart, blue **12.00**
    Keystone in circle, Patent Nov 30,
    1858, green, qt, zinc lid **8.00**
    Root, aqua, qt, zinc lid **4.00**
Mid West, Canadian Made, clear, qt, glass
lid, screw band **5.00**
Norge, clear, qt, glass lid, metal
band **10.00**
Opler Brothers, clear, qt, glass lid, wire
bail **5.00**
Peoria Pottery, gray pottery, brown glaze,
pt **20.00**
Perfect Seal, clear, qt, rubber seal **3.00**
Presto Wide Mouth, clear, ½ pt, glass lid,
wire bail **2.50**
Rhodes, Kalamazoo, MI, aqua, pt, zinc
lid **6.00**
Samco Genuine Mason, clear, 3 gallon,
zinc lid **15.00**
SC & Co, Mason, half gallon **10.00**
Standard, aqua, qt, wax seal **20.00**
Tropical Canners, clear, pt, zinc lid **4.00**
Universal, clear, qt, zinc lid **5.00**
White Crown Mason, aqua, qt, zinc
lid **10.00**
Woodbury, aqua, glass lid, metal
clip **25.00**
Young's Pat May 27, 1902, stoneware,
brown neck, metal clamp lid **20.00**

FUNNEL
Graniteware
    Acme, gray **40.00**
    Blue Diamond Ware, 9″ d **95.00**
Tin, red handle, combination funnel,
measure, and strainer **10.00**

FURNITURE
Baker's Stand, wrought iron, 48″ w,
14½″ d, 84″ h **225.00**
Chairs
    Arrowback, decorated, set of six side
    chairs, original dark brown paint, yel-
    low striping and floral decoration on
    crest, some wear, 17½″ seat, 33¾″ h,
    price for set of six **1,485.00**
    Plank Seat, decorated, set of six side
    chairs, old yellow–green repaint over
    earlier colors, striping, stenciled, free
    hand fruit and foliage, minor damage,
    33″ h, price for set of six **575.00**
    Windsor, bamboo, country, set of six
    side chairs, shaped seat, wide crest, old
    brown finish, 33¾″ h, price for set of
    six **630.00**

Crock Stand, country, three tier, oak, old
green repaint, 39″ w, 19″ d,
43¾″h **375.00**
Cupboard
    Corner, PA, pine cleaned down to
    traces of old blue paint, one pc con-
    struction, perimeter molding with un-
    usual applied scalloping, double top
    doors with eight panes of old glass,
    reeded and relief carved mid section
    panel, single paneled door flanked by
    two stationary panels, butterfly scal-
    loped top int. shelves, int. with arched
    baffle with cutout pinwheels, minor
    edge damage, 54½″ w,
    89¼″ h **6,500.00**
    Country, hanging, one piece, poplar,
    original red paint, dovetailed case with
    base and cornice molding, board and
    batten door, two int. nailed drawers,
    added turnbuckle latch, 22″ w, 11½ ×
    23¼″ cornice, 36½″ h **1,125.00**
    Country, wall, one piece
        Pine, reeded frame, paneled doors,
        scrolled base, refinished, repairs, re-
        placed 15¾ × 39¾″ crown mold
        cornice, 84¾″ h **400.00**
        Pine and poplar, old green and red
        paint, primitive, six small shelves,
        age cracks in backboards, 10″ w,
        6″ d, 41¼″ h **525.00**
        Poplar, red repaint, four paneled
        doors, two nailed drawers, one
        board cornice, damage to base, one
        nailed on back foot, edge damage to
        one drawer, 40½″ w, 20″ d,
        71″ h **1,210.00**
Dry Sink
    Country
        Pine, two raised panel doors set in
        reeded frames, apron drop on center
        stile, central well flanked by two
        dovetailed drawers, cutout feet, inte-
        riors and well painted blue, old
        mellow refinishing, 58¾″ w, 22″ d,
        32″ h **935.00**
        Poplar, old dark finish, well shaped
        cutout feet, two paneled doors, two
        dovetailed drawers in base, zinc
        lined well, hutch top with top shelf
        and two dovetailed drawers,
        61¾″ w, 21½″ d, 51″ h **2,200.00**
        Poplar and Walnut, old worn red re-
        paint with black brushed graining,
        black door panels over darker blue,
        39¼″ w, 19″ d, 36″ h **635.00**
    Grain Painted
        Poplar, one piece, hutch top, original
        brown flame graining, four paneled

doors, three dovetailed drawers, damaged zinc lined well, chamfered corners, cutout feet, cast iron and brass thumb latches, white porcelain pulls, wire nail construction, 36″ w, 19″ d, 74¼″ h **1,650.00**
Poplar, one secondary wood, original red vinegar graining on yellow ground, sunbursts, fans, X's, etc., well shaped bracket feet, paneled doors, one dovetailed drawer, open well, worn int. shelf, 42″ w, 19¼″ d, 31¾″ h **11,500.00**
Hanging, rectangular poplar box, scalloped ends, zinc lining, made to be taken off wall and used as water container, 15 × 30″ **225.00**
Hoosier Style Cabinet, Sellers, pine panels, oak frame, tambour door, flour bin, sliding porcelain work surface, bread drawer, sliding cutting board, painted white **350.00**
Jelly Cupboard
Pine, shaped crest, long drawer over two paneled doors, interior shelf, wood pulls, painted green **400.00**
Poplar, molded cornice, four panel door, shelved interior, molded base, slightly curved block feet, yellow repaint, 37¼″ w, 72″ h **1,540.00**
Kitchen Set
Rectangular gray laminated top table, one hidden leaf, chrome trim, four matching yellow and gray chairs, c1950 **300.00**
Rectangular oak table with porcelain top, four chairs, painted white **250.00**
Pie Safe, pine, slightly overhanging rectangular top, two doors each with three punched tin panels, diamond and circles design, three matching panels each end, single nailed long drawer, high square feet, worn bluish–green paint, replaced porcelain knobs, bottom side tins have rust damage **1,100.00**
Shelves, hanging, country, pine, old green paint, canted sides, three graduated shelves, age cracks in bottom shelf, 20½″ w, 7¼″ d, 22″ h **250.00**
Table
Drop Leaf, country, refinished maple with curl, turned legs, curved end apron, two board top, single board leaves, castors, opens to 47″ d, 28¼″ h **470.00**
Sawbuck, country
Pine and hardwood, old mellow refinishing, one board breadboard top, one end of horizontal cleat holding top to base is ended out, 90″ l, 25″ w, 29½″ h **1,000.00**

Pine, one board top with some stains and use scars, refinished, 43″ l, 21″ w, 26½″ h **500.00**
Work
Country, poplar, sturdy square tapered legs, refinished three board top, red repaint on base, 37½″ w, 56½″ l, 29″ h **200.00**
Hepplewhite, walnut, pine secondary wood, removable three board top, two cockbeaded drawers with replaced turned drawer pulls, square tapered legs, old mellow refinishing, replaced top is well made replacement, 33¼″ w, 59″ l, 29″ h **660.00**
Water Bench, country, poplar, old worn olive gray repaint, 48½″ w, 41″ d, 29″ h **450.00**

❧ G
GADGETS NO ONE CAN DO WITHOUT
Bar Utensil Set, chrome, green bakelite handles, five piece set **40.00**
Carrot Slicer, rectangular birch tray, center hole slides over blade, 2½ × 7¾″ **75.00**
French Fry Cutter, Maid of Honor, tin, stamped, 1930s **6.00**
Jar Wrench, Wilson Mfg Co, cast iron **12.00**
Pineapple Snip **20.00**
GRATER
Brass, scratched initials and mark, 4½ × 12½″ **165.00**
Cast Iron, cranked tin cylindrical grater, 11½″ l **70.00**
Graniteware
Cream and Green, flat **95.00**
Red, small **75.00**

Rare Yara chocolate grater, patent #2914, dates back to 1842. Courtesy of Bob and Kaaren Grossman, Chester, N.J.

Tin, Gilmore, patent 1897   8.00
Tin and Wire
  Ekco, two grating surfaces, 10½" l **8.00**
  Gadget Master Product No. 8,
  10" l   **10.00**

GRAVY BOAT
Aluminum, hand wrought, 7" l, curled
handle, matching underplate and ladle,
Hand Forged/Everlast Medal, price for
three piece set   **12.00**
Fiesta, Cobalt Blue   **50.00**
Franciscan
  Apple Pattern, underplate   **45.00**
  Coronado Swirl Pattern, attached un-
  derplate, yellow, satin   **22.00**
  Desert Rose Pattern   **45.00**
  Duet Pattern, underplate   **15.00**
  Ivy Pattern, underplate   **30.00**
  Starburst Pattern, original ladle   **45.00**
  Trio Pattern   **10.00**
Graniteware, blue and white, mot-
tled   **195.00**
Hall China
  Autumn Leaf   **20.00**
  Mulberry Pattern, original ladle   **25.00**
  Wildfire Pattern   **30.00**
Homer Laughlin
  Epicure Pattern, Turquoise   **20.00**
  Harlequin Pattern, Yellow   **10.00**
Knowles, Edwin, Yorktown Pattern,
pink   **18.00**
Metlox Pottery
  Aztec Pattern, Poppytrail line   **40.00**
  California Ivy Pattern, Poppytrail line,
  underplate   **25.00**
  California Provincial Pattern, Poppytrail
  line   **15.00**
  Homestead Provincial, Poppytrail
  line   **20.00**
  Navajo Pattern, Poppytrail line, under-
  plate   **30.00**
  Provincial Fruit Pattern, Poppytrail line,
  handled   **12.00**
Stangl Pottery, Apple Delight Pattern,
#5161, liner   **35.00**

GREASE JAR
Abingdon Pottery, daisy dec, No.
679   **40.00**
Anchor Hocking Glass, Vitrock, black cir-
cles and flowers   **35.00**
McCoy Pottery, cabbage head,
1954   **35.00**
McKee Glass, Seville Yellow   **37.50**

GRIDDLE
Cast Iron, Griswold Mfg Co, Erie, PA,
large emblem, round
  No. 9   **20.00**
  No. 10   **25.00**

GYPSY KETTLE
Brass, cast-iron bail, early, cleaned,
6½" d, 5" h   **40.00**

Cast Iron, small, 3 ftd, wire bail handle,
Wagner, 3 × 5"   **28.00**

↦ H
HONEY JAR
Ceramic, bee hive, bee finial, marked
"Occupied Japan"   **25.00**
Glass, figural, seated bear, metal lid **18.00**
HOT PLATE
Fire King, Oven Glass   **15.00**
HOUR GLASS
Egg Timer, turned wood, sand bulbs,
c1927   **20.00**
Primitive, clear blown glass, pine frame
with minor damage, 6¼" h   **400.00**
HOT PAD
Advertising
  Kriebel's Dairies, Hereford, PA, muslin,
  hemp backing, 4¼" sq   **1.50**
  Reddy Kilowatt, red, white, and yellow,
  c1950, 5½" sq   **30.00**
Autumn Leaf Pattern, accessory, tin back,
7¼"   **30.00**
Crewel Work, red, pink, yellow, gold,
and blue yarn, linen ground, initialed and
dated "H W 1767," 8" d   **775.00**
HOT PAD HOLDER PLAQUE
Black Memorabilia, plaster, boy and girl
holding watermelon slice, brass hook,
painted, 4 × 4", price for pair   **75.00**

↦ I
ICE BOX
Acme, ash, extra high, brass locks **750.00**
Economy, elm, golden finish, galvanized
steel lining, brass hinges, 45 pound ice
capacity, 41¼" h   **500.00**
Lapland Monitor, Ramey Refrigerator Co,
Greenville, MI, oak, three paneled doors,

Felt-backed pot holder advertised McFad-
den's Electric Coffee on its cotton front.

paneled ends, square feet, metal name plate, 35″ w, 20″ d, 48″ h **575.00**
North Pole, oak, applied decoration on two paneled doors, paneled ends, bracket feet, zinc lined, original hardware, metal name plate, 25″ w, 19″ d, 55″ h **475.00**
Victor, Challenge Refrigerator Co, Grand Haven, MI, oak, single raised panel door, paneled ends, zinc lined, original hardware, metal name plate, 22″ w, 15″ d, 40″ h **500.00**

ICE BUCKET
Aluminum, hand wrought
  Canterbury Arts, hammered finish, double walled, rubber weal, 8″ h **45.00**
  Hammered finish, ceramic lining **20.00**
Cambridge Glass, Decagon pattern, amber **25.00**
Chrome, round, wooden knob, penguins decoration **20.00**
McKee Glass, transparent green **20.00**

ICE CREAM DIPPER/SCOOP
Gilchrist No. 33 **145.00**
Maid of Honor, red bakelite handle, mint condition, original box **35.00**
Mayer, adjustable shank **250.00**
Mosteller No. 79 **195.00**

ICE CREAM FREEZER
Alaska Freezer Co., Winchendom, MA, North Pole model **50.00**
Kwik Freeze, galvanized tin, blue, paper label **50.00**
Tingley's Patent Horizontal, barrel churn, straight cylindrical sides, A–frame base, wood, iron bands on freezer, iron crank **135.00**

ICE CREAM MOLD
Basket, banquet size, French flared hinges, marked "Brevete, SGDG, Remarque Fabrique, CC" **200.00**
Chrysanthemum, marked "313" **55.00**
Grape Leaf, marked "E–256" **40.00**
Lobster, marked "S–175" **60.00**
Morning Glory, marked "S–239" **40.00**
Santa Claus, banquet size, marked "E & Co No. 194" **350.00**
Strawberry, marked "503" **65.90**
Turkey, dressed, pewter, 5″ l **20.00**

ICED TEA SERVER
Depression Era Glassware, frosted green, horizontal rib, "Frigidaire Iced Tea Server" **20.00**

ICE PICK
Advertising, Pevely Dairy, metal **12.00**
Wood, painted handle, steel pick **5.00**

ICE SHAVER
AC Williams Co., Ravenna, OH, lid monogrammed "ACW," cast iron, tinned **20.00**

Artic Ice Shave #3, Grey Iron Casting Co., Mount Joy, PA, cast iron **15.00**
Griswold, Erie, PA, cast iron and steel **35.00**

ICE TONGS
Cast Iron **30.00**
Forged Iron, 21″ l **35.00**
Wooden handle, cast iron, very worn advertising on handle **18.00**

❧ **J**

JAR, COV
Advertising, Kiss Me Gum slogan **95.00**
Fiestaware, Homer Laughlin, red, Kitchen Kraft **315.00**
Redware, ovoid
  5¾″ h, tooled strap handle, tooled line at shoulder, gallery lip with side spout and lid, edge wear and chips **200.00**
  6″ h, strap handle, dark orange glaze with brown splotches, lid, old chips **50.00**
  6½″ h, greenish yellow slip glaze with brown flecks, green and reddish brown flower like designs, old chips, badly chipped lid **2,000.00**
  6¾″ h, strap handle, rim spout, and lid, clear glaze with brown sponging, bottom imp "1½," minor chips **200.00**
Woodenware
  4⅜″ h, one pc of wood, inserted bottom, chip and scratch carved, original lid, repaired cracks **35.00**
  8½″ h, treen, ftd, good turnings, old refinishing, traces of old dark paint, glued break in foot **55.00**

JAR, OPEN
Morton Pottery, stoneware, Albany slip glaze, marked on side, two gallon size **65.00**
Stoneware
  8″ h, ovoid, imp label "Sipe Nichols & Co, Williamsport, Pa," cobalt blue brushed design, surface flakes **275.00**
  8½″ h, cobalt blue stenciled label "A. P. Donaghho, Parkersburg, W. Va." **95.00**
  10″ h, ovoid, imp label "Cowden & Wilcox 2," brushed cobalt blue floral design **440.00**
  11¼″ h, imp label "W. Flesher," brushed cobalt blue flourish on each side, stains **200.00**
  13¾″ h, imp label "White & Wood, Binghamton, N.Y. 4," cobalt blue quill work bird on branch, hairlines **415.00**
  15½″ h, ovoid, imp label "I. M. Mead, Portage Co, Ohio, 4," cobalt blue floral design, applied shoulder handles, hair-

lines and shallow chips, chip and hairline on lid   **275.00**
18½" h, ovoid, imp label "Hamilton, Greensboro, Pa. 8", applied shoulder handles, good brushed cobalt blue floral dec, badly cracked   **855.00**

JUG

Fiesta
  Cobalt Blue, two pint   **75.00**
  Green, cov, Kitchen Kraft   **170.00**
Hall China
  Chinese Red Pattern, Radiance
    #1, no lid   **35.00**
    #2, cov   **75.00**
    #4, cov   **75.00**
    #5, no lid   **45.00**
  Fantasy Pattern, Five Band, 2 pt **75.00**
  No. 488 Pattern, Radiance, #5, no cov   **50.00**
  Red Dot Pattern (a.k.a. Eggshell Polka Dot), cov, #2   **85.00**
  Red Popppy Pattern, Radiance, #5   **35.00**
  Wildfire Pattern, Radiance, #5 **55.00**
  Wild Poppy Pattern (a.k.a. Poppy and Wheat), Radiance
    #3, no lid   **35.00**
    #4, cov   **75.00**
Harker Pottery
  Deco–Dahlia Pattern, 6" h   **18.00**
  Mallow Pattern, cov   **25.00**
Homer Laughlin, Kitchen Kraft, cov **75.00**
McCoy Pottery, yellow, unmarked, 1950s   **20.00**
Stoneware
  9½" h, imp label highlighted with cobalt blue "J. Hayes & Co, Manchester, N.H.," minor lip flakes   **175.00**
  14" h, ovoid, incised long tailed bird, cobalt blue highlights, gray–tan salt glaze, chip on lip, ribbed handle   **900.00**
  15½" h, imp label "S. S. Perry & Co, W. Troy," brushed cobalt blue flower, ribbed strap handle   **250.00**
  17¼" h, imp "Nichols and Boynton, Burlington, Vt. 4," cobalt blue quillwork stylized floral design, large chip on lip, hairline in handle, flake on base   **126.00**
  18½" h, ovoid, imp label "I. M. Mead, Mogadore, Ohio," brushed cobalt blue floral decoration and "5," double ear handles, professionally restored   **385.00**
  "Penn Yan," two polka dot birds, cobalt blue quillwork "%", minor wear, short hairlines   **2,600.00**
  19½" h, ovoid, brushed cobalt blue labels "10" and "1882" on one side, "W. Lunn" on reverse, double ear handles, lip and one handle glued   **190.00**

K
KETTLE

Brass
  Cast, iron bail handle, 14" d, 7¼" h   **75.00**
  Spun brass
    11" d, iron bail handle, "Hayden's Patent" label, some damage, old repair   **50.00**
    17½" d, iron bail handle, marked "American Spun Brass Kettle," some damage   **110.00**
Wrought Iron, light blue swirl, marked "Wrought Iron Range"   **235.00**

KITCHEN SAW

Always Sharp, Charles Wohr, Lancaster, PA, adjustable steel blade, cast aluminum frame, 15¾" l   **15.00**
Keen Kutter, Simmons Hardware, carbon steel blade, wood handle, 13½" l **12.00**

KITCHEN SCALE

Hanson   **24.00**
Landers, Frary & Clark   **15.00**

Patent papers for this kitchen device show that it was invented by Lucius Goff of Richford, Vermont, who received a patent June 2, 1885 for his kettle lifter. According to the inventor, the object of his invention was to provide a new and improved device to facilitate lifting, carrying, tilting and otherwise handling kettles. Courtesy of Phyllis and Jim Moffet of Modesto, Ill.

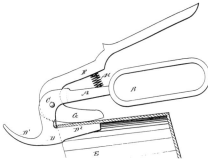

KNIFE BOX

Butternut, old worn finish, cutout handle in divider, baffle added to one side, bottom boards cracked, 9½″ w,
17¾″ l   75.00
Curly maple and other wood, old soft finish, well shaped divider with turned handle, minor old puttied repairs, 10¼″ w,
13¼″ l   150.00
Mahogany, dovetailed, scrolled ends, cutout handle in divided, old refinishing,
8¾″ w, 15¾″ l   200.00
Pine, divided, shaped center with cutout heart, old worn black repaint, 10¼ ×
14″   115.00

KNIFE, GLASS

Depression Era Glassware
  Air–Flo
    Crystal   50.00
    Green   75.00
  Block, crystal, 9″ l, original box   30.00
  Dagger, crystal   125.00
  Durex, Three Leaves, blue, 9¼″ l, original box   25.00
  Pinwheel, crystal, 8½″ l, original box   45.00
  Rosespray
    Amber, original box   250.00
    Crystal   85.00
  Steelite
    Santa Catalina, pink   110.00
    Treasure Island, pink   110.00
  Storex, green, original box   95.00
  Three Leaves, green, 8″ l, original box   32.00
  Three Star
    Blue, 8½″ l   32.00
    Dark Pink, 9½″ l   22.00

❧ L

LADLE

Aluminum, hand wrought, 14½″ l,
Argental Cellini Craft   18.00
Graniteware
  Blue and white, large swirl   70.00
  Red and white   22.00

LAZY SUSAN

Aluminum, hand wrought
  Everlast, rose and forget–me–not pattern, open mark, 14½″ d   15.00
  Rodney Kent, cov glass dish, ribbon and flower trim, marked "Hand Wrought Rodney Kent," 16″ d   15.00

LEMON SQUEEZER

Arcade, Freeport, IL, cast iron, pottery reamer insert   40.00
Sheet Metal, Walker's Quick & Easy No. 42, Erie Specialty Co, Erie, PA, frame clamps to table, iron lever, cast aluminum perforated cup, glass dish   50.00
Wooden, hand made   38.00

LINENS

Bread Tray Cover, filet crochet, white, motto "Staff of Life," c1925, 12½″ l   **5.00**
Dish Towel
  Embroidered, white textile background
    Designs and days of the week, seven piece set   **25.00**
    Mammy, days of the week, cross stitched, unused, set of 7   **150.00**
  Printed cotton, strawberries design, blue border   **8.00**
Napkins, damask, original paper labels, price for set of six, marked "Occupied Japan"   **45.00**
Tablecloth
  50″ sq, white, printed multicolored dec
    Mexican, minor repairs   **22.50**
    Strawberries   **25.00**
  52″ sq, blue, green, and white snowflake pattern   **12.00**
  54 × 72″, Autumn Leaf Pattern accessory, sailcloth   **75.00**
  55 × 64″, red and white, leaf design   **72.00**
  56 × 66″, white, printed multicolored floral and fruit dec, 1940s   **26.00**
  56 × 96″, linen, white, red Greek key design borders   **40.00**
Toaster Cover, fabric Mammy doll, original box, Bucilla Products, c1940,
16″ h   **225.00**

❧ M

MAGAZINE TEAR SHEET/COVER

Black Memorabilia, *Saturday Evening Post,* Nov 28, 1936, black Mammy cooking turkey and young boy watching on cov   15.00
Jello advertisement, Maxfield Parrish illustrator   35.00
Uncle Sam holding a "Health Bill" under his arm, looking at Cream of Wheat advertising billboard, copyright 1915, 5½ × 8½″   20.00

MATCH HOLDER

Advertising
  Ceresota/Prize Bread Flour of the World, diecut, full color litho tin, early 1900s   175.00
  De Laval   145.00
  Sharples Tubular Cream Separator, tin, cows in pasture scene above image of mother and child using separator, 2″ w, 7″ h   110.00
Black Memorabilia, bellhop, wood   45.00
Depression Era Glassware, Jeannette Glass, Delphite, round, "Matches" in black letters   88.00
Wall
  Advertising, Adriange Farm Machinery, multicolored, 7½″ h   165.00

Plastic, red 7.50
MEASURE, DRY
Graniteware
Gray, 4 quart, hanging ring, marked "4 Qt. NYC," L & G 90.00
Light blue and white swirl 35.00
Wood, iron bands, worn 30.00
MEASURING CUP
Advertising
Lenkerbrook Farms, Inc., Pyrex, 8 oz, red markings 5.00
Swans Down Cake Flour Makes Better Cakes," 1 cup, spun aluminum 15.00
Depression Era Glassware, Jadite
One–third cup 8.50
Four cup, handle 40.00
Federal Glass Company, amber, 1 cup, three spout, no handle 30.00
Fire King, 2 cup, sapphire blue 18.00
Fry Glass, Pearl, three spout 90.00
Hazel Atlas Glass Company, green, 1 cup, three spout 18.00
Jeanette Glass, Jadite, set of four measures, original box 75.00
McKee Glass
Clear, Glasbake, two cup 32.00
Fired On, red, two cup 20.00
MEASURING SPOONS
Advertising
A & P, tin 6.00
Dr Price's Baking Powder, stamped metal, four way, 4⅜" l 15.00
Robin Hood Flour, set of four 6.50
Towles Log Cabin, set of four 45.00
Tin, stamped, set of three riveted together marked "Original" 10.00
MEAT GRINDER
Family No. 1, Ellrich Hardware Mfg Co, Plantsville, CT, patent 1888 35.00
Gem Chopper, Sargent & Co., New York City, NY, cast iron, clamps to table, patent March 8, 1892]cm45.00
Perry's Patent No. 3, Ames Plow Co., cast iron, table mounts, large "S" crank handle, long turned wood grip, 9½" l 145.00
Russvin, 1903 15.00
MEAT SLICER
Dandy, tin, wood handle 12.00
General No. 208, white enameled metal, wood handle, 20th C 40.00
MEAT TENDERIZER
Cast iron round head, wooden handle, Yale Meat Scorer, 8¼" l 50.00
Stoneware drum with sharp points, thick turned painted wood handle, patent Dec 25, 1877 75.00
Wood, six sharp points, 9" l 15.00
MILK BOTTLE
Grasslands Dairy, qt 10.00
Thatchers Dairy, 1884, emb man milking cow 250.00

The four-way head rotates on this kitchen combination tool. It enabled the family cook to use it as a chopper, potato masher or meat tenderizer. Courtesy of Phyllis and Jim Moffet of Modesto, Ill.

MILK BOTTLE CAP
Christmas Seal Cap of 1939, Christmas Seal illus 5.00
Davol Anti Germ, rubber, fits over lip of milk bottle to keep out dirt, original container 8.00
Grade A Raw Milk, red and white .50
Heber Springs Dairy, Heber Springs, AR .25
I.O.O.F. Independent Order of Odd Fellows, Home Pasteurized Milk, Greensburg, IN .25
Kents Dairy Farms, Vitamin D, Olean, NY .20
Parker Goat Dairy, Raw Milk, picture of goat 1.25
Set, US Presidents, 35 in set, price for 35 piece set 12.00
War Cap, "Milk wouldn't be here if (large swastika) were" 5.00
MILK BOTTLE CAP OPENER
Brock Hall Dairy Products on front, Purity Protected Dacro Sealed Milk on back 5.00
Deerfoot Farms, Southborough,MA 5.00
MILK BOTTLE CAP PICK
Borden Select Milk 5.00
Forest Glen Creamery Co, combination pick and bottle opener 6.00
Sheffield Farms Co, Inc 5.00
MILK BOTTLE CARRIER
Metal, wire handle, holds six round quarts 10.00
MILK CAN
Brass nameplate showing name of shipper, ten gallon size 18.00
Dairy's name printed on front, ten gallon size 10.00
Plain, ten gallon size 10.00
MILK JUG
Morton Pottery, Woodland Glaze, yellow ware, brown and green spatter over transparent glaze, advertising on side, 4½" h 80.00
MILK PITCHER
Graniteware
Blue and White, large swirl, early 175.00

Bonnie Blue, small, marked **175.00**
Hull Pottery, Little Red Riding Hood, figural, standing, 8″ h **275.00**
Redware, 4⅝″ h, imp tooled dec bands, clear glaze, running brown, edge wear, small flakes **75.00**

MIXING BOWL
Anchor Hocking Glass Company, Vitrock, 10¼″ d, paneled **13.00**
Bauer Pottery, Gloss Pastel Kitchenware, c1942, No. 18, chartreuse **24.00**
Depression Era Glassware, green, 9″ d, slick handle **18.00**
Fiestaware, Homer Laughlin, nested set, No. 1 turquoise, No. 2 red, No. 3 cobalt blue, No. 4 yellow, No. 5 turquoise, No. 6 red, No. 7 turquoise, price for set **550.00**
Hall China, Pastel Morning Glory Pattern (a.k.a. Pink Morning Glory), Radiance, #2 **55.00**
Harker Pottery, Red Apple Pattern, 10″ d **30.00**
Homer Laughlin, Kitchen Kraft, 8″ d **20.00**
McKee Glass
  7″ d, Skokie Green, pouring spout **15.00**
  8″ d, Hamilton Beach, custard **10.00**
Morton Pottery, yellow ware, wide white band, narrow blue stripes top and bottom, 12½″ d **45.00**
  Pyrex Glassware, white, aqua kitchen utensils decor, nested set of five **40.00**

MIXING SPOON
Advertising, "Rumford Baking Powder," metal, slotted bowl, green wood handle, 10¾″ l **15.00**
Wooden, well worn, deep patina **5.00**

MOLASSES JUG
Graniteware, white, large, tin lid **35.00**

MUG
Advertising
  Dairy Dell **16.00**
  Elsie The Borden Cow, china, full color illus of Elsie dancing, c1940, 3″ h **65.00**
  Isaly Buttermilk, barrel shape, ironstone **75.00**
  Keebler Bakery Elf, plastic, F & F, 1972 **10.00**
  Mr Peanut, plastic, green, 1960s, 4″ h **50.00**
  Nestle Quick Rabbit, plastic, 1970s, 4″ h **20.00**
Ceramic
  McCoy Pottery
    Davy Crockett, marked "Brush" **35.00**

Stoneware, grape pattern, 1926 **110.00**
Occupied Japan
  Boy Handle, marked "Occupied Japan" **14.00**
  Indian Chief, marked "Occupied Japan" **35.00**
  MacArthur, marked "Occupied Japan" **55.00**
Graniteware, cobalt and white, large swirl, child's, price for pair **98.00**

MUSTARD JAR
Depression Era Glassware, white, hp dec **25.00**
Hull Pottery, Little Red Riding Hood, original spoon, 5½″ h **350.00**
Shawnee Pottery, Corn Queen **30.00**

❧ N
NAPKIN HOLDER
Aluminum, hand wrought
  Rodney Kent, hammered finish, decorative floral bands and feet **10.00**
  Trefoil shape, ftd, fruit dec **8.50**

NAPKIN RINGS
Bakelite, set of six round carved napkin rings, original box **85.00**
Bisque, cat, marked "Japan" **20.00**
Celluloid, figural, bear **6.00**
Franciscan Ware, Desert Rose Pattern **50.00**
Milk Glass, triangular **30.00**
Nippon China, hand painted floral decoration, green mark, 2″ d **60.00**
Silver Plated
  Parrot, rectangular base, Rogers Mfg Co **50.00**
  Ring, etched dogwood blossom **20.00**

NOODLE CUTTER
The Ideal, Toledo Cooker Co, rolling type, wire handle and frame, 14 blades, c1910 **15.00**
Vitantonio Mfg Co., Cleveland, OH, cast iron, tin, and wood, hand crank, table model **50.00**

NOTEPAD HOLDER
Black Memorabilia, figural, Mammy, red bandanna, yellow blouse, 1954 copyright, Miller Studio Inc., plaster, 5 × 9″ **50.00**
Celluloid, fruit decoration, wall mounted, pencil on string **8.00**

NUTCRACKER
Alligator, cast brass, 7½″ l **90.00**
Antelope, head, lever type, carved wood, glass eyes, long horns, 8⅞″ l **135.00**
Dog, cast iron, well defined hair, advertising "L. A. Althoff, Makers of Headlights, Stoves & Ranges, Laporte, IN," 11″ l **75.00**

This unusual nutmeg grater could be held in one hand, thanks to the finger holes the design contained. Photographed by Bob Cahn, Courtesy of *New England Antiques Journal.*

Nutmeg graters came in many shapes and sizes, showing that early inventors did their share of tinkering in the search for just the right device to do the job. Photographed by Bob Cahn, Courtesy of *New England Antiques Journal.*

There's a very hot market for nutmeg graters among kitchen collectors. This rare one is from the collection of Lois Carey of Michigan. Photographed by Bob Cahn, Courtesy of *New England Antiques Journal.*

Eagle, head, spring lever, cast iron, wood base, 6½" l **175.00**
Gold Fish, teeth in mouth, gold painted cast iron, glass eyes, spring loaded lever as upper fin, English, 1920s **95.00**
Pliers type, hand held, engraved steel, 5½" l **15.00**

NUT GRINDER
Climax, cast iron and tin, glass jar, threaded tin hopper, 1940s **12.00**
Lorraine Metal Mfg Co., green painted metal **25.00**

NUTMEG GRATER
Cast iron crank, wire handle, 7" l **75.00**
Tin
  Coffin type, stamped and punctured tin, storage box with sliding lid, embossed design, English, 6½" l **30.00**
  Cylinder and barrel, wood plunger, 4" l **85.00**
  Pocket, side unfolds, 2¾" h **95.00**

✦ O
ONION CHOPPER
Glass Jar, wooden knob, original paper label **10.00**

✦ P
PANCAKE SERVER
Nippon China, covered server, floral decoration, gold and cobalt blue borders, blue Maple Leaf mark **300.00**
PASTRY BLENDER
Wire, marked "Omar Wonder Flour" **8.00**
PEA SHELLER
Cast Iron, crank handle **27.50**
PEEL
Poplar, old refinishing, 33½" l **95.00**
PESTLE
Woodenware, curly maple, sturdy turned handle, good curl, refinished, minor age cracks, 11¼" l **40.00**

PICKLE FORK
Advertising, Dayton, OH, Finest Dairy
Products Co, 8″ l   6.00

PIE BIRD
Bird, Morton Pottery, white, multicolored
wings and back, 5″ h   22.00
Black Bird, white base   24.00
Black Chef, holding rolling pin   55.00
Chicken   48.00
Chinaman   50.00
Crow, black   40.00
Dog, baying, black spots, white back-
ground   50.00
Duck, wearing blue striped beret   50.00
Duckling, Morton Pottery, white, pink
base and wings, 5″ h   25.00
Elephant, standing on hind legs, white,
England   50.00
Funnel
  Inscribed "Nut Brown Pie Fun-
  nel"   50.00
  Yellow top, pie man followed by three
  children and dog   50.00
Mermaid, black face and arms, white hair,
green tail   52.00
Minstrel, black suit and hat, white face
with black features   52.00
Owl, stylized   45.00
Penguin, green scarf and hat   54.00

Rooster, Willow Ware, blue decoration,
white background   18.00
Woman, holding pie   50.00

PIE CRIMPER
Aluminum, Juice Tite Pie Sealer,
5½″ l   15.00
Wood, old patina, well shaped handle,
7″ l   185.00

PIE PLATE
Blue Ridge, Green Briar Pattern, 9″ d   4.50
Fiesta, Green, Kitchen Kraft   35.00
Fire King, Oven Glass, 9″ d   9.00
Graniteware, gray   20.00
Harker Pottery
  Colonial Lady Pattern   25.00
  Deco–Dahlia Pattern, 9″ d   17.00
  Pansy Pattern   30.00
Homer Laughlin
  Kitchen Kraft   25.00
  Mexicana Pattern, 9″ d   35.00
Morton Pottery
  Rockingham mottled brown glaze,
  9″ d   100.00
  Woodland Glaze, yellow ware, brown
  and green spatter over transparent
  glaze 9″ d   100.00
Pennsbury Pottery, Mother Serving
Pie   75.00

Delicate pie crimper has a paintbrush style
handle and bone jagging wheel. It is thought
to date from the second quarter of the 18th
century. From the author's collection.

Cruciform baker's tool of brass and wood is
thought to be English, from the 1800s, and
includes a jagging wheel plus a diamond-
shaped stamp and a round stamp. From the
author's collection.

Although it looks like someone's rendition
of a large insect, this kitchen antique served
a very useful purpose. The unusual-action
hot plate lifter or pie lifter kept the cook's
hands a goodly distance from the hot pots
and pans. Courtesy of Phyllis and Jim Moffet
of Modesto, Ill.

Redware, coggled rim, three line yellow
slip dec, small rim chips, 8⅝" d   **225.00**
Tin, Mrs Smith's, embossed name   **5.00**
Yellow ware, 11" d   **80.00**

PITCHER
Abingdon Pottery, ice lip, two quart, No.
200   **35.00**
Aluminum, hand wrought, ovoid, slender
neck, twisted handle, Buenilum Hand
Wrought   **35.00**
Bauer Pottery
  Gloss Pastel Kitchenware, c1942, 1
  quart, green   **32.00**
  Monterey Pattern, dinnerware line pro-
  duced from 1936 until 1945, 2 quart,
  Yellow   **40.00**
Fiesta, red, disc   **145.00**
Franciscan
  Apple Pattern
    Milk, 1 qt   **80.00**
    Water, 2 qt   **125.00**
  Desert Rose Pattern, milk   **85.00**
  Ivy Pattern, water   **125.00**
  Starburst Pattern
    Large   **95.00**
    Medium   **75.00**
Hall China, Red Dot Pattern (a.k.a. Egg-
shell Polka Dot), Baron   **95.00**
Homer Laughlin, Harlequin Pattern, wa-
ter, Medium Green   **70.00**
Jeannette Glass, Delphite, two cup, sun-
flower bottom   **80.00**
McCoy Pottery
  Clover Leaves, emb design, yellow,
  1948   **20.00**
  Elephant, white, marked "NM USA,"
  1940s   **45.00**
  Vegetable, transfer dec   **35.00**
McKee Glass, custard, red dots, two
cup   **25.00**
Metlox Pottery
  California Ivy Pattern, Poppytrail line,
  ice lip   **35.00**
  Red Rooster, Poppytrail line,
  6" h   **40.00**
Pennsbury Pottery
  Amish Woman, 5" h   **45.00**
  Red Rooster, 4" h   **27.00**
Redware, white slip with marbleized red,
green, and brown, some edge wear, glaze
flakes, 6¾" h   **45.00**
Roseville Pottery
  Bushberry, blue, ice lip   **225.00**
  Cow, c1916   **275.00**
  Creamware Medallion, 4" h   **55.00**
Shawnee Pottery
  Bo Peep, blue bonnet   **75.00**
  Corn King
    No. 70   **5.00**
    No. 71   **50.00**

Elephant   **25.00**
Grist Mill, No. 35   **10.00**
Little Boy Blue, No. 46   **50.00**
Stangl Pottery
  Antique Gold, No. 4052,
  14½" h   **35.00**
  Country Garden Pattern, 2 qt   **45.00**

PLACE CARD HOLDER
Celluloid, black base, two Mickey Mouse
figures, paper stick reads "Walt Disney
Enterprises Ltd/Japan," 1930s   **90.00**

PLATE
Ceramic, Occupied Japan
  Cabin Scene, chickens in yard   **18.00**
  Cherries, lacy edge   **25.00**
  Geisha Girls   **20.00**
Roseville Pottery, Jack Horner, rolled
edge, 8" d   **95.00**
Shawnee Pottery
  Corn King, dinner, No. 68   **15.00**
  Corn Queen, No. 69   **15.00**
Woodenware, burl, dense figure has pits
and some putty filled holes, old finish,
7⅞" d   **250.00**

PLATTER
Bauer Pottery
  La Linda Pattern, dinnerware line pro-
  duced from 1939 until 1959 oval,
  12" l, Yellow   **20.00**
  Monterey Pattern, dinnerware line pro-
  duced from 1936 until 1945, oval,
  12" l, Ivory   **32.00**
Blue Ridge
  Chrysanthemum Pattern, oval,
  12" l   **10.00**
  Garden Lane Pattern, Colonial shape,
  11¾" l   **10.00**
  Sungold #1 Pattern, Candlewick
  shape, 14" l   **22.00**
  Waltz Time Pattern, 14½" l   **25.00**
China, Blue Willow pattern, oval, 12" l,
marked "Occupied Japan"   **35.00**
Graniteware
  Blue and white, mottled, large   **70.00**
  Brown and white, swirl, bacon
  type   **195.00**
Fiesta, 15" d
  Cobalt Blue   **40.00**
  Red   **55.00**
Franciscan
  Apple Pattern
    12" l   **38.00**
    14" l   **42.00**
  Desert Rose Pattern, 14" l   **15.00**
  Duet Pattern, 15" l   **20.00**
  Ivy Pattern
    Oval, 13" l   **45.00**
    Turkey   **225.00**
  Starburst Pattern, oval
    13" l   **25.00**

15″ l	**22.00**
Trio Pattern, 14″ l	**16.00**

Hall China
Autumn Leaf, 13½″ l	**14.00**
Orange Poppy Pattern, 13″ l	**15.00**
Pastel Morning Glory Pattern (a.k.a. Pink Morning Glory), 13½″ l	**35.00**
Serenade Pattern, (a.k.a. Eureka Serenade), 13½″ l	**20.00**
Wildfire Pattern, oval, 11½″ l	**25.00**

Homer Laughlin
Dogwood Pattern, 11¾″ l	**9.00**
Riveria Pattern, 11½″ l, Yellow	**18.50**

Knowles, Edwin
Deanna Pattern, 12″ d, green	**15.00**
Yorktown Pattern, 12″ d, russet	**20.00**

Metlox Pottery
Aztec Pattern, Poppytrail line, 13″ l	**32.00**
California Provincial Pattern, Poppytrail line, 13½″ l	**25.00**
Homestead Provincial, Poppytrail line, 13½″ l	**20.00**
Navajo Pattern, Poppytrail line, 11¾″ l	**30.00**
Provincial Fruit Pattern, Poppytrail line, 13½″ l	**18.00**
Red Rooster, Poppytrail line, 13½″ l	**20.00**

Shawnee Pottery, Corn King, No. 96	**40.00**

POST CARD

Borden's Condensed Milk Plant No. 1, Brewster, NY, side view of plant, signed on front by plant manager, addressed to Borden's office in NYC **10.00**
Ebert Ice Cream Company, factory pictured **5.00**
Elsie, Elmer, and Beauregard, traveling representatives of Borden's family of fine foods, shows characters in traveling bedroom, explanation of bedroom furnishings on back, color **7.50**
Moxie, two children with cutouts and sign **25.00**

POSTER

Alaga Syrup adv, black and white Willie Mays photo, red lettering with black accents, c1958, 9¾ × 20″ **50.00**
Buckwheat Flour, flour bag shape, 19 × 10″ **25.00**
Coca–Cola–Yes, 1946 bathing beauty, Harold Sundblum, 11 × 27″ **150.00**
Coleman's Mustard, paper, trademark image in medallion insert, 16 × 22″ **150.00**
DelMonte Foods, garden show, dog knocking over flower vase, vegetable can in corner, c1970, 24½ × 35″ **15.00**
Evaporated Milk–Pure Cow's Milk, black and white cows, green ground, 1940 **8.00**

Healthy & Happy, colorful portrait of boy and girl eating bananas, milk, Lawrence Wileur, full color, 17 × 21″ **10.00**
Lion Coffee, c1910, 11 × 14″ **100.00**
Quaker Oats, "Today The Quints Had Quaker Oats," 1935, 14 × 32″ **65.00**
Rice's Seeds, paper, jolly man holding very large turnip, printed by Cosack & Co, 20 × 27″ **950.00**
Wheaties, model planes, multicolored, "Wheaties, Breakfast of Champions" at bottom, c1944, 16 × 36″ **85.00**

POTATO MASHER
Metal, double grid	**50.00**
Wood, well worn, deep patina	**25.00**

POTATO RICER

Handy Things, Ludington, MI, tinned metal presser and cup, iron handles painted red, c1940, 12″ l **10.00**

POT SCRAPER

Advertising, color lithography on tin, hole for hanging
Babitts Cleanser	**225.00**
Junket, curved	**250.00**
Sharples Cream Separator	**275.00**
Tin, triangular, plain	**15.00**
Wire rings	**17.00**

PREMIUM LIST

Mohawk Condensed Milk Co, can of Sweet Clover Brand Condensed Milk on front, can of Gold Cross Brand Condensed Milk on back, 40 pgs, 1927 **5.00**

PRESERVING JAR

Stoneware
6¾″ h, cobalt blue stenciled label: "Hartford City Salt Co, Dealers in Salt & General Merchandise, Hartford City, W. Wa," chips and hairlines	**275.00**
8″ h, cobalt blue brushed and stenciled design, small flake on base	**170.00**

The wire portions of potato mashers have been twisted into all sorts of interesting designs. This is one of the simpler ones, but it got the basic job done.

➡ R

RADIO
Advertising, figural
Pillsbury Doughboy, plastic, earphones,
1985, 6¼″ h   40.00

RAISIN SEEDER
Everett, marked "Patent Applied For,"
wood and wire   55.00
EZY Seeder, patent 1899, table model,
words "Scald the raisins" embossed on
side   75.00

RANGE SHAKER
Cinnamon, McKee, Jadite, Square, metal
lid   100.00
Flour
Jeannette Glass, Delphite, metal lid,
flour, 8 oz   165.00
McKee Glass, sq, Skokie Green   25.00
Pepper
Anchor Hocking, jadite   15.00
Depression Era Glassware, white, lady
watering decal   12.00
McKee Glass, custard, black vertical let-
tering and stripes   15.00
Salt
Blue Ridge, French Peasant Pat-
tern   50.00
McKee Glass
Roman Arch pattern, white, fired—on
red   7.00
Square pattern, Light Jadite, metal
lid   20.00
Salt and Pepper, price for pair
Purinton Pottery, Apple Pattern   25.00
Shawnee Pottery
Corn King   20.00
Dutch Boy and Girl   65.00
Pig   90.00
Roosters   45.00

Rare lever-action raisin seeder accepted two
grapes at a time, but dealing with a sizable
fruit crop still had to have been a tedious
task. Courtesy of Phyllis and Jim Moffet of
Modesto, Ill.

White Corn   30.00
Sugar, McKee, Square pattern, Light
Jadite, metal lid   24.00

REAMER
China and Ceramic
Austria, 2¾″ h, white, pink flowers,
green trim (D–106)   45.00
Bavaria, 3½″ h, two pieces white, red,
yellow, and green flowers, gold trim
(D–119)   50.00
Czechoslovakia, 6″ h, two pieces, or-
ange shape, white, green leaves,
marked "Erphila" (L–37)   35.00
England
3½″ h, white, orange and yellow
flowers (D–107)   45.00
3¾″ h, two pieces, orange shape, or-
ange body, green leaves
(L–20)   24.00
France, 3¼″ d, white, red, purple, and
yellow flowers, green leaves, gold trim
(D–112)   18.00
Germany
3½″ h, scrolling flow blue dec, white
ground (E–60)   55.00
5″ d, Goebel, yellow, (E–108) 50.00
Japan
3″ h, saucer type on pedestal, loop
handle, fruit dec (D–59)   40.00
3¾″ h, two pieces, strawberry shape,
red, green leaves and handle,
marked "Occupied Japan"   65.00
4½″, baby's orange, blue on white
(B–4)   28.00
4¾″ h, lemon, yellow, white flowers,
green leaves (L–40)   40.00
5″, orange, textured orange peel ext.,
yellow, green leaves, white int.
(L–39)   48.00
8½″, pitcher and tumbler, blue and
white windmill dec (P–87)   48.00
Limoges, 5¼″ d, scalloped, orange and
pearl luster, brown handle
(E–79)   125.00
McCoy Pottery, green, 8″ w,
1948   40.00
Nippon, 3¼″ h, two pieces, hp, white,
floral dec   75.00
United States
Ade–O–Matic Genuine, 9″ h,
green   95.00
Jiffy Juicer, large bowl with cone
center, elongated loop handle, ten
colors known, Pat 1938 (A–5) 60.00
Red Wing, 6¼″ d, gray, red and
blue design (A–16)   300.00
Universal, Cambridge, OH, 9″ h, two
pieces, pitcher, cream, lavender lilies,
green leaves, silver trim
(P–104)   155.00

Zippy, 3¼" h, 6½" d, hand crank cone, Wolverine Products, Detroit, MI, several colors (A–4)   **60.00**

Glass (Measurements indicate width, not including spout and handle)

Anchor Hocking Glass Co, 6¼" d, lime green, pouring spout   **22.00**

Depression Era Glassware

Cobalt Blue, Crisscross   **260.00**
Jadite, emb Sunkist   **45.00**
Pink, emb Sunkist   **75.00**
Seville Yellow, emb Sunkist   **55.00**

Fenton, transparent green, pointed cone, tab handle (131–7–5)   **95.00**

Fry, 6⁵/₁₆" d, opal, pouring spout **45.00**

Hazel Atlas

Criss–cross, two pieces, orange size, pink   **165.00**
Pink, tab handle, large (138–4–4)   **26.00**

Jeannette Glass Co

Delphite, Jennyware   **75.00**
Light Jadite, two pieces, two cup   **35.00**

Jenkins Glass Co, 5¼" d, green (N–212)   **50.00**

McKee Glass

French Ivory   **50.00**
Seville Yellow   **165.00**

US Glass Co, light pink, two cup pitcher set (151–2–1)   **35.00**

Metal

Aluminum

Gem Squeezer, two pieces, crank handle, table model (M–100) **10.00**
Handy Andy, table type, crank, red base, 6⅞" d, 10½" h   **20.00**
Knapp's, crank at top, hand held, patent 1930   **10.00**
Kwicky Juicer, pan style, Quam–Nichols Co (M–97)   **8.00**
Mason's Sealed Sweet Juicer, wall mounted, 1930s   **10.00**
Rival Mfg Co, Kansas City, MO, lever action, c1935   **40.00**
Wearever E–12–1, Ebaloy Inc, Rockford, IL, 6" h   **6.00**

Bernard Rice & Sons Apollo EPNS, 3¾" h, two pieces (PM–70)   **90.00**

Dunlap's Improved, 9½" l, iron hinged (M–17)   **32.00**

Hong Kong, 2½" h, two pieces, stainless steel, flat (M–205)   **8.50**

Nasco–Royal, 6" l, scissor type (M–265)   **8.00**

Presto Juicer, metal stand, porcelain juicer (M–112)   **60.00**

Wagner Ware, 6" d, cast aluminum, skillet shape, long rect seed dams beneath cone, hole in handle, two spouts (M–96)   **18.00**

Williams, 9¾" l, iron, hinged, glass insert (M–60)   **32.00**

Yates, EPNS, 4¾" d, two pieces (PM–73)   **130.00**

RECIPE BOX

Aunt Jemima, yellow   **110.00**
Metal, blue, filled with recipes   **10.00**

REFRIGERATOR DISH, COV

Depression Era Glassware

Crisscross, cobalt blue
4 × 4"   **35.00**
8 × 8"   **120.00**

Federal Glass, pink, vegetable emb lid, 4 × 4"   **8.00**

Jadite, 4 × 5"   **15.00**

Hazel Atlas, criss cross, cobalt blue, original label   **125.00**

Jeannette Glass, Chailane Blue, two small chips, 4 × 4"   **125.00**

McKee Glass

Seville Yellow, 4 × 5"   **15.00**
Skokie Green, 8 × 5"   **16.00**

Hall China

Chinese Red Pattern, Zephyr   **155.00**
Fantasy Pattern, loop handle   **145.00**
No. 488 Pattern, square   **60.00**
Orange Poppy Pattern, loop handle   **38.00**
Wild Poppy Pattern (a.k.a. Poppy and Wheat), sq   **125.00**

REFRIGERATOR JAR, COV

Jeannette, jadite, 32 oz   **24.00**
McKee Glass, Seville Yellow, 10 oz **17.00**

REFRIGERATOR WATER DISPENSER

McKee Glass, Skokie Green, original spigot, 11" l, 5" w, 4" h   **90.00**

RELISH TRAY

Aluminum, handwrought, Everlast, glass bowl, aluminum frame, Bali Bamboo pattern, open mark, 7¼" d   **10.00**

Blue Ridge

Buttons and Forget–Me–Nots Pattern, heart shape   **30.00**
Serenade Pattern, top handle shape, four sections   **60.00**

Franciscan, Desert Rose Pattern

Oval, 10¼" l   **25.00**
Three Part, 11" l   **50.00**
Duet Pattern, 7" l, handled   **10.00**
Starburst Pattern
6½" w, triangular, divided   **25.00**
7½" w, handled   **25.00**

Metlox Pottery, Provincial Fruit Pattern, Poppytrail line, rect, divided, handled   **12.00**

Nippon China, landscape scene, green mark, 8½" l   **125.00**

Shawnee Pottery, Corn King, No. 79   **22.00**

Stangl Pottery, Apple Delight Pattern, #5161   **22.00**

ROASTER

Graniteware, covered, oval
    Large, cream and red   30.00
    Small, cobalt blue   10.00

ROLLING PIN

Ceramic
    Amy Pattern, Harker Pottery   85.00
    Basket of fruits and flowers, Harker
    Pottery   75.00
    Cameoware Pattern, Harker Pottery,
    pink   110.00
    Countryside Pattern, Harker Pot-
    tery   115.00
    Deco–Dahlia Pattern, Harker Pot-
    tery   85.00
    Fruit Basket Pattern, Harker Pot-
    tery   85.00
    Petit Point Rose Pattern, Harker Pot-
    tery   100.00
Glass
    Depression Era Glass, blown
        Cobalt blue   80.00
        Light amber   145.00
    McKee Glass
        Custard   325.00
        Delphite Blue, shaker end   225.00
Wood
    Curly Maple, refinished, 18½" l   70.00
    Maple, one piece, 14" l   25.00

A 12-inch wide, double rolling pin was made with a cookie cutter on one end and a biscuit cutter on the other. Unmarked, it appears to have been factory made but is rare. Courtesy of Phyllis and Jim Moffet of Modesto, Ill.

❖ S

SAFFRON BOX

Lehnware, poplar, original painted decoration and decoupage flowers and strawberries in green, red, and other colors, pink background, glued break in foot, minor wear   470.00

SALAD SET

Aluminum, hand wrought, 13" d bowl, tulip dec, matching serving utensils, Buenilum Hand Wrought   20.00
Depression Era Glass, fork and spoon, clear, red teardrop handles   20.00

SALT AND PEPPER SHAKERS, PR

Bakelite
    Cubes, maroon, matching handled
    tray   15.00
    Dome top, red   12.50
    Half Moon, green and yellow, matching
    handled tray   18.00
    Shotgun Bullets, green   15.00
Blue Ridge China
    Blossom Top Pattern, Skyline
    shape   28.00
    Saratoga Pattern, Skyline shape   15.00
Ceramic, figural
    Bed and Pillow, Nester type pattern,
    black trim, white background   10.00
    Chilly Willy and Charlie Chicken,
    1958 Walter Lantz copyright,
    4" h   80.00
    Dutch Couple, sitting on bench,
    kissing   12.50
    Hammer and Nail, gray nail, brown
    and black hammer   12.00
    Kitchen Witch, blue dress, red hat, one
    with white apron, other holding
    broom, Taiwan, 1979   10.00
    Hat, one brown, one black, marked
    "Occupied Japan"   15.00
    Mammy and Chef, yellow, Brayton La-
    guna   95.00
    Penguins, glazed, black and white, or-
    ange bill and webbed feet, marked
    "Japan," 1930s, 3¼" h   19.00
    Pigs, large ears, marked "Occupied
    Japan"   12.00
    Pixies, blue outfits, yellow hair   10.00
    Smokey The Bear, yellow muzzle and
    hat, blue trousers, brown body, salt
    holding shovel, pepper holding bucket,
    1960s, 4" h   20.00
    Turtles, walking, dark green shell,
    brown bodies   6.00
Fiestaware
    Dark Green   40.00
    Red, Kitchen Kraft   75.00
Franciscan Ware
    Desert Rose Pattern
        Rosebud   14.00
        Tall   45.00
    Duet Pattern   15.00
    Ivy Pattern   30.00
    Starburst Pattern, tall   60.00
Hall China
    Autumn Leaf
        Handled, range   22.00
        Ruffled–D, small   14.00
    Fantasy Pattern, handled   32.00
    Mulberry Pattern   18.00
    Orange Poppy Pattern, handled   30.00
    Pastel Morning Glory Pattern (a.k.a.
    Pink Morning Glory), Teardrop   35.00
    Wildfire Pattern, Teardrop   35.00

Wild Poppy Pattern (a.k.a. Poppy and Wheat), handled **95.00**
Harker Pottery, Colonial Lady Pattern, small **16.00**
Homer Laughlin, Kitchen Kraft **28.00**
Metal, candelabra, silvered, black trim, clear plastic removable candle shakers, original box, 1950s, 5½″ h **18.00**
Plaster, figural, painted
Captain Midnight and Joyce Ryan, 1940s **100.00**
Dick Tracy and Tess Trueheart, Famous Features copyright, 1942, 3″ h **65.00**
Don Winslow and Red Pennington, blue outfits, white hats and accents, 1940s, 3″ h **40.00**
Little Orphan Annie, Annie and Sandy, 1940s, 3″ h **25.00**
Liza and Mose, original box, c1940, 2¾″ h **75.00**
Uncle Sam, glossy white, black, and red accents, red, white, and blue top hat, 1½ × 2½ × 2″ **45.00**
Plastic, figural
Aunt Jemima and Uncle Mose, figural, F & F, c1950, 5″ h **55.00**
Boy and Dog, Van Telligen **50.00**
Chef, black holding chicken, white holding cat **95.00**
Magic Chef, advertising, painted, red raised script, 1950–60, 5″ h **50.00**
Television Set, brown, gold accents, black and white picture of Art Linkletter on screen, on and off switch raises shakers, original box, 1950s, 3″ h **65.00**
World's Fair, New York, 1939, Perisphere and Trylon, orange and dark blue base, 4″ h **30.00**
Pottery
Little Red Riding Hood, Hull Pottery
Large, 5½″ h **125.00**
Small, 3¼″ h **50.00**
Shawnee Pottery
Bear, ivory and gold, 3¼″ h **55.00**
Corn King, 3½″ h
Dutch Boy and Girl **25.00**
Fruit, small **25.00**
Owl, green eyes, original paper label **30.00**
Roosters, 3¼″ h **40.00**
Sailor, small **18.00**
Watering Pail, 3¼″ h **45.00**
Winnie Pig, blue collars **60.00**

SALT BOX
American, hanging type
Mahogany, old mellow refinishing, one drawer, lift slant top lid, scalloped crest, 8½′ w, 13¾″ h **590.00**

Pine and poplar, long narrow crest, refinished, 35″ h **130.00**
Poplar, old red paint, interior of lid marked in pencil: "L. G. Adam, September 13, 1883," 8 × 8 × 8″ **220.00**
English, hanging type with spoon rack, oak, old worn finish, dovetailed, scalloped detail, age crack in backboard, incomplete crest, 23½″ h, 15″ w **275.00**

SAUSAGE STUFFER
Angers Perfect No. 1 Filler, Sargent & Co., tin and cast iron, spring loaded lever action, table top mounts **60.00**
Hubbard, cast iron, six quart **40.00**
Primitive, hand made, wood, long box, cranked turn screw, sliding lid, 25″ l, c1845 **150.00**
Wagner Stuffer Co 3, Salem Tool Co, Salem, OH, cast iron, crank type, mounted on board, c1900 **40.00**

SAUCE PANS
Brass, cast, bronze handle, polished, 6½″ d, 6¾″ l handle **40.00**
Copper
Dovetailed seams, cast iron handles, labeled "D. H. & M. Co. N.Y.," somewhat battered, 14½″ d **72.00**
Dovetailed seams, heavy, wrought copper handle, some edge damage, 5½″ d, 7¼″ h to handle **75.00**
Nesting set of four, cast iron handles, 7¾ to 10″ d **220.00**

SCOOP
Aluminum, cast, 11″ l, 4″ w, c1930 **15.00**
Copper, turned wooden handle, lip split, old soldered reinforcement, 14½″ l **75.00**
Graniteware, white, small **70.00**
Metal, wood on top of handle, grain type **10.00**
Woodenware, birch, little curl, old varnish finish, edge damage, 11″ l **195.00**

SIEVE
Bentwood, galvanized hardware cloth, 16″ d **25.00**
Tin, pierced bottom, minor wear **20.00**

SIGNS
De Laval Cream Separators, tin, round, woman using cream separator, child carrying cream pail, emb rolled border, 26″ d **2,000.00**
Golden Girl Sunspot, emb tin, green menu board, 1930s **115.00**
Heinz Mince Meat, paper, full color, 1930s, 12 × 22″ **75.00**
Jersey Creme, flange **400.00**
Morton Salt, tin **80.00**
Our Fresh Up 7–up, cardboard, diecut, easel back, elderly man and woman holding product, 1943, 12 × 18″ **35.00**

SKILLET

Cast iron, Griswold Mfg Co, Erie, PA, large emblem

No. 3	15.00
No. 4	35.00
No. 5	25.00
No. 6, lid	45.00
No. 8, lid	35.00
No. 9, smoke ring	35.00
No. 10, smoke ring	35.00
No. 12	95.00

SKIMMER

Brass, tooled wrought iron handle, 17″ l **245.00**

Graniteware, gray **28.00**

Wrought Iron, large flat bowl, 12″ d **40.00**

SPATULA

Advertising

Bucks County Bank & Trust, green handle, white plastic blade **2.00**

Rumford **6.00**

Wood, well worn **9.00**

SPICE BOX

Hanging Type, country

10″ w, 25″ h, hardwood, old finish, eleven drawers, porcelain pulls, faded spice labels, late wire nail construction, repaired crack in back at hanging hole **350.00**

14½″ w, 17⅜″ h, 7½ × 15½″ molded cornice, pine, old yellow–brown graining, ten nailed drawers, turned wooden pulls, int. of backboards branded name and "Bradford, Vt., Nov. 1873" **1,400.00**

Tin, eight drawers, old finish, 13¾″ h **225.00**

Tinware, decorated, round, six (of seven) original interior canisters, worn original brown japanning, gold stenciled labels, 7¼″ d **115.00**

Wood, scalloped wood frame, six open tin canisters, worn finish, 8¾″ d, 3″ h **110.00**

SPICE SET

Black Memorabilia, ceramic, emb Mammy and Chef, price for five piece set **125.00**

McKee Glass, custard, labeled jars, metal lids, original rack **50.00**

SPICE SHELF

Plastic, pink, cut–out letters, repaired crack **25.00**

Wood, hand made, three shelves, refinished **35.00**

SPOON

Graniteware, Blue Diamond Ware, long handle **48.00**

Primitive, hardwood, chip carved detail, old worn dark finish, 26″ l **40.00**

Wood, old varnish finish, 11″ l **80.00**

SPOON MOLD

Bronze, two piece mold used for casting pewter spoons, 9″ l **330.00**

SPOON REST

Aluminum, figural, head, relief black chef with wide open mouth, 1930s, 4 × 6″ **75.00**

McCoy Pottery, penguin shape, 1953 **35.00**

Nippon China, hand painted decoration, blue mark, 7¼″ l **85.00**

Plastic, chef holding two pans, white, black trim **7.50**

Shawnee Pottery, flower, green and yellow **18.00**

STOVE

Atlanta Stove Works, No. 8M, cast iron, coal or wood, two burner **300.00**

Atlas Stove, cast iron, coal, six burners, water reservoir, upper shelf projecting over warming oven, curved legs, nickel plated trim **1,200.00**

Gem Stove, No. 80, cast iron, coal, two burners **300.00**

STOVE LID LIFTER

Cast iron, embossed name

Eagle	12.00
Garland	10.00
Jewel	12.00
Plain, openwork handle	5.00
Radiant Home, nickel plated	10.00

STRAWBERRY JAR

McCoy Pottery, Bird of Paradise, brown and beige, No. 4, 1950 **32.00**

This unusual stove lid lifter's handle contained eight different words in reverse, which were to be used to mark the still-soft sealing wax on old canning jars. It hints at the inventory of foods on a home canner's shelves, thanks to the words it contains, "BLACKB," "STRAWB," "GOOSEB," "RASPB," "PEACH," "PEAR," "PLUM," and "TOMATO." Courtesy of Phyllis and Jim Moffet of Modesto, Ill.

STRING HOLDER

Advertising, Post Toasties, round, tin front 50.00
Ceramic, figural, apple 20.00
Chalkware, girl's head, wearing bonnet 45.00
China
  Mammy, stamped "Japan," 1930s, china, 7" h 75.00
  Shawnee Pottery, green and yellow 18.00
Woodenware, treen, holly or boxwood, turned detail, string hole in lid, turned finial with worn metal string cutter, 2⅞" h 185.00

SUGAR BOWL

American Art Pottery, bulbous, handled, blue, gray spray glaze, 3" h 10.00
Blue Ridge
  Sungold #1 Pattern, Candlewick shape 15.00
  Waltz Time Pattern 15.00
Franciscan
  Apple Pattern 35.00
  Ivy Pattern 35.00
Hall China
  Autumn Leaf, Radiance 15.00
  Mulberry Pattern 18.00
Homer Laughlin
  Epicure Pattern, charcoal 20.00
  Riveria Pattern, mauve blue 10.00
Graniteware, gray, tin lid, L & G 295.00
Hull Pottery, Little Red Riding Hood
  Crawling 225.00
  Standing 450.00
Metlox Pottery, Aztec Pattern, Poppytrail line 35.00
Shawnee Pottery
  Fruit Basket 24.00
  White Corn 30.00
Tinware, decorated, worn original red paint, brown and yellow comma type foliage, foot slightly battered, 3½" h 165.00

SUGAR BUCKET

Wooden, stave construction, old worn finish
  7¼" h, lid and intertwined bands, orange stain, minor edge damage 200.00
  8" h, worn old brownish–red finish, finger construction bands 115.00
  12" h, worn refinishing 85.00
  14½" h 95.00

SUGAR NIPPERS

8¼" l, wrought steel 200.00
9" l, wrought steel, tooled designs 100.00

SUGAR SHAKER

McKee Glass, transparent green, bullet shape 85.00
Shawnee Pottery, White Corn 60.00

SWIZZLE STICK

Black Memorabilia, Zulu–Lulu, plastic,

transparent brown, original display card, 1940s, 6" l, price for set of six 25.00
Plain, glass, red base, price for set of six 10.00

SYRUP PITCHER

Franciscan Ware, Desert Rose Pattern 125.00
Graniteware, brown, Onyx Ware, bulbous 365.00
Plastic, Aunt Jemima, hinged head, 1950s, 5½" h 75.00

❧ T

TABLE MAT

Dengler Dairies, Telford, PA, When Baking Use This Mat, When Cooking Use our Milk, There's Health in Every Drop, Dengler Dairies, Telford, PA 5.00

TEA CADDY

Tinware, decorated, 4¼" h, original red paint, stylized black, white, and yellow florals, minor wear 1,800.00

TEA CANISTER

Tinware, decorated, 7" h, original dark brown japanning, yellow and orange–red dec, worn 115.00

TEA KETTLE

Brass, cast, stationary iron handle, polished, 11" d 60.00
Cast Iron
  Erie, bowl like base, wire bail handle, marked "Erie," 11½" d 22.00
  Terstegge, Gohmann & Co, New Albany, IN, 1883, emb name on circular lid, 12" w including spout 45.00
  Wood Bishop & Co, Bangor, ME, wrought iron handle, sliding lid, 14" d 70.00
Copper, dovetailed
  6½" h, gooseneck spout, swivel handle 55.00
  8½" h, some battering, soldered repair, swivel handle 60.00
  8¾" h, gooseneck spout, well shaped stationary handle 140.00
  10½" h, gooseneck spout, brass trim, acorn, finial, well shaped stationary handle, maker's mark of intertwined initials "W.C. & S." 95.00

TEAPOT

Aluminum, hand wrought, 10 × 7", octagonal, wooden handle, Wagner Ware 35.00
Bauer Pottery
  Gloss Pastel Kitchenware, Aladdin, cov
    4 cup, Ivory 45.00
    8 cup, Burgundy 65.00
  Ring, 6 cup, wood handle, Orange–red 60.00
Blue Ridge, Kismet Pattern, Skyline shape 55.00

Bone China, blue, white, and gold, Wedgwood, c1905 110.00
Cast Iron, Norge, wall hanger 25.00
Ceramic, Black Memorabilia, Gone with the Wind type Mammy 29.00
China, floral, Victoria Carlsbad, Austria, 5" h 30.00
Cottage Ware, house, lid is roof, marked "Price Kensington, Made in England, Ye Olde Cottage" 28.00
Dragonware, 6 cup, raised dragon and coralene dec, gold trim, marked "Made in Occupied Japan" 30.00
Earthenware
  Brown, "Simple Yet Perfect", c1905 95.00
  Double spout, slip dec, c1890 80.00
Fiestaware
  Red, large, pinpoint flake on rim 100.00
  Yellow 90.00
Figural
  Bluebird, 6 cup, bright blue, Lefton China, Japan 30.00
  Cat, 6 cup, beckoning pose, black and white, green eyes and ribbon, paper label, Cortendorf, Germany 48.00
  Scottish Man, spout is nose, lid is cap, brown, yellow or green, Wade, England 40.00
  Snow White, lid is Snow White, body is her dress, dwarfs in relief, musical, marked "Walt Disney Productions," 6" h 50.00
  Whimsical man, spout is nose, pastel pink, blue, and yellow, marked "Japan," c1930 25.00
Franciscan Ware
  Apple Pattern 100.00
  Desert Rose Pattern 115.00
  Starburst Pattern 195.00
Graniteware
  Brown and White, swirl, gooseneck spout 145.00
  Cream and Green, gooseneck spout, 8½" w 75.00
Hall China
  Airflow, turquoise, gold trim 50.00
  Aladdin
    Chinese Red, oval infuser 100.00
    Cobalt Blue, gold trim, oval infuser 85.00
    Emerald Green, gold trim, oval infuser 85.00
  Basket, emerald ground, platinum dec 175.00
  Basketball
    Chinese red 750.00
    Turquoise, gold trim, some wear to handle 550.00
  Bellevue, cobalt blue, two cups 75.00

  Boston, cobalt blue, two cups 35.00
  Bowknot, pink 45.00
  Car, maroon 60.00
  Carroway, lettuce green 65.00
  Football, maroon 750.00
  French
    Cobalt Blue, four cup 45.00
    Royal Rose 50.00
  Globe, turquoise, gold trim 125.00
  Hollywood, Chinese red, 8 cup 200.00
  Hook Cover
    Chinese Red 135.00
    Cobalt Blue, gold trim 95.00
    Emerald Green, gold trim 95.00
  Kansas, ivory, gold trim 350.00
  Los Angeles
    Chinese Red, 4 cup 275.00
    Cobalt Blue 35.00
  McCormick, maroon, 6 cup 35.00
  Medallion (a.k.a. Colonial),
    Crocus 95.00
  Melody, Chinese red 175.00
  Moderne, marine blue 50.00
  Nautilus
    Maroon, gold trim 175.00
    Turquoise, gold trim 125.00
  New York, Chinese Red, 6 cup 125.00
  Orange Poppy, streamline 135.00
  Parade
    Canary Yellow 28.00
    Emerald Green, gold trim 175.00
    Turquoise, gold trim 50.00
  Pert, maroon, gold trim 95.00
  Philadelphia, Chinese Red, 6 cup 225.00
  Radiance, Chinese red, knob re-glued 125.00
  Rutherford (a.k.a. Alton)
    Chinese Red 250.00
    Orange Dot 250.00
  Star
  Delphinium 95.00
  Ivory 75.00
  World's Fair, cobalt ground, gold trim 750.00
  Streamline, canary yellow 95.00
  Surfside, emerald green, gold trim 125.00
  Thorley, Brilliant Series
    Harlequin, gold trim 125.00
    Windcrest, No. 1524, lemon yellow ground, gold trim 125.00
  Washington, marine blue, 6 cup 65.00
  Windshield
    Black, gold trim 125.00
    Cobalt Blue, gold trim 175.00
    Delphinium, gold trim 110.00
    Maroon 35.00
    Turquoise, gold trim 95.00
    Yellow 95.00

Homer Laughlin, Harlequin Pattern, Medium Green 60.00
Hull Pottery, Little Red Riding Hood 325.00
Ironstone, 2 cup, floral, Ellgreave, Wood & Sons, England 35.00
Jasperware, 2 cup, blue and white, Wedgwood, c1784 210.00
Knowles, Edwin, Yorktown Pattern, orange–red 50.00
Morton Pottery, brown Rockingham glaze, one cup, 4½"
    Acorn shape 30.00
    Pear shape 35.00
Musical, 6 cup, oval, Japan 10.00
Occupied Japan, china, colonial couple dec 20.00
Pottery, brown glaze, hp flowers, imp "Royal Canadian Art Pottery, Royal Dripless, Hamilton Canada" 30.00
Silver Luster, 6 cup, hexagonal, Sutherland, England 60.00
Shawnee Pottery
    Corn King, individual size, No. 65 100.00
    Flower
        Blue, gold trim 30.00
        Red 22.00
    Granny Anne 60.00
    White Corn 60.00
Stangl Pottery, Colonial Pattern, #1388, individual, Tangerine 30.00

TEA SET
Black Memorabilia, figural black clowns, teapot, creamer, and sugar, price for three piece set 45.00
McCoy Pottery, Pine Cone 40.00

TEA STRAINER
Graniteware
    Blue, star perforations 55.00
    Cream, circles 40.00
Nippon China, hand painted floral decoration, cobalt blue ground, lug handle, blue Maple Leaf mark, 6" l 125.00

TEA TILE
Franciscan Ware, Ivy Pattern 55.00
Hall China, Wild Poppy Pattern (a.k.a. Poppy and Wheat), 6" sq 85.00

TID BIT SERVER
Aluminum, hand wrought, two tiers, Continental Hand Wrought Silverlook, marked "No. 525" 30.00
Franciscan Ware, Apple Pattern
    2 tiers 42.00
    3 tiers 75.00
Hall China, Wildfire Pattern, 3 tiers 45.00

TIN
Coleman Mustard, round 105.00
Great American Tea, 2 lb, New York store image, black over red, 6" d, 7½" h 55.00

Colorful spice tins catch collectors' eyes and wallets whenever they're offered for sale.

Gustav A Mayer Champagne Wafers, bottle of champagne, glasses, and wafers, orange and black lettering, black highlights, orange ground, c1935, 5" w, 2¾" h 10.00
Horlick's Malted Milk, 10 lb can 45.00
Jackie Coogan, pail, black highlights, red ground, policeman chasing boy on back, emb lid, bail handle, sgd "Henry Clive," 1930s, 3¼" d, 3½" h 230.00
Nashes Liberty Bell Mustard 30.00
Peter Pan Peanut Butter, 25 lbs 195.00
School Boy Peanut Butter, 5 lb size 150.00
Up To Date Pure Candy, 5 lb, tropic scene, orange lettering, 1920–1950, 5" d, 8¾" h 15.00
Zingo Sweets, gold race car, black ground, 1910–20, 10¼" d, 8¼" h 45.00

TOASTER
Wrought Iron
    12½" w, twisted and scroll design, 22" l handle 190.00
    26" l, rotary, twisted and scroll design, pitted 350.00

TOAST RACK
Silver Plated, Art Deco design 28.00

TOY
Baking Set
    Aunt Jemima Pastry Mix Set, tin baking pans and baking sheet, plastic cookie cutter, wood rolling pin, plastic spoon, and seven boxes of pastry mix, original box, Junior Chef, 1950s 50.00

Little Orphan Annie, Gold Medal Pastry Set, baking utensils, Transogram Toy, 1930s **75.00**

Building Blocks, Uneeda Biscuit, cardboard boxes, set of six **175.00**

Dinnerware Set, Alice in Wonderland, service for four, beige, Plasco **40.00**

Hand Puppet
Great Root Bear, A & W Root Beer, 1976, 10″ h **30.00**
Snap, Crackle, Pop, Kellogg's Rice Krispies, rubber head, fabric body, 1950s, 8″ h, price for set of three **35.00**
Trix Rabbit, cloth and vinyl, 1960s, 12″ h **40.00**

Squeaker, vinyl
Campbell Kids, boy and girl, Oak Rubber, 1954 **75.00**
Charlie The Tuna, squeeze, 7″ h, vinyl, 1973 **25.00**
Chiquita Banana, 1950s **30.00**
Snap, Crackle, Pop, Kellogg's Rice Krispies 1975 premium, 8″ h **25.00**
Trix Rabbit, 1970s, 9″ h **25.00**

Tea Set, chromolithography on tin
Mother Goose, Ohio Art, eight cups and saucers, plates, two creamers, and tray **45.00**
Snow White, Ohio Art, eight pieces, original box **125.00**

Top, Haller's Oliver Twist Bread, "A Dickens of a Good Loaf," litho tin, fortune teller, red, white, and blue, 1930s, 1½″ d **25.00**

Windup, Raid Bug **175.00**

TRAY

Aluminum, hand wrought
14″ l, tulip motif, handles **35.00**
15½″ l, fruit design, handles **22.00**
17 × 23″, marlin fish scene, double fish hook handles, Wendell August Forge **120.00**

Graniteware, blue and white, mottled, corrugated, 19″ w, 25″ l, 1¼″ d **125.00**

Hall China, Fantasy Pattern, rect, 11½″ l, 10″ w **200.00**

Papier mâché, rectangular black ground, gold floral dec, marked "Occupied Japan" **8.00**

Plastic, red, 13 × 7″ **15.00**

Porcelain, portraits of George and Martha Washington, Mt Vernon, VA, "Washington's Home, Mt Vernon, VA" in center, multicolored, enhanced enameling, sq corners, gold trim, marked "Germany," 7½ x 11″ **75.00**

Tinware, decorated
9⅜″ w, 12¼″ l, original dark green–blue paint, gilt floral rim, center with detailed painting of village with stream, boat, and people minor edge battering **450.00**
10⅞″ w, 14⅜″ l, original black paint, gilt floral rim, well detailed painting of farmers meeting on country road **375.00**

TUB

Woodenware, burl, finely detailed, turned rings, maple lid with "S" shaped locking device, putty filled hole in bottom, 6″ d, 4″ h **525.00**

TUMBLER

Glass, decorated, advertising, Elsie The Borden Cow, clear, brown and yellow raised illus, 1950s, 5½″ h **35.00**

Graniteware
Blue and White, mottled, 5″ d **65.00**
White, small **10.00**

◆◆ U

UTENSIL RACK

Wrought Iron, high arched and scrolled back, five hooks, European, pitted, minor damage, 15½″ w, 17½″ h **200.00**

◆◆ V

VEGETABLE DISH

Bauer Pottery, La Linda Pattern, dinnerware line produced from 1939 until 1959 oval, 10″ l, Ivory **28.00**
Monterey Pattern, dinnerware line produced from 1936 until 1945, oval, divided, Green **45.00**

Blue Ridge
Chrysanthemum Pattern, 9½″ d **12.00**
June Bouquet Pattern, Colonial shape, 9½″ d **16.00**
Mountain Ivy Pattern, Candlewick shape **20.00**

Hall China
Autumn Leaf, oval **18.00**
Mulberry Pattern, open, 9″ sq **22.00**
Orange Poppy Pattern, round **20.00**

Harker Pottery
Colonial Lady Pattern **22.00**
Red Apple Pattern, 9″ d **28.00**

Homer Laughlin, Dogwood Pattern, oval **9.00**

Knowles, Edwin, Deanna Pattern, 8″ d, orange–red **18.00**

Metlox Pottery
California Provincial Pattern, Poppytrail line, 10″ d **20.00**
Homestead Provincial, Poppytrail line
8½″ l, two part, stick handle **22.00**
13″ l, three part, handled **22.00**
Provincial Fruit Pattern, Poppytrail line, 10″ d **18.00**

This factory-made vegetable slicer utilizes pendulum-style cutting action to make short work of vegetables. Its hinged "pusher" is spring-loaded to keep the pressure on the cabbage or whatever produce is being sliced. Courtesy of Phyllis and Jim Moffet, Modesto, Ill.

Wagner Ware offered an assortment of stove-top waffle irons in cast aluminum or cast iron.

Red Rooster, Poppytrail line, 10" d	15.00
Shawnee Pottery, Corn King, No. 95	40.00

VEGETABLE SLICER

A & J, Binghamton, NY, wood handle, twisted wire blade, c1930, 16" l	18.00

❖ W

WAFFLE IRON

Cast Iron, long wrought handles, one reattached, 28" l	140.00

WALL PLAQUE

Campbell Kids, plaster, hook in base, 1940s, 7" h, price for pair	75.00
Pennsbury Pottery	
Lafayette, B & O Railroad	45.00
NEA Centennial	24.00

WALL POCKET

Abingdon Pottery	
Butterfly, No. 601	65.00
Calla Lily, No. 586D	45.00
Cookbook, No. 676D	45.00
Leaf, No. 724	40.00
American Art Pottery, tree stump, applied woodpecker, brown spray glaze, 5" h	15.00
Hull Pottery, Little Red Riding Hood	450.00
McCoy Pottery	
Apple, 1953	35.00

Turtles, 5" h	40.00
Violin, turquoise, marked "McCoy USA," 1957	30.00
Morton Pottery	
Harp, white, hp underglaze floral dec, 10" h	14.00
Mary Quite Contrary, red dress, blue apron, 7½" h	10.00
Parrot on bunch of grapes, natural colors, 8½" h	18.00
Teapot, white, red apple dec, red finial, 6½" h	12.00
Violin, two musical notes, white, hp dec, 8¾" h, price for pair	20.00
Occupied Japan, violin	10.00
Roseville Pottery	
Bushberry, brown	145.00
Clematis, brown	100.00
Lotus, red	340.00
Sunflower, 1/85/1/2, 8" h	485.00
Zephyr Lily, brown	125.00
Shawnee Pottery, birdhouse, bluebirds	15.00
Stangl Pottery, Cosmos, green matte, No. 2091, 1937	40.00

WATER BOTTLE

Anchor Hocking, clear, original cover	10.00

WHETSTONE

Advertising, Cudahy's Blue Ribbon Meat Meal, pig, pocket size	35.00

WHIMSICAL

Bird Feeder, McCoy Pottery, hanging, brown, 1975   **12.00**

Bird House, made from sewer pipe, tooled bark like surface, 8½″ h   **525.00**

Flour Sack, Sleepy Eye Chief, dark blue, framed   **45.00**

Fruit

  Fabric, velvet, stuffed, worn hand coloring

    Apple   **60.00**

    Pear with leaf   **75.00**

    Peach   **60.00**

    Strawberries, pair, one deep pink, one pale peach, leaves, ribbons, and flowers, price for pair   **145.00**

  Stone, worn color

    Apple   **25.00**

    Banana   **35.00**

    Fig   **15.00**

    Grapes, bunch, wooden stem

      Black   **60.00**

      White   **50.00**

    Lemon, late   **10.00**

    Peach   **20.00**

    Pear, elongated neck, 7½″ l   **75.00**

    Plum   **40.00**

    Tomato, late   **10.00**

Ornament, carved hardwood, heart finial, two cutout hearts, chip carved edge, carved initials "E.R.," hardwood, good dark patina, 1¾″ w, 5½″ l   **200.00**

Seed Box, Rush Park, 1930s   **110.00**

Shelf Sitter, Little Boy Blue, marked "Occupied Japan"   **15.00**

WHISK BROOM

Advertising, Whiskbroom Cigars, cigar shaped   **30.00**

Natural broom, wooden Mammy handle, 4½″ l   **18.00**

WINDOW BOX

Roseville Pottery, Gardenia, green, 669–19   **115.00**

Wooden, primitive, worn finish, heart shaped handle   **65.00**

Index

●▸●▸ ●▸

ABC Pottery, 187
Abingdon Pottery, 187, 198, 211, 219,
  230
Ace Products, *100*
Advertising, *2*, *4*, *19*, *24*, *29*, *31*, *45*, 46,
  51, *54*, 61, 64, *69*, 79, *80*, *92*, *93*, *104*,
  141, 147, *148*, *151*, *158*, 168–231,
  200
African-American, 64
Allen, Bob, 65, 143
Aluminum, 28, 121, *178*
Aluminum, Hammered, 83, 168–231
Aluminum Ware Association, *29*
American Art Pottery, 174, 186, 189–190,
  226, 230
American Bisque, 107, 166
American Cookery, 24, 26, 28, 29, 31, 95,
  96, 100, 113, 115, 121, 206
American Electrical Heater Co., 200
American Harvest, 47
American Institute of Conservation, 117
American Pottery Journal, 81
American Reamer Collectors, 83
American Woman's Home, 134
Anchor Hocking, 71
Anderson, Hope-Vere, 55
Antique Advertising Association of
  America, 79
Antique and Art Glass Salt Shaker
  Collector's Society, 84

Antique and Collectors Reproduction News,
  165
Antique Bottle & Glass Collector, 80, 82
Antique Dinnerware, 121–122
Antique Trader Weekly, 57
Antiques Week, 49, 58, 87, 105
Apple Butter, 171
Apple Corers, 171
Applegate, Jane, 60
Apple Parers, *79*, 80, *131*, 132, *169*,
  171–172
Apple Slicers, *171*
Appliances, 46
Aprons, 44, 45, *45*, 46, 172
Archimedes Eggbeater, *69*
Armstrong World Industries, *27*, *30*, *32*,
  33, *35*, *37*, *38*, *39*, 157, 202, 204
Art Deco, 127, 155, 156, 200, 202
Auctions, 87, 99–105
Autumn Leaf, 82, 179, 186, 192, 211,
  220, 223

Baby Dish, 196
Badger, Chuck and Bonnie, 171
Bakers Chocolate, 140, 171, 175
Baking Pans, 172
Ball Collectors Club Newsletter, 82
Ball Corp, 61, 68
Ball Jug, 196
Bantock, John, 139

233

Barile, Mary, 65, 88, 96, 137, 143, *143*, 145, 146
Barlow, Ronald S., 63
Baskets, *42*, *47*, 64, 124, *124*, 129, 130, 172–173, 182
Basket Ware, 22
Batter Jugs, 173, 196
Bauer Pottery, 174, 179, 180, 187, 189, 190, 196–198, 216, 219, 226, 229
Bean Pots, 173
Bean Slicers, 173
Beard, James, 35, 37
Becton, Mrs., 134
Beecher, Catherine, 19–22, *19*, *21*, 61, 78, 122, 133, *134*
Beetles, 22
Bells, 173
Bennington Museum, 61
Bennington Pottery, 61, *62*, 75, *189*
Bensch, Christopher, 61
Bergevin, Al, 64
Bergner Apple Parer, *169*
Berne, Steffi, 66
Better Homes & Gardens, 42
Betty Crocker Kitchens, 28, 37, 185, 201
Biscuit Cutters, *168*
Black Memorabilia, 64, 168–231
Blenders, 200
Blue and White Pottery Club, 84
Blue Ridge, 174, 188, 189, 190–191, 197–198, 218, 219, 222, 223, 226, 229
Bohn, Carol, 40
Bonanza Apple Parer, 79
Bon Appetit, 37, 46
Bone Dish, 197
Booklets, Cookbook, 185–186
Borden Company, 35, 168, 169, 170, 198, 216, 220, 229
Boston Cooking School Magazine, 24, 134
Bottle Openers, 80
Bottles, 80
Bottles & Extras Magazine, 80, 82, 84
Bowls, 173–175
Boxes, 21, *62*, *104*, 175
Brantley, William F., 70
Brass, 117–119, *118*, 130, 161, 210
Breadboard, *16*, 175
Bread Box, 162, 175
Bread Knife, 176
Bread Machine, 132
Bread Maker, 176
Bread Plate, 176
Bread Toaster, *92*
Breakfast Set, 127
Brochures, 176–177
Broiler, *153*
Brown-Glazed Stoneware, 114
Brownfield, Marion, 28–29
Brush, 107, 166, 187
Butt, Jack and Barbara, 207
Butter Churns, *177*

Butter Crocks, 177
Butter Dishes, 161, 177
Butter Molds, *8*, *55*, *123*, 177
Butter Paddle, 177–178
Butter Print, 178

Cabbage Cutters, 178
Cahn, Bob, The Primitive Man, 49, 51, 217
Cake Board, *15*
Cake Breaker, *114*
Cake Decorations, 178
Cake Lifter, 197
Cake Mixer, 79
Cake Molds, 179
Cake Pans, 46
Cake Plates, 179
Cake Safes, 179
Cake Secrets, 135
Cake Tins, 179
Cake Turner, *73*, *178*
Calendars, 179
Calumet Baking Powder, *168*, 170, 186
Candle Related, 179, 197
Candy Americana Museum, 60
Candy Molds, 61
Canisters, 179–180
Canners, 180
Can Openers, *180*, 202
Carafe, 197
Carey, Lois, 217
Casseroles, 180
Cast-Iron, *6*, *51*, 73–74, 80, 88, 97, 98, 107, *112*, 119, *119*, 127, 130, 132, 161, 168–231
Catalogs, *47*, 180–182
Cavallo, Maria, 110
Celehar, Jane H., 23, 63
Celery Dish, 197
Ceramic Pudding Bucket, 117
Ceramic Ware, 46
Cereal Collectibles, 80, 170, 171, 176, 182, 186
Chafing Dishes, 200
Chalking, 122
Character Related, 47, 71, 72, *136*, 179, 182
Chargers, 182
Cheese Press, 182
Cheese Sieve, 182
Cheese Slicer, 182
Cherry (Pitter) Stoners, *111*, 131, *182*, *183*
Child, Julia, 35, 44, 111, 118, 136, 137
Child, Lydia Maria, 77, 78, 123, 133, 134
Children's Kitchenware, 47, 164, 228
Children's Pottery, 66, 183, 228
China and Ceramic Items, 168–231
Chocolate Mold, 74, 75, 161, 181, 183
Chocolate Related, 60, *61*, 168, 169, 171, 197, *210*
Chopper, 19, *206*

Chopping Knife, *101*, 207
Chop Plate, 197
Christmas, 46, *47*, *48*, 77, 87, *93*, *102*, 116, 127, *129*, *154*, 215
Civil War, 137
Coasters, 183
Coffee Mills, *4*, *88*, 127, *128*, 161, *183*, 202
Coffeepots, *73*, 152, *153*, *154*, 183, 184, 197, 201
Coffee Roaster, *184*
Coffee Urn, 184
Colander, 184
Colbert, Neva, 67
Coleman Lamp & Stove Company, 155, 205
Collector Glass News, 82
Collectors News & The Antique Reporter, 57, 166
Colonial Era, 17–18
Colonial Williamsburg, 13, 18, 60
Commemorative Items, 46
Compotes, 186, 197
Condiment Sets, 184
Congdon-Martin, Douglas, 64
Cookbook Collectors Club of America, Inc., 80, 143
Cookbook Collectors' Exchange, 81, 105, 139, 144
Cookbooks, 13, 45, 55, 60, 65, 80–81, 88, 89, 105, 133–146, *134*, *135*, *136*, *139*, *141*, *143*, *145*, *147*, *148*, 184–185
Cookery Book, *134*
Cookie Boards, *15*, 161, 186–187
Cookie Cutters, *8*, 65, *88*, 120, 130, 161, 187
Cookie Cutter Collectors Club, 81
Cookie Irons, 96
Cookie Jars, 47, 65, 87, 106, *107*, *126*, 127, 161, 165, 166, 187
Cookie Mold, *47*
Cookie Press, 188
Cooking Fork, 5, *110*, 116, 161
Cooking Light, 46
Cooking Magazines, 46
Cookstoves, 137
Cooler, 188
Cooling Rack, *111*
Copper, 51, 117–119, *118*, 161, 165, 207, 226
Copycats, 162
Corkscrews, *80*
Corning, 36, 60, 70
Corn Items, 81, *188*
Corn Items Collectors Association, 81
Cornstick Pan, *91*, 164, 172
Cornucopia, 188
Counter Scale, *131*
Country Decorating, 41–44, 150
Country Home, 42, 54, 87
Country Living, 54, 87

Crab Baking Set, 188
Cream City Ware, *102*
Creamers, 81, *129*, 168, 188–189
Cream of Wheat, 147, *148*
Cream Separator, *81*, 116, 179, 214
Cream Separator Association, 81
Creswick, Alice, 68, 165
Crockery, 21, 127
Crocks, 53, *75*, 99, 130, 132, *189*
Cruets, 197
Crumber and Brush, 190
Cuisinart Food Processor, 37, 45, 153
Cumberland Country Store, 163
Cunningham, Jo, 66
Cupboards, 51
Curtis, Tony, 55
Custard Cup, 190
Cutting Board, 190

Dairy Related, 81, 168, 169, 175, 177, 179, 182, 188, 189, 212, 215
Dandy Chopper, *19*
Davern, Melva, 76
Davis Apple Slicer, *171*
Dayton Power & Light Co, 60
Daze, 82, 83
Dazey Churn, *177*
DeBolt, C. Gerald, 67
Deep Fryer, 190
Demitasse, 190
DeMore, Dana, 49, 74, 79, 87, 90–92, 105, 118, 121, 165
DePasquale, Dan and Gail, 75
Depression Era Dishes, 53, 82, 174
Depression Glass, 66, 70, *83*, 161, 168–231
Dexter, *111*
Dickinson, Linda J., 65
Dinnerware, 66–68, 81, 190–198
Dinnerware Accessories Pieces, 196–198
Dippers, 198
Divone, Judene, 74
Dolls, 198–199
Doorstops, 199
Dormeyer Manufacturing, *69*
Double Boilers, 199
Dough Boxes and Trays, 3, 131, *199*
Dough Scraper, 199
Dover Eggbeater, *100*, *200*
Drippings Jar, 199
Drying Racks, 199
Dry Measure, 215
Dry Sinks, 131
Duke Cherry Seeder, *183*
Duke, Harvey, 67
Dust Pans, 199
Dutch Ovens, 199

Early American, 142
Edison, 152, 203

Eggbeaters, 40, 49, *52*, 68, 69, 87, *100*, 130, 199
Egg Cheese Mold, *112*
Egg Cookers, 201
Eggcup Collectors' Corner, 82
Egg Cups, 199
Egg Lifters, 200
Egg Scale, *98*, 200
Egg Slicer, 200
Egg Timer, 200
Egg Whip, *54*, 200
Electrical Appliances, 43, 68, *93*, 124–125, 150–160, 200–205
Electric Roasters, 153
Enamelware, *102*, 121, 130
Enterprise Products, *51*, *91*, *107*, *111*, *182*
Ephemera, 46, *147*, 171, 176–177, 179, 206, 207, 220
Ephemera Society of America, 79
Erwin, Sue, 139
Eureka Vacuum Cleaner Co., 202
Express Egg Beater, 49
Everhot Products, *159*, 202

Fakes, 162
Farberware, *153*, *154*, 160, 201
Farmer, Fannie Merritt, 134
Farm Pantry, 2
Fast Food, 72
Federal Glass, 163
Federation of Historical Bottle Clubs, 80
Fetter, Dawn, 13
Fiesta Collectors Quarterly, 81
Fiestaware, *41*, *50*, 53, 66, *126*, 127, 157, *174*, 180, 184, 189–192, 197–198, 211–213, 216, 218–219, 223, 227
Fire-King, 41, 53, 71, *174*, 218
Fireplace Cooking, 13–18, 205–206
Fireplace Tools, *14*
Fisher, M. F. K., 45
Fish Scaler, 206
Flatware, 206
Florence, Gene, 70, 163, 165
Flour Sifter, *8*, 202, 206
Flow Blue, 67, 68, 82
Flow Blue International Collectors Club, 82
Foley Food Mills, 87
Fondue Pot, 47, 127, 153, 157
Food & Wine, 37, 46
Food Chopper, 206
Food Fads, 77
Food Labels, 206
Food Mill, 87
Food Molds, 207
Food Press, *104*
Franciscan Ware, 177, 179–180, 184, 187, 189–192, 196–198, 211, 216, 223, 226, 227
Franklin, Linda Campbell, 62, 63
Frary & Clark, *96*, 176, 181

Free Inside, 80
French Chef, 45
Frigidaire, 36, 181
Fruit Crate Labels, 207
Fruit Jar Newsletter, 82
Fruit Jars, 61, 68, *71*, 82, *104*, 105, 130, 132, 208–209
Frying Pan, *6*, 47, *112*
Funnels, 209
Furnishings, 13–39, 209–210

Gadgets, 42, 43, 45, 210
Gaston, Mary Frank, 67
General Electric, 36, 90, *147*, *150*, 152, 153, *154*, 158, 181, 200–205
Gick-Burke, Barbara Loveless, 67
Gilbreth, Dr. Lillian M., 30
Glass, 82, 168–231
Glass Collector's Digest, 82
Glass, Hannah, 135
Glazes, 121
Glenwood Gas Range, *31*
Gold Metal Flour, *28*, 186
Goodell Co., 79
Good Shepherd Home Cook Book, *136*
Gore, Marian, 45, 144
Gould, Mary Earle, 77
Gourmet, 37
Graniteware, 42, 52, 72, 73, 82, 129, 168–231
Graters, 210–211
Gravy Boat, 211
Grease jar, 211
Greer's, 62
Greguire, Helen, 72
Griddle, *119*, 127, 205, 211
Griswold Cast Iron Collectors' News & Marketplace, 80
Griswold Manufacturing Company, 24, 73–74, 80, 98, 108, 164, 172, 179, 185, 190, 199
Groff, Betty, 109, 111, *112*, 120, 121, 132, *139*
Grossman, Bob and Kaaren, 51, 210
Guarnaccia, Helen, 76
Gypsy Kettle, 211

Hall China, 61, 67, 82, 173, 174, 177, 179, 180, 187, 189, 190, 192–193, *196*–199, 211, 213, 216, 219, 220, 223, 226–229
Hall China Encore, 82
Hammered Aluminum, 83
Hamilton Beach, *159*, 160
Hamilton Nut Cracker, *107*
Handy Maid, *52*
Hanford, Florence, 35
Harker Pottery, 67, *174*, 179, 180, 189, 190, 193, 197–198, 213, 224
Harlequin, 67
Harmer Rooke Galleries, 54

Harned, Bill and Denise, 74
Hazel Atlas, 68, *71*, *83*, 89
H. B. Meek Library, Cornell University, 60
Hearth Related, 13–18, 60, 143, 161, 165, 205–206, 228
Heinz, H. J., *99*, 170, 186
Herrick Dry Air System Refrigerator, *2*
Hervey, John, 72
Hess, Karen, 78, 134, 137, 146
Hill, Ellen R., 68
Holidays, 46, 75, 132
Holt Lyon Company, *52*
Homer Laughlin, 61, 174, 177, 180, 189, 193, 196–198, 211, 213, 218–220, 224, 226, 228–229
Honey Jar, 211
Hoosier Cabinet, *28*, 72, 131, 210
Horlick's Malted Milk, *69*, 169
Horsford's Baking Powder, 148
Hot Pads, *211*
Hot Plates, 202, 211
Hotpoint Electric Range, *28*, 202
Hour Glass, 211
Household Liberty Coal and Gas Range, *110*
Housewares, 72
Howard, Brian, 116, 118, 119, 120, 124
Hull Pottery, 67, 177, 179, 187, 189, 216, 224, 226, 228, 230
Huxford, Susan and Bob, 64, 66, 165

Iceboxes, 3, 131, 211
Ice Buckets, 212
Ice Cream Dippers, 73, 212
Ice Cream Related, *93*, *129*, 132, 212
Ice Cream Screamer, 81
Ice Picks, 212
Ice Shavers, 212
Ice Tongs, 130, 212
Imported Dinnerware, 121–122
Indiana Glass, 163
International Society of Antique Scale Collectors, 84
International Society of Apple Parer Enthusiasts, 80
International Willow Collectors, 82
Iron Kettles, *14*
Ironware, 21, 73–74, 168–231

Jadeite, 52
Jars, 212
Jasper, Joanne, 66
Jell-O, 147, 176, 186
Jelly Cupboard, 130
Jelly Jammers Club, 83
Jelly Jars, 83
Johnson & Wales University, 58–60
Johnson, Frances, 64
Johnson, Joan and Warner, 49
Johnston, Wendy, 87, 106, 165, 166
Judith Basin Museum, 60

Jugs, 54, 213
Juicers, 53
Juliet K. Rakow Research Library, 60
Junket, 145
Just For Openers, 80
Juvenile Pottery, 66

Kafka, Barbara, 37
Kalamazoo Range, *3*, *73*, 181
Keen Kutter, 164
Kennedy, Philip D., 72, 92
Kerr, Graham, 35
Kerr Manufacturing, 68
Kettle, 213
Kettle Lifter, *213*
Kettles 'n Cookware Cast Iron Newsletter, 80
Kilgo, Garry and Dale, 71
King, Phyllis, 144
KitchenAid, 98, *99*, *151*, 152, 155, 203
Kitchen Antiques & Collectibles News, 49, 105, 118
Kitchen Fork, 5, *110*, 116, 161
Kitchen Saws, 213
Kitchen Scales, 213
Klug, Ray, 64
Knapp-Monarch, 200–205
Knife Boxes, 214
Knife, Glass, 214
Knife Sharpener, 202
Knowles, Edwin, 177, 180, 189, 193, 196, 211, 220, 228, 229
KOOKS, 40, 78–79
Kosche, Eugene, 61
Kovel, Ralph and Terry, 66, 70
Kreamerware, 51
Kuck, Barbara, 58, 91

Ladle, 214
Landis Valley Museum, 13, 123
Lansky, Jeanette, 77
Lazy Susan, 214
Lead, 119, *122*
Lechner, Mildred and Ralph, 76
Lemmon, Jean, 42
Lemon Squeezer, 214
Leslie, Eliza, 133, 142
Library of Congress, 60
Lifshey, Earl, 72
Lifter, *218*, *225*
Lindenberger, Jan, 64, 74
Linens, 214
Longaberger Basket Company, 47
Longone, Jan, 135–144, 147, 164
Lowney's Cocoa, 62
Los Angeles Public Library, 60

MacLeod, Ruth Peck, 26–28
Magazine Advertisements, 51
Magazine Tear Sheets, *19*, *93*, *158*, *175*, 214
Maine Antique Digest, 57, 105

Majolica, 46, 176
Malleable Range, *16*
Maloney, David J., 58
Mandel, Abby, 37
Mandeville Library, University of
    California, 60
Manning-Bowman, 200–205
Manuals and Instruction Booklets, *16*, 142,
    159
Markowski, Carol and Gene, 71
Marmalade, 197
Martinus, Norman, 51
Mason's, *71*
Match Holders, 214
Maxwell House, *48*, 168, 176, 186
Mayonnaise Mixer, 116
McAllister, Lisa S., 76
McCoy Pottery, 65, 66, *107*, 166, 172,
    186, 187, 188, 189, 213, 219, 221,
    225, 230
McCurdy, Mike and Tessia, 55
McKee Glass, 174, 177, 180, 199, 200,
    212, 215, 216, 221, 223, 225, 226
McNerney, Kathryn, 63, 74, 75
Measure, Dry, 215
Measuring Cup, 215
Measuring Spoons, 215
Meat Grinders, 91, 215
Meat Slicers, 215
Meat Tenderizer, *206*, 215
Mechanical, *51*
Melmac, 154
Mergenthal, Bill, 162
Metal, 117–121
Metlox Pottery, 174, 176, 180, 186, 189,
    194, 196–198, 211, 219, 220, 222,
    226, 229
Michel, John L., 76
Michigan State University Library, 60
Microwave Oven, 62
Milk Bottles, 215
Milk Bottle Caps, 215
Milk Bottle Cap Openers, 215
Milk Cans, 215
Milk Jugs, 215
Milk Pitchers, 215–216
Milkshake Makers, 151, *159*, 200
Miller, Gary, 45, 68, 90, 98, 125,
    150–160, 164
Mirro, 36, 37, 203
Mitchell, Scotty, 45, 68, 89, 90, 98, 125,
    150–160
Mixers, 151, 203
Mixing Bowls, 216
Mixing Spoons, 216
Mixmaster, Sunbeam, *155*, 203
Modern Times, Early, 23–33
Moffett, Phyllis and Jim, 169, 183, 206,
    213, 221, 230
Molasses Jug, 216
Molds, 74, *129*, 207

Montgomery Ward, 200–205
Mortar and Pestle, *15*
Morton Pottery, 177, 215, 216, 218, 228,
    230
Mount Vernon, 13, 18, 206
Muffin Pans, 47
Mugs, 216
Mulberry Ironstone, 68
Mustard Jar, 197, 216

Napkin Holders, 216
Napkin Rings, 216
Nappy, 197
National Association of Milk Bottle
    Collectors, 81
National Association of Paper and
    Advertising Collectors, 79
National Autumn Leaf Collectors Club, 82
National Blue Ridge Newsletter, 82
National Early American Glass Club, 82
National Graniteware Society, 82
National Reamer Collectors Association, 83
National Toothpick Holders Collectors
    Society, 84
New England Antiques Journal, 217
Newman, Paul, *141*
New Standard Corp, *19*
New York Public Library, 60, 142
Nippon China, 179
Noodle Cutters, 216
Noritake China, 173, 176, 177, 179
Norton Pottery, 75, *189*
Notepad Holders, 216
Nouvelle Cuisine, 137
Novelty Salt & Pepper Shakers Club, 84
Nutcracker, *55*, *107*, 216
Nut Grinders, 217
Nutmeg Grater, 50, 52, 87, *121*, 130, *217*

Ohio Historical Society Museum of
    Ceramics, 61
Old Sturbridge Village, 13, 18, 60, 77
O'Neill, Rose, 136, 147, 176
Onion Chopper, 217
Oreo Cookies, *48*

Pamphlets, 142, 185–186
Pancake Server, 217
Paper Collector's Marketplace, 79
Parloa, Maria, *137*
Parrish, Maxfield, 136, 147
Pastry Blender, 217
Pea Sheller, 217
Peel, 217
Pennsbury Pottery, 179, 189, 197, 219,
    230
Pennsylvania Dutch, *124*, 126, *139*, 180
Pepin, Jacques, 37
Perc-O-Toaster, 157, 203
Pestle, 217
Peterson, Larry, 75

Philadelphia Electric Co, 35
Photograph, *2, 3, 21, 27, 28, 30, 32, 33, 35, 36, 37, 39*
Pickle Dish, 197
Pickle Fork, 218
Pickle Pusher, 102
Piebirds, 83, 218
Piebirds Unlimited, 83
Pie Crimper, *6, 41, 218*
Pie Plates, 218
Pie Server, 197
Pillsbury, *145, 148*, 168, 170, 186, 198, 221
Place Card Holder, 219
Plante, Ellen, 63
Planters Oil, 37
Plastics, 36, 74, 174, 179, 188, 224–226
Plates, 219
Platters, 219
Plimoth Plantation, 13, 17, 60
Popcorn Poppers, 151, 152, 203–204
Porcelier Toaster, 156, 201
Post Cards, 220
Posters, 220
Postwar to 21st Century, 33–39
Potato Creamer, *100*
Potato Masher, 163, *206, 220*
Potato Muddler, 98
Potato Ricers, 220
Pot Scrapers, *54*, 220
Pottery, 74–75, 84
Pratt Apple Segmenter, *169*
Premium Lists, 220
Preserving Jars, 220
Presto Industries, *154, 158*
Pretzel Jar, 198
Proctor Silex, *150*, 160, 200–205
Prudhomme, Paul, 47
Pudding Molds, 127
Punch Bowl Set, 198
Purinton Pottery, 180, 188, 197
Pyrex, 61, 70, 186

Quaker Oats, *48*, 175, 220

Radios, 221
Raisin Seeder, *51, 107*, 116, *221*
Ramekins, 198
Randolph, Mary, 78, 133, 137
Range Shakers, 221
Rawlings, Marjorie, 141
Raycraft, Don and Carol, 64, 74
Reagan, Ronald, 46
Reamers, *50, 83*, 161, 221
Recipe Booklets, 142, 185–186
Recipe Boxes, 222
Recipe Pamphlets, 46
Redware, *43*, 50, 74, 76, *122*, 129, 130, 174, 212, 216, 219
Red Wing Collectors Society, Inc., 84
Red Wing Pottery, *45*, 75–76, 84, 188

Refrigerator Dishes, 222
Refrigerator Jar, *71*, 222
Refrigerator Magnets, 87
Regal Ware, Inc., 37
Reissues, 162
Relish Trays, 222
Reno, Dawn E., 64
Reproductions, 161–166
Retro Style Decorating, 150
Rinker, Harry L., 44, 47, 86, 103
Riviera, 67
Roasters, 223
Robot, *153*
Rockingham Wares, 174, 177, 180
Rockwell, Norman, 147
Roerig, Fred and Joyce, 65
Roller, Dick, 68, 82, 99, 102
Rolling Pins, 40, 116, 124, 127, 161, 223
Rombauer, Erma, 136
Roosevelt, Teddy, 138
Roseville Pottery, 173, 174, 179, 188, 219, 230, 231
Rosgrove, Susan Tobier, 70
Royal Baking Powder, 140
Royal China Co., 194–195
Rumford Baking Powder, 73, 216

Saffron Box, 223
Salad Bowl, 198, 223
Salad Shooter, 46
Salt and Pepper Shakers, *42*, 60, 76–77, 79, 84, *90*, 161, 221, 223
Salt Boxes, 224
Salt-Glazed, 54
Sandwich Grill, 153
Santa, *47*, 164, 179, 187
Sauce Boat, 198
Saucepans, *118*, 224
Sausage Stuffers, 97, 131, 132, 224
Scales, 83, 84, *96, 98*, 131, 213
Schmidt, Dale, 96
Schneider, Chuck and Kathy McCue, 46, 52
Schneider, Mike, 76
Schlesinger Library, Radcliffe College, 60
Schneider, Mike, 65
Schremp, Gerry, 77
Schroy, Ellen Tischbein, 70, 89, 163
Scoop, 224
Sears, 37
Seasoned Cast Iron, 119
Sharples Tubular Cream Separator, *54*
Shawnee Pottery, 65, *126*, 174, 180, 188, 189, 219, 220, 222, 225, 226, 228, 230
Shirred Egg Dish, 198
Sieve, 224
Sifter, *8*
Signs, 224
Simmons, Amelia, 133, 135
Skillets, 225
Skimit Kitchen Cream Separator, *81*

Skimmers, 225
Skin Old Tin, 91
Slaw Cutter, *130*
Slice A Slice, *43*
Sloat, Caroline, 13, 77
Smith, Elmer S., 77
Smith, Kate, 136
Smith, Wayne, 73
Snyder, Jeffrey B., 67
Snyder, Judith, 16, 112
Sontheimer, Carl, 37
Spatula, 110, *111*, 225
Spice Boxes, 225
Spice Set, 225
Spice Shelf, 225
Spongeware, 161, 190
Spoon Molds, 225
Spoonrests, 46, 225
Springerle Board, *86*
Spry, 140, *148*, *186*
Stack Set, 198
Stahl, Thomas, 43
Stangl, *42*, 44, *67*, 67, 173, 179, 189,
    195, 196–198, 211, 219, 222, 228, 230
Steinhauer, Marcia Buan, 70
Stephens, Steve, 74, 98, 106, 107, 119,
    166
Stern, Jane and Michael, 32, 78, 142
Stew Pot, 88
Stickley, Gustav, 23
Stoneware, 7, 42, 50, 74, 75, 84, 99, 114,
    129, *131*, 132, 161, 173, 177, 188, *189*,
    212, 213, 220
Stoneware, Blue and White, 75, 84
Stove Lid Lifter, 225
Stoves, 225
Stowe-Day Foundation, *19*, 61
Stowe, Harriet Beecher, 19–22, *21*, 61,
    134
Strawbery Jar, 225
Straw Holders, 53
String Holders, 226
Strong Museum, 61
Sugar Bowls, 226
Sugar Bucket, *128*, 226
Sugar Nippers, 226
Sugar Shakers, 53, 226
Sullivan, George, 75
Sunbeam, *155*, *156*, 203, 204
Supple Network, 96–97
Swans Down Cake, *135*
Swiss Vegetable Peelers, 46
Swizzle Sticks, 226
Syrup Pitchers, 226
Szathmary, Louis, 58, *59*

Table Mats, 226
Taylor, Smith, and Taylor, 195
Tea Caddies, 226
Tea Leaf Club International, 82
Tea Kettles, 226

Teapots, *45*, 46, *126*, 203, 226–227
Tea Sets, 228
Tea Strainers, 228
Tea Talk, 84
Tea Tiles, 228
Teetsall, Ulysses Grant, *52*
Teflon II, 38
The Opener, 80
The Pleasures of Cooking, 37
Thornton, Don, 52, 68, 69
Tid Bit Servers, 228
Tin Containers Collectors Association, 79
Tinware, 21, 77, 118, 120–121, *129*,
    168–231
Toaster Ovens, 153
Toasters, Electric, 52, 53, 90, *150*, 151,
    152, 157, *203*–204
Toastmaster, 92, 157
Toast Rack, 228
Toleware, *129*
Tools, 53
Tomato Slicer, 86
Toothpick Holders, 84
Toys, 228
Travers, Carolyn, 17
Trays, 229
Tripp Bros, *171*
Tubs, 229
Tumblers, 229
Tvorak, April M., 71
Tyler's Ideal Fiber Cutter, *206*

Unglazed Dinnerware, 121
Uneeda Biscuits, *175*
United States Steel, 34
Universal, Landers, Frary & Clark, 96,
    176, 181, 200–205, 213
Universal Pottery, 195
University of Iowa Library, 60
University of Michigan, 143
Utensil Rack, 229
Utility Plate, 198

Vase, 198
Vegetable Dishes, 229
Vegetable Skimmer, *54*
Vegetable Slicers, *230*
Vernon Kilns, 195–196
Victorian Era, 19–23, 113, 127, *129*, 142,
    154
Victorian Society in America, 16
Vogelzang, Vernagene, 72
Vos, Jane, 25–26

Waffle Related, 115, 151, 153, 156, 164,
    181, 204–205, 230
Wagner Ware, 164, 182, 224, *230*
Waites, Raymond, 44
Wall Plaques, 230
Wall Pockets, 230
Warhol, Andy, 87

Waring Blender, *151*, 152
Waring, Fred, *151*
Washburn Crosby, 140
Wash Day, 10
Water Bottle, *196*, 198, 230
Watt Pottery, 82
Waxman, Nahum, 147
Weaver, William Woys, 16, 19, 77, 88,
  95, 111, 116–120, 122–124, 141, 146,
  164–166
Welch, Evelyn, 72
West Bend, 37
Westfall, Ermagene, 66
Westinghouse, *90*, 152, *196*, 200–205
Westmoreland Glass, 163
Wetherill, Phyllis S., 65
Whetstones, 230
Whimsical, 231
Whisk Brooms, 231
White Cross Electric Range, *31*, 153
White Mountain Freezer Co, *4*

Whitmeyer, Margaret and Kenn, 67
Wilbur Chocolate Company, 60
Wilkins, Jerry and Gail, 71
Williamson Farm, 1–8, *3*
Williams, Petra, 68
Williams-Sonoma, *47*, 163
Window Box, 7, 231
Wireware, 40, 130
Wolfert, Paula, 37
Women's Institute Library of Cookery, 120
Wooden Bowls, *14*, 132, 174–175
Woodenware, *14*, *15*, 16, 22, *86*, *123*,
  123–124, *128*, 130, 168–231
World's Fair, *145*
World War II, 32
Wright, Lydia McNair, 22–23, 119, *139*

Yellowware, 74, 76, *101*, 127, 129, 219

Zanol Products, 182
Zero Refrigerator Co., 182

IN TIME
AND WITH LOVE

Caring for Infants and Toddlers

With Special Needs

Volumes in the
Your Child at Play Series

～～～～～～～～

YOUR CHILD AT PLAY:
Birth to One Year

YOUR CHILD AT PLAY:
One to Two Years

YOUR CHILD AT PLAY:
Two to Three Years

YOUR CHILD AT PLAY:
Three to Five Years

YOUR CHILD AT PLAY:
Five to Eight Years

IN TIME AND WITH LOVE:
Caring for Infants and Toddlers With Special Needs

IN TIME
AND WITH LOVE

Caring for Infants and Toddlers
With Special Needs

SECOND EDITION

MARILYN SEGAL, PH.D.

WITH
WENDY MASI, PH.D.
AND
RONI LEIDERMAN, PH.D.

NEWMARKET PRESS   NEW YORK

10   9   8   7   6   5   4   3   2   1

Library of Congress Cataloging-in-Publication Data

Segal, Marilyn M.
    In time and with love: caring for infants and toddlers with special needs
by Marilyn Segal with Roni Leiderman and Wendy Masi.—2nd ed.
        p.   cm.
        Includes bibliographical references and index.
        ISBN 1-55704-445-7 (pbk.: alk. paper)—ISBN 1-55704-454-6 (hc.: alk. paper)
        1. Handicapped children—Care—United States—Handbooks, manuals, etc. 2.
Problem children—Care—United States—Handbooks, manuals, etc. 3. Developmentally disabled children—Care—United States—Handbooks, manuals, etc. 4. Child rearing—United States—Handbooks, manuals, etc. I. Leiderman, Roni. II. Masi, Wendy S. III. Title.
    HQ773.6.S44 2001
    649'.151—dc21   2001030310

QUANTITY PURCHASES
Companies, professional groups, clubs, and other organizations may qualify for special terms when ordering quantities of this title. For information, write to Special Sales, Newmarket Press, 18 East 48th Street, New York, NY 10017; call (212) 832-3575; fax (212) 832-3629; or e-mail mailbox@newmarketpress.com

www.newmarketpress.com

Interior photos by Lisa Nalven Photography
Book design by M. J. Di Massi
Manufactured in the United States of America

Acknowledgments

I would like to thank the following people who made substantial contributions to the writing of this book.

Betty Bardige—Since she was six years old, when her sister Debbie was diagnosed with cerebral palsy, Betty has committed her energy and talent to working with and advocating for infants and toddlers with special needs. Betty has collaborated in the writing and editing of all the books and articles I have written for parents, and was coauthor of the last volume in the "Your Child at Play" series. I am very fortunate to have a daughter who combines genius with commitment and generosity.

Thanks also to Dr. Debbie Schenck who counsels families with special-needs children. Debbie has accepted the role of setting up cluster groups of parents and grandparents who were willing to share their experiences as they met the challenges of raising a child with a handicapping condition.

To Suzanne Gregory, my ever-ready assistant, who turned my illegible scrawls into beautifully laid out pages.

To Ann McElwain who took on the mammoth task of setting up photo shoots.

To Lisa Nalven, who is responsible for most of the photos in this book. She has the uncanny ability to capture with her camera the activities, facial expressions, and parent-child interactions that illustrate the text.

And last but not least, to the parents and grandparents of special-needs children who shared their hopes, their questions, and their fears so that other parents and grandparents could feel they are not alone in their feelings.

Foreword

~~~~~~~~~~~~~~~~~~~~~~~~~~~~~~~~~~~

I have had the privilege over the course of the past twenty years to work closely with Dr. Marilyn Segal, and have observed countless families enter her office with their infants and toddlers in their arms. The parents often expressed feelings of isolation, confusion, disappointment, and fear. Their issues and challenges have varied but their questions inevitably remain the same. "Will our baby be okay?" "What is the future for our special-needs child?" "How can we cope with this overwhelming situation?" I have also watched as these same parents left Dr. Segal's office more confident, less anxious, and with a renewed sense of hope. They may not have definitive answers to all their questions, yet they do have a sense that someone cares, understands, responds, and supports them on the challenging journey upon which they have embarked.

For Dr. Segal, or Mickey, as parents and staff affectionately know her, is a true gift to families. She is the consummate professional who generously shares her wealth of knowledge. Mickey is a teacher and a mentor, an example to those of us who have the honor of working with her. Respectful of each child, Mickey celebrates who they are and honors their spirit. She carefully listens to parents, acknowledges their concerns, and is committed to maximizing every child's potential. In turn, children and their families respond. They allow relationships to develop, and as they experience trust and confidence, they begin to find many of their own answers.

In Time and With Love is a shining example of Mickey's commitment to families with special-needs children. It gives us the opportunity to ask the questions that explore our attitudes and feelings.

While addressing the complex challenges of parents, children, and professionals, the book offers practical suggestions for routine care and creative games and activities. It reminds us to discover and cherish the joy of interacting, playing with, and enjoying children while encouraging us to recognize their limitless possibilities. Most importantly, *In Time and With Love* is about the children, for they, too, are awaiting answers.

Roni Leiderman, Ph.D.
Nova Southeastern University

Contents

〜〜〜〜〜〜〜〜〜〜〜〜〜〜〜〜〜〜〜〜

Introduction   *xv*

SECTION I • A TIME OF ADJUSTMENT   1
Describes the emotional ups and downs families experience as they
care for a special-needs baby, as well as the importance of maintaining warm relationships with family and friends, despite the
time and energy you must expend looking after your baby.

CHAPTER 1 • *When Dreams Fade*   *3*
    Babies Born at Risk
    Babies Who Are Temperamentally Difficult
    Babies Who Are Medically or Developmentally Challenged
    Babies Who Remain a Puzzle

CHAPTER 2 • *Emotional Turmoil*   *10*
    Grief and Loss
    Anger and Frustration
    Depression, Fear, and Loneliness
    Guilt and Self-Blame
    Falling in Love With Your Baby

CHAPTER 3 • *Impact on Marriage*   *17*
    Stressful Times
    Nurturing Your Marriage

CHAPTER 4 • *Siblings*   *23*
    Secret Fears
    Jealousy
    Coping With Teasing
    Balancing Attention

Recognizing the Positives
Suggestions for Parents

CHAPTER 5 • *Family and Friends*   31
Communicating With Grandparents and Close Relatives
Relating to Friends
Communicating With Strangers
Seeking a Parent Support Group

SECTION II • EVERYDAY LIVING   41
Focuses on the routine care of your baby, including the importance of using daily routines—diapering, bathing, and feeding—as special opportunities to learn your baby's cues and engage in intimate communication. Offers playful suggestions to reduce the hassles that are likely to occur in the toddler years as your baby learns how to say "no."

CHAPTER 6 • *Tuning In to Your Baby*   43
States of Awareness
Temperamental Differences
• Easy babies
• Babies who are difficult to arouse
• Babies who are difficult to calm
Interpreting Signs of Stress

CHAPTER 7 • *Day-to-Day Care*   53
Feeding
• Breast-feeding
• Bottle-feeding
• Spoon-feeding
Dressing
Putting Your Baby to Sleep
Working Out a Daily Routine
Arranging Your Baby's Surroundings

CHAPTER 8 • *Day-to-Day Living With Your Toddler*   66
Challenging Routines
Coping With Challenging Behaviors

SECTION III • GROWING AND LEARNING   85

Describes ways in which parents can stimulate growth in different domains of motor, language, social, emotional, and intellectual development. Suggests games and activities that parents can enjoy with their babies and suggests ways of adapting these suggestions to their baby's special needs.

CHAPTER 9 • *Promoting Self-Awareness*   *87*
    Tuning In
    Reaching Out
    Making Discoveries

CHAPTER 10 • *Developing Motor Skills*   *109*
    Tuning In
    Reaching Out
    Making Discoveries

CHAPTER 11 • *Developing Language*   *126*
    Tuning In
    Reaching Out
    Making Discoveries

CHAPTER 12 • *Thinking Skills*   *139*
    Tuning In
    Reaching Out
    Making Discoveries

SECTION IV • PLAYTIME WITH FAMILY
AND FRIENDS   155

Underscores the importance of playful parent-baby interactions. Describes ways of encouraging pretend play, sensory exploration, musical experiences, storytelling, and fun family activities that capture your child's creativity and provide fun times that are every child's entitlement.

CHAPTER 13 • *Encouraging Creativity*   *157*
    Music, Rhythm, and Movement

Art Experiences
Pretend Play

CHAPTER 14 • *Toys and Books*   *167*
    Toys to Choose: Tuning In
    Toys to Choose: Reaching Out
    Toys to Choose: Making Discoveries
    Books to Choose for Babies and Toddlers

CHAPTER 15 • *Fun Times*   *177*
    Everyday Outings
    Vacation Time
    Family Time

SECTION V • TAKING CHARGE   183
Describes the tough decisions that parents are often faced with and
suggests some pros and cons of making some difficult choices. Offers parents a Bill of Rights and suggests ways that every parent can
become a child advocate.

CHAPTER 16 • *The Tough Decisions*   *185*
    Should We Have Another Child?
    Should We Both Go Back to Work?
    How Can We Select a Child-Care Arrangement?

CHAPTER 17 • *Making Informed Choices*   *197*
Specialists for Special-Needs Children
    Medical Specialists
    • Pediatricians
    • Neonatologists
    • Neurologists
    • Orthopedic Specialists
    • Opthamologists
    • Geneticists
    Nonmedical Professionals
    • Optometrists
    • Audiologists
    • Psychologists
    Therapists

- Speech and Language Therapists
- Physical Therapists
- Occupational Therapists
- Behavioral Analysts

Social-Service Professionals

- Hospital Social Workers
- Community Social Workers

Selecting a Specialist
Developing Relationships With Professionals
Choosing a Treatment Approach
Changing a Specialist or Therapist
Deciding on Medications and Alternative Treatments
Planning for the Future

CHAPTER 18 • *Your Role as an Advocate*   211
A Bill of Rights for All Parents of Children With Special Needs
The Importance of Record Keeping
Serving as a Child Advocate

CHAPTER 19 • *Coping With Illness and Hospitalization*   218
Home Care for a Child Who Is Ill
Preparing Your Child for a Hospital Stay
Keeping Informed About Your Child
Preparing Your Child for the Hospital Experience
When Your Child Is in the Hospital
Be an Advocate for Your Child
Going Home

AFTERWORD: *Some Final Thoughts*   229
Index   231
About the Authors   239

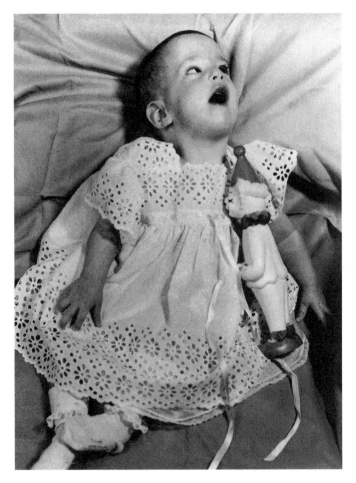

Debbie Segal, ten months

Introduction

~~~~~~

I have been on both sides of the fence. First, as the parent of a child with special needs, I have struggled with grief, pain, hope, and despair. I have desperately searched for a doctor who could tell me my baby would learn to walk. Second, as a developmental psychologist, I have watched parents go out of my office disappointed and angered by my inability to put their fears to rest. Both as a parent and as a professional, I have accepted the fact that there are questions that cannot be answered and problems that cannot be solved. At the same time, I have recognized the need for an authoritative handbook that would help parents mobilize their resources and build on the strengths of their baby, even when there are no firm answers.

In Time and With Love is written for parents who are concerned about their baby's development. It is a collaborative effort. It draws on my knowledge and experience as a mother and a developmental psychologist. It draws on the experience of my associate authors, Wendy Masi and Roni Leiderman, who have contributed both to its content and to its writing. It also draws on the experience of the staff of the Family Center at Nova Southeastern University, who work with parents and babies on a daily basis. Most importantly, it draws on the experience and expertise of thirty-six families who participated in focus groups and shared their personal stories.

Marilyn Segal, Ph. D.

A TIME OF ADJUSTMENT

"It is hard to tell you when I first found out that my baby was in trouble. I heard the words that the doctor spoke but the meaning of the words didn't penetrate. Like there was a filter between me and the doctor, and the only words that reached me were the words I wanted to hear. 'Your baby has a good chance of making it.' It was harder for my husband. He knew from the beginning that even if Angelica made it through the first few days she would still be a very sick baby."

CHAPTER 1

When Dreams Fade

~~~~~~

It is natural for an expectant mother to harbor dreams about the baby in her womb. She will be strong, healthy, and vibrant. She will be a responsive and engaging infant, and every day we spend with her will be sheer pleasure. During her growing years she will continue to delight us. She will accomplish every goal she sets, and we will be there to applaud her successes and snap a new photo for the family album. For many families the dream becomes the reality, but it doesn't always turn out that way. Some babies are born prematurely, and the first year is rocky. Some babies are born with a congenital problem, and the family is faced with an unexpected challenge. Some babies seem healthy at birth, but development goes off course during the early years and parents fear the worst. Some babies are temperamentally difficult, but their development is not in jeopardy.

In this chapter we recount the experiences of parents with four types of babies: infants who were born at risk, infants who are temperamentally difficult, infants who are medically and/or developmentally challenged, and infants who are developmentally different without a definable cause. For these parents, the baby they had fantasized about during their pregnancy has become a myth, and the real baby they gave birth to needs their boundless devotion.

BABIES BORN AT RISK

"I have to be brutally honest. When I went into the Neonatal Intensive Care and saw my baby lying there shriveled up, frightfully quiet, attached to stainless steel ma-

3

~~~

chines, I wanted to shout at the nurse, 'You've made a mistake. That's not my baby. Go get me the baby that belongs to me.'"

When an infant is born prematurely or with a medical problem, the anticipated joy of giving birth is replaced by disbelief, disappointment, and, above all, fear. "Will our baby survive? If we go home for the night, will he be alive in the morning?" For days and even weeks parents may find themselves on an emotional roller coaster. Their baby survives the first crisis, and they let down their guard. A new complication arises, and they are once again frozen with terror. Finally the last crisis passes, and parents cling to hope as their baby clings to life.

As soon as parents dare to believe that their baby is going to live, they are shaken by a different fear. "How can we bond with our baby if he spends all his time in the incubator? How long will it be before we can take him out of the incubator, feed him, and cradle him in our arms?" In many neonatal units the staff recognizes the emotional needs of infants and their parents and welcomes parental participation from the very beginning. In fact, parents are seen as a critical part of the medical team. According to recent research, babies are more likely to thrive and to spend less time in the neonatal intensive care unit (NICU) if parents participate in their care. As soon as possible, parents are encouraged to feed their baby, stroke their baby, and hold and rock their baby. They may also be taught how to massage and hold their baby skin-to-skin. Parent care not only improves the baby's physical health, it creates an emotional bond between the baby and the parents.

Unfortunately, some hospitals are not set up to invite parental participation. Concerns about sterility are paramount, and parents are often discouraged from entering the NICU. But whether parents have had an opportunity to participate in the care of their infant or have been placed in the role of onlookers, the day that they are given permission to take their baby home is a day of celebration.

"I'll never forget the day the pediatrician told us we could bring our baby home. What a warm, fuzzy, wonderful feeling! Now, for the first time, we felt that our daughter belonged to us and that we didn't have to share her with a whole bevy of medical experts. And yet, our joy was tempered with fear. Were we really ready to take care of such a tiny, fragile baby?"

No matter how thrilled the family is to bring their infant home, the first days and sometimes weeks can be frightening. Without a whole staff of nurses and pediatricians watching over their baby, how can they know for sure that they are doing the right thing? Many times parents will be so scared that something bad is going to happen, they will take turns staying awake and watching the baby sleep.

Even when parents are somewhat relaxed, taking care of a fragile infant is an exhausting task. Some babies require medical supports such as respirators, tube feedings, or apnea monitors. Some babies awaken every half-hour day and night, take a drop of milk, and then go back to sleep. Other babies sleep for long stretches, and parents keep wondering if their infant is getting enough nourishment. Fortunately, despite parents' fears, most preemies do gain weight despite their erratic feeding schedule.

Parents who talked to us about the first days at home with their preemies described a reluctance to have friends over. Partly they were concerned that the friend might be harboring a germ. Partly they were embarrassed because their infant had a "preemie look."

"When we brought Matthew home from the hospital, I was barraged with friends and family who wanted to come to visit. Except for people who were very close to me, I discouraged visitors. My ready-made excuse was that Matthew was still very fragile and I was concerned about germs. But it was really more than that. I didn't want to hear people oohing and ahhing about how cute he was when I knew perfectly well that Matthew was not an attractive baby. His eyes were puffy, his skin was wrinkled and jaundiced, one eye turned in, his head was too big for his body, and his legs were

like chicken bones. To make matters worse, he was constantly yawning, hiccuping, and sneezing, and at the least noise his whole body would start."

"I was upset in the beginning because my baby was constantly getting hiccups. The visiting nurse suggested that I might be trying too hard to keep my baby stimulated. She explained that preemies are easily stressed by too much stimulation. When my baby hiccuped, turned white around the mouth, arched his back, or curled his toes, it was a sign that my baby needed some rest and quiet time. After the nurse's visit, I continued to talk with my baby whenever he seemed responsive, but I was much more aware of when I was overstressing him and needed to back off. As she had predicted, the hiccuping decreased."

BABIES WHO ARE TEMPERAMENTALLY DIFFICULT

"The pediatrician keeps assuring us that there is nothing wrong with our baby, but I have my doubts. Jeremy is our fourth child, and he has done more crying in the first six months than all the others put together. The tiniest thing will set him off, putting him in the bath, wiping his nose, or dropping a pot lid on the floor. When I put him in the car seat and strap him in, you'd swear that I was abusing him."

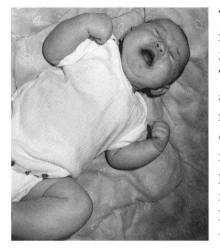

Temperament is an innate style of modulating emotions and responding to the world. Some babies have an easy temperament. They are calm, flexible, quick to warm up, and easily soothed. Other babies, whether or not they are premature or developmentally challenged, have more difficult temperaments. Most often babies with difficult temperaments have trouble regulating and modulating their emotions. On the one hand, they may be withdrawn, slow to warm up, nonresponsive, and difficult to arouse.

On the other hand, they may be hyperalert, over-reactive, irritable, unpredictable, and disorganized—easily disturbed by loud noises, bright lights, and rough textures. Relating to a nonresponsive baby who is difficult to arouse, or to a fussy baby who is difficult to comfort, is more than a full-time job.

BABIES WHO ARE MEDICALLY OR DEVELOPMENTALLY CHALLENGED

"I was devastated when the doctor told me that my baby has cerebral palsy. All I could think about was this child who lived next to me for several years. I would watch her lumber across the yard holding her mother's arm. She kept writhing with these uncontrollable movements. Would my beautiful little baby turn out like that? I brought her to three different doctors asking the same questions. Would my baby ever walk? Is my baby's brain okay? Will she be able to go to a regular school? What causes cerebral palsy? All I got from the doctors were these evasive answers. 'It's too soon to tell. All babies are different. Nobody knows for sure what causes cerebral palsy.'"

Whether a baby has cerebral palsy or a different congenital condition, parents have a strong need to know what caused the problem and what the future holds for their baby. When the physician is unable to answer their questions, parents are likely to feel frustrated and upset. It is particularly difficult for parents to let go of their need to know when their baby has a condition that is relatively common, like cerebral palsy, spina bifida, or Down's syndrome. Even when you are dealing with a well-known disorder like cerebral palsy, Down's syndrome, or spina bifida, every infant is different, and even the most informed physicians cannot tell you what your child will be like. In actuality, parents, although they can't predict what their child will be like in future years, are in the best position to know how well their child is progressing. Parents watch their child develop day by day, they know their child better than anyone else does, and they are likely to be so tuned in to their baby that they notice the subtle changes that are indicative of progress.

When an infant has a chronic medical problem, such as cardiac, pulmonary, or gastrointestinal abnormalities, the major focus of the family is the maintenance of their baby's health. Frequent trips to the hospital, special equipment at home, and struggles between being too protective or not protective enough become a way of life for the family. Partially because they want to be informed and partially because they have a need to know why it happened, parents of medically fragile infants keep looking for sources that describe their child's condition. Because of their single focus, parents are often informed as well as (or even better than) their doctors.

BABIES WHO REMAIN A PUZZLE

"I remember going to the pediatrician and asking every mother who came in how old her baby was. I compared their babies to my baby and then I subtracted two months because my baby was a preemie. One mother had this little eight-month-old boy who was crawling around the room pulling on everybody's shoelaces. I commented on how active he was, and she said that it kept her busy chasing him, but she didn't mind. He was two months premature, and chasing him around was her best assurance that he was right on target. At that point I looked at the limp baby in my arms and burst into tears."

While conditions that can be diagnosed at birth can be devastating for parents, conditions that are not diagnosed until later on—or perhaps not diagnosed at all—are very often the most difficult to live with. Parents are often the first ones who have an inkling that something is not right with their baby. Time and time again parents will tell us that that they knew something was wrong but when they went to the pediatrician, she assured them that the baby would grow out of it.

In defense of pediatricians, we have to recognize that in many instances pediatricians are right. Babies develop at different rates, and many of the behaviors or delays that parents worry about can be easily dismissed. At the same time, parents do know their babies better than anyone else, and when a parent is persistent about a concern it should be taken seriously.

Quite often, even when there is a general consensus that a child has a problem, the problem may not fall into a diagnostic category. For lack of a more precise diagnosis, therapists will often use terms like "developmental delay," "minimal brain damage," "hyperactive," or "sensory integration problems." In many instances these labels are a way of saying, "It is too early to give this child a label." Fearful that they are missing opportunities for early intervention, parents may take their child from specialist to specialist, seeking the definitive diagnosis.

CHAPTER 2

Emotional Turmoil

"I felt angry—like God was getting back at me for something. But I couldn't think of anything that I had done that was that horrible. All I kept thinking about was, why me?"

The turmoil that parents experience when they first suspect or are told that their baby has a problem has been described in different ways. Some professionals talk about a period of bereavement, in which parents face the loss of the perfect baby they once dreamt of. Others describe a sequence of emotions: denial, anger, depression, and, finally, reconciliation. As we talked with parents about their feelings, these descriptions seemed too simplistic. They leave out many factors that influence how parents feel: the moment-by-moment condition of their baby, the kind of support they receive from their spouse and their immediate family, the reactions of their friends, and the changing reactions of their baby's siblings.

As a way of exploring the emotional experience of parents with handicapped infants, the authors conducted a series of individual and group interviews. The interviewees included mothers, fathers, grandparents, and siblings. As parents talked about the emotional turmoil they had been through, they described painful and disturbing experiences over and over again.

Despite this common theme, each family's experience was personal and unique.

GRIEF AND LOSS

To explain their initial feelings about their child's problems, many parents went back to their pregnancy and talked about their dreams and expectations.

"I felt so close to my baby during pregnancy, listening to his heart beat, feeling his kicks. But the damaged baby I gave birth to was not the baby I knew."

Listening carefully to the mother of this brain-injured infant, we realized that she was struggling with the loss of a much-yearned-for perfect baby. Other parents expressed the same feeling of having lost the baby that should have been theirs.

"Every day I love him more, but I ache for that normal child."

"You kind of let your fantasies fade—that normal child growing up, ballet lessons, kindergarten, grade school, college."

ANGER AND FRUSTRATION

Whether parents found out at birth or later on that their baby had a problem, all parents we spoke with described feelings of anger and frustration. Sometimes this anger was an overwhelming sensation directed at no one in particular. More frequently it was aimed at the doctor or the hospital. Sometimes the anger was directed at family or friends, and sometimes at the child.

"I'll never forget that morning in the hospital. This stupid intern strolled into the room and asked if I had seen my baby. Then, just like he was talking about the weather, he said, 'She may look a little funny to you, but she's going to be okay. It's just that she has a cleft palate.'"

The anger expressed by parents of handicapped infants has often been described as self-defense against anxiety and guilt. There are other plausible explanations. Many people, including physicians and nurses, do feel uncomfortable talking with parents of an infant born with a problem. Obstetricians may feel that the birth of a handicapped baby is a challenge to their competence. Pediatricians may feel uncomfortable about talking with parents because they don't have good answers to the parents' questions. Feelings of inadequacy may interfere with the ability of medical personnel to be supportive with parents. Parents, in turn, are sensitive to professional's discomfort and respond with justified anger.

Similar dynamics may be in effect when anger is directed at friends and relations. A baby who is healthy and active, with a ready smile and a winning personality, makes friends for the parents. A baby who is irritable, sleepy, and unhealthy-looking makes people turn away. Parents interpret this reaction as rejection, not just of the baby but of themselves.

"My friends, they were no help at all. One woman said right to my face, 'I'm sorry about your baby,' like he died or got some horrible disease."

It is not uncommon for the baby to get the brunt of the parents' anger. A baby with a problem is often irritable, demanding, and difficult to soothe. The baby may not respond to the mother's efforts to comfort him or may turn away from stimulation as if rejecting the mother. Parents of an unresponsive baby feel inadequate and unwanted. Parents who are already tired, upset, and frazzled may react to the baby's fussiness by losing control.

"I spent all my time crying and hating her. It would have helped to have someone say that they felt that way, too. I wouldn't have felt so guilty."

"In the beginning, every day was terrible and every night was worse. One night, I literally walked the floor for three hours straight and she was still screeching that horrible, high-pitched, grating kind of screech. I finally told her to shut her mouth, and I practically flung her into the crib. Thank God for my husband. He came in the room and told me calmly to go to bed, and he took over with the baby."

DEPRESSION, FEAR, AND LONELINESS

Parents had little difficulty describing their feelings of anger, but they found sadness and fear more difficult to address. Most said they were initially overwhelmed by these painful emotions, but were able to resolve them and move on.

"I cried every day of the first week, then every other day, then once a month. Now I cry about the same things as any other mother with a normal child would cry about."

"Fright, that's one feeling I had. I was really scared. I didn't know exactly what Down's syndrome was. All I could think of was the retarded people that you feel sorry for in the store. I thought that there was no way I could raise my son, because I'd feel sorry for him just like I feel sorry for those people when I see them in the store."

A more subtle and perhaps more pervasive feeling that we identified in our interviews was a sense of vulnerability. Parents talked about how certain they had been that bad things couldn't happen to them.

"Other people have babies with encephalitis, and cerebral palsy, and spina bifida. My baby was going to be perfect, just the way everything else in my life had always been perfect. When the doctor told us about the spina bifida, I just couldn't believe it. Now I feel like I'm nude. Anything bad could happen to me."

"I'm not so much of a churchgoer, but I always believed that if you lived a good life and you cared about other people, God would take care of you. For the first time in my life I look up at the stars and I question."

Depression, vulnerability, and loneliness, like anger, are described in the literature as a natural part of the adjustment process. Although this is a reasonable and well-supported interpretation, characterizing such feelings as a passing phase may be misleading. Mothers of older handicapped children talk about these emotions recurring.

"Every time there is a transition like kindergarten, Sunday school, or Special Olympics, the fear and depression come back. I am up against a reality that I'll never be able to change."

GUILT AND SELF-BLAME

Of all the feelings that parents described, guilt and self-blame were the most pervasive and the most difficult to overcome.

"I was angry with everyone—the doctor, the hospital, the candy striper pushing the library cart—but, most of all, I was angry with myself. I should have been more careful during my pregnancy. People told me to take it easy, but I felt good and I just kept going full-steam. Then, all of a sudden, I got toxemia, they did a C-section, and the baby's lungs weren't developed. Now who knows what kind of life this baby is going to have? If I could only turn the clock backwards!"

"I kept going over and over my pregnancy in my mind. I knew I had been very careful about what I ate. I didn't drink, or smoke, or take medicine, or anything—but maybe there was something else. Then I'd get these really crazy thoughts that maybe I was being punished because I wanted this baby to be so perfect."

Guilt and self-blame are common, but they are also maladaptive. The problem is that parents who engage in self-blame can always find a tiny thread of truth. Maybe they did drink a little coffee or alcohol during their pregnancy. But it wasn't the cause of the problem. And even if they were in some part responsible for the problem, there is nothing to be done about it now. Feeling guilty will not make it better. When parents have difficulty handling these feelings, talking to a counselor may be helpful.

FALLING IN LOVE WITH YOUR BABY

No matter how much time parents spent describing their painful experiences, each wanted to tell us about the good times. Despite their conflicting feelings, they felt a real love for their child and they wanted us to know how much pleasure the baby had brought to the family.

"The deep hurt is there, the worrying about the future, the concerns about what will happen if something happens to us. But that is not what we think about most of the time. Most of the time we just enjoy her. It seems as if every day she is learning something new or doing something adorable. You know what she did the other day? Dennis came into the room wearing his cowboy hat, and Angela took the empty cereal bowl and stuck it on her head."

As they talked about fun times with their child, there was a dramatic change in mood.

"Donna may not be an Einstein, but she sure can hold her own. The other day she counted up to five and her brother said, 'Bet you can't do it backwards.' You know what she did? She turned her back to her brother and counted to five again!"

As parents talked about the pleasures they were getting from their baby, we realized that the literature describing the natural cycle of mourning does not tell the whole story. It is not just that parents go through a series of predictable stages and end up accepting their baby. From the beginning, the baby plays a vital and dynamic role in the parents' lives. As parents learn to interpret their baby's cues and respond to their baby's needs, the baby becomes more responsive and rewarding to his or her parents. There are always ups and downs, but, with time and love, feelings of anguish and pain are overshadowed by feelings of closeness and joy.

CHAPTER 3

Impact on Marriage

"Betty has been different since Jeffrey was born—like I can't really talk to her about anything. I guess she thinks I'm insensitive, but you can't spend your life in a blue funk."

Although the birth of a new baby is a traditional cause for celebration, the first few weeks are quite likely to be exhausting and stressful. New mothers must cope with hormonal changes that can elicit unexpected tears and, occasionally, postpartum depression. Both parents must adjust to a new family dynamic in which they have to share their spouse's attention with a baby. Both parents are physically exhausted. Friends and family arrive with gifts and congratulations, and parents feel bound to put on a happy face. But the kind of stress parents experience when a baby is born with a problem cannot be compared with the expected period of adjustment that follows the birth of a healthy baby.

No matter how strong the relationship with your spouse is, a baby born with a problem can put a strain on your marriage. As you and your spouse deal with your separate fears and guilt, you may be uncommunicative when you need each other most.

In this chapter we explore ways couples relate to each other as they face the reality of parenting a handicapped child. We are concerned with the kinds of conflicts that occur, the differences in perspective that underlie these conflicts, and the kinds of compromises and resolutions that enable husband and wife to maintain a supportive relationship.

STRESSFUL TIMES

As we talked to couples about their baby's disability, we found out that many husbands and wives disagree with each other when they talk about their baby's problem. This is particularly true when the baby shows signs of developmental delay but has not been diagnosed as handicapped. In these situations, mothers, who often have closer daily contact with the child, were usually first to suspect the problem. Some of the husbands we spoke with made light of their wives' concern.

Husband: "What do you expect? He's only a baby. He should recite the Gettysburg Address?"
Wife: "You know what I expect. He's a year old and he should be making sounds. Pretending there isn't a problem isn't going to help."

In situations where either the husband or the wife continued to deny the problem, heated arguments were inevitable. Some couples tried to avoid these arguments by agreeing not to talk about the baby. This lack of communication augmented their fears, and they reached out to others for support.

"I'm so thankful that I found a support group. For a man with 20/20 vision, my husband is blind as a bat. He's made up his mind that there's nothing wrong with the baby and that I'm just being neurotic."

In many situations parents are able to agree on the nature of a problem but disagree violently on how to manage it. One spouse may believe strongly in letting nature take its course, while the other tries to speed up development through nonstop infant stimulation.

"My wife drives herself and the baby crazy. All he wants to do is sleep, and there she is, shaking the rattle and squeaking that darn rubber duck."

Another area of philosophic difference is child management. Disagreements can arise over any aspect of child care. Should the baby be allowed to cry? Can the baby be left with a sitter? Should the baby sleep in the family bed? When parents are already tired and tense, minor disagreements turn into major battles.

"Handicapped or not handicapped, I don't want Alicia to turn into a spoiled brat. The way my husband gives in to her every whim, we're going to have a monster on our hands!"

NURTURING YOUR MARRIAGE

Even when couples are in agreement about how to parent, a baby with a handicap can jeopardize a marriage. In some situations, one parent, often the mother, has to stop working in order to take care of the baby. The nonworking parent may feel angry about being stuck at home. The working parent may feel overwhelmed by the burden of being the sole financial support of the family. Although couples may recognize that they have worked out the only plausible compromise, feelings of resentment can persist.

An even greater threat to a marriage may be overzealousness. When one or both parents make a conscious decision to devote their whole life to the baby, the marriage has to suffer.

"When we found out that Jerod was deaf, we made a pledge on the spot. No matter what we had to do, no matter how much we had to sacrifice, we would do everything in our power to make life easier for Jerod."

Parents who devote their lives to their baby are always in danger of devoting too little time to each other. This is particularly true when the time commitment of the couple is uneven, with one parent taking on most of the child-care responsibility. Tensions between husband and wife can begin to feed on themselves. Disagreements

turn into resentment, and couples who need each other very badly find themselves drifting apart. Recognizing that having a child with a problem adds stress to marriage, parents need to seek ways of nurturing their relationship. The following suggestions come from parents who have been through tough times and have come out with their marriages intact.

- Find time on a regular basis to be alone with your spouse. The extra stimulation you may have provided your baby or the tears you may have prevented are not as important as your marriage. If the problem is finding a baby-sitter, make it a top priority and don't be too proud to ask favors of friends.
- Set aside time for yourself on a daily basis. Read a magazine, go for a walk, listen to music, engage in a sport, or visit a friend. Every human being, no matter how strong or energetic, needs time for self-renewal. The better care you take of yourself, the more available you will be to your baby and your spouse.
- Talk to each other about your feelings and try to understand each other's point of view. Perhaps your spouse resents the amount of time you are devoting to the baby, and perhaps he or

she feels you are spoiling the baby by being at her beck and call. Perhaps your spouse feels that you are not taking your share of responsibility with the baby or that you don't recognize how needy the baby is. When you make a special effort to understand each other's point of view, it is easier to come up with some reasonable compromises.

- Avoid sending mixed messages. Parents often ask for help and then criticize the helper. Perhaps your partner can't change a diaper as quickly as you can or hasn't got the knack of getting up the burp. If you find yourself hovering over your spouse to make sure he or she does everything right, it may be a good idea to leave the room. Your partner's involvement is important for you and your baby, and a little bit of awkward handling is not going to hurt your child.
- Do not pretend with each other. Share your bad feelings as well as your good ones. All parents have moments when they look back longingly to the days before the baby was born, when they were free of worry and responsibility. It's all right to say out loud that sometimes you resent the baby. When husband and wife give voice to their bad feelings, they become more supportive of each other.
- Spend time together enjoying your baby without worrying about therapy. Silly, playful moments are tonic for the whole family.
- Seek counseling or marital therapy if you feel that, despite your best efforts, your marriage is failing.

Siblings

"Tony is one of those really happy-go-lucky, good-natured children. He is unbelievably patient with his little sister, who has cerebral palsy. He lets her walk all over him. One day Tony had a fever, and we decided to take him to the doctor. He put up such a fuss you wouldn't believe it. Finally he asked us in this really scared voice, 'Is the doctor going to say I catched cerebal palsy?'"

Children seem to have a sixth sense. Even when parents are careful not to have disturbing discussions in front of them, they know their parents are concerned about the new baby. Sometimes children react to their parents' concern by developing secret fears. Maybe the baby is going to die, and everyone will get sad. Maybe cerebral palsy is catching, and they are going to get sick.

In this chapter we discuss how a handicapped child affects the dynamics of the family. We explore the impact of a handicapped child on older and younger siblings and describe positive and negative sibling reactions. Finally, we suggest ways parents can help their nonhandicapped children deal with the problems and reap the rewards of having a handicapped sibling.

SECRET FEARS

Parents are often surprised when their nonhandicapped child expresses an irrational fear associated with the baby's disability. When Tony talked about catching cerebral palsy, his mother's first reaction was to laugh at such a silly idea. When you think about it, however, you really can't expect a four-year-old to make the distinction between the condition a child is born with and the diseases that are contagious.

While some of the secret fears that siblings harbor can be attributed to a lack of information, their most haunting fears may reflect a sensitivity to nonverbal communication. When parents are worried and upset about the baby, the other siblings sense it. Often, children are too afraid to ask questions, so parents become convinced that they have protected their children from worry.

It is common for siblings, like parents, to harbor a secret fear that they are to blame for the baby's problems. A common fear is that the baby has problems because they didn't want a brother or a sister.

JEALOUSY

In families with more than one child, a certain amount of jealousy is inevitable. It is certainly not surprising to find jealousy intensified in families with a special-needs child. But many children discover at an early age that expressing jealousy about a handicapped sibling is not acceptable. A child's logical solution is often to get his or her share of attention by helping with the baby. As siblings fuss over the baby, they gain center stage as mother's or father's little helpers.

Another strategy for gaining attention is to imitate the baby. Older siblings cling, whine, and act like a baby, or develop an array of symptoms that provoke a sympathetic response. Recognizing the reasons for their behavior, parents often go overboard to give the older child a fair share of attention. Unfortunately, too much attention to imaginary illnesses can make matters worse. Children and parents find it increasingly difficult to distinguish between real and imagined complaints.

A third strategy for gaining attention in a preoccupied family is to act out. Young children discover that breaking a lamp, spilling a glass of orange juice on the floor, or grabbing the rattle out of the baby's hands gets them attention, even if it is negative. Children are often very up front about their jealous feelings.

"That's why I broked it, 'cause I'm mad. Tim gets all the presents, and he don't do nothing good. He cries, and he spits, and he poops in his diaper, and he stinks!"

When children use these strategies to gain their share of attention, parents have little trouble reading and responding to their cues. The children who appear to show no resentment or jealousy are the ones who need closer watching. Occasionally the sibling of a handicapped child accepts the situation and makes no demands at all. These children may be undervaluing themselves. They may believe that because they do not have a handicap they are not very important and can make no demands.

"Mommy can't come to school to see our play. She's got to watch my brother. He's got zebra palsy."

"I'll give my balloon to my sister. She isn't allowed to go to parties."

Quiet, compliant behavior becomes a way of coping, but, like boisterous behavior, it can also cover up hurt. If parents miss the cues, this coping strategy can rob children of their childhood.

Children who grow up with a handicapped older sibling have less difficulty with adjustment than those with a younger handicapped sibling. Very often the older handicapped child becomes a playmate for the younger child, and a healthy friendship develops. In this situation sibling problems may be kept to a minimum. Exchanges like the following occur in many such families.

Brother: "Mom, can I bring Angela to Terry's birthday party?"
Mother: "Did you ask Terry if it's all right?"
Brother: "He won't mind, 'cause she's my sister."

COPING WITH TEASING

Brother: "Jeremy says that Susan is an idiot."
Mother: "That must have made you feel angry."
Brother: "Yeah, that made me mad. What's an idiot?"

Parents with a handicapped child are always concerned when their children are teased about their sibling. Sometimes children are ostracized by the neighbors because they have a funny-looking brother or sister. Fortunately, in recent years, through the efforts of the media and the schools, people are becoming more knowledgeable about handicapping conditions, and families with a handicapped child are less likely to be stigmatized.

BALANCING ATTENTION

Siblings of handicapped children can also suffer from getting more than their share of attention.

Some families overindulge their nonhandicapped children to shield them from the insensitivity they may have to face. Other families may put too much pressure on the nonhandicapped child, making him or her the focus of all their hopes and dreams. No child is perfect, and living up to unrealistic expectations can be a heavy burden. The nonhandicapped sibling may become too grown-up, too studious, or too responsible. The end product could be an overanxious child who hasn't learned the art of having fun.

RECOGNIZING THE POSITIVES

We have talked so far about the negatives of having a handicapped sibling. But there is a flip side. Children with a handicapped sibling quite often feel confident, successful, and good about themselves. They develop a special talent for playing with their handicapped sibling, which delights their parents and earns them genuine praise. Their interaction with a handicapped sibling makes them sensitive and empathetic, and they have little trouble making friends. Finally, parents who live with a handicapped child are tuned in to the special accomplishments of their nonhandicapped child and boost their child's self-confidence.

Suggestions for Parents

Although most studies show that siblings of handicapped children fare very well in the long run, it is important for parents to help their children cope with some of the inevitable problems and avoid unnecessary hurt.

- Tell your child about the baby's problem in a matter-of-fact way and in words he can understand.

"Jeremy is a baby with Down's syndrome. This means that he will walk, talk, and learn new things more slowly than other children. Down's syndrome is something you are born with, like some people are born with red hair. It is not something that you catch."

"Alicia has cerebral palsy. The part of her brain that tells her arms and legs what to do doesn't work very well. Alicia is going to have trouble learning to walk and may have to use crutches or a wheelchair. She's lucky to have a big brother to help her learn to use crutches or push her around in the wheelchair."

"Tarren is hearing-impaired. Something went wrong before she was born, and she can't hear noises or voices the way you and I can. The hearing aids we put on her will help her learn to hear a little bit. Because Tarren has trouble hearing people talk to her, it will take a long time for her to learn to talk. You and I will have to be very patient when we help her talk."

- Help your child find words to describe her negative feelings.

"You're feeling angry with your baby brother. He does a lot of crying, and he takes up so much of our time."

"You felt sad today when your friends made fun of Eric. People sometimes make fun of things that they don't understand. Maybe one day you can invite your friends over and we'll tell them about autism."

- If your child shares her feelings spontaneously, be a good listener. Accept her feelings without being judgmental and adding to her resentment.

Child: "I hate her, I hate her, I hate her, and I wish she never got borned. Now we can't even go to Grandma's house 'cause she went and got sick."

Parent: "You really feel awful about not going to Grandma's house. Too bad Susie is running a fever."

Child: "Andrew is going to die, and then you and Mom are going to die and leave me all alone."

Parent: "It's scary when Andrew gets sick and we have to take him to the hospital. I'm glad he's feeling better. You know, your mom and I are not going to die for a very long time, and we will never leave you alone."

- Set aside a special time every day to spend with each of your children, even if it's only five minutes. Tell your children how important this special time is to you.

"Our baby keeps us busy. But I'm glad we have this special time for me and you to be together."

- Avoid making your children feel guilty. Instead of saying, "You're selfish to eat that cookie in front of your brother," say, "Eat your cookie in the other room so Paul won't see it." Instead of saying, "Don't make your sister sick by kissing her when you have a runny nose," say, "You have a runny nose. You better not kiss your sister."
- Read your child books about special-needs children. A sensitively written book can help a child understand and empathize with his or her handicapped siblings. Look for books that describe the reactions of siblings to their handicapped brother or sister. It will help your child realize that other children have felt jealous, left out, and resentful, too.
- If your nonhandicapped child is between three and six years old, you may want to try role-playing. Give your child an opportunity to practice answers to the questions people are likely to ask about her handicapped sibling. Take turns asking the question and giving the answer. "Why does your brother keep flapping his arms in the air?" "My brother has autism. Children with autism often flap their hands because it makes them feel good."

CHAPTER 5

Family and Friends

"When Martha brought the baby home from the hospital, it was the first time I had ever seen my sister's baby close-up. It was kind of a shock; his eyes seemed to be too big for his face and his mouth looked distorted. I tried to hide my shock by saying something comforting. 'He's such a lovable little boy. Is it okay if I pick him up?' I don't know what I said wrong, but my sister started to sob."

Part of the joy of childbirth and child-rearing is sharing the new baby with close friends and family. Grandparents and siblings can be especially important. Their expressions of delight as they admire the new baby enhance the celebration. Even couples who distanced themselves from their parents as they cemented their own marriage may sense a new camaraderie with their family and friends. Tensions and conflicts are set aside as the baby takes center stage. When there is a problem with the baby, the joy is mixed with tension and concern. New parents and close relatives may have difficulty sharing their feelings. Perhaps they try to hide their feelings in order to protect each other. Perhaps they express their anxiety in ways that are hurtful.

COMMUNICATING WITH GRANDPARENTS AND CLOSE RELATIVES

Many parents find it difficult to break the news to their close relatives about their baby's problem. A new mother may want to protect her parents or avoid a painful subject. She may want to spare herself the pain of seeing her parents hurt.

"The hardest part of this whole thing was telling my mother. She had been so excited about this baby. When I finally told her, she put up a real brave front. She put her hand on my arm and said in this cheerful voice, 'Well, it's a tough break, but we've had tough breaks before and we always come out on top.' And then her mascara started to run, and I knew she was fighting back tears."

In some situations it is the grandmother who guesses that there may be a problem with the baby and tries to protect the mother. Often the best of intentions backfire, and her probing of the doctors for information is interpreted as interference.

"My mother is giving me a hard time. She's trying to find out more about the problem and keeps looking for something worse. She never tells me directly, but I know what she's up to."

When families have difficulty communicating openly about a child with problems, it can often be traced to long-standing conflicts. A mother and a daughter who were never really close might have fantasies that sharing a new grandchild will put an end to their conflicts and mark a turning point in their relationship. Grandparents expect their children to be less judgmental when they discover firsthand what it is like to be a parent. Daughters expect to be treated as equals as they step into the parent role. Unfortunately, the birth of a handicapped child is likely to increase rather than decrease existing tensions. Old issues like sibling rivalry, struggles with separation, and conflicts over autonomy appear once again.

"My mother practically lives in my kitchen, and she's always there with an opinion. 'You spend too much time holding the baby. She'll never develop her muscles if you hold her all the time.' 'Why don't you let her cry? It's good for her lungs.' 'Shouldn't she be wearing a warmer outfit? It's freezing in this house.' 'I don't want to interfere or anything, but shouldn't you be giving her vitamins?'"

Yet establishment of a new mutually supportive mother-daughter relationship is not impossible.

"We used to fight all the time, but things are better now. At least we can talk about things. I'm glad about it, because I know that Katherine needs all the love and support she can get."

Suggestions for Parents

- If you feel your parents have overstepped their boundaries, discuss the problem openly. It is natural for parents who have always shouldered responsibility for their children to continue in that role. It is up to you to explain that, although you need and appreciate their love and support, you are in charge of your baby.
- If you think your parents are not spending enough time with their grandchild or are not helping out enough, discuss that too. Perhaps your parents are trying so hard not to interfere that they don't realize how welcome they are.

- Help your family feel comfortable about taking care of the baby. It is natural for relatives to lose their confidence if they believe the baby is fragile. With a little practice and guidance, they will learn to trust themselves with the baby.
- Give your family very clear messages. Don't just hint that you would like some financial help or that you need them to do more baby-sitting. It is much easier on everyone if you make your needs explicit.
- If grandparents are reluctant to baby-sit, do not take it as a rejection of your baby. Perhaps your parents don't like to go out at night, or perhaps they are nervous about the responsibility of taking care of the baby. Talk about it openly. Your parents may be more comfortable if you bring the child to their house, or they may volunteer to pay for a baby-sitting service.
- Find specific ways to involve grandparents in taking care of the baby. Try teaching them how to play a language game or showing them how to exercise the baby. This active involvement builds your parents' confidence, gives you an extra pair of hands, and creates a closer bond between grandparent and grandchild.
- If you have tried everything with your parents and nothing seems to work, give it time. Just as your children have a way of making you love them, grandchildren have a knack for winning over their grandparents.

Suggestions for Grandparents

When a baby is born with a problem, grandparents are in double jeopardy. Your first thoughts are for your own children and the kind of pain they are experiencing. Your second thoughts are for your grandchild. When you see your own children hurting, your instinct as a parent is to rush to their side and help them in any way you can. You feel that the best help you can give your children is to focus on their well-being. And yet your children are so focused on

the new baby that they may half resent the attention you are paying to their comfort. This is especially true if your daughter has had a difficult birth.

- Ask your children if they know of reading material that would increase your understanding of your grandchild's problem.
- Ask your children to be honest about the way they feel you could be most helpful. Assure them that you will be just as honest with them about your own limitations.
- Make sure that you don't talk to your own friends about your grandchild's problems until your children are ready to talk about the problem with their own friends.
- If your children ask you to accompany them to the pediatrician, let your children ask the questions.
- If you are upset about your grandchild's condition, be open about your feelings. If you try to hide your feelings, your children will see right through you.

- No matter how right you know you are, don't criticize your children for what they did in the past. It won't change anything.
- Talk openly with your children. If you are concerned about asking too many questions, share your concern with your children: "Matthew is very special to me. I want to know as much as you feel comfortable telling me. I don't want you to feel as if you have to protect me."
- Let your children know that you understand what they are going through. An empathetic word goes a long way.
- If you are uncomfortable about handling the baby, be honest with your children and let them know this. You can find other ways of being supportive until you feel ready.
- Don't be a Pollyanna. Assuring parents that their child will outgrow the problem makes facing up to the problem more difficult.

Suggestions for Close Relatives

- Be careful about giving advice unless it's solicited.
- Be a sympathetic listener. Sometimes parents will need to share with you something especially encouraging about their baby. At other times they may want to share a deep concern. Do not automatically try to either modify their enthusiasm or belittle their concerns. It is important for parents to feel free to share feelings.
- Do not keep asking the mother or dad how you can help. Rather, assure them that you are always there for them and pitch in every way you can.

RELATING TO FRIENDS

"I don't know what's the matter with Robin. I met her at the dentist's, and she acted very cold. Like she didn't even know me. She had her baby with her. I think he may

have Down's syndrome. And when I started to talk to him she whisked him away, saying she was in a hurry."

When a couple has a handicapped baby, particularly if it is a first child, established friendship patterns are likely to change. Some of the reasons for this change are obvious. Admittedly, time is a factor. Free time is at a premium, and finding a sitter with enough experience to care for a handicapped child is not easy. When there is time for socialization, it is natural for couples to gravitate toward other families who have similar problems.

Couples who keep in touch with old friends agree it takes special effort. The first encounter is always the most difficult. Inevitably the old friends ask about the baby, and it's hard to know how much to tell. Do they really want to know about the delivery, or are they making polite conversation? It takes time for couples to break down their defenses and talk comfortably with each other.

If the old friends are already parents, the renewal of the friendship may be particularly difficult. Couples may find themselves in an approach-avoidance conflict. On one hand, they really want to visit with their friends and talk about old times. On the other hand, they are concerned about seeing a baby who is developmentally on target and bound to outperform their baby. A father described his reactions to a visit from his college roommate:

"I was glad to see them, but at the same time it was a shock. I never really believed that Samantha was behind until we spent some time with Joey. That kid was all over the place, digging up the houseplants, climbing on furniture, splashing the water in the toilets. It's not that we cared about the mess he was making. It's just that it hurt so much to watch Samantha just sit there, unable to move."

Whether or not your old friends have children, you may feel uncomfortable about reestablishing the friendship. The experience of having a special-needs child can play havoc with your self-confidence, and you may think of yourself as socially unattractive.

"My wife and I lived like hermits for a while. Frankly, we were embarrassed about having a funny-looking kid with a big head. No, it was more than that; we felt inadequate and disgraced. I know it doesn't make sense, but that's the way we felt. And then a funny thing happened. A neighbor came to the house and started playing with our kid. Jeffrey started laughing, and then we started laughing, and from that moment on things started getting better."

After the ice is broken, most couples report that keeping up with friendships has been an important part of getting their lives back in order. As their friends get to know their baby, talking gets easier and they regain their confidence.

COMMUNICATING WITH STRANGERS

Even when parents have gotten over the hurdle of socializing with friends, they may still be challenged when they take their baby out in public. Parents often tell stories about insensitive strangers who ask impertinent questions or give unsolicited advice. "Is your baby a Mongoloid? You know you could get him operated on. I saw it on TV." But most of the strangers who come up to the stroller are simply attracted to babies. If they ask how old the baby is, they are probably just making conversation, not checking out developmental milestones.

As a defense against questions that make them feel uncomfortable, parents can develop some pat answers that discourage further questions without creating embarrassment.

Acquaintance: "That baby looks like he's too big to carry."
Mother: "He is getting big. I'll be glad when he learns to walk."

Acquaintance: "Your baby looks like she's going to fall asleep any second."
Father: "Yes, she does look sleepy."

Acquaintance: "Is your baby a Mongoloid?"
Father: "She has Down's syndrome."

SEEKING A PARENT SUPPORT GROUP

Even when parents have overcome their "stranger anxiety," they may find themselves becoming less social and more reclusive. Laughter can be jarring when you are worried or depressed, and putting up a good front when you are feeling down is not always easy to do. While some reclusiveness is natural during the adjustment period, it is important not to make it a habit. For the sake of your child as well as the rest of the family, try to keep yourself in the mainstream, inviting social encounters and maintaining your circle of friends.

When parents are ready to reach out and make new friends, the most accessible prospects may be parents with disabled babies. These are the people who are most likely to understand how you feel and to share your joys and concerns. Unfortunately, despite the availability of already established support groups, many parents have difficulty taking the first step. You may perceive the decision to join a support group as a confirmation of your baby's handicap and as an abandonment of hope. Even when parents do decide to join a parents' group, it may take them a while to find a group that really meets their needs.

"I went to a support group meeting for mothers of babies with Down's syndrome. All these women kept talking about how great it was to have a Down's syndrome baby. I had to leave. I couldn't deal with it. I figured there was something wrong with me, thinking all the time that it would have been best if my baby had died."

"It wasn't easy for me to join the Family Center group. When I first saw all those babies with handicaps sitting around in a circle, I wanted to run away. My son wasn't

going to look like that! He was just developmentally delayed, and he would outgrow his problem. But then, when a parent urged me to come into the room, I saw my son's reaction. He was clapping his hands to the music and having a wonderful time. Pretty soon I heard myself saying that next week I'd bring the snack."

One of the major benefits of joining a parent support group is the opportunity you gain to give as well as receive support. As you reach out to help another parent, you will reinforce your own coping skills. At the same time, your baby will have the opportunity to be with other children.

In this chapter we have made some suggestions to ease the tensions and improve communication between new parents and grandparents, friends, relatives, and others. Remember, a technique that works beautifully for one family can be a disaster for another. Each family brings its own mixture of understanding, caring, education, social customs, emotional stability, and a host of other characteristics. How these mesh will probably determine what kind of relationship is possible. Our advice is to read about the experiences of other families and the resolutions they have reached, and select those ideas that may be helpful for your family.

EVERYDAY LIVING

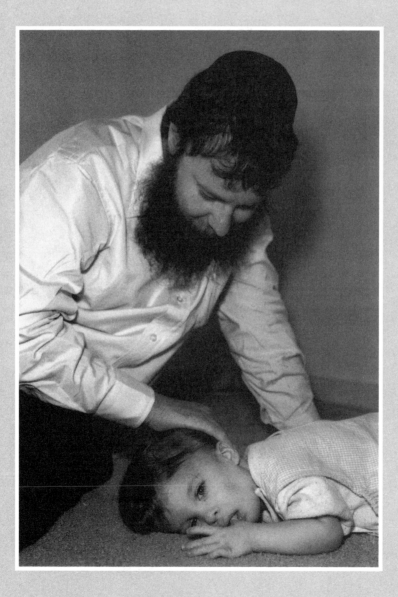

"I feel uncomfortable when I'm away from Brett. I know he's just a baby and he'll be fine without me, but somehow I feel that no one can take care of him quite as well as I can. I know by the sound of his breathing and the way he moves that he's going to awaken, and I lift him out of the crib before he starts to cry. I know just how to hold him, cradle, rock, and soothe him, and get him back to sleep. It's as if I'm part of him and he's a part of me."

CHAPTER 6

Tuning In to Your Baby

~~~~~~

According to many parents we talked with, the best way to free yourself from the emotional turmoil of having a special-needs child is to focus your energy on the daily care of your child. Many of the concerns that parents of special-needs children express are the same concerns expressed by parents with a typical child. *"How can I leave my infant and go back to work?" "How can I find a caregiver I can trust?" "How can I get my infant to sleep through the night?" "What should I do when my toddler has a temper tantrum?" "How can I discipline my toddler without destroying his free spirit?"*

Every child, whether preterm, developmentally challenged, or healthy and robust, comes into the world helpless and alone. The baby's survival depends on his ability to make his needs known and to invoke caregiving behaviors. During the early years, the connections that the baby makes with parents or caregivers are his lifeline. They are the baby's way of rising out of helplessness and developing an awareness of self and a sense of security, control, and purpose.

Just as your baby is affected by the quality of care you give him, your baby is affecting you by the quality of his responses. The infant who cries when hungry and calms down when fed has initiated an unspoken dialogue: "I need, you respond, and I'm comforted."

A critical task of the infant is to signal his needs to his caregiver. In turn, a critical task for the caregiver is to interpret and respond to these signals. As the signal-and-response system takes hold in infancy, infant and parent are tuned in to each other and a love bond is cemented. In infants at risk, where the cues are indistinct, hard to read, and often confusing, the bonding process may be slower. For a while you may feel inadequate as you struggle to interpret those muted cues. In the long run, however, the energy and the effort expended by infant and parent can make bonding all the stronger.

In this chapter we explore the ways in which you, by reading and responding to subtle behavioral cues, come to know your baby. First we look at natural fluctuations in behavior, recognizing that every baby has times during the day when he is quiet and alert, times when he is drowsy, and times when he is agitated. Second, we examine differences in temperament, activity level, sensitivity to stimuli, adaptability, and quality of mood. Finally we suggest ways you can recognize and respond to your baby's cues and signals.

STATES OF AWARENESS

As your newborn baby awakens from sleep or goes from wakeful attentiveness to agitated crying, you will recognize the various states of her sleeping/waking cycles. These different ways of responding to the outside world are described as the baby's state of arousal. Different parts of the brain control the different states of your baby's behavior.

- In deep sleep, your baby is sleeping quietly. Her breathing is regular, and there are no visible eye movements.
- In wakeful or REM sleep, the baby is asleep but restless. REM stands for rapid eye movement, because the baby's eyes can be seen moving back and forth under her almost closed lids. Her breathing is likely to be irregular.
- In the drowsy state, the baby is awake but inattentive. Her eyes look glazed and unfocused.
- In the state of quiet alertness, the baby's eyes are focused. She looks interested and aware, and is ready to take in new information.

- In the state of active wakefulness, the baby is less focused. Some babies will kick and wave their arms. Others will stiffen, squirm, and begin to fuss.
- In the state of crying, your baby's face is distorted. Her eyes may be open or tightly closed.

Babies who have well-established sleep/wake cycles move from one state to the next in a smooth and predictable way. The baby who is in a quiet alert state, for instance, may be going up the cycle, in-

creasing her activity level until she reaches crying, or down the cycle into drowsiness and sleep. Babies who are premature or developmentally challenged may take several months to establish these six distinctive states.

As your baby's states become distinctive enough to identify, you will want to maximize the amount of time that your baby is quiet and alert. You can bring your baby up from a state of drowsiness to a state of quiet alertness by introducing the right amount of stimulation. You will also find ways of quieting your baby when she is crying or active in order to bring her back down to a state of quiet alertness.

When a baby is either actively crying or looking drowsy and half-awake, it is natural to assume that the baby should be comforted and put to sleep. In actuality, a drowsy baby may be in the process of awakening, and a crying baby may be ready for some active play-time. If your baby is drowsy but appears to be awakening, approach the crib talking in a soft but high-pitched voice, and see if your baby responds by making eye contact. If your baby is crying or fussy but not hungry, cradle her in your arms or place her in a bounce chair, or hold her in a "baby sling." Talk to her softly, making sure that she can see your face and watch your lips move. She may enjoy some "conversation" before she falls asleep.

TEMPERAMENTAL DIFFERENCES

Since the early 1960s, researchers have tried to identify individual differences present at birth that have significance for later development. The task has not been easy. Infants change very rapidly, and behaviors that characterize an infant one day may be gone the next. Also, babies are sensitive to caregivers, and both the significance and the predictability of a characteristic are related to the caregiving environment. At the same time, an infant who is irritable at birth may be experiencing a physiologic adjustment, becoming accustomed to living in the world outside the warm surroundings of his mother's uterus. If the parent interprets the infant's behavior as signaling a permanent characteristic or as a reflection of her own inexperience, her negative reactions could stabilize the trait.

To identify temperamental characteristics that are present at birth and stabilize over time, researchers have followed the same babies through their growing-up period. They have scrutinized the individual differences present at birth as well as parenting styles and characteristics. Through these studies, they have been able to identify dimensions of difference in infancy that affect caregiving needs. They have also recognized clusters of characteristics that make it easier or more difficult to parent a newborn child.

Babies who from the start are placid and easy to soothe, who adapt easily to new situations, who are predictable in terms of sleeping and eating, and who are neither too easy nor too difficult to arouse are thought of as "easy babies." Babies who are sluggish, difficult to arouse, disturbed by new stimuli, and irritable, or babies who are active, irregular, easily aroused, and hard to soothe are considered to be "difficult babies." Unfortunately, many of the characteristics that are associated with a difficult temperament are also associated with babies who have some sort of disability.

Easy Babies

An easy baby makes life easy for his parents. The easy baby can be thought of as "forgiving." If the parent takes a long time to get the bottle ready, the baby tolerates the wait. If the parents decide to visit a friend, the baby is content to go to sleep in a strange place. The baby does a lot of smiling and little crying, giving parents the unspoken message, "You are doing fine." The baby is a joy to hold and cuddle, and his pleasant behavior is reinforced.

Babies Who Are Difficult to Arouse

Preterm babies, disorganized babies, or babies who have a difficult beginning may have some, but not all, of the characteristics of an easy baby. They may spend a lot of time sleeping and fall back to sleep with no difficulty after a period of wakefulness. Unlike easy babies, however, they spend little time in the beginning in a state of quiet alertness. Parents have the special challenge of providing modulated stimulation that engages their baby's attention and helps him achieve a quiet alert state.

Here are some examples of modulated stimulation. Notice that only one sense is engaged at a time:

- Stroke your baby softly on the cheek or play gently with his fingers and toes.
- Sing or chant a lullaby or ring a small bell with a pleasant tinkle.
- Swing or rock your baby, slowly and easily, in an infant seat.
- Show your baby a colorful ribbon or scarf.

If your baby responds to modulated stimulation without showing signs of overload, increase the stimulation gradually. You may want to sing quietly as you wave the ribbon or bounce the infant seat with a little more vigor. Babies who respond well to modulated stimulation do not usually like sudden changes in activities or in the intensity of the stimuli.

Babies Who Are Difficult to Calm

When a baby is hyperalert or difficult to calm, the role of the parent is much more challenging, particularly in the first year. If the baby is easily aroused by stimuli such as light, sound, and touch, he will be disturbed by a mild increase in stimulation. The slightest noise will startle him; a room full of people may set off a panicked cry. If a baby is slow to warm up, he may react negatively to any kind of change or new experience. The first bath may be a disaster, and changing the blanket on his crib may provoke a bedtime crisis. Babies who tend to be irritable or hard to soothe may respond to being handled by crying louder or by extending their arms and legs. Parents may feel rejected.

Babies who are easily aroused or hyperalert are also likely to be slow to warm up. These babies require sensitive and caring parents who recognize how easily they are overloaded and seek out ways to modify and control the environment. Parents need to be alert to the particular kind of stimulation that is disturbing to their baby. Some babies are especially sensitive to noises, some to bright light, and some to changes in texture. Other babies may be upset by quick and jerky movements. When you can anticipate the kinds of stimuli or changes in stimulation that your baby has difficulty with, you can introduce modifications that build up your baby's level of tolerance. The task becomes even more demanding when your baby responds inconsistently, rejecting being cuddled one day and enjoying it the next.

Although hypersensitive and slow-to-warm-up babies are not necessarily at risk, extreme hypersensitivity is usually associated with prematurity or a developmental disability. Babies with cerebral palsy may be particularly sensitive to quick movement or sudden noises. A dropped rattle can make them start or quiver. A vision-impaired or hearing-impaired baby may be upset by an unexpected touch or tickle.

If your baby is sensitive to bright light, make sure to pull down the shades if there is too much sunlight. When you need the room to be brighter, turn on a lamp with a low-wattage bulb. When your baby has adjusted to this amount of light, you can turn on an overhead light or a full-wattage lamp. Some parents find a light on a rheostat (dimmer switch) helpful.

If your baby is sensitive to noise, tone down those noises that are likely to disturb him. Turn the ring on your telephone to its lowest level and muffle a noisy doorbell. Talk to your baby in a soft voice and gradually raise the volume. If the problem persists, consider installing acoustical ceiling tile or adding heavy drapes to help control extraneous noises.

If your baby is sensitive to texture, be careful about the sheets you put on his crib, the clothes you wear, and the clothes you dress him in. If he is used to a cotton sheet on his crib, buy another cotton sheet rather than a polyester one. Wash a new outfit before you put it on him to make sure it is soft enough. Let him touch it or play with it. Pay attention to the texture of your own clothes. If you are wearing a rough-textured shirt or sweater, you may want to slip on a housecoat before you begin his feeding.

If your baby is disturbed by new experiences, modify your daily routine so that any new experience is introduced slowly. The first time you give your baby a bath, let him watch you make the preparations. Be sure to choose a quiet time during the day so that he won't be bombarded with other kinds of stimulation. Place him on a towel or sponge in a baby tub with very little lukewarm water. Every few days increase the amount of water until his body is submerged. Talk to him gently as you bathe him to keep him calm and relaxed.

If your baby is difficult to soothe, try to identify and avoid situations are potentially upsetting. Hard-to-soothe babies are often distressed by sudden changes in the amount of stimulation, or by an increased level of stimulation over a relatively long period of time. A room full of company that most babies can ignore or tune out might

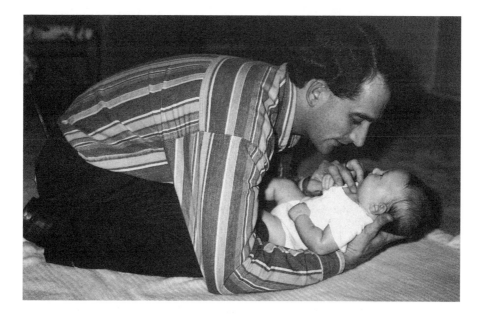

really upset a hard-to-soothe baby. No matter how hard you try to stay away from these stressful situations, there are times when they are unavoidable. There will also be times when your baby becomes agitated and frantic for no identifiable reason.

The best way to calm a hard-to-soothe baby is to reduce the amount of stimulation. It may be possible to bring your baby into a quiet room and rock him gently. For some babies even this may not be enough; their own active thrashing in your arms may maintain their overload. When this happens, put your baby down in the crib in a quiet, darkened room. Once he is down, talk to him softly, pat him gently and rhythmically, and cover him with a familiar blanket. When he has discharged his energy through active crying, he is likely to calm himself and fall quietly to sleep.

As parents adjust their own behavior in response to their baby's temperament, it is important to recognize that a baby's temperament is something he was born with and does not reflect their adequacy as parents. Hard-to-soothe babies or babies who are too easily aroused are not rejecting their parents. On the contrary, they are sending out a message that says, "I need your special kind of caring. I am easily overwhelmed."

INTERPRETING SIGNS OF STRESS

Just as babies are born with a set of reflexes that have survival value, they also have distinct ways of signaling and reacting to stress. In the early months a baby will react with her whole body to any type of stress situation: a bright light, a loud noise, a sudden change in position, or an over-stimulating caregiver. Parents become sensitized to the special ways their baby signals stress or overload, and either modify the environment or help their baby cope.

The ways in which babies signal stress are often very subtle: a change of expression, a tightening of the lips, a curling of the toes, or a slight change in color. Other stress signals include hiccuping, spitting up, turning dusky, or having a bowel movement. When your baby is showing signs of stress, it is important, of course, first to reduce the amount of stimulation. Equally important is helping your baby organize her own resources and learn self-calming strategies. Sometimes putting your hand on your baby's stomach or back is enough to help her reorganize. At other times you may be able to give her a pacifier, or put her arms close to her body with her hand close to her mouth. If self-calming techniques are not successful, hold your baby close in your arms and move gently from side to side.

Tuning in to your baby, recognizing her unique needs and special characteristics, and identifying ways to meet these needs is a never-ending challenge. Babies are capable of sudden spurts in development that modify their needs and change their capabilities. Often you will find yourself walking a tightrope. On one hand, you want to be there for your baby, protecting her from discomfort. On the other hand, you want your baby to learn to self-regulate, cope, and adapt to changes in her environment.

CHAPTER 7

Day-to-Day Care

~~~~~~

"Seven and a half pounds, and our whole house is full of baby diapers, cradles, carry-cribs, baby bottles in the sink, nighty-nights in the shower, and everyone in the house at her beck and call."

A full-term and thriving newborn baby can place the household on active twenty-four-hour duty, particularly in the first few weeks when the baby and the household are adjusting to each other. When the baby is born premature or at risk, the period of active twenty-four-hour duty may continue for a very long time. The baby's erratic sleep and eating patterns make it difficult to establish a schedule, and parents find themselves chronically overtired. The calm and organized household that parents want so much for the baby is almost impossible to achieve.

This chapter focuses on the routines of daily living. We look at eating, sleeping, holding, changing, and other caregiving routines that take up a significant part of each day.

FEEDING

In the early months, parents spend more time in feeding their baby than in any other caregiving activity. When feeding routines go smoothly, other routines are likely to follow suit. In most situations, however, parents do have some concerns associated with feeding their special needs baby.

When you have a choice between breast-feeding and bottle-feeding, most doctors agree that breast-feeding has nutritional advan-

~~~~

tages. Breast milk contains the appropriate ratio of carbohydrates to fats and proteins, and a good supply of calcium and other minerals. It also provides immunity against certain infections. From the point of view of the mother it is usually easy, pleasant, and comfortable. Breast-feeding provides a special opportunity for the mother to feel close to her baby.

Despite the advantages of breast milk, mothers with at-risk babies are less likely to breast-feed than mothers with normally developing babies. There are several reasons for this, including problems with sucking, prolonged hospital stays, and stress-related problems with milk flow. Fortunately, commercial formulas are good substitutes for breast milk, and bottle-feeding has some advantages. Bottles provide a way of measuring intake and provide fathers with the opportunity to share in the feeding routines. In addition, nipples can be modified, or specialized nipples can be purchased for babies who have sucking difficulties or other problems coordinating their tongue, lips, and palate.

Whether they are being breast-fed or bottle-fed, preterm and developmentally delayed babies are likely to have problems with sucking. To suck, an infant must purse his lips around the nipple and rhythmically move his tongue up and down. This creates a vacuum that draws the milk into the infant's mouth, where it is reflexively swallowed. Problems can occur with babies who have difficulties with positioning, with pursing their lips, or with tongue control.

Whether the baby is being fed from breast or bottle, a beginning step to help a baby who is having difficulty with sucking is to modify the feeding environment.

- Make sure that the room is cool and quiet and that the lights are dim.
- Sit in a comfortable chair with an armrest.
- Let the baby feel your skin or touch your breast as he sucks.
- Begin feeding, whenever possible, before your baby is crying frantically. A distraught baby may have difficulty sucking.

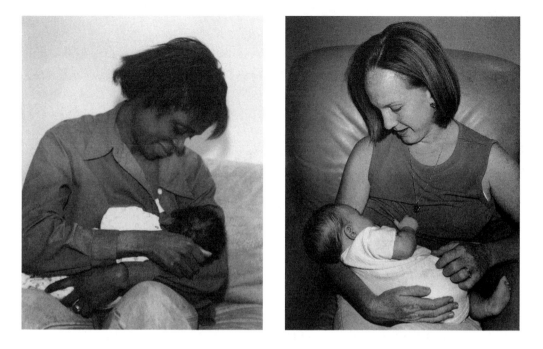

- If your baby tends to fall asleep after just a few sucks, awaken him fully before you begin the feeding. Keep a light on in the room and sing and talk to him during the feeding.
- If your baby is wide awake and crying before a feeding and then falls asleep as soon as he sucks on the nipple, it may be that your baby is seeking comfort rather than crying because he is hungry. Try to stretch out the feedings by giving him a pacifier when he awakens crying. If he rejects the pacifier at first, be persistent. If you hold the pacifier in his mouth as you rock and soothe him, he will gradually learn to accept it.

Breast-feeding

- Make sure that you are eating a well-balanced diet; avoid chocolate, spicy foods, caffeine, and over-the-counter medications. Note what you have eaten when your baby is particularly fussy after a feeding.

- Drink plenty of water throughout the day.
- Try to get a few minutes' rest before you begin to breast-feed. When you are feeling relaxed, your baby's hunger cry will trigger a let-down reflex, and your milk will begin to flow spontaneously.
- Position your baby for breast-feeding by placing him in the crook of your arm with your hand supporting his buttocks.
- If your milk does not start dripping spontaneously, expel a few drops manually from your breast to get the feeding started.
- When you put your baby to the breast, rub your nipple on his cheek. This will stimulate him to turn his head, open his mouth, and actively search for the nipple.
- Aim the nipple toward your baby's mouth by holding your breast around the areola.
- Make sure that your baby gets the whole areola into his mouth and not just the nipple. Compressing or flattening the areola with your hand just before the baby begins sucking may be helpful.
- Make sure that the baby's nostrils are not covered by your breast.
- Never pull the nipple out of your baby's mouth. If your baby chews on the nipple, insert your finger in the side of his mouth and ease the nipple out gradually.
- Breast-feed on demand.
- Regardless of how much milk you feel your baby has taken in, limit each feeding to 15 to 20 minutes per side.
- Feed your baby with both breasts at every feeding.
- If your baby resists the breast, discontinue the feeding temporarily. Soothe your baby and try again.
- Try using a breast pump for a few days to increase the flow of milk.
- If you are having trouble with your nipples, get a pamphlet or advice from La Leche League or consult your obstetrician. Do not get discouraged if it takes a week or two to establish a com-

fortable routine. If your baby continues to have difficulty with breast-feeding, call your pediatrician.

If you would like additional suggestions for breast-feeding your baby, you can find more information in one of several good books on the subject. Ask your librarian or local bookseller for help.

Bottle-feeding

- Experiment with different positions until you find the one that is most comfortable for both you and your baby.
- Adjust the size of the nipple hole to accommodate to your baby. If he keeps choking, the nipple hole may be too large; if he falls asleep without getting enough milk, it may be too small.
- Experiment with different types of nipples.
- Throw nipples away when they begin to get soft and gummy.
- Some babies enjoy soft music while they are feeding. Try it with your baby.

Make sure to let your pediatrician know if problems with sucking persist.

Spoon-feeding

Many premature or otherwise at-risk babies have real difficulties managing baby food. A hypersensitive baby, or one who adjusts slowly to change, may have difficulty getting used to the sensation of food in his mouth. A child with abnormal muscle tone may either bite down too soon on the spoon and prevent the food from entering his mouth or not close his jaw at all. This happens frequently with babies with cerebral palsy. The Down's syndrome baby is likely to push the food out of his mouth with his tongue.

Babies who have difficulty accepting food into their mouths will also have problems chewing. They may not be able to achieve the rhythmic movement of the jaws or to use their tongues to move the food around.

To help your child accept food:

- Make sure that your baby is looking at you before you put the spoon in his mouth.
- Use a small, rounded spoon. Make sure the spoon is at room temperature before you put it in your baby's mouth.
- Feed your baby small amounts at a time, and place the food well back in his mouth.
- Begin by giving your baby cereal for which you can control the consistency by adding more or less liquid. Finding the exact consistency that is right for your baby is a matter of trial and error.
- If your baby is sensitive to temperature, make sure the food is at room temperature.

- Never introduce more than one new food at a time.
- Stop feeding your baby when he shows the first signs of disinterest. Never force your baby to eat.

Babies with developmental disabilities are often prone to hiccups. Hiccups are a spasm of the diaphragm and are usually of no consequence. Hiccups usually disappear within a few minutes, whether or not you give the baby a bottle. If hiccups persist for more than twelve hours, call your pediatrician.

Many babies, whatever their status, are likely to spit up small amounts of food after a feeding. Spitting up in immature babies is usually caused by esophageal reflux. The muscular part of the esophagus that normally keeps food from backing up functions improperly, and the food surges back from the stomach. If spitting up is excessive (a large amount at every feeding), or projectile, call your pediatrician.

To limit hiccups and spitting up:

- Feed your baby frequently and on demand.
- Make sure to burp your baby several times during the feeding. Some babies burp more easily if held over your shoulder. Other babies do better if you lean them forward in a sitting position, holding up their chin with your hand. It may help to rub your baby's back gently, but do not slap or pound his back.
- Hold your baby in a sitting position for a few minutes after each feeding.

As long as your baby continues to gain weight and look healthy, don't worry about a little spitting up. In most situations the best solution with a young baby is to keep a diaper or towel handy.

Colic

Colic is a common digestive disorder that affects many young infants, whether or not they are premature or disabled. A baby who has colic experiences abdominal distress during or right after feeding. Often a baby will appear to be hungry and search frantically for the nipple. Then after a couple of sucks the baby will reject the nipple, draw up his legs, and cry out in pain. These attacks of colic may occur once or several times in the course of the day.

Although colic is disturbing to parents as well as infants, it is not a serious condition. It is simply an indication of an immature digestive system and is likely to disappear by the time the baby is three months old. While some "colicky" babies do better with a change of formula, for the most part colic is something that the baby simply must outgrow. Some pediatricians claim that colicky babies may be somewhat soothed by the sensation of riding in a car. There is even a device available now that attaches to a crib and simulates the sound and movement of a car. But for the most part, the best you can do is try to make your baby as comfortable as possible. Try carrying him on your shoulder, stretching him stomach-down across your knees, swaying or moving up and down while you carry him, or rocking him in a cradle.

DRESSING

Simple routines like dressing, diapering, and bathing can become a challenge with babies who are hypersensitive or with babies who have poor postural control.

With hypersensitive babies there is always a fine line between overdressing and underdressing. Dressing the baby in an undershirt and an overshirt provides you with some flexibility if your baby tends to get too warm as the day goes on. Hypersensitive babies are also sensitive to changes in texture. A stiff outfit or a tag in the back of a shirt is enough to make some babies irritable. Be sure to wash all new baby things with a mild soap and a double rinse to avoid irritation.

Babies with postural disorders or motor dysfunctions provide other challenges. A cerebral palsy baby may scissor her legs when

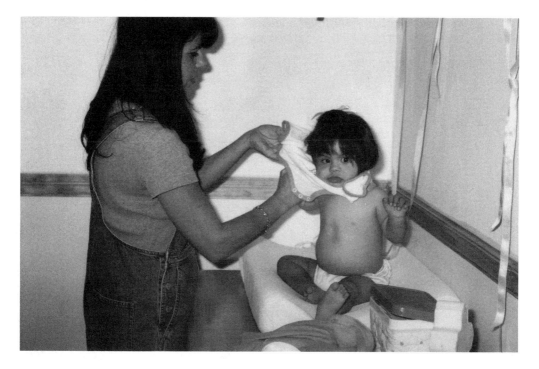

you try to put on slacks or develop clonus (ankle spasms) or toe curling when you try to put on her shoes. If your baby is difficult to dress, it may help to modify her clothes. Babies can usually get along without shoes, and loose-fitting two-piece outfits can simplify the dressing chore.

PUTTING YOUR BABY TO SLEEP

Sleep problems are common with developmentally disabled babies, who usually take longer to settle into a routine and may awaken frequently and for long stretches during the night. One problem may be sleep position. A child who lacks neuromuscular control may not be able to readjust her posture during sleep. Still another problem may be parental concern. Parents of disabled babies may rush into the room before their baby has a chance to put herself back to sleep.

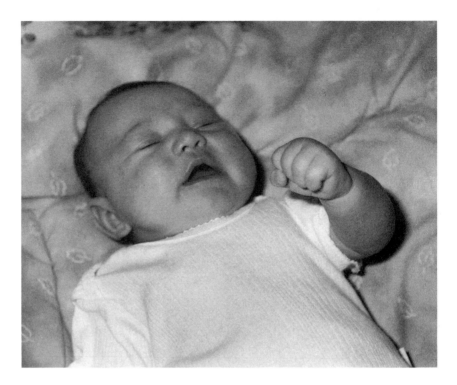

These suggestions may help your child form successful sleep habits:

- Put your baby to sleep in the same place and at approximately the same time every night. Sleeping is habit-forming!
- Let your baby fall asleep in her crib or cradle rather than in your arms. It is important for her to associate the crib with falling asleep.
- Find a soft blanket that your baby seems to like, and keep it in the crib at all times. The blanket can be an extra cue that will help your baby fall asleep.
- If your baby is six months old or more, avoid giving her a bottle right before she falls asleep. A very wet diaper is disturbing.
- Help your baby learn to sleep through the night. Rather than picking your baby up as soon as she begins to cry, give her a reassuring pat and let her fall back to sleep.

- If the pat didn't work and your baby begins to cry again, wait four or five minutes and pat her gently again.
- Unless you are willing to keep it up for a very long time, avoid the temptation of putting your baby in your bed.

If you would like to read more about sleep problems and solutions, *Crying Baby, Sleepless Nights: Why Your Baby Is Crying and What You Can Do About It* by Sandy Jones is an excellent reference.

WORKING OUT A DAILY ROUTINE

In the first section of *In Time and With Love* we discussed the importance of making time for yourself. One of the best ways to accomplish this is to begin to schedule your baby. Advice about scheduling varies greatly. Before Dr. Spock, babies were scheduled by the minute hand. In the post-Spock era, demand feeding was the rule. We tend to disagree with both positions. Most babies do better on a schedule as long as it isn't rigid. Most important, all parents, no matter how dedicated they are to their baby, need time for themselves and time to be together.

As you begin to schedule your baby, pay attention to the cyclical patterns your baby has developed on his own. If your baby is relaxed by a bath, schedule it for the time of day when your baby is most likely to fuss. Plan regular brief play periods at the times when your baby tends to be quiet and alert, or when you find it easy to help him achieve this state. If weather permits, take your baby on an outing at the same time every day. If you like to sing, select a jaunty tune for playtime and a quiet song for sleep time. After a while, your baby will associate a tune with playing or falling asleep. Dim the lights when it is sleep time, and make them bright for playtime. Gradually stretch out the time between feedings by giving your baby water or a pacifier.

ARRANGING YOUR BABY'S SURROUNDINGS

No matter how much planning you do, it is difficult to arrange the house to accommodate the baby until you have the baby home and find out what you need. And your needs will change as your baby grows older. But be sure to baby-proof your house before your baby starts to creep around.

Post emergency telephone numbers beside every telephone. Hopefully, you will not have to use them.

Arrange your house so that there is a comfortable place for your baby in each room where you spend a lot of time. This may involve buying or improvising an extra cradle or bassinet.

Before putting up mobiles, pictures, and crib toys, think about your baby's temperament. If your baby is sensitive to loud noises, take his tolerance level into account as you choose musical toys.

Make sure not to put up a sound mobile that you cannot turn off. If your baby is overly quiet and placid, you may want to encourage alertness with stimulating mobiles, chimes, and musical toys.

Take into account your baby's particular type of disability as you arrange the house. Visually impaired babies need an environment in which there is tactile and auditory stimulation and cues. An area rug in the bedroom could define play space for your baby and keep him from bumping into furniture.

Hearing-impaired babies need special opportunities to develop residual hearing. Hanging a bell by your baby's door lets you signal to your baby that you are coming into the room.

Babies with mobility problems need the opportunity to see the world from different perspectives. Keep a stroller in the house so you can wheel your baby from room to room, or carry your baby in a "Snuggly," or other baby carrier. Arrange places in different rooms where your baby can be propped in a safe and comfortable sitting position.

When a baby has a disability, the routines of daily living are seldom routine. With some babies, some of the routines are especially easy. A preterm baby may fall asleep easily after feeding, and a baby who is slow in motor development may not pose a threat to houseplants or bric-a-brac. More frequently, the daily care of a special needs baby puts heavy demands on the household. On one hand, these demands can push you to the point of exhaustion. On the other hand, satisfying your baby's persistent demands strengthens the bond between parent and child.

CHAPTER 8

Day-to-Day Living With Your Toddler

~~~~~~~~~~~~~~~~~~~~~~~~~~~~~~~

"Jeremy was almost two when he took his first step. I'll never forget it. He was stand-ing with me. I was holding Jeremy in an upright position. My husband was squat-ting down about three feet away and held out his arms. I let go of Jeremy and he walked right into his father's arms. Jeremy walks pretty well on his own now, and I've discovered it's a mixed blessing. If I don't watch him every second he's into something else."

In this chapter we describe day-to-day living with a toddler. We discuss characteristic toddler behavior, daily living routines, and ways of managing disruptive behavior.

The term "toddler" is traditionally used to describe the baby who is just learning to walk. Recognizing that some children with handi-

caps may learn to walk when they are older or perhaps not at all, we use the word toddler to refer to youngsters between one and three years old, whether or not they are mobile.

Toddlers are reputed as ornery and unpredictable. At one moment they appear to be quite grown-up, insisting on doing things by themselves and resisting help or suggestions; at the next moment they turn back to baby behavior, clinging to their caregiver and exaggerating their helplessness. For most toddlers, "no" and "mine" are the most overused words in their vocabulary. The constant "no" as well as the "mine" are the toddler's way of declaring his emerging sense of self. "I am a person with a will of my own, with the right to make choices, to resist commands, and to claim sole ownership of important possessions." While the inquisition of a sense of self is an important developmental milestone, it also adds to the challenge of living with a toddler.

CHALLENGING ROUTINES
Mealtime

Mealtime for many toddlers is an opportunity to assert their will. Some toddlers are insistent about eating the same food as the rest of the family. If dad is drinking coffee, they want coffee. Other toddlers become increasingly selective about what they eat. As their appetite decreases their "don't like" list grows, and parents will describe them as being "finicky" eaters. They are aware of small differences in taste and texture. A lump in the bowl of oatmeal, a new spaghetti sauce, or a piece of meat that has to be chewed can precipitate a hunger strike. For parents who are aware of the importance of nutrition, mealtimes that had been associated earlier with talking and cuddling can become the stage for a power struggle. This is particularly true of special-needs toddlers who are hypersensitive to new sensations, or who have difficulty with chewing. Families that have faced mealtime challenges or tantrums describe techniques that have been successful with their children.

"*When my toddler began throwing food on the floor that he didn't want to eat, we made a special point of giving him meals with the rest of the family. I put a plastic tablecloth under his high chair and gave him a plastic plate with very small portions of a variety of table foods. It didn't do much to increase his appetite, but it did stop him from throwing his food. I guess he understood that throwing food around was not an attention-getter, and he became a much more pleasant dinner companion.*"

"*My daughter is two and a half, and unless I gave her Rice Krispies or mashed potatoes she wouldn't eat anything. I found a solution that worked for us. I give her Rice Krispies and mashed potatoes at every meal for a week. By the end of the week she asked for a banana. She is still not a great eater, but every couple of weeks she will try something new. She seems healthy enough, and I've decided not to drive myself crazy giving her a balanced meal.*"

Weaning

Making a transition from breast or bottle is a particular problem for many special-needs youngsters. The bottle or breast becomes a kind of security blanket, a way of calming a fussy child or of helping a child fall asleep. Weaning is especially difficult when milk is the staple in a child's diet. Choice of a time to begin weaning is influenced both by the parent's and child's readiness. Some parents feel that as

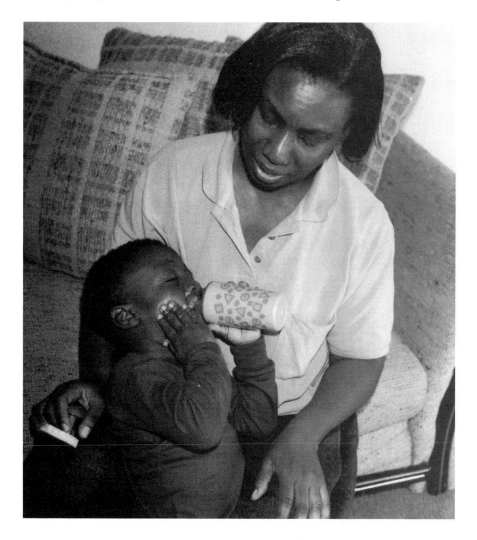

long as their child wants breast or bottle, they are not about to wean them. Other parents associate drinking from a cup or glass as being an important part of growing up. If parents do feel strongly about weaning their special-needs baby, there are ways of making the transition easier.

- Select a time to focus on weaning when there are no other changes taking place in your or your baby's world. It is particularly important not to change sleeping arrangements or introduce toilet learning at the same time you are weaning.
- When it is feasible, establish a schedule for bottle or breast that is consistent with the family's mealtime schedule.
- If your youngster has difficulty drinking from a regular cup, try to find a weaning cup that she is able to manage.
- Invite to lunch or dinner a same-age youngster who is drinking from a cup.
- If your child is drinking from a bottle, gradually water down the milk. Your youngster will recognize that undiluted milk from a cup tastes better.

If weaning has become a hassle between you and your youngster, you may want to postpone it until she is ready.

Sleeptime

"I don't know what's the matter with Genia. I've never had a sleep problem with her. By the time she was three months old she'd fall asleep as soon as I put her in the crib—and sleep through the night. Now she not only puts up a fuss at bedtime, but she wakes up during the night and won't go back to sleep until we let her sleep in our bed."

Genia's mother's complaint has been echoed by many parents of both typically developing toddlers and toddlers with special needs. Unfortunately, there is no magic formula that guarantees success with every toddler. Changes in sleep patterns can be attributed to many causes, including teething, head colds, apnea, night terrors, changes in daily routines, and tensions or disturbances in the family.

Problems going to sleep

Going to sleep at night is a learned behavior. Parents who establish nighttime routines such as a bath followed by a massage, reading or telling a story, singing, kissing each of the stuffed animals, or listening to a tape of lullabies, are less likely to have problems with putting their toddler to sleep. It also helps to give a toddler a transition object such as a blanket or a doll.

One of the issues that parents often face is whether or not to cosleep. In actuality, cosleeping is practiced in many countries and in many families in the United States. Cosleeping has both an upside and a downside. The upside is that toddlers are less likely to resist bedtime if they go to sleep with a parent. From the parent's point of view, if their toddler awakens during the night it will be less of a struggle to put her back to sleep. On the downside, toddlers who cosleep spend less time in quiet sleep and may not be well-rested. At the same time parents, particularly parents with a special-needs child, may need private time together as well as a full night's sleep. A greater concern has been expressed by the Pediatric Society. There have been consistent reports of babies being crushed or suffocated when their parents accidentally turned over in their sleep. Whether or not to cosleep is a decision that parents must make in accordance with their own priorities.

Night waking

Toddlers awaken during the night for many different reasons. Some reasons are associated with physical reasons such as difficulty breathing or gastrointestinal problems. More frequently, night waking is psychological. Some toddlers, like infants, have learned to self-comfort and put themselves back to sleep. Others have become dependent upon an adult.

Napping

In contrast to infant sleep patterns, toddlers are likely to sleep at night and nap for short periods during the day. Young toddlers may require two naps during the day, while older toddlers are more likely to fall into a one-nap routine. Depending on the child, daytime naps last for one to three hours. Toddlers in childcare are likely to become accustomed to an after-lunch nap that extends from an hour and a half to two hours. Even if older toddlers do not fall asleep during naptime, an after-lunch rest time helps the children manage the day without getting cranky, over-tired, or wound up. Children with special needs and/or children whose night sleep is interrupted may maintain the two-nap routine until they are two or three.

Toilet Learning

An advantage of disposable diapers is that parents are likely to feel less pressured to begin toilet teaching before their toddler is ready. The usual rule of thumb is to put off toilet teaching until your toddler remains dry for stretches of at least two hours. There are different schools of thought on the best method of helping children with toilet learning. A popular method is placing the toddler on the toilet or potty at regular intervals and rewarding him for voiding or moving his bowels. A method that seems more natural to many parents is to introduce toilet learning in a gradual and nonpressured way. Several options can be used:

- Invite a sibling or friend who will let your child watch as he or she uses the toilet.
- Let your toddler watch as you put a doll on the toilet and tell the doll what is happening.
- Read a favorite book to your toddler as she sits on a potty chair.
- Show your pleasure when your child "makes" on the potty, but don't be too lavish with your praise.

Remember that toddlers with special needs, particularly when there is a physical problem, may not be ready for toilet learning at two or three years old. Attempting to toilet-teach a child before he is ready inevitably backfires.

Most toddlers take longer to stay dry overnight than they do during the day. They are also likely to establish bladder control before they establish bowel control. Be realistic in your expectations. Don't be concerned if your toddler appears to be perfectly trained and quite suddenly regresses. When a toddler is stressed or ill, accidents are the rule rather than the exception.

Whether you use a "reward" approach, a "modeling" approach, or simply place your toddler on the toilet on an hourly basis, always make sure that toileting is a positive experience.

Bathing

Most toddlers enjoy taking a bath. When toddlers are provided with toys, bathtime is a good opportunity for relaxed conversation. It is also an excellent time to introduce pretend play ideas or practice new skills. Children love to pour water from one container to another or wash a baby doll.

For some toddlers, the part of the bath they don't like at all is having their hair washed. One experience with soap in their eyes can create a long-time fear. "No tears" shampoos alleviate the problem to at least some degree, but it is usually a better idea to find ways of keeping the shampoo away from her eyes. Techniques that are likely to work include washing her hair with a washcloth, holding a toy over the toddler's head to hold her head back, or washing her hair with a watering can. Giving a toddler a chance to wash her doll's hair can work very well with some toddlers.

COPING WITH CHALLENGING BEHAVIORS

Babies who have a tough beginning often exhibit difficult behavior as they make a transition from infancy to toddlerhood. This is not surprising. The baby who had trouble organizing his behavior during infancy is likely to exhibit some disorganization as he faces the new demands of the toddler period. At the same time, as a parent of a special-needs child, you may not be in a hurry to impose limits on your toddler. You recognize that some misbehavior is a sign of developmental progress.

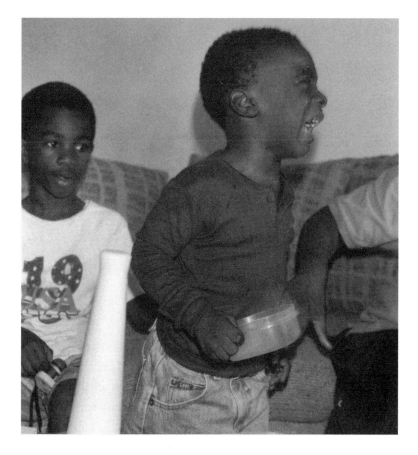

Impulsiveness

All children have problems with impulse control during toddlerhood. They have to accept the fact that their needs will not be met immediately and that they can't always have their way. They also need to develop self-regulating techniques, avoid impulsive reactions, and learn ways of calming themselves when they are upset or overly excited. For toddlers with special needs, these lessons are hard to learn.

Most parents recognize the importance of providing behavioral guidelines and setting consistent limits. They recognize that allowing their child to have and do whatever she wants is irresponsible, and that their child must learn to live in harmony with other people. When we ask parents if the same principles hold for their disabled child, the answer is very often, "Yes, but..."

"...but he really doesn't understand about not breaking his brother's toys."

"...but we can't say 'no' to him. He gets into a terrible tantrum and can't get himself out of them."

"...but right now our concern is to get him healthy."

"...but he has a right to scream and lash out. How would you like to be blind?"

As we listen to parents give reasons for not disciplining their handicapped children, we recognize their dilemma. Saying "no" and imposing limits are much more difficult with a handicapped child. Parents who continue to blame themselves for their child's problem feel guilty when they discipline. Parents with children who are physically fragile are fearful of endangering their child's health. Parents who have mixed feelings toward their handicapped child may feel paralyzed when it comes to discipline.

Despite the difficulties associated with discipline, a lack of behavioral limits can be devastating to a child. When parents give up the responsibility of helping their child develop socially appropriate behavior, they are imposing an extra handicap that their child may never outgrow.

The following guidelines and techniques may be helpful in teaching your toddler to develop impulse control.

- If your child continues a prohibited behavior, it is time to distract him. Learning "no" takes time.
- When children have learned to attend to differences in their parents' tone and expression, they are ready to learn the meaning of "no."

- In the beginning reserve the word "no" for situations with a clear-cut danger. Say "No, hot!" as you pull your child away from the stove. Whenever possible, get your child to look at you when you are saying "no."
- Always keep your voice calm and firm when you say "no," and simultaneously remove the child from danger or danger from the child.
- Always provide your child with an alternative. He may not dig up the houseplants, but he may dig in the sand.
- Remember that special-needs children may take longer than other children to understand the meaning of "no." If your child stops for a minute, looks at you, and then continues with the prohibited behavior, it is a good sign. He is beginning to make the connection. Be persistent. After a while he will understand that "no" means "stop."
- If your child continues the prohibited behavior, after three or four tries it is time to distract him. Learning "no" takes time.
- Children who are ready to learn the meaning of "no" are also ready to learn the meaning of "yes." As you teach your child to

hand you the napkin, throw away the banana peel, or pick up a toy, you are giving your child a first lesson in taking responsibility. At the same time you are helping her engage in behaviors that gain your approval and applause.

- When your child has the ability to do a simple chore, seek out every opportunity to let her practice, and give her praise and encouragement. For example, if your child is ready to throw, give her a chance to throw a piece of paper in the wastebasket and thank her for being a big girl.

- If your child half-completes a chore, praise her for what she has done rather than criticize her for what she has not done. For example, if your child gets distracted in the middle of picking up her toys, you might say, "I like the way you picked up all your blocks. Do you suppose you could pick up your stuffed animals? They don't like it on the floor."

- Sing simple songs with her that go along with her chores. "It's clean-up time, it's clean-up time. Everybody helps with clean-up time." Or, "This is the way we pick up the blocks, pick up the blocks, pick up the blocks. This is the way we pick up the blocks, so early in the morning."

Temper Tantrums

"I am the first to admit it, looking after Denny is a full-time job. But despite the challenges, I wake up every morning looking forward to the day. My boy is fun to be with."

Unquestionably, parents of toddlers, whether or not their toddlers have special needs, are faced with challenging behaviors that tax their patience and keep them on their toes. But despite the challenges, parents describe their toddlers as charming, delightful, and full of happy surprises. At one moment their toddler may be shy and fearful, clinging to their pant leg or hiding behind their back. At the very next moment he insists on being the center of attention,

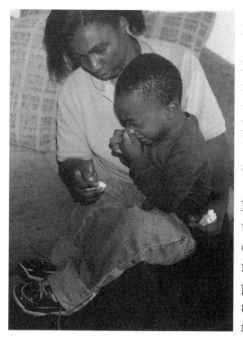

proudly showing off a new skill or feat to an admiring audience. At one moment he seems helpless and naïve. At the next moment he lets you know that he understands more than you realize. You pour his milk in a cup and tell him it's coffee. "Want coffee," he tells you emphatically as he pushes the cup away.

Temper tantrums are a part of the behavioral repertoire of practically every toddler. Unfortunately, with special-needs children, temper tantrums may be more frequent, longer-lasting, and harder to prevent or control. If your child throws a temper tantrum, observe the following rules:

- Do not shout or try to impose discipline while the tantrum is going on.
- Never hit, spank, or shake your baby. Shaking is particularly dangerous for infants because it can cause brain damage.
- Put your child in a safe place and remain aloof and nonjudgmental until the tantrum is over.
- If your child's behavior is out of control, so that she doesn't know what she is upset about, you may have to help her calm down. Pat her gently. Hold and rock her, but don't take back the "no" that got the tantrum started.

Aggressive Behaviors

Never let your child physically hurt you or another person. Although you may think it's cute when an eighteen-month-old baby gets cross and gives you a slap, if hitting gets to be a habit, it isn't cute anymore. Furthermore, it is very difficult for a child to learn that it is okay to hit Mommy or Daddy, but it is not okay to hit a baby or a dog. *The "no hitting, no biting, no hurting" rule must not have exceptions.* Here are some ways you can help your child learn this rule:

- If your child hits you or anyone else, your immediate response should be, "No hitting."
- Help your child learn the difference between hitting and stroking. If she hits the dog, say "No hitting, make nice." Be sure to praise her when she strokes the dog.
- If your child hits another child, take her away from the child immediately and repeat the admonition, "No hitting."
- If your child persists in hitting, begin a time-out procedure. Tell the child what she did wrong and what is going to happen. "No hitting. You have to sit in the time-out chair." Sit your child in a chair away from the play for a brief period. (It sometimes helps to use an egg timer.) Until your child understands the time-out procedure, you may have to hold her in the chair. Face your child in the chair away from you and hold her gently but firmly. If your child plays nicely after a time-out period, be quick to praise her: "I like the way you're playing."

Atypical Behaviors

Parents of special-needs children are disturbed when their toddlers engage in atypical behavior. With some behavior, such as head-banging, the concern is that the child is going to hurt himself. With other behaviors, such as spinning or hand-waving, they are concerned about the baby's appearance. Parents are right to pay attention to "self-stimulating" behaviors. Once the behaviors begin they can easily become a habit.

Some babies bang their heads when they are having a temper tantrum. Other babies do it because they find it pleasurable. Depending on where he is banging his head, pad the back and the side of the crib, or put a cushioned helmet on your baby's head. Without the bang, the head-banging loses its appeal.

If your baby is in the habit of spinning or hand-waving, keep him busy and interested in toys and games.

If your toddler has lost interest in playing with his toys, place him in a swing or hammock or on a rocking horse. This will provide the motion he is looking for without becoming habit-forming.

Biting

"My toddler is going through a biting phase. The caregiver at the child-care center keeps telling me about how often he bites other children. I don't know what to do about it."

Biting is a common problem with older toddlers. The question of why some toddlers bite does not have a single answer. Toddlers biting can be a way of getting attention or producing a reaction, a way of satisfying an oral need, or an instinctive reaction to frustration. The most effective way of dealing with biting is to prevent it from happening. Caregivers need to be aware of the precursors of biting or the situations that prompt biting and intercede before the biting takes place. Scolding a toddler or placing a toddler in time-out is not likely to be effective.

Pay attention to what was happening before your child bit. When you know the kind of stimuli that precipitates biting you can restructure his environment or his schedule so that biting is less likely to occur. At the same time, if you can figure out what he was trying to achieve by biting, you may be able to find other ways to help him achieve his goal. For instance, if he wants another child to play with him, teach him more effective techniques like saying, "Play with me" or handing the other child a toy.

No matter how vigilant we are, toddlers who have a tendency to bite will find a victim to bite before we can stop them. Here are some "after-bite" suggestions:

- Comfort the child who has been bitten before you turn your attention to the biter.

- Give your child a clear message. "No biting. Biting hurts."
- Give your child something to bite on like a teething ring or hard apple.
- Avoid using old-fashioned methods like biting back, slapping, or putting her in time-out.
- Give him chewy foods at mealtime that satisfy his urge to bite.

Getting Into Everything

"Now that my toddler has learned to walk I don't have a minute's peace. She is into everything. She pulls at electric wires, pulls leaves off plants, splashes in the toilet, and pulls down any bric-a-brac she can reach. I have toddler-proofed my house until it's barren, but I can't expect my friends to do the same."

When babies take their first steps, whether they are early or late walkers, it is a joyous and exciting day for parents as well as for their babies. But as thrilling as it is to watch a baby master the two-legged stance, parents learn soon enough that there is a downside. Toddlers are curious. Once they are able to walk, they have all kinds of new opportunities to explore and experiment. What will happen if I pull on the end of the tablecloth or the cord that is attached to the lamp? Will the vase break into pieces and make a nice noise if I drop it on the floor?

While parents are quite adept at toddler-proofing their house, it becomes increasingly more difficult to take their toddler for a visit. Saying to a toddler "do not touch" is paramount to saying "do not learn." Unwilling to accept this alternative, parents either keep their toddler at home or resign themselves to turning a supposedly casual visit to a friend's house into a game of "chase and catch." Another alternative that parents may want to try is teaching their toddler to "touch gently." Parents practice the "touch gently" game by showing their youngster how to touch the leaves of a plant without pulling them off or how to use their fingers to stroke a figurine.

Fortunately, even if the only technique that works is "chase and catch," toddlers eventually become more focused in their interests and household ornaments lose their appeal.

Resisting Transitions

"My toddler is easy to get along with until I try to change activities. For instance, she loves to ride in the car, but if I suggest a car ride when she's busy playing with her blocks she is sure to protest."

Most toddlers have difficulty with transitions. They do not want to stop what they are doing just because an adult says it is time to do something else. They are especially likely to resist when doing something else involves going to another place, like home from a visit, to an appointment, or to bed.

Make transitions easier for your child by:

- Talking about where you are going in an upbeat tone. Even if he doesn't understand language, he will recognize by your tone that something new is about to happen.
- Prepare your child for a transition several minutes ahead. You might say to him, "I'm going to help you put your toys away so we can go outside."

Poor Social Skills

Although we may not consider the lack of social skills a challenging behavior, parents are quite rightly concerned when their child is reluctant to play with other children. Special-needs children are likely to spend a great deal of time around adults where they don't have to share toys, take turns, or even make social overtures. Parents of special-needs children need to work hard at finding peers for their children to play with.

Many special-needs children shy away from other children. A child who is temperamentally shy, slow to warm up, or easily over-stimulated may not be comfortable around other children. If your child withdraws or becomes irritable when he is with other children, introduce him to one child at a time. Select a child who is either much older or much younger, so that your child will not feel threatened by a peer.

Praise your child for all friendly overtures even if your child does no more than watch other children who are playing.

Do not expect your child to share toys spontaneously. Your child has just learned the meaning of "mine," and it is difficult to make the distinction between sharing a toy and giving a toy away. It is easier to teach children to "take turns" with toys than to "share" them. "Let Katie have a turn for a minute, and then it will be your turn again." Keep the "turns" very short until both children get the idea.

When children with special needs are ready to begin a school situation, the most important challenges they will face are controlling impulsive behavior and getting along with other children. If you begin as early as possible to help your child accept limits, take responsibility, control aggressive behavior, and play with other children, he will have a much better chance of doing well in school. With many children, the problem in school is not that they cannot learn but that they have learned maladaptive behaviors that interfere with learning.

GROWING AND LEARNING

"My baby has always been small for her age. You know, in some ways it's an advantage because people who don't know about her just assume that she's much younger than she is. As a matter of fact, I brought her to a parent-child class with my cousin's baby who is six months younger. It was great—she was doing the very same things her cousin was doing. When I stop comparing her with her same-age peers, I can just focus on the new things she is doing and learning. The other day my husband and I went into the pediatrician's office, and they had this chart on the wall telling about the milestones babies achieve at different ages. I refused to look at it. My husband says I am in denial, but that's not true. I am interested in what my baby is doing, and I am not going to be bothered if she's a little behind other children her age."

CHAPTER 9

Promoting Self-Awareness

～～～～～～～～～～～～～～～

"When the doctor told me my baby had spina bifida, I didn't want to see her. I wanted them to take her away and put her in an institution. I knew that if they ever put her in my arms she would be mine and I would love her."

Babies come into the world uniquely programmed to win their parents' love. With few exceptions, a newborn baby has the built-in capacity to focus on his mother's face and to tune in to his mother's voice. The mother, too, is programmed to respond. The softness of the baby's skin invites the mother's stroke, and milk flows in the nursing mother in response to the baby's cry.

In this chapter and subsequent chapters in this section, we trace infant development through three qualitatively different stages. In the first stage, Tuning In, babies are adjusting to life outside the uterus. Equipped with a built-in capacity to recognize likes and differences, babies listen to voices, make eye contact, and experience the comfort of touch. In the second stage, Reaching Out, babies actively initiate contact with the world of objects and people and anticipate a response. In the third stage, Making Discoveries, babies explore objects and social relationships and are actively involved in goal-oriented behaviors. Babies enter these stages at different chronological ages and are likely to be at different stages in different domains of development.

～～～～

TUNING IN

In the first stage, parent and infant develop a special kind of closeness that is rooted in biology. Psychologists call this close relationship bonding, and describe it as a love affair between parent and child. The baby, who has lost the safety and predictability of life inside the uterus, is protected outside the uterus by the strength of parental love.

When babies are born full-term with a well-organized nervous system, a mutually supportive relationship between baby and mother begins at birth. Nursing releases a hormone into the mother's system that gives her a feeling of well-being as she nourishes her baby. The baby responds to the gentle stroking, rocking, and soothing of his mother by becoming quiet, alert, and organized. Preterm or "at-risk" babies are not as well organized as healthy full-term babies. They may be easily overwhelmed by new sensations

and may have difficulty regaining their composure. With babies who are disorganized and difficult to soothe, a mutually supportive relationship between parent and infant may take longer to achieve.

As parents and infants play out their love affair during the Tuning In stage, several important developments take place simultaneously. Babies spend a greater amount of time in the quiet alert state, which allows them to focus on their environment. They become increasingly aware of the potential of their own bodies. They learn ways to comfort themselves when the stress in their environment is more than they can handle, and they learn the joy of social interactions.

Suggested Activities

- Remember that your baby has different ways of being awake or asleep, and different states of awareness, deep sleep, wakeful sleep, drowsiness, quiet alertness, activity, and crying. Babies are most aware of their surroundings and most ready to learn when they are in a state of quiet alertness. Calming your baby if he is active or crying, or stimulating your baby if he is drowsy helps him reach a state of quiet alertness. Help him maintain this state by capturing his interest. Talk, change your tone of voice, smile, play with his fingers and toes, or show him an object that interests him.

- Help your baby learn about his body. As your baby kicks his feet, gazes at his hands, or strokes your face with his fingers, he is making important discoveries about his own body and its many capabilities.

- Give your baby the opportunity to watch the movement of his own hands. Babies get very excited when they first discover what fun it is to wave their fingers in front of their eyes. When your baby lets his fingers fall out of sight, he may appear upset. It takes a baby a while to coordinate his hands and eyes and to realize that he has the power to put his hand back into his visual field.

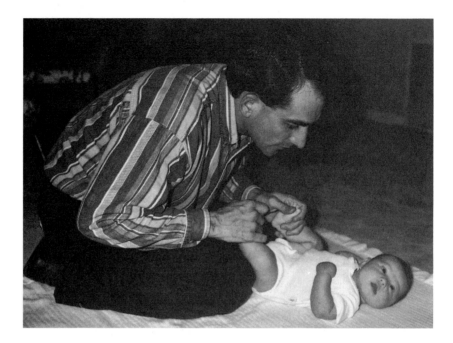

- Place a colorful sock on one of your baby's hands. It will increase the fun of hand-watching and help your baby with the ongoing task of learning about himself.
- Bathtime provides an excellent opportunity to increase body awareness. Massage your baby's arms and fingers, then legs and toes, as you dry him after his bath.
- When the temperature of the room is appropriate, give your baby an opportunity to kick his legs without wearing a diaper. This self-generated activity helps him learn how his body is organized.
- Babies differ from each other in the kinds of stimulation they find stressful, in the amount of stress they can tolerate without becoming disrupted, and in the strategies they develop to cope with stress. While you should be concerned with protecting your baby from overly stressful situations, you also ought to give your baby opportunities to develop coping strategies. By watching your baby closely and experimenting with different

techniques, you will find ways to help your child experience and deal with moderate stress.

- Lie flat on your back and hold your baby in the air. He will be interested in seeing your face from a different perspective.
- When you are holding your baby, let him touch your face and feel your skin. Your baby is coming to know you as mother or father by the sound of your voice, they way you hold him, the way you look, and the way you feel.

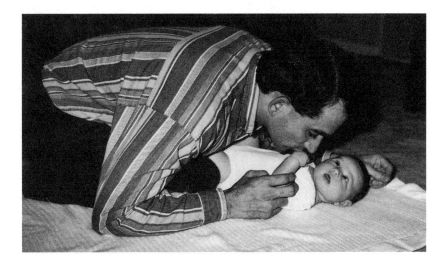

- Provide opportunities for the baby's father to carry on his own conversations. Fathers and mothers have different ways of playing, different voice qualities, and different skin textures, and it is important for your baby to have this double experience.
- Be sensitive to your baby's cues. An animated conversation can be tiring. When your baby stops trying to coo or talk, he is saying "I've had enough for now." Babies who are small and not very strong may signal "I've had enough" in very subtle ways. They may grimace or yawn or shut their eyes. They may turn pale or red, start to shake, extend their arms, or perhaps turn limp. Be sensitive to your baby's way of telling you when he needs time out from stimulation.

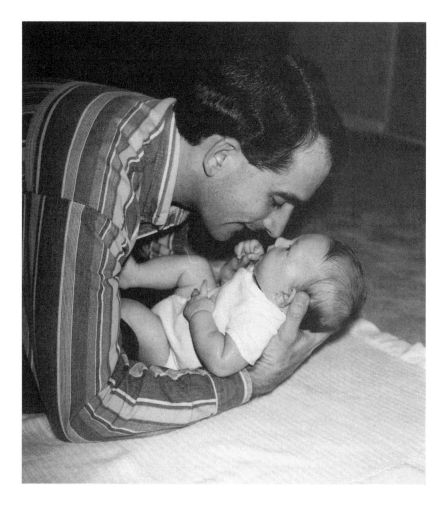

Modifications

For babies who are visually limited

- Hang wind chimes in one or two rooms of the house in front of a window. When your baby is crying, lift him to your shoulder and let him hear the tinkling of the chimes.
- Help your baby discover his own hands by placing bands with bells on your baby's wrists. As he moves his hands in front of him he will hear the ringing of the bells. (You can make a wrist-

band by cutting off the cuff of an infant sock, sewing the bell securely on the inside, folding the cuff over the bell, and sewing the seam shut.)
- Wear a special cologne to help your baby recognize you as you approach the crib.

For babies who are hearing-impaired
- When your baby is in a state of quiet alertness, place your lips close to her ear and talk softly. Give each ear a turn. Speaking directly into your baby's ear is like fitting her with a hearing aid.
- Wear special cologne that your baby will recognize. This will help her know you are coming when she cannot hear your voice.

For babies who are physically impaired
- If your baby has difficulty with arm control, position him in your lap with his arms in front of him. Place his hands together so that he has the sensation of feeling his own hands.
- Hold your baby's hand and help him stroke your face and feel your nose and mouth. Blow gently when his fingers are over your mouth.

For babies who are hypersensitive or tactile-defensive
- Talk to your baby in a gentle voice as you stroke her hands with a firm touch.
- Avoid taking her to places that are noisy, busy, or overstimulating.
- If your baby is hypersensitive to touch (tactile-defensive) and gets upset or withdrawn when you hold or stroke her, you will have to help her adapt to new sensations.
- If she is tactile-defensive and flaccid or floppy, stroke her arms and legs with a firm and steady stroke. If she tends to be rigid and jittery, use a more gentle touch and avoid sudden movements.

- Some tactile-defensive babies will tolerate and even enjoy gentle stroking with a feather or a paintbrush.
- Tactile-defensive babies are likely to reject a pacifier. Try different kinds of pacifiers until you find one your baby will accept. A Sassy pacifier is especially good for small babies with a weak sucking reflex.

For babies with Down's syndrome

- Babies with Down's syndrome may take longer to respond to stimulation and may be more muted in their responses than other babies.
- Be patient with your baby. It may take him a month or more before he can sustain a state of quiet alertness.
- When your baby establishes eye contact with you, do not expect an immediate smile or cooing. Your baby will learn to smile and coo, but it may take longer than you expect.
- Continue to talk to your baby even when you do not get a distinct response. Your baby is aware of your overtures and will learn to respond in time.

REACHING OUT

The second stage of development, Reaching Out, is characterized by your baby's growing ability to initiate social interactions. Your baby is becoming more and more social, reaching out with her arms to an approaching parent, actively seeking out people to engage in vocal play. In the early phase of Reaching Out your baby smiles happily at anyone who smiles back. After a while she becomes more discriminatory, reserving her biggest greetings for the people who are most familiar.

Suggested Activities

In the first developmental stage, self-awareness was characterized by your baby's ability to recognize and coordinate different parts of her body. Now your baby is exploring the relationship between her own body and the outside world. She is reaching out for the mobile over her crib, smiling at herself in the mirror, picking up a cracker and putting it in her mouth. At the same time she is making new discoveries about her own body, discovering a set of toes, passing toys from hand to hand, and pulling at one ear and then the other.

A few props can help increase your baby's self-awareness:

- Put up a safety mirror over the changing table or inside the crib. Your baby will enjoy getting acquainted with her own image.
- Put colorful socks on your baby's feet, Now that she has discovered where to find her toes, you can add an element of surprise.
- Give your baby some special practice bringing her hand to her mouth. Let her dip her finger in her cereal or fruit, even if she gets a bit messy.
- Increase opportunities for social interaction. Your baby's social world is expanding. She not only makes distinctions between mother and father, she is making distinctions between children and adults and between old friends and strangers. She is fascinated with other children and delighted by a playful sibling.
- As your baby develops an increased capacity to remember past experiences, you will see a change in reactions to new people. She will become wary when a stranger gets too close. You will also notice a difference in the way your baby relates to you. Your baby will become watchful when you start to leave the room and give you a special greeting when you return. This special love for special people is called attachment behavior. It begins in the second developmental stage and continues through the third stage.

Just as special-needs babies may differ in their development timetable from other babies, they may differ in their attachment behavior. Some special-needs babies take longer to develop attachment and continue to interact with anyone who is willing to play. Other special-needs babies appear to get overattached and have difficulty with any kind of separation.

- Playing games with your baby that involve separating and coming back together helps to strengthen attachment behavior and give your baby the assurance that you will always reappear.
- Play different versions of the peek-a-boo game. Peek-a-boo allows your baby to know that you can be out of sight for a second without disappearing. Put your hands over your face, and take them away quickly, saying, "Peek-a-boo!" Put a scarf over your baby's head and pull it off quickly, saying, "Peek-a-boo!"
- Making a parachute using a sheet or towel is a more elaborate game that is fun when there are several adults to make the parachute go up and down.
- Interactive pull-push games, like peek-a-boo, help your baby understand that mother or father can go away and come back.
- When your baby is strong enough to sit with support, sit face-to-face with your baby and hold her hands. As you recite "Seesaw, Margery Daw," lean backwards and come forwards. Then help your baby take a turn leaning backwards and forwards.
- Play catch with your baby. Sit her in a corner. Push a beach ball toward her and let her push it back. During this game as with any game, talk about what you are doing. When you push the brightly colored beach ball to your baby, say, "Here comes the ball! Whee, you caught it! Good, now push it to Daddy."
- Hold one end of a scarf and let your baby hold onto the other end. Pull tight and then let loose. See if your baby will join the game.
- With an increased capacity to hold an image in memory, your baby is ready for interactive games involving imitation and anticipation.

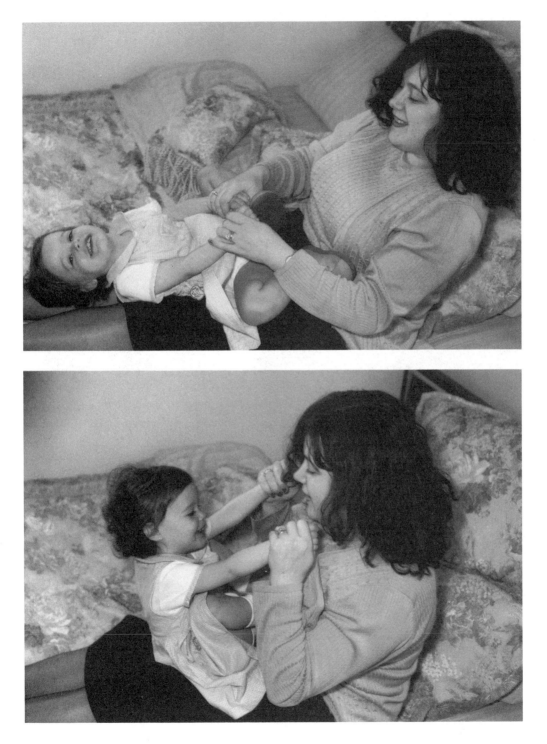

- Show your baby a Jack-in-the-box. Does she laugh out loud when Jack pops out of the box?
- Turn a cake pan over and bang it. See if your baby will imitate the banging.
- Blow bubbles for your baby. She will enjoy watching them float away. She might even imitate your blowing.
- Sing the song "Trot, Trot to Boston" or "Pop Goes the Weasel." See if your baby laughs as you come to the last stanza. In "Trot, Trot to Boston" let your baby drop halfway through your knees at the end. In "Pop Goes the Weasel," turn in a circle and lift her in the air when you come to "Pop."

Modifications

For babies who are visually limited

- Guide your baby through a tasting experience. Place her hand in the cereal and then in her mouth. After a while she will finger-feed herself.
- Place socks with bells on your baby's feet. Make sure that the bells are very securely sewn on.
- Use very bright multicolored beach balls for your rolling back-and-forth games.

For babies who are hearing-impaired

- Before you initiate a back-and-forth game with your baby, be sure to establish eye contact. Let your baby feel your lips as you begin to talk.
- When you sing a song to your baby, bounce your baby on your knee in rhythm with the song. Your baby will feel the rhythm of your song.
- Continue to talk to your baby even though she may not babble back.
- Hold your baby's hand in front of your mouth as you chant these rhymes:

Ba, Ba, Ba, Bumblebee
Ba, Ba, Ba, Bumblebee
I will say Ba to you
You will say Ba to me.

Pop, pop, pop, POP
My popcorn pops
Pop, pop, POP, POP
And now it stops.

For babies who are physically challenged

- Play a special version of the pull-push game. Place your baby on a mat between you and your spouse. Take turns pulling baby and mat toward you. Greet the baby with a special "Hi" as you pull her to your side.
- Invent your own modification of "Trot, Trot to Boston" and "Pop Goes the Weasel." If your baby cannot sit up, you can move her legs up and down as you recite "Pop Goes the Weasel." When you reach the "Pop," release your baby's legs for a second and then catch them again.
- Avoid quick movements in all the games you play so that your baby will not be startled.

For babies who are hypersensitive or tactile-defensive

- Play a special version of seesaw. Thread a long silk scarf through a paper towel spindle and tie the ends together. Place the scarf around your baby's back when she is in a half-sitting position. Put your baby's hands and yours on the spindle. see-saw gently up and down.
- Use a crib sheet as a hammock. Let your partner hold one end while you hold the other. Gently swing your baby in the hammock as you sing "Rock-a-Bye-Baby." When you come to "the cradle will fall," drop the hammock gently and give your baby a kiss.
- Your baby may not like sticky fingers. Do not expect her to enjoy a fingerpaint-with-food activity.

For babies with Down's syndrome

- Select games and activities that you and your baby enjoy. If your baby does not show a visible reaction to a game such as bubble blowing or banging on a cake pan, continue your efforts but do not play more vigorously. Remember that your baby may need some time to take in new information and express her delight. If you are playing the cake-pan-banging game, for instance, don't bang harder because she seems to ignore the first few bangs. A loud bang could turn off an emerging smile.

- With all the games, keep in mind that you are not looking for perfect performance, but rather the fun of participation. Make sure you praise your baby for every nascent attempt.

MAKING DISCOVERIES

In the third stage, Making Discoveries, your baby is interested not only in reaching out and exploring the world outside himself, but also in making discoveries about how things outside him are connected. He is exploring objects to see if they come apart or fit inside each other. He is exploring spaces and places: Can he fit himself in-

side a box or under the sofa? He is exploring relationships with other people: Can he make his mother laugh at his newest stunt?

As your baby practices his motor skills and plays rough-and-tumble games, he increases his knowledge of his own body and the ways the parts of his body are connected with each other. You can spot signs of developing self-awareness. When you play "This Little Piggy Went to Market," your baby will look down at his toes as soon as the game begins. If he gets a mosquito bite on his arm he will find the spot and scratch it.

Another indicator of increased self-awareness is a new level of mirror play. At some time during this stage your baby will make the connection between the baby in the mirror and himself. If you put a hat on his head and show him his image in the mirror, he will learn to reach for the hat. If you place a toy beside him while he is looking in the mirror, he will reach down and pick up the toy.

Perhaps the most exciting indicator of this new level of self-awareness is your baby's readiness to repeat a stunt that draws laughs. If he puts the salad bowl on his head and the family bursts out laughing, he will try it again. Your baby is telling you without words that he knows that he is a person and can make other people react to the things he does.

Suggested Activities

To help your baby make discoveries, try these games:

- While your baby is standing in front of the mirror, put a toy beside him. Does he reach for the toy in the mirror, or does he look down at the floor?
- Put a piece of Scotch tape on your baby's toe and let him pull it off.
- Put a sticker in the middle of your baby's forehead and let him look at himself in a mirror. Does he watch his image in the mirror as he pulls the sticker off his forehead?

During stage three, your baby will demonstrate an increased awareness of others. He has become a people-watcher, interested and alert each time a new person comes into the house. He listens to adult conversations, watches facial expressions, and gives his own reactions in easy-to-read ways. If a new person approaches too quickly, he may bury his head in Daddy's shirt. If his sister or brother comes into the room, he can express his delight with happy squeals.

Help your baby explore his newfound awareness to others:

- Invite other children over to play. Remember that even when your child is ready to play around other children, you will need to be on hand. Babies don't understand sharing and can get into a struggle over toys. Take on the task of passing toys to your child and his friend—to keep the time a happy one.
- When a new person approaches your baby, discourage him or her from immediately lifting up the baby. Babies make friends more easily if the visitor gives them warming-up time and offers them a toy.
- Make separation easier for your child. Play a leave-taking game with your baby. Wave "Good-bye," leave the room for a second, and come back saying, "Hello."

As your baby becomes physically more adept, you will increasingly notice signs of psychological attachment. Your baby will keep a close watch on your whereabouts when a stranger is around or when you take him on a visit. He may be happy to explore new areas, but only if he can maintain eye contact with you and check back from time to time. When he comes on something new, he will look at you to make sure it is safe before he continues exploring. If you look approvingly he will continue to play.

- Help your baby explore the relationship between together and apart with a few simple games like tag and "I'm going to get you."

• When your baby is good at crawling or creeping, play a simplified version of hide-and-seek.

One problem such young explorers face is distinguishing between rules of play and rules of day-to-day living. When parents say "no" in a firm voice, the baby will often stop what he is doing, look up for a second, and then proceed with the mischief. The baby is not making a distinction between a "no" that is for real and a "no" that is a back-and-forth game. It's hard for a baby to understand why splashing in the bathtub is encouraged and splashing in the toilet is forbidden, or why it's good to dig in the sandbox and bad to dig in the plant box.

• Help your child explore with ease by making the distinction clear. Use a word like "dirty" or "yucky," when he gets into something you don't want him to touch. This changes the message from "I don't want you to explore" to "I don't want you touching that yucky thing."

In the Reaching Out stage your baby was able to imitate the actions that were in his repertoire. In the Making Discoveries stage your baby's imitative skills are more advanced. With a better under-

standing of his body parts and how they work together, he is able to imitate actions that he hasn't tried before. If you pat your head or pull your ear, your baby may follow suit.

A second kind of imitation that is beginning to emerge is called "deferred imitation." Your baby will imitate an action several hours after he has seen it performed. If your baby has seen you talk on the telephone, he will pick up the receiver and hold it to his ear. If your baby has seen you pat the dog, he will try out his own version of patting when the dog ventures into his territory.

Encourage your child to develop his imitating skills:

- Play body-part games with your baby—"Touch your nose," "Touch your eyes," "Touch your mouth." After a while your baby will enjoy a more complicated version: He touches your nose and you touch his. When he can play touching games with some degree of success, you can create your own little songs to accompany the command.

Touch my eye
Touch yours too.
First touch me
And then touch you.

- Play a copycat game like "So Big" or "Patty-Cake."
- Sing action songs with your baby, changing the words to match your baby's skills. "The Wheels on the Bus Go Round and Round" could become "The Wheels on the Bus Go Clang, Clang, Clang" as you and your baby clap knees.

Pretending is a sophisticated skill that is just beginning to emerge in the Discovery stage. Early pretending is an outgrowth of imitation. As with deferred imitation, your baby has to remember an action and replay his version of it later. When your child first starts to pretend, you will have difficulty making a distinction between pretend play and imitation. He picks up an empty cup and holds it to his mouth. Is he imitating you drinking coffee, or is he pretending to drink some milk? The distinction will become clearer as your baby continues to play. Perhaps he will offer his teddy bear a drink from the cup, or perhaps he will pick up an alphabet block and use it as a cup.

Make pretending fun and easy by providing the right props:

- Place old hats, shoes, and scarves in front of a mirror and watch what your baby does. Dress-up is a wonderful game to feed your baby's growing imagination.

- Give your baby some nonbreakable dishes and bring in stuffed animal "guests" to a tea party.
- Bring your baby a teddy bear and a blanket. Perhaps he'll put teddy to sleep.
- Give your baby a purse to play with. He may decide to go shopping.

Modifications

For babies who are visually limited

- Place a band with a bell around his ankle. (Remember to sew the bell securely onto the band.) See if your baby reaches for his ankle and starts to finger the bell.
- Talk to your baby from the minute you enter the room. Do not stop talking until you have left the room.
- Hide-and-seek is a good game once your baby is mobile. First, make sure that there is nothing in the room that could hurt your baby, such as a table with sharp corners or a lamp cord. Move across the room and challenge your baby until he discovers where you are.
- If your baby is walking, play follow-the-leader by each holding on to a hula hoop. Talk to your baby about where you are walking. "We are walking on the sidewalk." "We are walking through the grass."

For babies who are hearing-impaired

- Always begin a game by calling his name and getting his attention. You may want to say, "Thomas, it's playtime." If your child does not respond to your voice alone, hold his hand as you call his name.
- Use words when you play imitation games even if you think your child does not hear the words. Your child may have more residual hearing than you realize.
- Make sure that you play your games in a quiet room. Your baby will have trouble tuning in if there are competing sounds.

For babies who are physically challenged

- Provide "self-awareness" challenges that he can be successful with. For example, instead of putting Scotch tape on her toe, put a cotton pad between her toes.
- When you choose imitation games, make sure that your baby is able to perform the actions he is expected to copy. If your baby has difficulty with hand clapping, clap your hand on your knee and let your baby follow suit.

For babies who are hypersensitive or tactile-defensive

- Your baby may not enjoy playing imitation games that include touching his face. Play the same game with a doll or large stuffed animal.
- Avoid playing imitation or pretend games that involve wearing a hat. Your baby may get so upset by the feel of a hat on his head that he won't want to play at all.

For babies with Down's syndrome

Some babies with Down's syndrome seem to have more fun playing with toys than with people. It may be that adults are not always as patient as toys and do not let the baby set the pace. When you play with your baby, don't be in a hurry. It takes time for your baby to join in the fun.

As you select activities from this chapter, don't be surprised if you find yourself choosing some games suggested for one stage and some games suggested for another. When we talk about activities that babies enjoy at a particular stage, we are making generalizations. But your baby has distinct needs and tastes. Select the games that you and your baby enjoy wherever you happen to find them. When you are both relaxed and having fun, you know that you have made good choices.

CHAPTER 10

Developing Motor Skills

"As far as John and I are concerned, it was the best day in our lives. Andrew had been a real pain all day—constantly whining, and fussing, and refusing to take a nap. By the time we got him settled for the night we were both worn out. He hadn't been quiet for more than five minutes when he started calling again. I went into his room really mad. I couldn't believe my eyes. He had pulled himself up and he was standing in his crib. I shouted for John, and the two of us just stood there and cried."

The development of gross motor skills and the achievement of motor milestones have a profound effect on all areas of a baby's development. The baby with poor head control may be slow to locate sounds or objects even if she has no visual or auditory problems. The baby who has difficulty with sitting may be slower than others in exploring the properties of objects because he has had less opportunity for two-handed manipulation.

This chapter describes motor development throughout the three developmental stages: Tuning In, Reaching Out, and Making Discoveries. Within each development stage we detail the motor skills the baby is working on and suggest ways parents can arrange the environment to enhance their development; we do not describe therapeutic intervention. If your baby has a motor problem and is being followed by a physical therapist, you may want to skip this chapter, or discuss the ideas with your therapist.

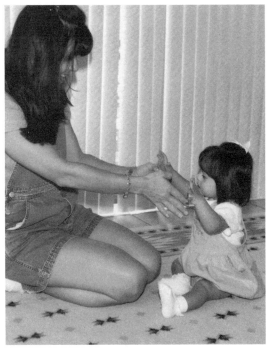

When discussing the development of motor skills in babies, many parents focus their attention on specific milestones such as sitting up, standing, or taking a first step. These events are genuine cause for celebration. While the importance of such milestones should not be minimized, we also need to recognize that the quality of the performance is just as important as the timing. Flipping accidentally from back to stomach is very different from a purposeful roll.

Whatever motor skills your baby is working on, you need to be aware of the subtle changes that are taking place in the quality of the movement. Is your baby pulling up with less effort? Does it take her less time to stand up? Does she pull up over and over again for the sheer joy of practicing? You also need to realize that the sequence as well as the rate of motor skill achievement differs for each baby. Some babies, even if they do not have disabilities, will skip one or more of the typical milestones. It is not true that all babies must crawl before creeping and creep before walking.

TUNING IN

In the Tuning In stage of development, your baby is working on primary coordinations. She is learning to raise and turn her head as she watches a mobile, kick her legs rhythmically, and wiggle her fingers in front of her eyes. Each new skill she achieves gives her access to information that helps her understand her world.

Suggested Activities

Head control

Head control is the first and certainly the most important motor skill your baby will develop. Head control is a component of all the motor milestones. Also, when your baby has good head control, it will be easier for her to track objects and identify the source of sounds. You can encourage the development of head control in a variety of ways:

- Place your baby facedown on the floor. Sit a doll or a teddy bear in front of her. See if she will lift her head to look at the doll's face.
- Lie flat on the floor. Place the baby facedown on your stomach. This position will encourage your baby to lift her head in order to watch your face.
- Hold your baby on your shoulder. Encourage her to look at a toy or out the window.
- Place your baby on a blanket on her stomach and pull the blanket slowly across the floor. She will improve both head control and balance as she enjoys this magic carpet ride.
- When your baby has gained enough head control to hold up her head easily, you may want to hold her on a large beach ball. As you rock baby and ball back and forth very gently, your baby will hold up her head, strengthening the muscles in her neck.
- When head control is established, play seesaw with your baby, pulling her up to a sitting position. She will have the fun of seeing you from different positions while she is practicing head control.

Kicking

Babies have a natural inclination to kick when placed on their backs. At first they kick in an uneven and spasmodic way, but after a while their kicking becomes more rhythmic, and they appear to be peddling an invisible bicycle.

Kicking does more than give babies an opportunity to exercise. It is an important way for the baby to learn about her own body and how it is located in space. You can encourage your baby to try kicking by providing stimulating environments:

- When the room is warm, place your baby on the floor on her back with just a diaper on. When she begins to kick, turn on some music. Does the tempo of the music affect the rate of her kicking?

- Play bicycle with your baby by moving her legs in a bicycle motion while she is on her back. Make sure to bicycle in a forward direction as an early preparation for walking.
- Place a large beach towel in the bottom of the bathtub and fill the tub with about two inches of water. While you are watching, let your baby lie on her back in the water and practice her kicking. She will enjoy the sound and feel of the splashing.
- Make a "kick-mobile" by tying rattles or bells onto short lengths of ribbon or elastic. String the mobile between two chairs. Place your baby on a mat on the floor between two chairs so that she can activate the "kick-mobile" and listen to the jingle of the bells. Safety check: Always stay close by when your baby has access to ribbon or elastic. There is always the chance of her getting entangled.

Hand and arm exercises

Most newborns hold their hands in a tight-fisted position and keep their arms close to their bodies. During the Tuning In stage, your baby will learn to thrust her arms in play and open and close her fists. These new skills help keep the outside world within reach. Help guide your baby to use her hands and arms:

- Place your finger in your baby's palm. At first she will grasp it reflexively. After a while she will learn how to tighten and loosen her fingers.
- While your baby is on her back, move her arms gently up and down and in and out. Adding a rhyme to the exercise can turn it into a game.

Up and down, up and down,
This is what we do.
Up and down, up and down,
This is fun for you.

- Hold your baby between your legs in the bathtub and help her splash with her arms.
- Sing a familiar song with your baby as you clap her hands gently together. You might try "If you're happy and you know it, clap your hands!"

Modifications

For babies who are visually limited

While sighted babies lift their heads for the joy of looking around them, babies who are visually limited do not have such impetus for gaining head control.

- A good way to help a very young visually limited baby strengthen her neck muscles and develop head control is to hold her against your shoulder in an upright position. Support her head with your hand just enough to keep her head from swaying or falling back.
- Bath play, where the fun is in the feel and the sound of the water, is particularly appropriate for the visually impaired baby.
- When you make a kick-mobile for your baby, make sure the

sound effects are interesting. Use very pliable squeak toys, bells, and rattles.

For babies who are hearing-impaired

Hearing-impaired babies need extra practice in head-lifting in order to build their neck muscles and gain good head control. Hearing babies hear a parent coming and naturally lift their heads to watch Mom or Dad approach.

- Call your baby by name in a loud, clear voice every time you approach the crib.
- Hold your baby over your shoulder as you introduce her to new sights around the house.
- Create a special kick-mobile or cradle gym that is appealing to your hearing-impaired baby. Substitute an interesting sight for an interesting sound by attaching bright-colored ribbons or scarves that flutter when your baby kicks.

For babies who are physically challenged

Babies who are physically impaired are likely to be slower in attaining motor milestones and in gaining muscle strength, balance, and coordination. If your baby has cerebral palsy, spina bifida, or other neurological impairment, early consultation with a physical therapist is important before beginning an exercise routine.

- Avoid sudden movements that startle your baby and make her jump, quiver, or stiffen up.
- If your baby stiffens her legs, do not bend them by force. Try to help your baby relax by talking to her, massaging her legs, or carrying her in an upright position. Once she is relaxed, help her flex her legs by applying steady and gentle pressure.
- If your baby enjoys a bicycling exercise but tends to cross or scissor her legs, place a small pillow between her legs before you begin that exercise.

- If your baby has tight ankles, flex her foot gently up and down several times a day.
- Avoid pulling your baby to a sitting position if she reflexively stiffens her legs and gets into a standing position.
- If your baby holds her hands in a tight-fisted position, play gently with each finger as a way to help her relax.

For babies who are hypersensitive or tactile-defensive

- Find a warm room in the house where you can "dress down" your baby, place her on a sheet, and let her practice kicking.
- If your baby is sensitive to the texture of grass or sand, spread out a blanket or towel.

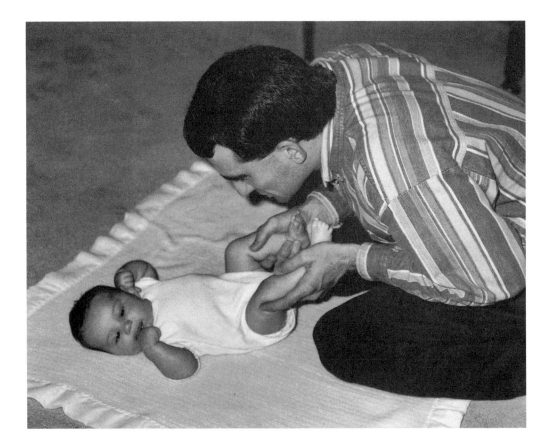

For babies with Down's syndrome

- Down's syndrome babies tend to be flexible and flaccid. Massage your baby's arms and legs to increase muscle tone.
- Find different safe ways to carry your baby: place her in a baby carrier, cradle her in your arms, hold her upright on your shoulder. Each different position helps your baby strengthen different sets of muscles.

REACHING OUT

In the Reaching Out stage, typically developing children are developing an increased interest in object play at the same time they are developing new physical skills. Maintaining a sitting position frees their hands, allowing them to manipulate toys, and learning to crawl gives them the ability to go after the toys they want. For a baby with special needs, motor development and cognitive development may not be in synchrony. They may be interested in active play with toys before they have achieved the balance to stay in a sitting position. By the same token, they may develop a special preference for a certain toy but not have the motor skill to fetch it.

When motor and cognitive development are out of synchrony, it is important for parents to prop their babies in a sitting position, and keep a variety of toys within the baby's reach.

Suggested Activities

Rolling over

The ability to roll over from stomach to back and back to stomach may be achieved in either the Tuning In or Reaching Out stage.

Roll your baby gently from side to side to get him used to the rolling motion. Sing a song to the tune of "Row, Row, Row Your Boat" to increase the fun.

Roll, roll, roll we go,
Roll from side to side.
Merrily, merrily, merrily, merrily,
What a way to ride!

Help your baby learn to roll over by putting him on an incline. You can create an incline by setting the crib mattress on the floor and lifting it just a little on one side. Make sure to position your baby so that his arms don't interfere with turning over.

Improving balance

- Use pillows or a swim ring to help your baby maintain his balance when he is first learning to sit.
- Use a large beach ball to further improve your baby's sense of balance. Hold your baby on the top of the ball and roll it gently from side to side.
- Bounce your baby on your knee while you listen to music or sing a song.
- Place your baby in a door swing. He will enjoy the motion and improve his balancing skills.

Leg exercises

As your baby improves balance and coordination, he will be able to catch his own toes and use his feet for kicking.

- String a cradle gym over the foot of his crib so that he can kick it with his feet.
- Put different-colored socks on each of your baby's feet to increase the fun of foot watching.

Crawling

Some babies begin to crawl during the Reaching Out stage. For a baby, moving about under his own power is an exciting step, bringing new horizons closer. To crawl, the baby must have enough strength and coordination to push forward with his feet from a prone position. A little encouragement will help your baby reach this important stage.

- With one hand, pull your baby's favorite toy just out of reach. Let your baby propel himself forward by pushing against your other hand.
- If your baby tries to crawl forward and ends up crawling backward, let him use your hands to push off.
- Place a blanket on a slight incline in the yard or park. Crawling downhill is easier than crawling on a flat surface.
- If your baby is becoming an accomplished creeper, increase the challenge by encouraging him to creep up the incline.

Modifications

For babies who are visually limited

Balance, like head control, is difficult for the visually limited child, who lacks the visual cues to help him with spatial relationships. (Try closing your eyes when you're standing on one foot and you'll understand the problem.)

- After your baby has achieved some head control, he will be ready for a blanket ride or a roll on a large beach ball. Introduce these activities slowly so that he will feel secure.
- Begin balance exercises with your baby while he is safely on your knee to give him a sense of security. Once he is able to maintain his own balance sitting supported on your lap, give him a little push so he can learn to right himself.

For babies who are hearing-impaired

- Continue to cue your baby by calling her by name before every exercise.

- Play music as you exercise your baby. Even if your baby has a profound loss, she will feel the vibrations.
- Help your baby associate changes in position with changes in your voice. Lift your baby up and down as you say this rhyme:

Up, up high (use high voice)
Down, down low (use low voice)
Up, up, up
And down we go.

For babies who are physically challenged

Swimming is a fine exercise for your baby as long as the water is warm. Introduce your baby to the water gradually. You may begin by pouring water on his hands and feet. Next, help him splash with hands and feet. Then, hold him against your body face-to-face as you walk waist-deep in the water. Finally, turn your baby away from you and let him kick in the water. Continue to hold your baby firmly, and do not put his head under the water until your pediatrician approves. Talk and laugh with your baby as you play together in the water.

For babies with Down's syndrome

Your baby may need help in developing sitting balance. A fun way to work on balance is to sit with your baby on a chair swing or glider, holding your baby firmly on your lap as you swing back and forth.

MAKING DISCOVERIES

As babies make the transition from the stage of Reaching Out to the stage of Making Discoveries, their field of exploration is expanding. Once again there is a synchronization of the development of motor skills and social-emotional skills. Newly emerging creeping and walking skills allow the baby to explore more territory and investigate more objects. The emotional attachment to her caregivers keeps her within the safety range. A baby who has a good, strong emotional attachment to her parents is ready to explore new territory when her mother or father is constantly within view to serve as a base of security.

As you work to provide opportunities for your baby to practice her emerging motor skills, be sure to keep safety precautions in mind. With each new motor skill an infant achieves, there is a new set of hazards to guard against.

Suggested Activities

Crawling

Crawling is a more advanced skill than creeping. A baby creeps stomach-down like a turtle, pulling with her arms and pushing with her legs. A baby crawls on hands and knees with stomach off the floor.

- The best surface for a baby to crawl on is a carpet. A textured carpet provides traction and keeps the baby's knees from slip-

ping. If your baby seems to be ready to crawl, dress her in soft and loose-fitting slacks or jeans.

- If your baby is trying to crawl but keeps collapsing, give her some practice with knee standing. Help her get into a kneeling position and hold her arms to help her keep her balance.
- Invite a crawling baby for a visit. Babies often learn by imitating each other.

Crawling, like creeping, has its own set of hazards. Stairs, doors to the outside, closets, and cupboards may be accidents waiting to happen. Babies who creep around the floor can also find small things and put them in their mouths, pull on lamp cords or tablecloths, and get their fingers into dangerous spots. Baby-proofing the house is absolutely critical when your child has learned to move around on the floor.

Pulling up

Pulling up is a precursor of walking. When your baby is first learning to pull up, it may be an all-consuming activity, for parents as well as the baby. Inevitably, babies learn to pull up before they learn to let themselves down again, and they can easily get themselves locked into a standing position.

The safest way for a baby to learn to pull up is by holding her parent's hands. For beginning pull-ups, support your baby's forearms or hold your baby around the waist. As your baby gains strength and control, she will use your hands to push off.

When your baby is learning to pull up to a standing position she may discover that a low coffee table is almost as useful as a parent's hands. Be sure to clear off the tops of low coffee tables.

Many babies pull up for the first time in their cribs. Often they find out that getting back down is not as easy as pulling up. If your baby gets stuck in a standing position, gently help her bend her knees to let herself down.

Bureaus and dressers are especially dangerous when babies reach the pulling-up stage. Your baby may open a drawer to pull up, and the whole dresser will fall on her head. Be on the watch at all times.

Beginning walking

As a baby practices her creeping, cruising (walking while holding on to furniture), and walking skills, she is learning more about her own body, what she can make it do, how high she can reach, where she can fit, and what she can climb. If your baby is slow to progress from cruising to walking, try the following ideas:

- Take your baby on a walk holding hands.
- When your toddler takes her first steps, help her gain confidence by walking from mother to dad and back again.
- Let your baby learn to walk by pushing a small sturdy chair, a large box, or a walking toy around the room.
- Increase her confidence by letting her hold on to one end of a scarf while you hold the other. After a while, just holding the scarf without you on the other end will be enough to help her walk alone.
- Provide your baby with safe places to practice climbing skills. Use pillows and bolsters to create an obstacle course.
- Cartons of all sizes provide wonderful opportunities for practicing climbing skills. If you leave an empty carton within reach, your toddler will struggle to get inside. Because toddlers can find their way into grocery boxes, it is important that empty boxes be clean inside and free of cash register slips, or anything you don't want your baby to put in her mouth.

Although the early attainment of motor milestones is not related to precocious intellectual development, the mastery of physical skills contributes to skill development in other domains. The mastery of a new motor skill increases confidence and self-awareness and provides new opportunities for exploration and discovery.

Modifications

For babies who are visually limited

Motor skills for sighted children depend in large part on visual cues. Early walking, for instance, is facilitated by watching other people walk, and reinforced by the new perspective toddlers get when they view their world from a standing position. Infants and toddlers who are visually impaired enjoy the feeling of motion, but are likely to be delayed in the development of motor skills.

- Lift your baby into different positions; hold him upright, upside down, or in a prone position. He will learn to judge his position in space by experiencing gravitational cues.
- Put your toddler on a swing. He will enjoy the motion and improve his balance. At the same time, you will have the opportunity to teach him positional language—up-down, high-low, back and forth.

For babies who are physically challenged

If your toddler is receiving physical therapy, make sure that you stay with him through the session. With the help of the therapist, learn exercises that you can repeat at home with your baby. Toddlers are always more secure and usually more cooperative when parents take over the exercises.

For babies with Down's syndrome

Toddlers with Down's syndrome are likely to be flaccid. Work with a physical therapist to learn exercises that help your toddler develop muscle tone.

CHAPTER 11

Developing Language

Although it may be a long time before your baby can speak in words, the development of language begins at birth. Your baby awakens and cries, and you take him to your breast or give him a bottle. At first your baby does not know that his crying brought you to him, but after a while he makes the association. When your baby is a little older he will send out different signals, and you will be able to interpret them. You will differentiate the cry of pain from the cry of hunger, and the fretting sounds of a sleepy baby from the distress sounds of a baby who is uncomfortable or upset. He will turn his head when he doesn't want any more cereal. He will raise his arms when he wants you to pick him up. He will welcome you into his room with a great big smile that tells you how much he loves you.

Learning language involves learning the sounds of language, the meaning base of language, the grammar or syntax of language, and the "rules" of carrying on a conversation. It also involves learning to interpret nonverbal signs and gestures. Given that a baby must develop all these skills in order to communicate, the fact that children do acquire speech in such a short period is nothing short of a miracle.

As we trace the course of language-learning in babies and toddlers, we recognize stage-related changes just as we did in social-emotional and motor development. We have once again labeled these stages Tuning In, Reaching Out, and Making Discoveries.

TUNING IN

In the first developmental stage, Tuning In, your baby is making the transition from an inward to an outward focus. He is learning to organize his own behavior and attend to the events around him. When he catches sight of his fingers, he watches how they wiggle. When he hears the sound of a rattle, he searches for it with his eyes. At the same time he is becoming aware of his own ability to produce sounds. He listens to the sounds he makes and reproduces them. He engages in sound-making games with his parents: cooing, listening, and then repeating his coo. He practices a variety of vocalizations including grunts, gurgles, squeaks, and sucking sounds.

Suggested Activities

- Increase your baby's attentiveness to sounds by giving him new listening experiences. Offer him different sounds such as rattles, squeak toys, bells, the tick of a clock, or the sound of a music box. Introduce some of the sounds in a quiet manner. Your baby may be even more attentive to quiet sounds.

- See how your baby responds to sounds. When he is lying down, talk to him very slowly, then faster, and then slowly once more. Is he kicking his legs and moving his arms in rhythm with your voice?

- Help your baby produce noises by himself. Hold a rattle in his hand and shake it up and down gently. After a while he will make the connection between the sounds he is hearing and the feel of the rattle in his hands. Or you can try making a rattle wristband by sewing a piece of Velcro to his sleeve and a second piece onto a rattle. As he waves his arm, he will hear the rattle jingle. The faster he moves his arm, the louder the jingling will sound.

- Try some spoken sounds as well. Snuggle your baby comfortably in a position where he has a clear view of your mouth. Make pleasant vocal sounds with different mouth positions. Try "ooh, aah, eeh." Or extend your tongue and wiggle it. With a little encouragement, your baby will try to copy your mouth positions. You may even be surprised by your baby's cooing as he tries to imitate your vowels.

- Bring your lips three to four inches from his ear and make the same sounds in a quiet voice. This gives him time to hear you at close range after he has just seen your face. Be sure to give each ear a turn. Talking into your baby's ear is especially important for the child with frequent ear infections or upper respiratory infections.

- Try more complex sounds by holding your baby as you sing lullabies. Talk to him in highly inflected phrases, in a loving tone. Avoid shouting or arguing near your baby. He is much more likely to practice his language when the sounds he hears are pleasant.

- Allow your baby some quiet time to practice his own vocabulary. When you approach his crib, try to repeat some of the

sounds you heard him make. Or let him listen to his own baby talk by recording one of his conversations and playing it back.

- Engage your baby in a playful activity that creates out-loud laughing.

Modifications

For babies who are visually limited

- Your baby is missing some early language experience when he cannot see your lips. Let your baby feel your lips as you carry on a babble conversation.
- Some visually impaired children spin around in a circle or rock rhythmically back and forth. This is a baby's way of stimulating himself. It is a good idea to distract your baby with an interesting activity before he gets into a habit that is difficult to break.

For babies who are hearing-impaired

A hearing-impaired baby babbles just like a non-hearing-impaired baby until he is three or four months old. Respond to your baby's babble with lots of smiling and touching. If your baby learns to associate his own babbling with your enthusiastic response, his babbling is more likely to continue.

REACHING OUT

In the second developmental stage, Reaching Out, your baby is actually seeking out stimulation, initiating games, and actively making contact with the world outside herself. The back-and-forth conversations become more vigorous, and your baby is often the initiator.

As she continues with these back-and-forth conversations, your baby is becoming more adept at making different sounds. Soon her repertoire will include babbling and calling out, playful coughs, spitting, "raspberries," and a variety of throaty sounds. Her babbling or repetition of consonant sounds will sound more and more like real speech as she experiments with changes in inflection. At different times she will seem to be asking a question, making a statement, or giving a command. Some babies learn to "sing along" with a familiar tune or imitate the consonant sounds they already know. Help your child expand her vocabulary by joining in her conversations.

Your baby is learning new ways to produce language. She is also tuning in more to the language she hears. During this stage she may learn to recognize her name, react to "no," respond differently to different tones of voice, or listen intently when you are talking on the telephone.

Suggested Activities

- When your child plays at making sounds, echo the sounds she makes. The exchange will encourage her to make more sounds and listen to herself. When your baby makes a playful cough, imitate her. She will enjoy playing a back-and-forth coughing game. Before she tires of the cough, change to a raspberry. See if she will change with you.
- Make a tape of your child's vocal play. Playing the tape will encourage her to talk back to herself and increase her babble repertoire.
- When your baby is babbling, position her in front of a mirror where she can watch her mouth.
- Listen to the consonant sounds your baby makes when she is alone in the crib. Make up rhythm songs to sing with her that repeat her newest sounds.

Pa-pa, Pa-pa, Pa-pa Jim,
Pat my nose and pat my chin.

Ba-ba-ba, ba-ba-ba, ba-bumble bee,
I ba to you and you ba-ba to me.

Da-da-da-da, da-da-da, Daddy Doo,
Da-da loves baby and I love her too.

- Place a shatterproof mirror over your baby's crib or changing table so that she can watch her mouth as she babbles.

Modifications

For babies who are visually limited

- Begin to build your baby's vocabulary by introducing words that your baby can experience. Say "up" every time you lift your baby out of the crib.
- Call your baby by name during feeding, bathing, and diapering. Substitute her name in songs and nursery rhymes.

Seesaw, Margery Daw,
Georgia shall have a new masters

- Play speech and gesture games with your baby, such as "Patty-Cake," "This Little Piggy," and "So Big." Help her imitate the gestures by moving her hands until she learns the pattern
- Call your baby's name before you enter the room. Is she searching for you with her eyes as you enter the room? Start softly and gradually increase your volume until she responds. Be sure to repeat her name after she has found you with her eyes.

- Say "nose" as your baby feels your nose and "mouth" as she touches your mouth. Say "cold" as your baby touches an ice cube.

For babies who are hearing-impaired

- Establish eye contact with your baby before you begin a conversation. Make sure she is watching your lips.
- Continue to show how pleased and excited you are with your baby's efforts to babble.
- As you sing to your baby, let her feel your lips and your throat muscles.
- When your baby makes a vowel or consonant sound, play back the sound into her ear.
- Keep a hand mirror in a convenient place. Let your baby watch her own lips when she plays with sounds.

MAKING DISCOVERIES

In the third developmental stage, Making Discoveries, your child is making the transition from focusing on the sound of language to focusing on its meanings. Through vocal play, conversations, and back-and-forth language games, your child has become familiar with the sounds of language and with the turn-taking "rules" of conversations. Now your child is ready to focus on the meanings of words and phrases and to engage in meaningful conversational exchanges. In the months ahead, he will learn that language can serve a variety of purposes. He will learn to use language to ask questions, make requests, play games, give directions, name and describe the things he sees, and play word games.

An important jumping-off point for learning the meanings of language is making the association between a word and the person or thing it refers to.

By now, your child may be attentive when you call his name. He may not realize that the name you are calling belongs to him especially, but he has picked up the concept that name-calling means "Pay attention." The next important step is recognizing that a particular name stands for a particular person.

Much remains unknown about the way children learn language. But there is general agreement that word meaning begins when a parent imposes meaning on the baby's spontaneous babble. The baby may playfully shriek out, "Da, da, da, da." The father hears his baby call and says, "Your daddy is coming." As the baby happily repeats, "Da, da," Daddy comes into the room. After a while the baby makes a clear association between his "da, da" babble and his daddy. This type of interaction helps the baby turn his babble into a meaningful word.

The expansion of language skills in the Making Discoveries stage is associated with the baby's increased ability to imitate and recall sound combinations. When the baby is playing with a ball, Mother is able to say "ball," and the baby says "ball" back. This allows Mother to help her baby make the association between the ball he is playing with and the word he is saying.

While your baby is improving his skills with word repetition, he is also getting better at expressive jargon. He is able to imitate intonation (the rise and fall of pitch), volume, and can put a string of sounds together that sounds like a real sentence. After a while your baby will use these pseudosentences as a way of giving commands, scolding, or inviting you over to play. You can encourage your baby's emerging control of language by playing word games with him.

Suggested Activities

- Play "show me" games with your baby. When you first introduce a "show me" game, choose something that is especially interesting to him, like a new pair of shoes or the "booboo" on his finger. Don't be upset if your baby says words wrong or makes up his own words for things. What is important now is the association of words with objects, body parts, and people. He will learn the exact word later.

- Exchange greetings with your baby. Say "Hi" when you come into the room and "Bye-bye" when you leave. Your baby will learn that words can stand for actions as well as objects.
- Let your baby play with an unplugged telephone. The telephone helps your child learn the turn-taking quality of a conversation.
- It won't be difficult for you to show your delight when your baby says his first words. Repeat these words after him and show him you know what he means.
- Spend time every day reading books with your baby. Show your baby a picture album and point out pictures of the family. Make a scrapbook with pictures of familiar things.
- When your baby begins to use single words, guess from the situation what he is telling you and expand his one-word sen-

tence. If your baby says "car," you might say, "Yes, that's a car." If your baby says "cookie," you can say, "You want a cookie?"

- Say nursery rhymes with your baby. Even though he may not know what the words mean, he will enjoy the cadence.
- Put familiar objects such as a ball, a shoe, a toy dog, and a rubber duck into a basket. Play a naming game with your baby. Ask your baby to find the shoe. Or name each object as your baby pulls it out of the basket.
- When you are bathing, feeding, or changing your baby's diaper, tell him in words what you are doing: "I am drying your toes."
- Even if your baby does not respond, continue to talk to him. Children who are slow talkers are most in need of language experience.

Modifications

For babies who are visually limited

- If possible, buy a pet for your visually impaired child. A visually impaired child who enjoys the experience of petting a dog is likely to learn the word "dog" without any problems.
- Make a "feel book" for your baby. Say "smooth" as she touches the silk, "rough" as she touches the sandpaper, and "hard" as she touches the board.
- Name the food your baby is eating. Let her feel and smell the food before she tastes it.

For babies who are hearing-impaired

- Listen to the sounds your baby makes spontaneously and find words to associate with the sounds. For example, if he says "daw-daw," show him a toy dog. Repeat "dog" into his ear as he makes the dog walk. For "puh-puh," you might say, "Putt-putt, the little engine goes putt-putt." As you let him play with a toy train or show him a picture of an engine, let him feel your throat and touch your lips as you say "putt-putt."

- Always speak clearly to your baby and let him watch your lips as you talk. Do not use exaggerated mouth movements or talk in a very loud voice.
- Use gestures as you talk to your baby. It is natural to communicate with your hands, your body language, and your facial expressions as well as with your voice.

Language is a unique skill that differentiates humans from all other species. The development of language depends both on maturation and a critical set of experiences. This set of experiences includes opportunities to hear and practice the sounds of language, opportunities to hear language spoken in a meaningful context, and opportunities to practice language with a responsive and appreciative teacher. Your baby will benefit more from your talking with him about the mundane chores you are doing—particularly those tasks the two of you do together—than from an expensive "educational toy." For every child, the first and best language teacher is a loving, caring parent.

CHAPTER 12

Thinking Skills

Newborn infants, whether preterm or full-term, healthy or at-risk, have a built-in need to take in and organize information. This need to learn is as powerful as the need to take in nourishment. No matter how much food they are given, babies who are not held and played with cannot thrive. On the other hand, babies who are brought up in a responsive and enriching environment can grow and flourish despite incredible odds.

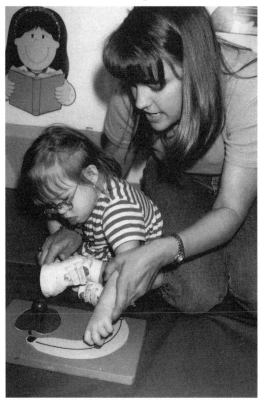

In this chapter we look at the intellectual development of children during the infant and toddler years. We discuss the development of both motor and sensory skills that help babies investigate their world. As we describe each facet of development, we suggest games and activities that parents can initiate to enhance emerging skills. Our discussion is organized according to the three stages of infant development: Tuning In, Reaching Out, and Making Discoveries.

TUNING IN

During the first phase of development, babies notice and respond to a variety of stimuli. Right from the

start, babies have the ability to tune into new information and to ignore information that is redundant. The newborn startles at the sound of a bell the first two or three times, then gets used to the sound and stops responding. When presented with a different sound, the baby will react again. This ability to discriminate between same and different, familiar and novel, serves as the basis for more complex learning.

There was an old belief that babies could not see until they were one or two months old. Now we realize that babies are not only able to see at birth, but they can focus their eyes and follow a moving target. During the early months babies are developing their visual skills and are using their eyes as a major source of information.

Touch is the first and most powerful way you have of reaching your baby. As you touch and stroke your newborn, you are providing a special kind of nourishment that fuels infant development. Experts who have studied the effects of touch on the newborn recognize the critical role that touch plays in helping an infant organize her behavior and integrate her experiences. At the same time, touch serves as a control system. A crying infant can be calmed by a soothing touch, a drowsy infant alerted by gentle stroking.

Parents instinctively recognize the importance of touch and seek out opportunities to stroke their infant or hold her skin-to-skin. Some babies seem to crave this kind of touching, and parents describe them as being soft and snuggly. Other babies may show some resistance to touch and withdraw or show agitation when they feel the touch of a hand. When babies show distress at being touched, sensitive intervention is especially important. Slowly, gradually, and ever so gently, parents must help their babies adapt to different kinds of touch.

As your baby coordinates the information from different senses, she becomes increasingly aware of where the parts of the body are and how they relate to each other.

Suggested Activities

- Use gentle stroking or massaging as a way to help your baby quiet down. If your baby's skin is dry, you may want to put nonmineral baby oil on your hands. Make sure your hands are warm.
- Rub your face against your baby's or stroke your face with your baby's hand. Her favorite feel is skin-to-skin. Fathers with beards should let their baby feel the inner surface of their arm. Short beards or "five o'clock shadows" may be too scratchy for a baby.
- Your baby's most exciting toy is your face. Hold your baby in your arms near the window so that the light is shining on your face while your baby's face is shaded. Talk and sing to your baby.
- Put a finger puppet on one of your fingers and let your baby watch as you move it up and down. Or let your baby focus on a colorful rattle. Move it from side to side while your baby is watching. After a while your baby will watch the rattle as it crosses from left to right and back again. When your baby has learned to follow the rattle from side to side, move it up and

down, in and out, in a circular motion, and, finally, in a diagonal. Move your hand a little faster, watching your baby's eyes to make sure she is following the rattle.

- Your baby will also enjoy watching objects that flutter and twirl. Hang a mobile over the crib. Make a mobile out of a colorful silk scarf and hang it in front of an open window, close enough for your baby to watch, but not close enough to touch.

- Gauge your child's listening skills. Ring a dinner bell close to the baby's crib. Does your baby stop moving and notice the sound? If she has been crying, does she quiet? Squeak a toy near your baby's crib. At first she will appear to be listening, and then she will "habituate" or stop paying attention. When she appears to have stopped listening, change to a different squeak toy and see if she renews her interest.

As your baby learns about objects—the way they look, the way they feel, and the sounds they make—she begins to make connections. When you ring a bell over her head, she searches for it with her eyes. When you lean over the crib to talk to her, she responds with cooing and kicking. When you place a rattle in her hand, she may bring her hand to her mouth. As you watch your baby's reactions during the Tuning In stage, keep track of the different ways she responds to information received through different senses.

Modifications

For babies who are visually limited

Touching experiences are especially important for a visually impaired child. Take advantage of her quiet alert time to introduce touching experiences. Even if you think your baby cannot see, introduce visual games. Use bright colors with sharp contrasts or shiny materials such as Mylar.

For babies who are hearing-impaired

Almost all hearing-impaired children have some residual hearing. Introduce the suggested sound games. If your baby responds to one or more of the games, redouble your efforts.

For babies who are physically challenged or hypersensitive

All sensory experiences, whether they involve feeling, seeing, hearing, or a combination, should be introduced gradually. The more tactile-defensive a baby appears to be, the more important it is to introduce early touching experiences. Stroking your baby very gently while she is taking a bottle or falling asleep may be the first step in helping your baby enjoy being touched.

Remember that babies with a physical disability or babies who are hypersensitive are easily overwhelmed. Introduce new sensations one at a time. Proceed slowly and cautiously. If she startles, quivers, or tenses up, give your baby time to rest before you begin again. If she appears to enjoy or at least tolerate your efforts at stimulation, continue for a short time and stop before she is tired.

For babies with Down's syndrome

Down's-syndrome babies may not respond to sensory stimulation as quickly as other babies. Begin by introducing tactile sensations. Use firm rather than gentle touching. Introduce a variety of feeling experiences: brush your baby's tummy with a paintbrush, use a spray bottle during bathtime as a shower, and rub her arms, legs, and back with cornstarch or unscented baby oil.

REACHING OUT

In the Reaching Out stage the baby changes from passive observer to active participant. No longer content simply to watch and listen for the information that comes in, your baby becomes a busy and active investigator. Instead of simply waving his arms in response to an interesting sight, he coordinates his hands and eyes and reaches out to grasp the interesting thing he sees. As he grasps the objects around him, the baby is making a whole new set of associations— the rattle shakes and the rubber ducky squeaks, the birds on his mobile flutter and twirl.

During the Reaching Out stage your baby is making two generalizations on a nonverbal level. He is recognizing that objects can be

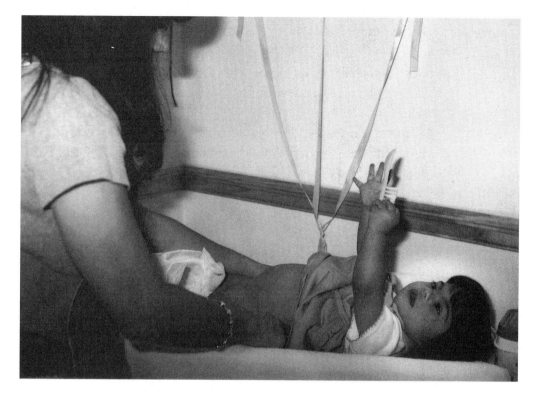

classified or grouped according to functions—rattles are for shaking, bells are for ringing, and rubber toys are for squeaking, while paper crushes. He is also recognizing that certain actions can be tried out on different objects with different results. When you bang on the table, it makes noise. When you bang in the bathtub, there's a splash.

When your baby first reaches out toward an object, he is likely to bat at it rather than grasp it. If the thing he is batting does something interesting, like spin around or make a noise, he will probably bat it again. After a while your baby will learn to use his hand to bring the object toward him. As this reaching behavior becomes better-coordinated, your baby will adjust his hand in anticipation of the object he is reaching. After trying the object out "for taste" he will begin a more intensive investigation—turning the object upside down, passing it from hand to hand, and trying to make it squeak.

Suggested Activities

- Give your baby experience with a variety of objects, including both toys and everyday things like plastic spoons and pots and pans.
- Watch your baby's reaction to a squeaky toy. Some babies laugh at the sound and others show distress. If your baby seems to enjoy the sound, let him reach for it himself. Once he learns to make the toy squeak he will be ready to try a different kind, or perhaps he will try to bite the toy, making it squeak in his mouth.
- Give your baby the lid of a small plastic bowl. See if he will hold it with two hands or pass it from one hand to the other.
- Give your baby a washcloth to hold. When he discovers that shaking it doesn't make it squeak or rattle, he may try bunching it up and transferring it from hand to hand.
- Hand your baby several balls of different sizes. He will learn to adjust his hand as he reaches in anticipation of the size of the ball.
- Wrapping paper that crinkles holds a special fascination for babies. Watch carefully if your baby gets hold of a piece of paper. It could easily end up in his mouth.
- Put a patterned sheet on your baby's crib. He will make scratching motions as he tries to pick up the design.
- Curlers that fit into each other make an interesting toy. If you fit two curlers inside each other, your baby may learn to pull them apart.
- Improvise a cradle gym using large curtain rings, plastic bracelets, and pot holders. See if your baby bats at the pot holders and grasps the rings.
- As your baby reaches for and plays with different toys and objects, you will discover that there are certain favorite toys that he always comes back to or seeks out. This is an important development that signals the ability to recall specific experiences.

If you watch carefully, you will see more and more evidence of your baby's increasing memory power.

- Half cover up your baby's favorite toy with a diaper. Can he recognize it and retrieve it?
- Drop a colorful ball onto the floor while your baby is watching. Does your baby look down on the floor in anticipation of where the ball will land?
- Put a floating toy in the bathtub. Chasing and grasping it will be a challenge. Your baby gets better with practice—another indication of increased memory power.
- Using a piece of elastic, string a stuffed animal from the ceiling or curtain rods. As he tries to grasp it, your baby will laugh in anticipation of its springing back.

Modifications

For babies who are visually limited

- Give your baby extra opportunities to handle objects of different shapes, weights, and textures.
- Present objects in pairs that are almost alike. This pairing technique gives your baby early practice in identifying similarities and differences on the basis of feel. Here are some examples: a wooden block and a rubber block, a plastic ball with holes and a similar ball without holes, a squeaky toy fish and a squeaky toy duck.
- Make your baby a texture box by turning a large carton on its side and gluing different textured material on the inside. Stringing bells from the topside can make it even more fun.

For babies who are hearing-impaired

Play hiding games in a quiet room, preferably with a rug on the floor. Hide a music box or a radio under a diaper while the baby isn't looking. See if she can find the toy by listening to the music.

For babies who are physically challenged

If your baby has difficulty with grasping, find toys that can be grasped easily, such as dumbbell rattles, small cloth animals or dolls, and clutch bells.

For babies who are hypersensitive or tactile-defensive

Use toys with bells rather than squeaky toys. A high-pitched squeak can disturb a sensitive baby.

- If your baby shows extreme tactile defensiveness and refuses to touch or pick up a toy, try putting baby socks halfway over your baby's hands. Your baby will shake his hands and watch the socks flutter. After a while he will adjust to the sensation of having his hands covered.

For babies with Down's syndrome

If your baby is having trouble with a finger-thumb grasp, let him practice a grasping activity with a built-in reward. Make gelatin thicker than usual and cut it in cubes. Let your baby finger-feed himself first with one hand and then with the other.

MAKING DISCOVERIES

As your child reaches the third developmental stage, Making Discoveries, she is able to use her new skills and information to solve more challenging problems. She is interested now not only in the different ways she can manipulate an object, but she also is trying to find out how objects relate to each other. She is poking, prodding, pushing, pulling, and presenting herself with new challenges. She may puzzle over such questions as: I have a block in each hand already—how can I pick up a third block? Can I find my favorite toy at the bottom of the toy box? Can I pull open a cabinet door and play with the things I find? What can I find that I can empty or fill, pull apart, or break into bits? With each new discovery that the baby makes, you will find new areas in your house that need to be baby-proofed.

Suggested Activities

Help your child find new ways of investigating objects. Encourage her to combine her investigation in complex ways:

- Let your baby discover that some objects come apart and fit together. Improvise a stacking toy by covering two to three empty cans of different sizes with contact paper.
- Let your baby watch as you bang two toys together, and then give her a turn. Let your baby extend her banging and pounding skills. Give her a short-handled wooden spoon and a kitchen pot. If she is really into banging, try out a xylophone.
- Let your baby discover the fun of filling and emptying. Give her tennis balls and a muffin dish, or let her put pom-poms into an egg carton.
- If your baby is ready for opening and closing, turning wheels, or pushing down levers, let her play with a busy box.
- If your baby has good control of her hands and is no longer putting everything in her mouth, you may want to let her scrib-

ble with a soap crayon, spread Crazy Foam or shaving cream on a placemat, or manipulate peanut-butter clay.

- Pouring is a special skill that requires lots of practice. Begin pouring activities in the bathtub or swimming pool.

As your baby carries out her complex investigations of objects, she is learning through experience that objects continue to exist even when she can't see them or feel them. As she gains this new insight, she will enjoy playing hidden-object games.

- Hide a toy under a diaper while your baby is watching and see if your baby will move the diaper to get the toy.
- Hide a toy behind a plastic tray. Will your baby try to reach through the tray, or will she figure out how to reach around it?
- Find a hard rubber toy that sinks in the bathtub. Will your baby reach into the water to retrieve the toy? Bubbles in the bathtub increase the challenge of the fishing game.

Here are some other advanced activities to challenge your baby's problem-solving ability:

- Give your baby a spindle toy. Placing a ring over the spindle is a challenge in itself. It will be a while before your baby can put a spindle toy together with the rings in the right order.
- Puzzle play is an extension of filling and emptying. Homemade box puzzles are easy to make and even more successful than commercial puzzles. Start with a simple one-piece knob puzzle with a round inset or make your own puzzle by cutting out a square hole in a shoe box top for a block-dropping game.
- See if your baby can retrieve a toy by pulling on a string. Attach strings to her wheel toys. When she is in the high chair, tie a ribbon to a favorite toy. Will she toss it on the floor and pull it back up by pulling in the ribbon? Add a special element of fun by tying a bagel to the end of the ribbon.

- Put a doll or a teddy bear on a blanket close to her when she is seated on the floor. See if she will pull the blanket toward herself to retrieve the doll.

As your baby becomes more skillful with imitation and solving problems, she is laying the foundation for learning self-help skills. Children who have the ability to do things for themselves can cope with challenge without becoming overly dependent. For children with handicaps, it is especially important to encourage self-help skills at the earliest possible age. Adaptive devices of various sorts can facilitate early independence.

- Let your child drink from a cup. Several different cups are on the market that prevent extensive spilling and create a smooth transition from breast or bottle to cup.

• Pour milk into a small lightweight pitcher and let your baby pour the milk into her cereal bowl. At first you will need to guide her hand.

Modifications

For babies who are visually limited

• Give your baby extra practice with the concept of "inside." Get a set of cardboard stacking blocks. Glue different pieces of fabric on the inside of one or two of the blocks. Your baby will put her hand inside the block to discover the interesting texture.
• Make a shape game for your baby out of a large coffee can with a plastic top. Cut a two-inch circle in the lid and tape the lid securely on the can. Guide your baby's hand as she drops Ping-Pong balls through the hole. The sound of the ball bouncing in the tin adds interest to the game.
• Put a sock on one of your baby's hands. She will enjoy the challenge of pulling off the sock.
• Put something that your baby really likes, perhaps a toothbrush, inside a shoebox. Tape the top on, but make a large hole on one end of the box. Let your baby put her arm inside the "tunnel" to fish out the toothbrush.

For babies who are hearing-impaired

Play hide-and-seek with a transistor radio. Hide the radio behind a chair or under a cushion, turn up the volume, and see if your baby can find it. This will give her practice in locating the source of a sound.

For babies who are physically challenged

• If your baby has difficulty picking up toys, place the toys within her reach in a flat box with sand in it. The sand will keep the toys from slipping away as she tries to grasp them.
• If your baby is not mobile, play a special version of hide-and-seek. Bury a toy in a box full of sand and see if she can find it.

As your baby becomes more active, you will find that he discovers his own problems and invents his own challenges. The more adventuresome he becomes, the more watchful you have to be. If he has learned to pull a toy by a string to make it follow him, he may try pulling the cord of a lamp, or the corner of a tablecloth. If he has learned about the fun of filling and emptying, he may dump out the contents of your purse and jewelry box or fill up the toilet with a stack of unopened mail.

After a while the explorations do become less vigorous, and babies begin to understand that there is some off-limits behavior. During the transition period it is important for parents to remember that their child is adventuresome rather than naughty, and that the experiences that babies accumulate are the basis for later learning.

PLAYTIME WITH FAMILY AND FRIENDS

"I know that my family disagrees with me, but I think we're making a big mistake. We're spending so much time dragging my son to all kinds of therapists that we're not giving him time to have fun. Sure, he has problems that need to be worked on, but he also has the same needs and rights as any other child. I feel that the worst thing we can do to him is to take away his playtime."

CHAPTER 13

Encouraging Creativity

W̱hile no one would claim that an infant is an artist or a musician, every infant, from the moment of birth, has creative potential. The newborn recognizes the sound of his mother's voice and the rhythm of her heartbeat. The two-month-old is attracted to visual patterns that are moderately complex and differentiates between a pattern that is new and one that is familiar. The six-month-old moves in rhythm to a lively beat and is quieted by a lullaby. Throughout the early years children continue to refine their

appreciation of beauty and to develop ways of expressing their own creative responses.

In this chapter we look at different ways in which infants and toddlers express their creativity. First, we describe ways in which children respond to different types of musical and rhythmic experiences. Second, we describe ways in which toddlers create artistic products. In the final section of the chapter we discuss the gradual emergence of imaginative play.

MUSIC, RHYTHM, AND MOVEMENT

Infants and toddlers are cosmopolitan in their taste for music. They are aware of differences in tone, timbre, melody, rhythm, and cadence. They show their pleasure in listening to music in different ways. There is evidence in the literature that listening to music, especially classical, has a positive effect on brain development. As infants instinctively identify patterns in the music as it is played, they build up circuits in their brain that facilitate later learning. Although music is certainly an important way of stimulating problem-solving skills, the most critical outcome of a musical experience is cementing the emotional bonds between parent and child. When a parent sings a song to her baby, the baby associates the sound of her mother's voice with the gentleness of her touch, creating in the infant feelings of trust and security. During the first year of life, parents can use songs in many different ways. You can sing special songs that go with different routines thus helping your infant anticipate and accept what is going to happen. "This is the way we wash our face" prepares babies for the approaching of the wet washcloth. A soft lullaby like "Tender Shepherd" helps babies know it is time to fall asleep. Songs can also be used as a way of introducing your child to games with motion. "Row, Row, Row Your Boat" encourages your baby to rock back and forth as you support her with your arms.

Suggested Musical Activities

- Provide your child with a variety of musical experiences. Children enjoy classical music, popular music, and traditional children's songs.
- Pay attention to the kind of music that your child enjoys most and the kind of music that seems to disturb him.
- Play music that you enjoy as well as what your child likes. He will sense and share your pleasure.

- Some babies react negatively if music is played too loud. Lower the volume if your child shows signs of distress.
- Play musical games with your child. Children enjoy shaking noisemakers and banging with a spoon, keeping time with their favorite songs.
- Special tapes saved for playing in the car make car rides more enjoyable.

- As children grow older they will enjoy creating their own rhythms and will "sing" along with music.
- With older toddlers you can also use songs as a way of teaching language. "Old MacDonald Had a Farm" helps children learn the sounds that different animals make.
- All infants and toddlers enjoy the experience of dancing to music. As soon as babies learn to stand with support they love to bounce up and down as the music plays.
- Whether your toddler is standing or sitting in a chair, give him a silk scarf that he can wave as the music plays.
- Make homemade drums out of cereal boxes and use wooden spoons as drumsticks. Your toddler will enjoy participating in a rhythm band with other family members.

ART EXPERIENCES

Newborn babies are genetically programmed to look into their parents' eyes. This eye-to-eye contact ties a love knot between infants and their parents that can last a lifetime. Throughout their growing-up years, children continue to derive pleasure from visual images. Beginning perhaps with making sand cakes, blowing bubbles, or scribbling with a crayon, children discover their own capacity to create a pleasing display.

Your baby's fascination with art is closely akin to her fascination with music. Art and music are built on patterns, which are repeated and reconfigured. Learning to recognize different patterns satisfies an infant's innate drive to make sense out of her world and producing images on her own satisfies the urge to create that is in every child.

Suggested Art Activities

- Watch your infant carefully as you introduce a new mobile. The same mobile that delights and excites one infant may be frightening to another. If your infant avoids watching a particular mobile, you may want to find another mobile that is either more or less stimulating.

- "Read" a classic children's book with your baby. Even if she can't understand the words she will enjoy the illustrations.
- Give your infant practice in discriminating between like drawings. Draw a happy face on one side of a paper plate and a sad face on the other side. Observe you baby's reaction as you show him each side of the plate.
- Put food coloring in a glob of shaving cream and spread it out on a plastic placemat. Your toddler will enjoy finger painting with this delightful concoction.
- Make peanut butter playdough and give your toddler the opportunity to reshape the playdough.
- Give your toddler a large crayon and a sheet of stiff paper. Play a lively record and encourage him to draw on the paper keeping in time with the music. Encourage him to create a second drawing. This time play slow and soft music.
- Give your toddler soft blocks and allow her to construct her dream house.

Peg·Pérego

- Give your toddler the opportunity to tear up pieces of colored tissue paper. If he is ready, help him glue the pieces onto a sheet of paper to make a collage.
- Take your toddler with you to an art museum. Both you and your toddler will enjoy the experience.
- If it is holiday time, take your infant on short shopping trips. He will love looking at the holiday decorations in the store windows.

PRETEND PLAY

Engaging in pretend play is the crowning achievement of the preschool years. Pretending requires self-recognition. Before a child can pretend to be or pretend to do he must image himself as separate and distinct from other people. At the same time he must image other people also as being agents with the ability to initiate actions and make things happen. Although a young child may not have the language to express his intuitions in words, the ability to engage in pretend play is a confirmation of his ability to think abstractly. "I can be myself and pretend to be a puppy." "I can put a block in my mouth and pretend it is a cookie."

Imitation is the precursor of pretending. Many infants as young as two months old have the capacity to imitate a tongue thrust or a facial expression. During the second phase of development when the child is reaching out and actively investigating his world, his ability to imitate becomes more exact. He can imitate many actions that

are already in his repertoire, like banging on the table or shaking a rattle. Another giant step in pretending is when he can imitate an action that he has not done before, like clapping his hands together or waving goodbye.

In the Making Discoveries stage of development we can watch the gradual evolution from imitation to pretend play. The toddler will imitate an act that an adult does with an object, like sweeping with a broom or talking into a telephone. At first he will imitate the action only when he sees it. After a while he will associate the action with the object. When he sees the telephone, he will hold it to his ear. When he is given a toy broom, he will begin to sweep. Then, as a final step, he will hold one hand to his mouth and one hand on his ear and pretend he is talking on the phone.

Toddlers with special needs are less likely than typical toddlers to engage in imitation or pretending. There are many reasons for this. Some toddlers lack the motor skills to imitate an action. Some toddlers have not developed an image of their own body. They mean to tap their nose. They have no problem touching your nose but they can't see their own nose and they don't know exactly where it is. Some children may have mastered imitation but they have not defined themselves as being separate individuals. They cannot pretend to be someone else if they don't understand "self."

Suggested Activities to Promote Pretending

- An important precursor of pretending is interactive play. Hold your baby in your arms. Establish eye contact. Coo to your baby. If your baby begins to coo, wait until he stops cooing and then coo again. If your baby turns away he is letting you know that he needs a break. Wait for a few seconds and then renew your cooing conversation. If your baby learns to babble, do your best to imitate his babble sounds.
- Another interactive game that your baby may enjoy is "raspberry," sticking out your tongue and making a silly sound.

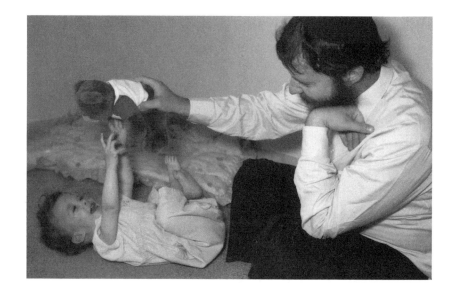

When your baby discovers how to make a raspberry sound, try to repeat the sound he is making and see if he will engage in a raspberry conversation. Will he play the game if you make the first raspberry sound?

- Play patty-cake with your baby. At first you are best off holding her hands while you say the patty-cake jingle. Next, alternate between clapping your hands and clapping her hands. After a while she will clap her hands when you clap your hands or when you recite the patty-cake jingle.

- While your toddler is watching, place a doll facedown on a blanket. Pat the doll on its backside and say "nighty-night." Perhaps your toddler will take a turn patting the doll. It may also encourage imitation if you give the doll a hug.

- Beginning when she is a baby, place the same doll or stuffed animal in your baby's crib at night. Give the doll a name and say goodnight to it when you say goodnight to your child. For many toddlers a familiar doll becomes a security object. When your child responds by settling down when you put the doll in her bed, she is animating the doll. This may be the first indication of her emerging ability to pretend.

CHAPTER 14

Toys and Books

"I sometimes get so annoyed with people. My child has cerebral palsy and everyone keeps bringing her presents. I know they mean well but Angela can't even hold a rattle, let alone look at a book or watch a video. The more stuff she gets, the more I realize how limited she is."

When an infant has special needs it is natural for family and friends to shower the baby with gifts. It may be a way of compensating the baby for her disability or a way of expressing their concern for the baby's health and well-being. But it takes a parent or caregiver who is with the baby on a daily basis to select a toy, book, or videotape that captures the baby's interest and helps to build her strengths.

Before you go to a toy or a music store, think about the kinds of things your baby likes to do and the skills she is attempting to acquire. You may conclude that she already has enough appropriate toys or that you can create or improvise a toy or book that would be just as good or better than a toy or book you could buy.

In this chapter, our goal is to provide guidelines for the selection of toys, books, and videotapes and to provide suggestions for toys and books that a parent can create or improvise at home. The joy of buying a new toy is anticipating how

happy it will make your child. When your child has no interest in the toy you bring home it is bound to disappoint you. The challenge of buying a toy for a child with special needs is to find a toy that is both easy to manipulate and fun to play with. Naturally there is always an element of trial and error. What appears to be the perfect toy for your youngster might be not stimulating enough or may be over-stimulating and scary.

TOYS TO CHOOSE: TUNING IN

Visually Appealing Toys

Before an infant is able to grasp a toy, he will enjoy looking at an interesting pattern, especially if it is moving back and forth. Infants are attracted by mobiles that are hung over their crib or homemade visuals that hang from the rails of the crib. They enjoy watching a mobile with contrasting colors and prefer designs that have a center focal point. Once your baby has shown an interest in focusing on a pattern, you may want to give her opportunities to track a moving object. Almost any small brightly colored infant toy can be used for tracking. As you move the toy slowly either up and down or from side to side, your baby is learning to coordinate the movement of his head with the movement of his eyes. A simple mobile hung over the crib will have the same effect.

If your baby loses interest in focusing on a particular visual display, it may be time for a change. With little work or imagination you can make your own visual toys. Draw a face or a simple design on a paper plate and attach it to a craft stick. Attach the stick to the side of the crib or on a carry crib or car seat. Other simple toys that invite visual exploration and tracking are hand puppets, nonbreakable mirrors and brightly colored wristbands.

Sound Toys

Babies are tuned in from the moment of birth to the sound of their mother's voice. In the first days and weeks after birth, babies with intact hearing and motor skills develop the skill of turning their head to the source of sound. If you shake a rattle a few inches from her head on one side or the other, she will turn her head and search for the rattle. The ability to coordinate sight and sound is an important sensory achievement. Before long your baby will focus on your lips when you talk or sing.

A second skill that your baby achieves in the Tuning In stage is the ability to recognize and assign meaning to different sounds. When you open the door to her room, she will look toward the door in anticipation of your arrival. She will show preferences to particular sounds. She may respond positively to a rattle, a bell, or a music box, and show distress when she hears other sounds such as a squeak or a scraping sound. Many babies are startled by sudden unexpected sounds, high-pitched sounds, or loud noises.

As babies show their ability to differentiate sounds and search for their sources, toys with sound effects become appealing. In addition to music boxes and rattles many babies enjoy the sound of bells, tambourines, and xylophones. In the Reaching Out stage, your baby will be able to activate sound toys on his own.

Feel Toys

Just as your baby is learning to differentiate different sounds and images, he is also capable of differentiating different types of "feels." Babies are unique in their reactions to different feels. Some babies like soft and gentle touches. Other babies enjoy vigorous rub. If your baby likes gentle touches you may want to tickle him with a soft paintbrush or rub his face with a silky fabric. If he enjoys a rigorous rub, stroke him with a rougher fabric, like a nubby washcloth or a swatch of corduroy.

TOYS TO CHOOSE: REACHING OUT

In the Reaching Out stage, babies acquire the ability to investigate their world by reaching out and grasping. Now they are not satisfied by just listening and watching. They want to play with their toys. They will bat at a cradle gym and watch to see what happens. Did the ring on the cradle gym swing back and forth? Did the cradle gym make a noise? The baby bats the cradle gym over and over, pleased with the effect.

In selecting toys for your baby think about the kinds of things your baby is learning to do. What happens when she grasps a rattle and gives it a vigorous shake?

Responsive Toys

The most popular baby toy since time immemorial is a rattle. There is a good reason for this. Rattles are easy to grasp and always responsive to a shake. A good first rattle is shaped like a dumbbell. Baby's can grasp it by tightening their fingers around it and can make it shake just by moving their arm.

Other popular responsive toys include crib gyms, squeaky toys, simple busy boxes, and different types of musical toys. Crib toys with large rings that babies can grasp have the greatest play value. Squeaky toys are most fun when they are made of soft pliable rubber. Musical toys for young babies including bells, shakers, and drums help babies learn to play without adult help.

As you choose toys for your baby in the Reaching Out stage, think about the kinds of things she enjoys doing or is learning to do, and let that be your guide in the selection of toys. If she likes to pick up a toy and shake it, buy several rattles. At first she will do best with a dumbbell rattle because it is easy to grasp. After a while change to more challenging rattles that can be grasped from only one end. Squeaky toys can also provide graded challenges. Begin with a soft rubber toy that responds to a light squeeze and then buy squeaky toys that are not quite so easy to squeeze. Other toys that are appropriate for the Reaching Out stage include bells that ring with the twist of a wrist, teething rings, clutch balls, lever-type toys with pop-up effects, and busy boxes.

Not all responsive toys have to come from a toy store. As children get more adept at handling objects, they will enjoy banging a pan with a wooden spoon, crinkling a piece of Mylar, or clanging aluminum pie plates together.

TOYS TO CHOOSE: MAKING DISCOVERIES

Babies in the third developmental stage, Making Discoveries, are ready to solve problems. They enjoy all kinds of toys that pose a challenge and provide opportunities to discover their own capacities. They also enjoy toys that resemble the kinds of objects that adults use and provide opportunities for imitation and language learning.

Children in the third developmental stage are making exciting discoveries. They are learning that

- Objects exist even when they have disappeared from sight.
- Some things fit inside other things.
- Balls come back when you throw them against the wall.

- Wheel toys move faster when you give them a big push.
- Cupboards open when you pull their knobs.
- Pulling on a tablecloth can make the dishes move.

Problem-Solving Toys

Babies enjoy toys that present them with problems to solve and give them a sense of accomplishment.

Toys that encourage problem-solving include

- spindle toys
- fill-and-dump toys
- lock boxes

- snap beads
- busy boxes
- jack-in-the-box toys
- shape boxes
- pop-up toys
- pounding toys
- nesting blocks
- oversized pop-out beads
- rolling toys
- wheel toys
- riding toys
- large peg boards
- inset puzzles
- toys with knobs, levers, or screw-on lids

In addition or as substitutes for toys you can buy in the store, you can improvise problem-solving toys using household materials.

- Save tubes from paper towels or wrapping paper and show your toddler how to drop a Ping-Pong ball through the tube.
- Save cardboard boxes or coffee cans with plastic lids. Put a cracker in the box or can and cover it. See if your child can take off the lid and retrieve the cracker.
- When your child is sitting in a booster chair at the kitchen table, put a cracker out of her reach. See if she can retrieve it using a wooden spoon.
- Line up three margarine tubs. While your child is watching, put a small toy in the tub nearest to your child. If she retrieves it, place the toy in the tub that is furthest away. Don't be surprised if she searches for the toy in the first tub. It will take her a while to figure out your game.
- In selecting a toy for your toddler, take into account her level of dexterity as well as her problem-solving skills. Remember that toddlers with special needs may take longer than other toddlers to reach the discovery stage.

BOOKS TO CHOOSE: BABIES AND TODDLERS

Babies, even if they are in the Tuning In stage, enjoy looking at a book or having it read to them. The following criteria are useful for the selection of first books:

- Find board books that allow babies to turn the pages either on their own or with minimal help.
- Choose a book that has clear, bright illustrations that are not overstylized.
- Find books with everyday objects that your baby will recognize and eventually be ready to name.
- Find books that are without words so that you and your baby can focus on the illustrations or choose books with rhyme and rhythm that your baby will enjoy hearing over and over again. Babies enjoy and learn from repetition.

- Avoid books with moving parts. They will not survive your baby's first pull.
- Keep away from cloth books. The colors are not bright enough and the book will not hold your baby's interest.
- When your baby begins to understand language, your choice of books becomes wider. Select books that invite your baby's participation.
- Choose books that depict objects that your child can recognize and/or name.
- Find books where the same object is shown on each page so that your child can enjoy finding the object.
- Read books to your child that you enjoy.
- Find books like a farm or zoo book where your baby can repeat the noises that the animals make.
- Find a book with a repetitive line so that your child can anticipate the line and perhaps join in.
- Find books where you can read the illustrations rather than reading words.
- Reserve a special book for naptime or bedtime. *Goodnight, Moon* is a perennial favorite.
- Select books with lyrical prose or rhymes so that your child will appreciate the sound of the language even if he does not understand the words.
- Babies enjoy books they can manipulate. Scratch-and-sniff books, books like *The Very Hungry Caterpillar* where you can put your finger through a hole, books that can squeak, books that open like an accordion, or books that play a song are fun for some children and frustrating for others.

When your child becomes fond of a book, don't hesitate to read it over and over again. Babies love and learn from repetition.

CHAPTER 15

Fun Times

~~~~~~

"Today, for the very first time, I took my toddler to a birthday party. We had been invited to parties before but I always explained that my schedule was just too packed. This was true, I suppose, but it was also true that I was afraid of being embarrassed. Supposing Jimmy started to scream when he heard a balloon pop, or supposing he bit one of the other children? Well, guess what. He did cry when a balloon popped, but other than that he had a great time. He clapped his hands when they sang 'Happy Birthday' and he let me put him down in the middle of the floor when the birthday boy opened his presents."

Parents who have babies with special needs are likely to have very full days. Between caring for their baby, taking care of household chores and carving out time for the rest of their family, there seems to be no time left for having fun with their baby. Sometimes we have to remind ourselves that our baby with special needs has the same need and the same right to fun time as any other child.

In this chapter we talk about three ways of having fun with our child on everyday outings, special excursions, and special times with the family.

EVERYDAY OUTINGS

With a baby or toddler who is medically fragile or physically limited, the primary concern is to protect the baby's health and conform to therapeutic routines. We see only the downside of taking her out on a walk, bringing her to a store, or taking her on a shopping excursion. Yet every baby needs a change of scene, just as we need changes of scene. Every baby also needs to develop coping skills, to adjust to differences in temperature, sounds, sights, and different levels of stimulation.

- Unless the weather is too extreme, take your baby on a daily walk. Sing to her or play a tape as you walk along.
- If your child is lying flat in a carriage, talk about the things within her line of vision: leaves fluttering on a tree, a big truck driving by, or a child peering into her carriage.
- If your child is sitting up in a stroller, take her for a walk to a playground, a house with a flower garden, or a line of store win-

dows. Talk to her about the sights that attract her attention. She may not understand what you are saying, but the more you talk about the things she sees and hears, the faster she will learn language.

- When you go to a store, take your child with you. If the hustle and bustle or the long line in the grocery store makes her uncomfortable, she may enjoy a quick stop in a bookstore, a toy store, or a drugstore. After a while she will learn to tolerate a longer shopping expedition.
- Taking an infant or toddler to a restaurant, whether or not he has special needs, takes a little more courage. Even a fast-food restaurant can involve waiting time, and very few youngsters can put up with waiting for food.
- Make a habit of bringing along your child's preferred foods. If your baby is not ready to eat the food that you can order in a restaurant, he may not enjoy the experience.
- Be sure to choose a restaurant that is not crowded or noisy.
- Bring your spouse or a friend to the restaurant with you so that you can make a temporary exit if your baby gets upset.

VACATION TIME

"We haven't taken a vacation since Veronica was born. In the first place, it's too much of a hassle to take along all her equipment. In the second place, we don't feel comfortable spending money when we don't know what the future holds."

Parents with special-needs babies may feel that taking a vacation is a luxury they can't afford. Other parents are concerned about the amount of paraphernalia they will have to take along, with interruptions of the therapy schedule, or with the lack of easy access to medical help. These concerns are understandable, but with some creativity and flexibility they can be overcome.

Weigh the benefits of a vacation against the liabilities. Even a minivacation or a vacation at home can have a positive effect on your emotional and physical well-being.

If you feel that the equipment you need is not portable or that you can't afford a real vacation, treat yourself to a schedule of day-long vacations. Think of yourself as a tourist and visit places in your area that a tourist would enjoy. Think about parks, museums, attractions, country roads, outdoor concerts, fairs, or sports events. When you are relaxed and having fun, your baby reaps the benefits.

Talk to your baby about your vacation. Even if he doesn't understand your words, he will catch your enthusiasm.

Don't worry about missing a few days of therapy. Nothing is quite as therapeutic as having fun with your parents.

FAMILY TIME

"Our family has always recognized the importance of preserving holiday traditions. Each member of the family hosts one holiday per year. We have Easter Sunday at our house, and my children help me dye and decorate dozens of Easter eggs. Unfortunately, I have to skip the tradition this year. I am too busy with the baby to spend all that time messing around with Easter eggs. I think I'll just buy chocolate eggs and hide them in the yard."

Family traditions provide children with a host of happy memories that they will always treasure. In most families these traditions are associated with special holidays. Children are given a special role to play in preparing for the event, such as decorating a Christmas tree, polishing a Menorah, dyeing Easter eggs, or baking batches of cookies for the Labor Day family picnic. Skipping a part of the tradition is like breaking up a memory.

Parents of babies with special needs find themselves in a quandary. How can they take time away from their baby to carry out a tradition that has no meaning for them?

As you make decisions about whether to follow a family tradition, remember that if you have other children and decide to skip a tradition, you may be sending a negative message. "Things won't be the same any more now that we have a baby."

Memories are built over time. Even though you feel that a family tradition like watching fireworks on the Fourth of July, carving a pumpkin on Halloween, or baking a Christmas turkey for the homeless is not meaningful to your baby, you are creating memory traces that take on meaning with time. Furthermore, holidays marked by traditions provide children with a way of understanding the passing of time. "Wait until Christmas" has more meaning to a youngster than "wait until next year."

- Take holiday photos and make an album for each holiday.
- Let your child put stickers on a wall calendar to mark off special days.
- String holiday cards where your baby can see them.
- Create unique family traditions like singing special bedtime songs, collecting and pressing autumn leaves, serving pancakes on Sunday morning, or tying a balloon to a chair on the breakfast table of the birthday girl or boy.
- Think about your own childhood. What family traditions were meaningful to you? Whenever it seems feasible, pass along these traditions to the next generation.

Providing opportunities for your special-needs child to have fun is the most effective therapy you will ever find. With all children, the quality of their daily lives has a profound effect on their future. It influences their capacity to learn, their ability to form meaningful relationships, and, most important, their ability to experience pleasure. No matter what disabilities your child may have, a large dose of fun and laughter is her most effective tonic.

SECTION V

TAKING CHARGE

"I have never been an assertive person. If someone in authority told me to do something, I did it. I resisted taking stuff back to a store, even if it was damaged or defective. When a doctor or a dentist told me that some procedure had to be done, I never questioned their judgment. But since Allison was born, I realize that now I have to be in charge. I ask lots of questions and insist on getting answers. I explore alternatives before I follow the advice of the first professional I visit, and when I have doubts about something, I seek another opinion. I realize that I am Allison's mother and I have to take over the reins and be her advocate."

CHAPTER 16

The Tough Decisions

"When Aletia was a baby, everything went so smoothly. We decided ahead of time that I would stay home for the first year and then put my baby in family child care. Then, when she was three, I would transfer her to a preschool. It's different with Beatrice. It's so difficult to plan for her future because we don't know what her future will bring."

Like Beatrice's parents, other parents of special-needs children are continually faced with tough decisions that no one can make for them. Often, the decisions they have to face can affect not only their special-needs child but the well-being of the whole family.

In this chapter, we look at some tough decisions that many families are faced with. Should we have another child? Should I go back to work? What kinds of child care arrangements should we make for our baby? What sorts of intervention programs should I consider? And how do I know if I've made the right choices?

SHOULD WE HAVE ANOTHER CHILD?

"My husband and I are at loggerheads. Gina is two years old; she has cerebral palsy. My husband is convinced that we should have another child. He feels that it would be good for Gina to have a little sister or brother. It would get her playing more. I disagree. I can't imagine having another child. I am worn to a frazzle with Gina—carrying her around everywhere and running from appointment to appointment. There is no way I could manage another child."

"We have the same problem in our family, only it's the other way around. I want to have another baby, and my husband is dead-set against it. I'm selfish. I'll admit it. I want another baby for me. I want to experience the joy of watching a baby smile when I sing a silly song or hearing a baby babble away when I walk into the room. My husband keeps saying, 'How do you know the next baby won't be deaf, too?'"

"I'm pregnant now, and I'm not at all sure we did the right thing, even though we went through the amniocentesis and this baby is going to be okay. I worry about what it's going to do to Timothy. How is he going to feel when his little sister walks and talks before he does?"

"I can answer that. Andrew was only sixteen months when Mercedes was born. Mercedes is the best thing that ever happened to this family. Andrew absolutely adores her, and my husband is like a new man. Sure, it's busy and the house looks like a disaster area half the time, but there's also laughter and silliness. And you know, now that we're not on top of him all the time, Andrew is doing much better."

"I could never do it. I could never have another child. I'd feel as if I were letting Terrence down. He needs all my time, all my energy, and all my love."

As we listen to parents struggling to make a decision, we recognize how complex an issue expanding the family can be. The fear, guilt, and self-doubt come to the surface again. "Am I capable of having a normal child?" "Will I still love this damaged baby if the new baby is healthy and well?" "Do I have the energy, strength, and desire to take care of another child?"

The decision about whether to have another child is a very personal one, and every family must grapple with it alone. Our best advice is to make no decisions until you have asked all the questions and talked out all the issues. Some of the questions can be resolved by talking with your spouse. Other questions may require input from your obstetrician, a pediatrician, or genetic counselor.

Consider the question of genetics. Is your baby's condition related to a genetic disorder? If so, have you had genetic counseling? A geneticist can investigate your family and determine the risk factor for a particular disorder. If you do fall into an at-risk category, the geneticist will suggest prenatal testing. Fortunately, over three thousand genetic defects can now be detected in the prenatal stage.

What are the chances, according to a professional, of your having another child with a similar condition? If your unborn child has a similar condition, could it be detected *in utero* in time for a therapeutic abortion? Would you have difficulty deciding whether to have an abortion if you did find out that your unborn baby had a genetic disorder?

A second consideration is whether you are currently prepared to take care of a new baby. Given the expenses you have at the moment, how much strain would a new baby place on your budget? When you take into consideration the amount of time and energy your baby is taking now, do you have the financial resources and the emotional reserve to meet the demands of a newborn? If you delay having a baby now and wait until you are older, will you be capable of conceiving? How long did it take you to become pregnant before?

Consider the effect of a new child on your handicapped baby. Have you talked with families with handicapped older children and nonhandicapped babies? Were there serious problems of jealousy? Did the older child enjoy the opportunity to play with an active younger sibling? If you had a healthy baby to take care of, would it be easier for you to accept your first baby's problem?

Look at the big picture. Imagine your family with the new baby. Would your family have an easier time or a more difficult time if there were one or more nonhandicapped children in the family?

SHOULD WE BOTH GO BACK TO WORK?

Parents agonize over the question of when and how to separate from the baby. They try to balance the needs of the baby and the needs of the rest of the family.

"I have to go back to work—I can't afford to stay home, but I don't know how I could ever leave my baby."

"I was really resistant at first, but things are so much better since I've gone back to work. Alex is in a special program. He's there during the day, and he's home nights and weekends. I come to him fresh, and he comes to me fresh, and we enjoy each other more."

"I just can't do it—put him in a program at two years old. I wouldn't send a normal kid to school that young, so how could I do it to Jeff? He wouldn't have any way of understanding what was happening to him."

"I was really against sending him to school so young, but you know, it's been great. I can't get over how many new things he has learned. The therapists are so good, and they have all kinds of toys and equipment. I couldn't possibly do as much at home."

Placing a very young child in a program is a big step, and it is very difficult to know the right thing to do. Often parents are caught, feeling that their baby is too young to go to a school, but that if they don't send him immediately, he may not get into the program. Before making a decision, ask yourself the following questions:

- Is there a high-quality program available in your area that would be appropriate for your baby?
- Does the pediatrician think that exposure to other children would affect your baby's health?
- If your baby were placed in a half-day or full-day program, what would you do while your baby was in the program? How beneficial would this activity be to you and the rest of your family?
- Do you enjoy being at home with your baby?
- Do you feel that your baby needs more stimulation or more therapy than you can provide at home?
- Are there other alternatives that you could explore, in which your baby could receive the stimulation she needs without being separated from you?

- If you keep your baby at home until he is older, will you have missed the chance of getting him into a good program?
- Do you feel pressured by friends or relatives to make a decision that you are not comfortable with?

HOW CAN WE SELECT A CHILD-CARE ARRANGEMENT?

"It took my wife and me a long time to decide how we would manage child care when I went back to work. Finally we made a great plan. My wife and I have different working hours so one of us is always home to take care of the baby."

"You know, we can honestly say that since our baby was born we have never left her with anyone but my mother—and even then never for more than two hours. Sometimes I wonder if that is good for her."

"I have to go back to work—I can't afford to stay home, but I don't know how I'll ever find someone who can take care of my baby."

"I was really worried about hiring an au pair for my baby while I was out working, but you know, it's been great. But I lucked out and got a really good au pair. I can't believe how well it has worked out."

A parent's decision about going to work often depends on whether or not she can find adequate child care.

Finding a caregiver situation is never easy, but the challenge is always more difficult when baby has special needs. A good starting point is to identify the options that are open to you, and then consider the pros and cons of each of these options. Once you have determined the option or options you would like to pursue, then you need to plan how you will go about it. It is helpful to make a list of the kinds of questions you need to ask as you pursue an option.

Sharing Child Care With Your Spouse

One option is to arrange your work schedules so that either you or your spouse is always at home with the baby.

Pros:

- Your baby will have the security of being in his own home, cared for by his own parents.
- You will not have to budget for child care.

Cons:

- This arrangement is difficult to work out and limits your ability to change positions.
- Husbands and wives drastically reduce their time together.
- Your baby, as well as your other child(ren), have fewer opportunities to do fun things with both parents.
- This type of schedule is difficult to maintain and can be exhausting.

Leaving the Baby in the Care of a Close Relative

You can select a relative, a parent, or a sibling with whom the question of trust is not an issue.

Pros:

- Your baby will not have to relate to a new person. Neither will he have to adjust to a new situation if the relative can come to your house. This is particularly important if your infant or toddler needs special equipment.

Cons:

- This leaves you without a backup if your selected relative is ill or has another engagement.

- Tensions may arise when you disagree on an aspect of caregiving. It is difficult to be critical of a relative who has agreed to take care of your infant.
- In this situation, a baby or toddler can develop a strong attachment to the person who cares for him during the day. This can create feelings of jealousy, dependency, and/or resentment.

Bringing a Caregiver Into Your Home

Pros:

- Your baby will remain in a familiar setting.
- You will have an opportunity to watch your baby with the caregiver before you leave them alone together.

Cons:

- Finding an excellent caregiver who is able to manage a special needs baby may be very difficult.
- You may have to try out more than one caregiver before you find the right one. The adjustments may be difficult for you and your baby.
- This does not provide you with a backup if your caregiver is ill or leaves the job without giving you adequate notice.
- This option can be expensive.

Here are some suggestions that can guide your selection of a caregiver.

1. Recruit from as large a pool as you can identify. This may include friends, members of a support group, your church or synagogue, an ad in a local newspaper, or a response to ads you place in a local newspaper.
2. Arrange face-to-face interviews with each respondent.
3. Describe the job to the applicants in full detail.
4. Develop a written list of questions for each respondent:

- Where did you work last, how long did you stay, and why did you terminate?
- May I check your recent references?
- Have you had experience working with special-needs babies?
- Do you have reliable transportation?
- Is your home situation and your health such that you are unlikely to be absent?
- What are your expectations in terms of time off and holidays?
- What kind of training and experience have you had with special-needs youngsters?
- Have you had a background check that included fingerprinting?

Placing Your Child in Family Child Care

Family child care is considered by many professionals a viable choice for infants, toddlers, and children with special needs.

Pros:

- You can select a situation where a family-child-care home is licensed by the county or state, and accredited by an early childhood professional organization.
- You can develop a personal relationship with the provider.
- You can visit the center before you enroll your infant or toddler.
- You can check references with parents and professionals.
- Your toddler will have the opportunity to interact with same age children.

Cons:

- It may be difficult to find a quality child-care home that is accessible and affordable.
- Your baby or toddler will have to adjust to being out of his familiar environment.
- Your selected caregiver may not be trained to meet the special needs of your baby.
- Your baby may be exposed to germs from the other children.

Questions to ask before you select a child care home

1. How long has your home been opened?
2. Are you licensed or registered? (Ask this question only if this is an option in your state.)
3. Are you a member of a child-care provider association?
4. May I telephone other parents who have used your services?
5. Do you have written contracts that you sign with new parents? (If yes, ask to see it.)
6. Have you had experience and/or training in working with special-needs infants and toddlers?
7. What coverage do you have in case of emergency?
8. How many children do you take care of at a time? What are their ages?
9. Do you have an assistant?

Placing Your Child in a Child-Care Program That Welcomes Special-Needs Children

Pros:

- You can rely on the center being open even if a caregiver is ill.
- You can find centers that are licensed by the county or state and accredited by an early childhood professional organization.
- You can visit the center before you enroll your infant or toddler.
- You can check references with parents and professionals.
- Your toddler will have the opportunity to interact with same-age children.

Cons:

- Quality centers can be too costly.
- Your toddler will be exposed to many children.

Questions to ask before deciding on a program:

1. What is your program's philosophy and curriculum?

2. Are typically developing children included in your program?

3. Are you licensed and/or accredited?

4. Do you have written policies?

5. What is your child-to-adult ratio?

6. How large are your groups?

7. What are the training and/or educational backgrounds of the teachers?

8. What kind of in-service training is provided to your teachers?

9. What means do you use to communicate with parents?

10. What percentage of your teachers is turned over in a year?

11. What are your observation policies?

Observations to make on your visit:

1. Is the center clean, organized, and attractive?

2. Do the teachers talk individually with the children?

3. Is the noise level reasonable?

4. Do the children seem happy?

Once you have thought out the pros and cons of the option or options you would like to investigate, consult your pediatrician to be sure that he or she feels that your child's health will not be jeopardized by the option you select.

CHAPTER 17

Making Informed Choices

"I went to this support group for parents of children with Down's syndrome. I couldn't believe how knowledgeable they were. They knew so much about specialists, medications, and therapeutic programs. I need to go back to college and take a crash course so that 1 can make some intelligent decisions."

In this chapter we look at decisions parents must make as they chart a course for their child. We begin by describing some of the specialists who work with special-needs children. Second, we describe different types of therapeutic programs and discuss some of the considerations that come into play when parents select a therapeutic option. Third, we look at the financial decisions that parents must make as they plan for their child's future.

SPECIALISTS FOR SPECIAL-NEEDS CHILDREN

Parents of babies with developmental problems are often bombarded by specialists. Sorting out the functions of the different specialists and knowing what services they perform is important and not always easy. In general, specialists who work with disabled babies fall into four categories: medical specialists, nonmedical professionals, therapists, and social work professionals.

Medical Specialists

Pediatricians

Pediatricians are physicians who specialize in the care of children. Because the pediatrician is responsible for monitoring the growth and development of the child, he or she is the lead member of the treatment team. Pediatricians are certified as specialists by the American Academy of Pediatrics.

Neonatologists

The neonatologist is a pediatric specialist who works in a hospital setting with newborn babies. He or she evaluates babies who are at risk and supervises their treatment. Hospitals with intensive care units for high-risk infants are likely to have one or more neonatologists on their staff. Neonatology is recognized as a specialty by the American Medical Association.

Neurologists

Neurologists are specialists in disorders associated with the central nervous system. They are likely to be called in by the neonatologist or the pediatrician when an infant is suspected of having some type of nervous dysfunction or seizure disorder such as cerebral palsy or epilepsy.

Orthopedic specialists

The orthopedic specialist is concerned with injuries or disorders associated with the muscular and skeletal systems. He may be called in to examine an infant suspected of having a birth defect or congenital disorder.

Opthalmologists

The ophthalmologist is a medical doctor who specializes in diseases and disorders associated with the visual system. Pediatricians will ask for a consultation if there is concern about the baby's vision, or if there are medical problems for which an examination of the eye could provide diagnostic information.

Geneticists

A geneticist is concerned with inherited or genetic disorders. The geneticist studies the chemical and physical nature of genes and chromosomes to determine how a disorder is inherited and the risks of its recurrence. Parents who are concerned about having a child with a genetic disorder can seek counseling at a genetic clinic.

Nonmedical Professionals

Optometrists

The optometrist is concerned with the diagnosis and treatment of visual problems. He or she measures visual competency and prescribes glasses when needed. The optometrist is not a medical doctor and does not treat eye disease.

Audiologists

The audiologist is concerned with the measurement of hearing. He or she uses a variety of procedures to determine whether an infant or child has any type of hearing loss or problem. When a hearing loss is detected, the audiologist may prescribe a hearing aid. Audiologists are certified by the American Speech-Language-Hearing Association (ASHA).

Psychologists

A psychologist is a nonmedical therapist trained to observe and measure behavior and treat emotional or behavioral disorders. Psychologists are responsible for assessing the baby's developmental progress and for helping the family with child management skills. The American Psychological Association is the professional association that certifies psychologists.

Therapists

Speech and language therapists

Speech and language therapists are concerned with the identification and treatment of speech and language problems involving the ability to reproduce language sounds, interpret spoken language, and use language to convey meaning. They are also concerned with potential speech problems that may manifest themselves originally as disorders in chewing and swallowing. Speech and language pathologists are licensed to practice by their state and are certified professionally by the American Speech-Language-Hearing Association (ASHA).

Physical therapists

The physical therapist is concerned with the child's strength, coordination, and motor development. In addition to physical therapy, the physical therapist can provide information about a child's muscle tone that has diagnostic value. Physical therapists can also help a family identify adaptive equipment, such as special highchairs, infant seats, and walking and standing boards that are appropriate for a particular child. Physical therapists are licensed by the state and certified by the American Physical Therapy Association (APTA).

Occupational therapists

The occupational therapist is trained to work with a child in the activities of daily living. Occupational therapists help children attain self-help skills. They are licensed by the state and certified by the American Occupational Therapy Association (AOTA).

Behavioral analysts

Behavioral analysts are professionals licensed by the state who are concerned with the diagnosis and treatment of behavioral problems. They help families, educators, and professionals within institutions to determine the underlying causes of undesirable behaviors and initiate therapeutic programs.

Social-Service Professionals

Hospital social workers

The social worker is a trained professional with expertise in working with families. In pediatric hospitals or hospitals with neonatal or pediatric units, the social worker is usually a member of the treatment team. Part of the social worker's job is to take a family history, seeking information that might be helpful in understanding the baby's problem or in planning for follow-up services. Another part of the social worker's role is to help the family work out problems and identify resources.

Community social workers

Social workers who do not work in hospitals are usually associated with public or private agencies. In addition to providing family therapy, the social worker may lead a family support group or help a family develop a treatment plan. Social workers are licensed by the state and certified by the National Association of Social Workers (NASW).

SELECTING A SPECIALIST

"I don't know how I lived through that morning. I had a C-section, and Marty came in my room. We didn't even get a chance to talk to each other when this doctor came in. I asked him how the baby was and he started beating around the bush— like he didn't have the guts to tell us. Thank God my husband was there. He looked him straight in the eye and told him, 'This is our baby, and we want to know the straight story.'"

One of the most difficult tasks for parents with a disabled child is to identify specialists with the expertise and personality characteristics to meet their special needs. The most common way to identify a specialist is to ask your pediatrician to make a referral. This method assures a good flow of communication between the specialist and the pediatrician, but there are disadvantages. If you are uncomfortable with the professional selected by your pediatrician, it may be harder to make a change. Fortunately, you have several viable alternatives.

- Ask your pediatrician to recommend more than one specialist so that you can make a choice.
- Compile a list of the qualified specialists in your area who can provide the service you are seeking. Depending on the type of specialist you are looking for, consult the County Medical Association, the Community Service Council, the state or county professional associations, the Yellow Pages, a local or regional hospital, a university or medical school, the school system, and/or the health and rehabilitative service departments in your area.
- If you belong to a parent support group, talk to different parents about the specialists they are using. Ask specific questions

about their availability to parents and their rapport with children. Ask the parents to describe how the specialist benefited their children. Use the information from the other parents to adjust your list of specialists.

- When your list has been finalized, call to set up an interview with each specialist. The interview can take place over the telephone or in the specialist's office. Check the fee schedule and the insurance assignment policy with the receptionist before making the appointment.

- During your interview with the specialist, provide as much information as you can about your child. If your child has an unusual problem or condition, make sure that the professional feels comfortable about treating your baby. As you talk with the specialist, keep in touch with your own feelings. If you have confidence in the person and would like to work with him or her, you have probably made the right choice.

DEVELOPING RELATIONSHIPS WITH PROFESSIONALS

"It was like yelling down a dark tunnel and no one was there."

Because having a handicapped baby is an emotionally charged situation, it is not surprising to find that parents are often angry with the physician who was involved in the original diagnosis. Sometimes the message is confused with the messenger, and parents project their anger on the bearer of bad tidings. Sometimes doctors who are charged with the responsibility of delivering an unwelcome message let their own discomfort affect the delivery of the message. Parents are occasionally too frightened to hear what the doctor has to tell them, and some doctors don't listen to parents' legitimate concerns.

As different parents talked to us about their experiences with professionals, we realized that some of the negative experiences could have been avoided if parents and professionals had given more credence to the parent-professional partnership. Professionals would do well to abandon the "mightier than thou" attitude and recognize that parents have spent a very long time observing their own children; they know more about their own children than anyone else. Parents can benefit by taking a much more "in charge" position when they discuss treatment with the professional. The following list of suggestions may be useful to parents who want to take a more active role in planning for their baby:

- Set up a meeting to talk about the baby when your spouse can be with you and when the baby can be left at home.
- Make sure that the therapist you are visiting receives the reports on your baby from other therapists before the visit. As an extra safeguard, bring copies of the reports with you.
- Write down the questions you have before you come to an meeting. It is easy to forget once you are there.
- Keep a diary of activities associated with your baby. Record telephone calls, prescriptions, tests, and office meetings.
- Be businesslike with the therapist; ask about fees, credentials, and meeting policies. You are the consumer.
- If you want another opinion, or if you want to change therapists, don't make up excuses. Tell the truth: "We're concerned about Tina's progress, and we'd like to take her to the medical center."
- If you don't understand what the therapist means, ask him or her to describe it again in different words. You have a right to know.
- Ask the therapist for written material. It will help you review what you have been told and share information with relatives who were not at the meeting.
- At the end of an meeting with a therapist, review what was said during the interview, including actions that must be taken: "I'm going to call you on Wednesday to report Gina's reaction to the medicine. You're going to call Dr. S. to make arrangements for the X ray."

- If you feel that you did not get all the information you needed in a meeting, ask for a second meeting.
- Make a special effort to be on time for all meetings. If you have to cancel a meeting, do it as far in advance as you can.

Some of the suggestions we have offered may seem to violate the traditional dynamics of the patient-doctor relationship. The goal is not to undermine the relationship, but to strengthen it. As you assume the role of partner to the therapist, you share your knowledge and expertise, and your baby comes out the winner.

CHOOSING A TREATMENT APPROACH

Parents have to grapple with a confusing array of treatment options. Whether or not you have a pediatrician who is coordinating your baby's treatment, as parents, you are the final decision makers. Difficult decisions are up to you. Should you change professionals? Should you try a different therapy? Should you agree to give your baby a medication with the possibility of side effects? Parents struggling to make the right decision find themselves caught in dilemmas that are difficult to resolve.

"I read about this program that was developed in Philadelphia. My pediatrician is dead-set against it, but I feel we have nothing to lose."

"The school wants our daughter on medication. They say that when she takes it she is much more subdued and easier to manage, but I just hate to give it to her. She's really out of it when she's on the medication."

"The neurologist that we go to is absolutely set against physical therapy. He says that Tina is too young and it wouldn't do her any good. But I've seen other babies like Tina who have really been helped by a physical therapist, and even if the therapist

did no more than show me how to carry Tina or what sorts of equipment to get for her, I feel it would be helpful."

The dilemmas that these parents describe are very real. Part of the problem is that decisions are seldom clear-cut, and in many situations even the professionals do not have the answers. There are professionals who are misinformed or unethical who continue to make promises that cannot be substantiated. Often it is difficult to distinguish between false claims and genuine breakthroughs, and parents who will do anything in the world to help their baby are in a vulnerable position.

"Sometimes I feel as if I am being tossed from pillar to post. My pediatrician sends me to a specialist, and the specialist sends me to one or two other specialists. Each of the specialists has a different opinion about what I should do next, and I feel as if I'm further away from knowing what to do than when I started out on the circuit."

Making decisions that affect your baby requires careful deliberation. As you go through your deliberations, take into account the following.

Before putting your child in a program or on a treatment regime that your pediatrician questions, investigate the program carefully. "It can't do any harm, and it may do some good" is not a strong enough rationale. Any program that takes time and money and promises benefits it cannot deliver is doing some degree of harm.

Make sure that the people who are offering the program and treatment have the appropriate licenses. Call the local or state branch of the professional association that regulates the specialty area of the treatment. If it is a medical specialty, for instance, call the American Medical Association. Ask for the references for published research on the program or treatment. Testimonials that are a part of the program's publicity are not useful.

Talk with other parents whose children are currently in the program. Talk to parents who have left the program because they were not satisfied.

If there is a special-interest group associated with your baby's condition, speak with a knowledgeable person within the association and ask about the program. Request literature or references. Ask for an interview before beginning treatment and before putting money down. Make sure to find out the cost of the treatment and the expected duration. Call your insurance company and find out if the treatment offered is covered by insurance.

There are situations in which a particular treatment or therapy meets all professional standards but may not be appropriate for your child. If you do not feel comfortable following your pediatrician's advice regarding a treatment or therapy issue, you may want to request a consultation for a second opinion.

It is extremely important to be up-front with your baby's doctor before you arrange for a consultation. "My wife and I have given this a lot of thought. Before we go ahead with the treatment you have recommended we would like to have her seen by Dr. Z." In most situations you will find that your primary physician appreciates your honesty and will arrange for or support the referral.

CHANGING A SPECIALIST OR THERAPIST

Changing professionals is always difficult, and many parents find they want to make the change without letting the original professional know.

This is bad policy for several reasons. First, reputable professionals are unlikely to agree to see a child unless an appropriate referral has been made. Second, it is always important to have all the records sent on ahead before you see a new professional. You don't want your baby to have unnecessary tests or be given a treatment that has already proven unsatisfactory. Third, you don't want to burn your bridges. You may want to go back to the original professional.

When you decide that you would like to change professionals, be honest about the reason. "I would like to take my baby to

_____. They have special expertise with my baby's condition." "I appreciate all you've done for the baby. For financial reasons, I would like to change to _____."

DECIDING ON MEDICATIONS AND ALTERNATIVE TREATMENTS

Decisions related to medication are generally made by the physician. It is up to parents, however, to ask in advance about side effects and to watch for and report unexpected reactions as soon as they occur. If you are uncomfortable about giving your child a medication that your pediatrician has prescribed, you may want to consider an outside consultation.

In some situations, the pediatrician will prescribe a medication on a trial basis. This is particularly true with medications prescribed to control hyperactivity. If your doctor has prescribed medication on a trial basis, begin by administering the medication at home where you can keep a record of behavioral changes and side effects. If your baby is fine at home without medication but is overactive or out of control when you send him to school, it is a good idea to go to the school and observe his behavior. Sometimes a child's behavior is quite different when there are other children around. It may be better to modify or change your child's program rather than to place him in a program where he requires medication.

From time to time you may read about a medication or other treatment regimen that your own physician has not prescribed. Show the article to your pediatrician. He may say that he hasn't heard of it but will make inquiries. Or he may say that the treatment is effective for some disorders but could be harmful to your child. Or the treatment could be perfectly safe for your child, but ineffective. Unless the pediatrician is fully convinced that the treatment you read about cannot hurt your baby, it is not a good idea to go against his or her advice.

PLANNING FOR THE FUTURE

Perhaps the most difficult and sensitive area to talk about is planning for the future. For many parents, just talking about the future is like giving up on their child.

"I don't want to hear about insurance policies or trust funds or how to make out my will. I can't even think about what I should make for dinner. Besides, I refuse to be that glum about things. Sure, my baby has a problem, but that doesn't mean he has a life sentence. I'm not giving up on Jimmy."

"Planning ahead doesn't mean you're giving up. You don't buckle your seat belt because you're planning to have an accident, and you don't make out a will because you think you're going to die. What worries me is if something did happen to Fred and me, what would happen to Gina?"

Unfortunately, even when parents do want to plan ahead, it is difficult to know whom to listen to and how to select among options. The best advice that we can give you is to be as informed as possible.

- If you have not already worked out your insurance, go to an insurance agent and find out about the pros and cons of different insurance plans. Do not select a plan that does not cover existing conditions.
- Talk to an accountant about setting up a trust fund for your children. Inquire about the tax benefits of different kinds of funds.
- Make out a will in which you assign custody of your child to the people you feel are most capable of taking care of her. Make sure to rewrite your will if there are important changes in your family or financial situation.
- Consult with a lawyer on a regular basis to keep in touch with changes in the law.

Fortunately, most difficult decisions do not have to be made quickly. There is almost always time to gather information, consult knowledgeable people, and weigh alternatives carefully. Although there is never a guarantee that you will make the perfect choice, you will not go wrong too many times if the decisions you make are carefully thought out and informed.

CHAPTER 18

Your Role as an Advocate

"I have never been a political animal. Sure, I vote, but that's as far as I go. My friends in the Down's support group are always bugging me to write a letter to a legislature or make a phone call to the White House. I tell them I'll do it but I can never find a free minute."

Although you may be reluctant to spend time on advocacy, it is one of the responsibilities that parents of exceptional children are often forced to assume. In addition to becoming an advocate for your own child you will be called on by other parents to advocate for laws that would benefit all special-needs children. Much of the legislation that supports exceptional children has been inspired by parent groups that have learned from firsthand experience how critical it is for society to protect its vulnerable children.

We begin this chapter by crafting a "Bill of Rights" for parents of special-needs children. Then we describe ways in which parents can advocate for their child. In the final section of the chapter we describe ways in which parents can serve as advocates for all children with special needs.

A BILL OF RIGHTS FOR ALL PARENTS OF CHILDREN WITH SPECIAL NEEDS

The Right to Know

"It took weeks for the doctor to get me my son's records. I realize he was trying to protect me, but I don't think he realized how painful it was waiting for an answer. Once I know the truth I can accept it and go on with my life."

As a parent you have a right to find out all you can about your child's condition. Whenever you request them, you should be able to secure hospital, physician, therapist, and school records. It is never the right of a practitioner or other professional to withhold information from you, even if she feels you are not ready to receive it. It is up to you to decide what you are ready to hear.

The Right to Ask Questions

"I know I should have asked more questions. I was just too embarrassed to tell the doctor that I couldn't understand his jargon."

Sometimes your physician will use jargon without realizing that you do not understand what she is trying to tell you. At other times she may use jargon because it is difficult for her to find ordinary words to explain what she is trying to tell you, or because the ordinary words sound too blunt. Whatever the reason, it is appropriate for you to let her know that you don't understand and ask her for a clearer explanation. Another concern that parents have described is a fear that they are taking up too much of the doctor's time. It is always appropriate to tell a physician that you have some questions to ask him. If he tells you he is pressed for time, ask if you could make an appointment to talk with him at a more convenient time. When you come back be armed with written questions. It is easy to get nervous and forget what you wanted to know. Use this same strategy with a therapist or a teacher.

The Right to Make Treatment Decisions

"My husband read about this new treatment that can cure a child of autism. We're thinking of trying it. After all, we have nothing to lose. "

No intervention or medical decisions should be made lightly either by parents, physicians, therapists, or educators. In most medical situations, decisions about treatment are clear-cut. A hot appendix should be removed, and a broken arm should be set. However, even in medicine there are many situations where the course of treatment is controversial, and it is the responsibility of parents to exercise their decision-making right. With special-needs children, a treatment with clear-cut benefits may have physical or emotional risks, and a highly touted new medication may have serious side effects that are not immediately apparent. When a course of treatment is controversial, parents are wise to consult with other professionals before making a decision. This is particularly true when parents are considering alternative treatments or experimental drugs.

The Right to Protect Your Rights

The first step to protecting your rights is to become familiar with the legislation that defines these rights. IDEA (Individuals with Disabilities Education Act) is the most comprehensive piece of legislation that spells out the rights of special needs children. This law makes a clear statement that every child with a handicapping condition has the right to a free education in the least restrictive environment. ADA (Americans with Disabilities Act) describes the rights of all people with handicaps. It includes accessibility codes that require that all buildings open to the public have wheelchair access. Once parents are familiar with the rights of their child as prescribed by law, they are in a position to recognize and protest if these rights are violated.

The Right to the Pursuit of Happiness

Parenting a child with special needs takes work and dedication. It is all too easy to take your responsibility so seriously that you deny yourself the right to have fun. Remember that the well-being of your family depends on your physical and emotional health.

THE IMPORTANCE OF RECORD KEEPING

"You know, it's a funny thing. I was faithful about keeping a baby book on my first child. I kept track of every little thing she accomplished, and my husband took enough photos of her to practically paper the walls. Unfortunately, Colton's baby book is full of blank pages. When the doctor asked me when he first turned over, I couldn't even tell him. I guess a part of it was, I didn't want to admit to myself how slowly he was developing."

One of the primary reasons for keeping a baby book is to keep a record of fun events and happy times. Particularly with a first baby, there is something to write about almost every day. When your child is old enough to understand, she will love it when you tell her stories about when she was a baby. When we have a premature or other special-needs child, we may have neither the time nor the will to record daily events. But even if we do not fill out a baby book, we need to develop a record-keeping system that allows us to keep track of important information.

One way of setting up a record-keeping system is to keep separate files for different types of information.

Medical Files

In your medical file you could keep listings of medical appointments that describe the reason for the visit, the outcome, suggested treatments and prescribed medications, and any allergic reactions to the medications. Your file should also include copies of all test reports and an updated record of medications and their dosages. In addition, you may want to include abstracts of articles that relate to your child's condition.

Therapy Files

Like the medical file, your therapy file should include a calendar of therapeutic appointments with the name of the therapist, progress reports, and any recommendations for home activities. It should also include abstracts from articles and reports that focus on your child's condition.

Progress Files

This file should include a biweekly or monthly update on your child's behavior, health, and developmental status. Depending on your child's condition, it could include food intake, sleep patterns, seizures, positive and negative behaviors, mood, energy level, social behavior, play behavior, and developmental achievements.

SERVING AS A CHILD ADVOCATE

"I don't have time to care for my own baby. I certainly don't have time to worry about anyone else's problems. Maybe when Marvin is older I'll change my mind."

Although they might not have time to be active when their child is still a baby, parents of children with special needs are the most com-

mitted advocates for exceptional children. The experience of living with a special-needs child gives you first-hand knowledge of the kinds of obstacles that parents have to face and makes you keenly aware of the kinds of accommodations that parents have a right to demand.

Advocating for children can be accomplished in different ways. Even with very little time you can make a phone call or write a letter to your senator. As your child gets older, your days won't be quite as busy and you will find new ways of taking on an advocacy role.

- Study the laws, policies, and issues related to rights and resources for special-needs children.
- Become aware of current issues that require legislative action. When a policy is controversial, be familiar with the arguments both for and against the policy.
- Join advocacy groups that share your concerns about a certain issue.
- Become a member of a national organization for exceptional children.
- Become knowledgeable about resources within your own and other states.
- Talk with a political strategist to identify ways of getting your issues heard.
- Get to know your legislators in person. You will be surprised how responsive they will be to a persistent and well-informed voter.
- Get to know your legislator's aides. They are most likely to have the ear of their legislator.
- Maintain contact with the media.
- Keep track of the voting record of your senators and representatives. Thank them when they support a position that you have been advocating.
- Learn about the fiscal implications of policies and issues you support.
- Participate in fund-raising drives that raise money for advocacy.
- Arrange for a field trip to your state capital with fellow advocates when an issue you are concerned about is being debated in Congress.
- Participate in activities that galvanize public opinion.

CHAPTER 19

Coping With Illness and Hospitalization

Coping with a baby's illness is difficult for any parent. For babies who are developmentally at risk, even a minor illness can be frightening. One parent whose baby was subject to ear infections said to us, "I know this sounds silly, but when Benjamin gets an earache I keep wishing that I could suffer for him." In this part of the chapter we will talk about effective ways of taking care of an ill child, preparing a child for hospitalization, and caring for a child when he is in the hospital.

HOME CARE FOR A CHILD WHO IS ILL

When babies are struck with an illness, parents find themselves on twenty-four-hour duty. Some babies will not be quiet unless they are in their parent's arms, and parents may find themselves walking the floor day and night. Other babies cope with illness by sleeping long hours, sometimes putting parents in a quandary about whether to awaken the baby to give him his medicine. Another problem parents face is knowing when to call the pediatrician. On the one hand, they want to keep the physician informed of any change in their baby's condition. On the other hand, they feel that if they call the pediatrician too often, she may not respond quickly enough if they have a serious problem.

Obviously there are no hard and fast rules for caring for an ill child, but here are some suggestions that you may want to consider.

- Don't be afraid that you will spoil your baby by constant attention. One lesson she will learn from her illness is that her parents are there when she needs them.
- Take your baby with you when you go to a different room. If she still fits in a portable crib, this is a good time to use it. You can also use a bassinet, a cradle, a stroller, or a carriage.
- If your baby is on medication, be sure to introduce it when she is relatively quiet and relaxed. Special baby medicine spoons that you can buy in the drugstore are worth trying out.
- If your baby has a security blanket, a favorite doll, or stuffed animal, make sure that it is always on hand.
- If your child's beloved object gets wet or soiled, tell your child that you are going to give the blanket or stuffed animal a nice warm bath. Avoid sneaking the beloved object away when your child is asleep. Some babies have an uncanny way of knowing when the beloved object is gone.
- Relax about therapy when your child is not feeling well. Two or three days of not doing exercises will not make a difference.
- If your child is interested in playing, find toys that are easy to manipulate. When children are ill, they are unlikely to want a toy that presents them with a challenge.
- Don't hesitate to call your pediatrician if you have a concern. No one knows your baby as well as you do and if something worries you, you should discuss it with your pediatrician.

When your child is recuperating from an illness, you may find yourself having to cope with a host of new problems. Your baby may surprise you by being whiny and demanding, by refusing food or medication, or by being angry and difficult to manage. Parents are torn between giving in to their baby because he has been ill and disciplining their child because they don't want him to be spoiled.

Fortunately, these negative behaviors are usually short-lived. After a few difficult days your child is likely to be himself again.

PREPARING YOUR CHILD FOR A HOSPITAL STAY

Whether your child is going to the hospital for a surgical procedure, a diagnostic work-up, or medical treatment, hospitalization can be frightening for parents. Even if the child is going to the hospital for a routine procedure, parents worry about the remote possibility that something might go wrong. They are also concerned about the impact of a hospital stay on their child's psyche. These fears may be fueled by their own memories of a traumatic hospital experience. Fortunately, in recent years hospitals have become much more family-friendly. Most children's hospitals make accommodations for parents who want to stay in the room with their children. Many are equipped with playrooms and include on their staff child-life specialists who help children and their families cope with the hospital experience.

Hospital Policies and Procedures

Before you bring your child to the hospital, contact a hospital administrator to find out all you can about the policies and procedures that will affect your child's hospital stay. Here are some of the questions you may want to ask.

- What accommodations are made for parents who choose to stay in the hospital with their baby? Does the hospital provide parents with a bed or a recliner so that they can sleep in the room with their child? Is there a place where parents can shower and change their clothes? What arrangements are made for parent meals? Can parents accompany their child when he goes into a treatment or pre-op room? Are parents allowed to go into the recovery room?

- What kind of room will my child have? Will he have a private room or will he have a roommate? How are the rooms set up? Is there a television and/or a VCR in the room?
- What are the visiting policies? What are the visiting hours? How many people are allowed at a time? Are there any restrictions on bringing food or particular toys? Are siblings allowed to visit?
- Does the hospital have a pediatric floor? Is there a playroom my child can visit? Are his siblings allowed in the playroom? What hours is the playroom opened? Is the playroom staffed? What kinds of toys are in the playroom? Is there a life specialist who visits with the children and the family?
- What are the admission procedures? What procedures do parents follow in order to admit their child? How long a wait is there likely to be before a child is assigned a room?

KEEPING INFORMED ABOUT YOUR CHILD

In addition to finding out about hospital policies and procedures, it is important to find out as much as you can about the treatment, diagnostic work-up, or surgical procedure your child is going to receive. These questions should be addressed to the pediatrician and/or medical specialists who will be treating your child.

- Why is this particular operation or procedure being performed? What are the expected benefits? What are the risks of not doing it? What are the possible complications? Is there any literature that describes the procedure?
- What type of anesthetic or sedation will be used? How long will the surgery take? Can parents accompany the child into the

treatment room, pre-op room, and/or recovery room? How will my child feel after the surgery? What type of pain medication will my child be given? When can I find out the results?

PREPARING YOUR CHILD FOR THE HOSPITAL EXPERIENCE

Once you have been informed about hospital policies and have found out about the procedure or surgery, you are ready to prepare your household and your child for a stay in the hospital. The way you prepare your child for a hospital stay depends on your child's age and language proficiency.

Preparing a Baby or Nonverbal Child

With a very young child who has not learned to talk, the best way to prepare for surgery is to remain calm and upbeat when you are with him. Babies are very tuned in to their parent's mood. If you act anxious and upset, your baby will be anxious and upset. It is a good idea not to talk about the impending hospitalization when the baby is with you. Babies may recognize when their parents are tense or troubled, even when they don't understand their words.

Preparing a Toddler

Toddlers, even if they have acquired speech, have difficulty understanding what it means to go to the hospital. If the hospital permits it, it is a good idea to let your toddler visit the hospital before she is admitted. Parents choose to tell children about the hospitalization in different ways and at different times. For some children, it is better to tell them a while in advance, allowing them time to get used to the idea. For other children, telling them too soon either makes them feel that it isn't going to happen or gives them time to build up their fears.

- Be matter-of-fact when you tell your child about the hospital-ization. If the hospital permits it, take him on a tour of the hospital. If they do not permit a tour, drive to the hospital and play for a while in the lobby. The thought of going to a hospital is not quite as scary if you know what a hospital looks like.
- Using a toy doctor's kit as a prop, play out a hospital scene. Pretend with your child that her doll or stuffed animal is in the hospital. Let your toddler listen to the doll's chest with the stethoscope, take the doll's temperature, and give the doll a shot.
- Let your child help you pack her suitcase. Ask her to choose her favorite pajamas, a set of clothes, and her favorite toys and books.
- After your toddler packs her suitcase, let her help you pack your suitcase. That will help reassure her that you will be with her in the hospital.

Preparing the Siblings

If your toddler has older siblings, explain to them that their little sister has to go to the hospital and that you are going with her. Answer all their questions as honestly as possible, but be careful not to frighten them. Remember that young children may think that any-thing that happens to their siblings might also happen to them. Here are some other ways of preparing your older child or children.

- Wait until two or three days before your scheduled hospital stay to tell your children about it. If you tell them too early, their fears can build up. They will worry both about what will hap-pen to their sibling and about your going away and leaving them at home.

- Tell your children about the arrangements you have made for their care. Be very specific.
- If children are allowed to visit the hospital, explain the visiting procedures to your children. Take them to a store and let them choose a present they can bring to their sibling.

Other Preparations

- Post the hospital number and the number of a friend who could be called in an emergency near every telephone before you leave the house.
- Select little gifts that can be given to the child at different times throughout the stay.
- Be sure that your child brings a doll or favorite stuffed animal to the hospital. Most hospitals will put a bracelet on a favorite doll and allow your child's doll to accompany him to the operating room.
- Bring a number of different toys, games, and books to keep your child busy and distracted: The fewer the pieces, the easier to manage. Look for favorite books, inset puzzles, coloring books, drawing tablets like Etch-A-Sketch, hand-held electronic games, busy boxes, and bubble sets.
- Some children are more comfortable if they have their own pillow in the hospital.
- When you pack your own suitcase, include clothes that are comfortable and washable. Bring along a sweater because hospitals are usually kept cold. You may also want to bring along your own pillow and some light reading. If there is a VCR in the room, include some tapes that your child enjoys. You might also bring a tape recorder and your children's favorite audiotapes.

WHEN YOUR CHILD IS IN THE HOSPITAL

Make certain that you and your spouse or another family member stays with your child. The hardest part of being in a hospital is being separated from parents, brothers, sisters, and pets and from the comfort and familiarity of home. A child's hospitalization can rob both you and your child of a sense of control, leaving you feeling helpless. Your major goal in the hospital must be to give your child back his sense of power and to add cheerfulness and fun even when you are feeling down.

Befriend the Hospital Staff

Get to know the names of different members of the staff. If your child is going to be in the hospital for more than a few days, bring a box of candy or a basket of fruit to the nursing station. Do as much of the routine care of your child as you can. Your child will be more comfortable if you are the one who gives her a bath, feeds her, and gives her medication. It will also relieve the nurses.

Give Your Child Choices

If your child is old enough to let you know his preferences, take every opportunity to let him make decisions. "Do you want to wear your Pooh Bear pajamas or your train pajamas? Would you like apple juice or cranberry juice? Would you like to color or blow bubbles? Would you like to drink your medicine from a cup or would you rather have it mixed in applesauce?"

Decorate Your Child's Room

Bring pictures of the family and the family pets and put them on the table. Decorate the walls and windows with posters, pictures, and get-well cards. Encourage your friends to continue sending cards.

Prepare Your Child for an Operation or Painful Procedure by Acting Out What's Going to Happen

For example, you might give his doll a shot, make it cry, and then comfort it. Rather than saying to your child, "the doctor will put you to sleep (which may make a child afraid to go to sleep)," say "the doctor will give you medicine that will make you feel sleepy."

Encourage Visitors, but Not Too Often

Both you and your child will enjoy having visitors, so long as they don't stay too long or interrupt when you are playing with your child.

Help Your Child Cope With Pain and Discomfort

Young children and certainly babies don't tell you in words when they are not feeling well. If your child starts to get fussy when you are playing with her, it may mean that she is tired or uncomfortable. Try changing the activity. Put on a tape or read her favorite story. It may be time to rub her back, hold her in your arms, or lay on the bed beside her.

Change the Smell of the Room

Many children are stressed by hospital smells. Try using a potpourri or aromatherapy.

BE AN ADVOCATE FOR YOUR CHILD

It is both your responsibility and your right to assume control of your child's treatment. Be sure you know what kinds of medication your child is receiving and what kinds of treatment regimes and procedures are planned. Don't ever hesitate to ask questions. You have the right to know about your child's condition and treatment and the right to refuse a procedure if you are concerned about its efficacy.

- Ask about pain medications and medicine to control nausea. There are usually several options. There is also a cream that can be applied to the skin a half-hour before a procedure that has a numbing effect.
- Keep a log of the medications your child has received and his reaction to these medications. You may want this information at a later time.
- Take photos of the hospital playroom, your child's room, and the staff who took care of your child. Showing these photos to your toddler when you get home will help him process the hospital experience.
- If your child refuses hospital food, find out if you can bring food from home.
- Find out in advance about discharge procedures. What time of day will your child be discharged? Do you have to pay a hospital bill or get clearance from the finance office first?
- Ask for a list of the phone numbers of all the physicians who treated your child. Remember that you have the option to get a copy of your child's records and X rays if you want a second opinion.
- Be sure to obtain a copy of your discharge instructions before you leave the hospital.

GOING HOME

"Theresa was like an angel when she was in the hospital. She smiled and babbled to the nurses and didn't even cry when they put the IV in her foot. But the day she came home, she was impossible. She screamed every time I left the room, spit out her medicine, and wouldn't let her Grandmother anywhere near her!"

Theresa's behavior is not at all unusual. When a baby is in the hospital, his parent's major concern, and rightly so, is to minimize his or her child's pain and fear. When the baby is better and comes home from the hospital, the rules are likely to change. Parents stop responding to every whim and expect their baby to settle into the old routines. Babies, on the other hand, are not ready to accept these changes. They have been through a traumatic experience and they desperately want to be coddled.

- This is a good time to invite friends and relatives in to help. Many of your friends and relatives may be anxious to help out and are waiting to be invited.
- Talk to your toddler's doll or stuffed animal about the hospital experience, "Big Bear, are you happy to be back home? You were a very big boy in the hospital. Let's take your hospital bracelet off your wrist."
- Put the photos you took at the hospital in an album. Show your child the album and talk about the photos. Even if your toddler isn't talking yet, retelling the story of the hospital experience will help her understand what happened.

Young children are remarkably adaptable. An illness or hospitalization that has been handled proactively is not likely to leave emotional scars. As children replay or retell the event, they can focus on the special gifts they got or the games they played, the people they met, the new words they learned, the equipment and procedures that intrigued them, and their own heroic role. The pain of the operation or illness becomes less salient in their memory.

Some Final Thoughts

In the Introduction to *In Time and With Love,* I talked about my daughter Debbie and the difficult times we went through. Although I urge parents not to try miracle cures as I did, I realize what it is like to feel desperate and grasp at any straw. Through the years I have continued to talk with parents. I have recognized when parents are blaming themselves for their child's problem and have repeated over and over that some things just happen and it is not their fault. At the same time I have told parents about the special joys their handicapped child can bring and about the real progress that continues to be made in early intervention, treatment, and adaptive technology.

I am the mother of five children. Each of my four older children has been enriched by having Debbie as a sister. Debbie brings her own brand of humor, which her siblings continue to appreciate. And she has made advocates of them all. Even more important, Debbie has helped her family recognize that success can be defined in different ways. When Debbie was a young child, I wrote a book called *Run Away Little Girl.* I described how all the family joined the struggle to help Debbie learn to walk. My "runaway little girl" never overcame her physical handicaps and never learned to walk. But Debbie is a success. She has learned to appreciate who she is and has discovered ways to find happiness within her limitations.

As I talk to families about their hopes and fears about their children's futures, I cannot promise them a rose garden. But I can say from experience that children with special needs can be a source of joy and celebration.

Dr. Marilyn Segal and Debbie Segal

Index

A

abortions, 188
ADA (Americans with Disabilities Act), 213-14
advocacy role, 211, 229
   Bill of Rights for parents of special-needs children, 212-14
   child advocate, serving as, 215-17, 226-27
   hospital stays, during, 226-27
   record keeping, importance of, 214-15
   rights, protection of, 213-14
aggressive behaviors, 79-80
anger of parents, 12-13
apnea, 71
attachment behavior, 95-96
audiologists, 200
autism, 30
awareness
   language development. *See* language development
   Making Discoveries stage of development, 101-8
   mirrors, 95, 102, 131, 132
   modulated stimulation, 48-49
   Reaching Out stage of development, 94-101
   sounds, attentiveness to, 127-29
   states of, 44-47
   stress, signs of, 52, 90-91
   Tuning In stage of development, 88-94

B

baby slings, 47
balance, 118, 119, 120
bathing, 50, 71, 74, 90
behavior problems, 74
   aggressive behaviors, 79-80
   atypical behaviors, 80-81
   biting, 81-82
   getting into everything, 82-83
   hitting, 79-80
   impulsiveness, 75-78
   "no" and "yes," 76-78
   poor social skills, 83-84
   temper tantrums, 78-79
   transitions, resistance to, 83
Bill of Rights for parents, 212-14
biting, 81-82
bonding, 88-94. *See also* Tuning In stage
books and reading, 136, 162, 175-76
bottle-feeding, 57
   weaning, 69-70
bounce chairs, 47
bowel movements, 52
breast-feeding, 53-57
   weaning, 69-70
brothers and sisters. *See* siblings

C

cardiac abnormalities, 8
cerebral palsy, 7, 23, 24, 28, 49, 57, 60-61, 167, 185

child care, 190-91
    close relative as caregiver, 192-93
    family child care, 194-95
    in-home caregiver, 193-94
    sharing care with spouse, 192
    special-needs children, for, 195-96
choices. *See* decision making
chores and responsibility, 78
chronic medical problems, 8
clonus, 61
colic, 59-60
crawling, 118-19, 121-22
creativity, 157-58
    art experiences and activities, 161-63
    music, rhythm, and movement, 158-61
    pretend play, 105-7, 164-66
crying
    calming difficulties, 49-51
    responding to, 43-47
    temperamental differences, 47-51

D

decision making, 184, 185
    abortions, 188
    advocacy role. *See* advocacy role
    another child, having, 185-88
    changing specialists or therapists, 207-8
    child care arrangements, 190-96
    medications and alternative treatments,
        208
    planning for future, 209-10
    specialists for special-needs children.
        See specialists
    treatment options, choosing among,
        205-7
    work, going back to, 188-91
depression of parents, 13-14
developmental stages, 86-87. *See also*
        specific stages
    Making Discoveries stage, 101-8,
        120-25

    Reaching Out stage, 94-101, 117-20
    Tuning In and bonding stage, 88-94,
        110-17
diagnosis, difficulties in, 8-9
difficult babies, 47-48
    arousing, 48-49
    calming, 49-51
discipline, 76-78
    aggressive behaviors, 79-80
    biting, 81-82
    rules of play and day-to-day living, 104
    saying "no," 76-77
    temper tantrums and, 79
    time-out procedure, 80
    "touch gently" technique, 82
doctors, 198-99. *See also* specific types of
        physicians
dolls, 166
Down's-syndrome babies, 7, 28, 36-37,
        38, 39, 57, 94, 100-101, 108, 197
    intellectual development, 144, 148
    motor skill development, 117, 120, 125
dressing baby, 60-61
drinking from cup, 151

E

easy babies, 47, 48
emergency telephone numbers, 64, 224

F

family
    child care by relatives, 192-93
    grandparents and close relatives, 31-36
    parental emotions. *See* parental
        emotions
    siblings. *See* siblings
    traditions and fun times, 180-82
fear
    hospital stays, regarding, 220, 222-23
    initial reactions of parents, 13-14

siblings' secret fears, 23, 24, 29
feeding baby, 53-55
   bottle-feeding, 57
   breast-feeding, 53-57
   colic, 59-60
   mealtime for toddlers, 67-68
   scheduling, 63
   spoon-feeding, 57-59
   weaning, 69-70
first steps, 66
friendships, 36-38
fun times, 177-78
   everyday outings, 178-79
   family time and traditions, 180-82
   vacation time, 179-80
future, planning for, 209-10

G

games
   attachment behavior, strengthening, 96
   discovery games, 102-4
   imitation games, 96, 97, 104-5, 107-8
   language development games, 131-33, 135-37
   leave-taking game, 103
   music, songs and rhymes, 98, 99-100, 105, 114, 117-18, 131-32, 133, 137, 158-61
   object investigations, 150-51
   pretending, 105-7, 164-66
   Reaching Out stage of development, in, 96-101
   tag and hide-and-seek, 103-4, 107
gastrointestinal abnormalities, 8
geneticists, 187-88, 199
grandparents, 31-36
   advice for, 34-36
grief reactions of parents, 15
guilt
   initial reactions of parents, 15
   siblings, feelings of, 30

H

habits, 129
hand and arm exercises, 113-14
hand-waving, 80, 81
head banging, 80
head colds, 71
head control, 111-12, 114, 115, 119
hearing-impaired babies, 28, 50, 65, 93, 99, 107
   intellectual development, 143, 147, 152
   language development, 130, 134, 137-38
   motor skill development, 115, 119-20
hiccups, 5-6, 52, 59
hitting, 79-80
hospitalization. *See* illness and hospitalization
hypersensitive babies, 49-51, 60, 93-94, 100, 108, 116, 143-44, 148

I

IDEA (Individuals with Disabilities Education Act), 213
illness and hospitalization
   advocacy for child, 226-27
   going home from hospital, 227-28
   home care, 218-19
   keeping informed about child, 221-22
   operation or painful procedure, preparation for, 226
   pain and discomfort of child, 226
   preparing child for hospital experience, 222-23
   preparing for hospital stay, 220-24
   siblings, preparation for, 223-24
   smell of hospital, 226
   time in hospital, 225-27
   visitors, 226
imitation
   anticipation and, 96, 97

imitation (*continued*)
    deferred imitation, 104
    games, 96, 104-5, 107-8
    pretending, 105-7, 164-66
impulsive behaviors, 75-78
intellectual development, 139
    Down's-syndrome babies, 144, 148
    hearing-impaired babies, 143, 147, 152
    hypersensitive babies, 143-44, 148
    Making Discoveries stage, 149-53
    objects, functions and reactions of,
      144-47
    objects in relation, 149-52
    physically-challenged babies, 143-44,
      148, 152-53
    Reaching Out stage, 144-48
    touching and being touched, 140-44
    Tuning in stage, 139-44
    visually-impaired babies, 143, 147,
      152

K

kicking, 112-13, 114-15, 118

L

La Leche League, 56
language development, 126-27, 138
    back-and-forth conversations, 130-31
    greetings to baby, 136
    hearing-impaired babies, 130, 134,
      137-38
    listening experiences, 127-30
    Making Discoveries stage, 134-38
    making sounds, 127, 128-29, 130-34
    meanings, learning of, 134-38
    name, awareness of, 131, 134-35
    nursery rhymes, 137
    Reaching Out stage, 130-34
    reading to baby, 136
    therapists, 200

    Tuning In stage, 127-30
    visually-impaired babies, 129, 133-34,
      137
loneliness of parents, 13-14
love
    initial reactions of parents, 15-16
    responding to baby, 43-44

M

Making Discoveries stage, 101-2, 120-21
    activities, 102-7, 121-24, 135-37
    crawling, 121-22
    games, 102-4
    imitating and pretending, 104-7
    intellectual development, 149-53
    language development, 134-38
    modifications for impairments, 107-8,
      124-25, 137-38
    motor skill development, 120-25
    objects in relation, 149-52
    pulling up, 122-23
    toys for, 171-74
    walking, 123-24
marriage, 17, 86
    care of child, disagreements regarding,
      19
    levels of concern, differences in, 17,
      18-19
    mixed messages, avoidance of, 22
    nurturing of, 19-22
    therapy for, 22
meals, 67-68. *See also* feeding baby
medications, 208, 219, 222, 226, 227
mirrors, 95, 102, 131, 132
motor skills, 109-10
    balance, 118, 119, 120
    crawling, 118-19, 121-22
    hand and arm exercises, 113-14
    head control, 111-12
    hearing-impaired babies, 115, 119-20
    kicking, 112-13, 114-15, 118

Making Discoveries stage, 120-25
physically-challenged babies, 65, 115-16, 120, 125
pulling up, 122-23
Reaching Out stage, 117-20
rolling over, 113-14
swimming, 120
Tuning In stage, 110-17
visually-impaired babies, 114-15, 119, 124-25
walking, 123-24
musical toys, 64-65, 169
music and rhymes, 98, 99-100, 105, 114, 117-18, 131-32, 133, 137, 158-61

N

naps, 72-73
neonatal intensive care unit (NICU), 3-4
neonatologists, 198
neurologists, 199
night terrors, 71
"no" and "yes," 76-78, 131
nursery rhymes, 137

O

ophthalmologists, 199
optometrists, 199
orthopedic specialists, 199

P

parental emotions
anger and frustration, 12-13
Bill of Rights for parents, 212-14
bringing baby home, 5-6
decision making required. *See* decision making
depression, fear, and loneliness, 13-14
diagnostic uncertainties, 8-9
falling in love with baby, 15-16
friendships, maintenance of, 36-38
grandparents, difficulties with, 33-34
grief and loss, 11-12
guilt and self-blame, 15
marriage, stress on, 17-22
strangers, reactions of, 38-39
stress, helping baby with, 52
support group, seeking, 39-40
taking charge, in. *See* decision making
temperament of baby, 51
turmoil, 10
pediatricians, 198, 219
uncertainty of, 8-9
physically-challenged babies, 65, 93, 100, 108
intellectual development, 143-44, 148, 152-53
motor skill development, 115-16, 120, 125
physicians, 198-99. *See also* specific types of doctors
planning for future, 209-10
postural disorders, 60
pouring action, 150, 152
premature babies, 3-5, 8, 53, 54, 65, 88-89
pretending, 105-7, 164-66
psychologists, 200
pulling up, 122-23
pulmonary abnormalities, 8

R

rattles, 127, 128, 144, 145
Reaching Out stage, 94
activities, 95-98, 117-19, 131-32
attachment behavior, 95-96
balance, 118, 119, 120
crawling, 118-19
games, 96-101
intellectual development, 144-48
language development, 130-34
leg exercises, 118

Reaching Out stage (*continued*)
  modifications for impairments, 99-101,
    119-20, 133-34
  motor skill development, 117-20
  objects, functions and reactions of,
    144-47
  rolling over, 117-18
  social interactions, 95-96
  toys for, 170-71
reading to baby, 136, 162
record keeping, 214-15
restaurants, 179
rolling over, 113-14
Run Away Little Girl (Segal), 229

S

scheduling, 63
self-awareness. *See* awareness;
    developmental stages
separation, 95-96, 103
sharing, 84, 103
shyness, 83-84
siblings, 23
  balancing attention on, 27
  decision to have another child,
    185-88
  fears of, 23, 24, 29
  hospitalization of child, preparation for,
    223-24
  jealousy in, 25-26
  positive aspects, 27
  suggestions for parents, 28-30
  teasing from other children, 26, 28
skin color, 52
sleep
  calming baby, 49-51
  napping, 72-73
  putting baby to bed, 61-63
  toddler challenges, 70-73
  waking at night, 72
social interactions

attachment and separation, 95-96,
    103-4
  discoveries of others, 103
  poor social skills, 83-84
social-service professionals, 201-2
songs and rhymes, 98, 99-100, 105, 114,
    117-18, 131-32, 133, 137, 158-61
sounds
  attentiveness to, 127-29, 143
  making sounds, 127, 128-29, 130-34
  See also language development
specialists, 197. *See also* specific type
  changing professionals, 207-8
  child care, 195-96
  medical specialists, 198-99
  nonmedical professionals, 199-200
  record-keeping system regarding,
    214-15
  relationships with professionals,
    developing, 203-5, 212-13
  selection of, 202-3
  social-service professionals, 201-2
  therapists, 200-201
  treatment options, choosing among,
    205-7, 213
spina bifida, 7
spinning, 80, 81
spitting up, 52, 59
stimulation, modulated, 48-49
stores, visits to, 179
strangers, communication with, 38-39
stress, signs of, 52, 90-91
strollers, 178-79
support groups, 39-40
surroundings for baby, 64-65
swimming, 120

T

tactile-definsive babies. *See* hypersensitive
    babies
teething, 71

temperamental differences, 6-7, 47-51, 64-65

temper tantrums, 78-79

therapy and therapists, 219
  behavioral analysts, 201
  changing therapists, 207-8
  file on, 215
  marital, 22
  occupational, 201
  physical, 125, 200
  speech and language, 200
  support groups, 39-40

thinking skills. *See* intellectual development

time-out procedure, 80

toddlers, 66-67. *See also* specific subject areas
  aggressive behaviors, 79-80
  atypical behaviors, 80-81
  bathing, 71, 74
  biting, 81-82
  discipline for, 76-78
  first steps, 66
  getting into everything, 82-83
  habitual, atypical behaviors, 80-81
  hospital stay, preparing for, 222-23
  impulsiveness, 75-78
  mealtime challenges, 67-68
  misbehaving challenges, 74-84
  poor social skills, 83-84
  sense of self, 67
  simple chores for, 78
  sleeptime, 70-73
  temper tantrums, 78-79
  toilet learning, 70, 73-74
  transitions, resistance to, 83
  weaning, 69-70

toilet learning, 70, 73-74

touching and being touched, 140-44

toys, 166, 167-68
  feel toys, 170
  improvised toys, 173-74
  Making Discoveries stage, 171-74
  musical toys, 64-65, 169
  problem-solving toys, 172-74
  Reaching Out stage, 170-71
  responsive toys, 170-71
  sound toys, 169
  Tuning In stage, 168-70
  visually appealing toys, 168-69

traditions, 180-82

transitions, resistance to, 83

Tuning In stage, 88-89
  activities, 89-90, 111-14, 127-29, 141-43
  hand and arm exercises, 113-14
  head control, 111-12, 114, 115
  kicking, 112-13, 114-15
  language development, 127-30
  modifications for impairments, 92-94, 114-17, 129-30, 143-44
  motor skill development, 110-17
  touching and being touched, 140-44
  toys for, 168-70

Tuning In stage
  intellectual development, 139-44

V

vacations, 179-80

visually-impaired babies, 49-50, 65, 92-93, 99, 107
  intellectual development, 143, 147, 152
  language development, 129, 133-34, 137
  motor skill development, 114-15, 119, 124-25

W

walking, 66-67, 123-24

weaning, 69-70

work, back to, 188-91. *See also* child care

About the Authors

MARILYN SEGAL, PH.D., a developmental psychologist specializing in early childhood, is professor of human development and dean emeritus of the Family Center at Nova Southeastern University in Fort Lauderdale, Florida. The mother of five children, she is the author of nineteen books, including *Making Friends*, *Just Pretending*, and the five-volume series, *Your Child at Play*. She is also the creator of *To Reach a Child*, a nine-part television series for parents.

WENDY MASI, PH.D., has been working in the field of early education and family support for more than twenty-five years. She received her Ph.D. in developmental psychology from Nova University and is currently the dean of the Family Center of Nova Southeastern University. She has been interviewed on NBC's *Today*, *Later Today*, and *Weekend Today* shows.

RONI COHEN LEIDERMAN, PH.D., is the associate dean of the Family Center of Nova Southeastern University, the executive director of the Baudhuin School of Nova Southeastern University, and the director of the Birth to Five Program at the Family Center of Nova Southeastern University.

PARENTING/CHILDCARE BOOKS FROM NEWMARKET PRESS

Ask for these titles at your local bookstore or use this coupon and enclose a check or money order payable to: **Newmarket Press**, 18 East 48th Street, New York, NY 10017.

Amelia D. Auckett
Baby Massage
____ $11.95 pb (1-55704-022-2)

Elissa P. Benedek, M.D., and Catherine F. Brown, M.Ed.
How to Help Your Child Overcome Your Divorce
____ $15.95 pb (1-55704-461-9)

Sarah Cheyette, M.D.
Mommy, My Head Hurts: A Doctor's Guide to Your Child's Headaches
____ $21.95 hc (1-55704-471-6)

Lee F. Gruzen
Raising Your Jewish/Christian Child
____ $16.95 pb (1-55704-414-7)

Debra W. Haffner, M.P.H.
Beyond The Big Talk: Every Parent's Guide to Raising Sexually Healthy Teens
____ $24.95 hc (1-55704-472-4)
From Diapers to Dating: A Parent's Guide to Raising Sexually Healthy Children
____ $23.95 hc (1-55704-385-X)
____ $14.95 pb (1-55704-426-0)

Sally Placksin
Mothering the New Mother, Rev. Ed.
____ $18.95 pb (1-55704-317-5)

Teresa Savage
The Ready-to-Read, Ready-to-Count Handbook
____ $16.95 pb (1-55704-413-9)

Dan Schaefer & Christine Lyons
How Do We Tell the Children? Third Ed.
____ $24.95 hc (1-55704-430-9)
____ $14.95 pb (1-55704-425-2)

Frederick Leboyer, M.D.
Inner Beauty, Inner Light: Yoga for Pregnant Women
____ $18.95 pb (1-55704-315-9)
Loving Hands: Traditional Baby Massage
____ $16.95 pb (1-55704-314-0)

Lynda Madaras & Area Madaras
My Body, My Self for Boys
____ $12.95 pb (1-55704-440-6)
My Body, My Self for Girls
____ $12.95 pb (1-55704-441-4)
My Feelings, My Self
____ $12.95 pb (1-55704-442-2)
The What's Happening to My Body? Book for Boys
____ $22.95 hc (1-55704-447-3)
____ $12.95 pb (1-55704-443-0)
The What's Happening to My Body? Book for Girls
____ $22.95 hc (1-55704-448-1)
____ $12.95 pb (1-55704-444-9)

Robert Schwebel, Ph.D.
Keep Your Kids Tobacco-Free
____ $14.95 pb (1-55704-369-8)
Saying No Is Not Enough, Rev. Ed.
____ $14.95 pb (1-55704-318-3)

Marilyn Segal, Ph.D.
In Time and With Love
____ $18.95 pb (1-55704-445-7)
Your Child at Play: Birth to One Year, 2nd Ed.
____ $27.95 hc (1-55704-334-5)
____ $17.95 pb (1-55704-330-2)
Your Child at Play: One to Two Years, 2nd Ed.
____ $27.95 hc (1-55704-335-3)
____ $16.95 pb (1-55704-331-0)
Your Child at Play: Two to Three Years, 2nd Ed.
____ $27.95 hc (1-55704-336-1)
____ $16.95 pb (1-55704-332-9)
Your Child at Play: Three to Five Years, 2nd Ed.
____ $27.95 hc (1-55704-337-X)
____ $16.95 pb (1-55704-333-7)
Your Child at Play: Five to Eight Years, 2nd Ed.
____ $29.95 hc (1-55704-402-3)
____ $17.95 pb (1-55704-401-5)

For postage and handling, please add $3.00 for the first book, plus $1.00 for each additional book. Prices and availability are subject to change.

I enclose a check or money order payable to **Newmarket Press** in the amount of $ _____

Name _____

Address _____

City/State/Zip _____

For discounts on orders of five or more copies or to get a catalog, contact Newmarket Press, Special Sales Department, 18 East 48th Street, New York, NY 10017; phone 212-832-3575 or 800-669-3903; fax 212-832-3629; or e-mail mailbox@newmarketpress.com

IT&WL.0401